The Charlton
Standard Catalogue of

CANADIAN
DOLLS

3rd EDITION

By
**Evelyn Robson
Strahlendorf**

**W. K. Cross
Publisher**

The Charlton Press
Toronto, Ontario • Birmingham, Michigan

EDITORIAL

Editor	Jean Dale
Assistant Editor	Nicola Leedham
Graphic Technician	Davina Rowan

CONTRIBUTORS

Heartfelt thanks are due to the collectors whose dolls are represented here and all those who wrote and generously sent photographs of their dolls to be identified and added to the book. Without the help of so many doll collectors, this book would not have been completed. Special thanks to the late Chris Needham who shared his knowledge of the G.I. Joes that were made in Canada; to Jane Kupka for help with the Barbies; to Joan Grubaugh of Van Wert, Ohio for her research on the Canadian made Gerber Baby; and to Marion Field and Phyllis McOrmond of British Columbia, and Diane Richards of Saskatchewan.

A big thank you to my husband Carl who patiently photographed and developed dozens of pictures to be added to the third edition.

Marina Adamson, Calgary, Alberta; **Edie Barlishen**, Edmonton, Alberta; **Dobhran Beauvais**, Ottawa, Ontario; **Jan Belcher**, Stittsville, Ontario; **Connie Bishop**, Ottawa, Ontario; **Elva Boyce**, Regina, Saskatchewan (deceased); **Mrs. Roy Brown**, Campbellford, Ontario; **Mrs. Marjorie Cameron**, Nova Scotia; **Lorraine Chapman**, Edmonton, Alberta; **Mrs. Eileen A. Chouinard**, Saskatoon, Saskatchewan; **June Clark**, Halifax, Nova Scotia; **Lynne Copeman**, Regina, Saskatchewan; **Donna Custonguay**, Almonte, Ontario; **Jackie Dean**, Calgary, Alberta; **Rebecca Douglass**, Dartmouth, Nova Scotia; **Margaret Edmonds**, Halifax, Nova Scotia; **Jean Edmondson**, Hamilton, Ontario; **Eva English**, Edmonton, Alberta; **Edna Epp**, Langham, Saskatchewan; **Marion Field**, Powell River, British Columbia; **Sheila Folk**, Fall River, Nova Scotia; **Sheila Forster**, St. Albert, Alberta; **Madeline Goodkey**, Stirling, Ontario; **Mary Haffermehl**, Biggar, Saskatchewan; **June Harrison-Leier**, Whitecourt, Alberta; **Margaret Hayes**, Musquodoboit Harbour, Nova Scotia; **Betty Hemus**, Calgary, Alberta; **Irene Henderson**, Winnipeg, Manitoba; **Dina Heuschop**, Calgary, Alberta; **Pat Homan**, Edmonton, Alberta; **Wanda Istace**, Kindersley, Saskatchewan; **Moyra Jameson**, Burnaby, British Columbia; **Gloria Kallis**, Whitecourt, Alberta; **Elizabeth Kanigsberg**, Musquodoboit Harbour, Nova Scotia; **Mrs. John Ketcheson**, Stirling, Ontario; **Frieda Krakowetz**, St. Louis, Saskatchewan; **Lina Lamb**, Saskatoon, Saskatchewan; **Stella Lamont**, Kindersley, Saskatchewan; **Jennifer Larson**, Calgary, Alberta; **Connie Leask**, Bettleford, Saskatchewan; **Erin de Laroque**, Edmonton, Alberta; **Paddy de Laroque**, Edmonton, Alberta; **Heather Browning Maciak**, Calgary, Alberta; **Ruth McAra**, Caron, Saskatchewan; **Phyllis McOrmond**, Victoria, British Columbia; **Ethel Mandigo**, Edmonton, Alberta; **Bev Martineau**, Halifax, Nova Scotia; **Elsie Martinson**, Langham, Saskatchewan; **Edwina Mauck**, Calgary, Alberta; **Christina Mont**, Nova Scotia; **Andrea Morrow; Anne Muttice**, Ottawa, Ontario; **Chris Needham**, Ottawa, Ontario; **Hennriette Nehman**, Winnipeg, Manitoba; **Margaret Olson**, Alberta; **Roberta LaVerne Ortwein**, Olds, Alberta; **Margaret Pablicoover**, Alberta; **Sue Pearson**, Waterloo, Ontario; **Judy Pedman; Joanne Penicud**, Orleans, Ontario; **Elaine Penn**, Saskatoon, Saskatchewan; **Sonya Piaskoski**, Calgary, Alberta; **Kathleen Pontefract**, Ottawa, Ontario; **Jean Potvin**, Ottawa, Ontario; **Mary Prue**, Winnipeg, Manitoba; **Lillian M. Pruitt**, Winnipeg, Manitoba; **June Rennie**, Saskatoon, Saskatchewan; **Mrs. Reynolds**, Richmond, Ontario; **Dianne Richards**, Kenosee Lake, Saskatchewan; **Connie Royal**, Winnipeg, Manitoba; **Sharon Schwartz**, Saskatoon, Saskatchewan; **Lesley Stuart-Smith**, Calgary, Alberta; **Dena Thompson**, Halifax, Nova Scotia; **Coco Van Maanen**, Cornwell, Ontario; **Marie Varey**, Little Current, Ontario; **Kim Warren**, Calgary, Alberta; **Shirley Washer**, Palgrave, Ontario; **Marilou Will**, Saskatoon, Saskatchewan; **Lillian C. Wilson**, Calgary, Alberta

A SPECIAL NOTE TO COLLECTORS

We welcome and would appreciate any comments or suggestions in regard to The Charlton Standard Catalogue of Canadian Dolls that you might have. If you would like to participate in pricing or supplying new data please call Jean Dale at (416) 488-1418.

CANADIAN CATALOGUING IN PUBLICATION DATA

The National Library of Canada has catalogued this
publication as follows:
Strahlendorf, Evelyn Robson
The Charlton standard catalogue of Canadian dolls
2nd ed. (1992) -
Biennial
Continues: Strahlendorf, Evelyn Robson. Charlton
price guide to Canadian dolls.
ISSN 1188-8873
ISBN 0-88968-140-6 (3rd ed.)
1. Dolls - Canada - Catalogs - Periodicals.
2. Dolls - Prices - Canada - Periodicals. I. Title.
NK4894.C3S87 745.592'21'0971 C92032428-2

**Printed in Canada
in the Province of Ontario**

The Charlton Press

**Editorial Office
2040 Yonge Street, Suite 208
Toronto, Ontario M4S 1Z9
Telephone: (416) 488-1418 Fax: (416) 488-4656
Telephone: 1-800-442-6042 Fax: 1-800-442-1542**

TABLE OF CONTENTS

PREFACE TO THE THIRD EDITION

The third edition of The Charlton Standard Catalogue of Canadian Dolls has grown once again and contains many dolls that were not in the second edition. Five years have elapsed since the second edition was published in 1992. That edition has been sold out for several years, and judging by collectors' requests, the third edition will be equally popular.

The last few years have not been very good for the Canadian economy, and this has resulted in a rather erratic doll market. Generally, prices have dropped for the more common dolls, and yet some of the dolls that are much in demand, such as the Shirley Temple dolls, have seen enormous price increases. Ever-popular dolls, such as the Barbara Ann Scott and hard plastic Toni dolls and wartime dolls in uniform, have increased in demand and therefore in price. This is particularly true of dolls that are in mint condition and have all of their original costume.

Dolls are not like any other collectable because the reasons why a collector wants a certain doll tend to be emotional. Perhaps it was a childhood doll they remember fondly or a doll they wished to have as a child. When the reason is emotional, sometimes a collector is willing to pay considerably more than book value to own the doll.

The Wis-Ton Toy Mfg. Company was the last factory making vinyl dolls in Canada, and it closed in 1991, when the owner Salvatore Manganaro died from a heart attack. Sam, as he was called, began working for Star Doll in Toronto when he was 14 years old. When Star closed in 1970, he worked for Regal Toy until he opened his own business in 1983. When Wis-Ton closed its doors, it was the end of an era of dollmaking in Canada.

Although there are no more vinyl toy dolls being made in Canada, collectors of Canadiana can turn to original artist dolls. Dolls made by our artists compete with the best in the world and bring home awards and honours for their work. Their dolls are made of every type of material imaginable and show a technical mastery of their medium and great creativity.

A doll that is made in a very small edition is more expensive to buy than a doll produced by the hundreds because it is rarer. Not every collector can pay a handsome price for a rare doll, but sometimes the same artist will sculpt a doll for a company that makes many copies and sells them for much less. Several of the large companies that produce their dolls in China or Korea have signed contracts with Canadian artists to create an original doll to be sold worldwide. This not only pays the artist royalties, but makes the artist very well known among doll collectors.

There have been some interesting finds in the doll world, such as a 17-inch hairbow doll by Dominion Toy turning up in mint condition, complete with her hang tag. Her hang tag doesn't give her a special name, but she certainly predates Reliables Hairbow Peggy.

Another doll by Noma Toys of Owen Sound has turned up. She is a large stuffed-vinyl doll, originally made by Effanbee in the United States and licenced to Noma Toys. She has an electronic talking device in her tummy, made by Noma.

Unfortunately, she doesn't say a word anymore, although when she was new, she spoke both English and French. The American made version spoke only English but wore the same dress as the Canadian version.

A baby doll by Commercial Toy was discovered, which was a very exciting find. Commercial Toy was only in operation in Toronto for a year in 1917, and surviving dolls are very rare. It is dolls like this that make collecting such a fascinating hobby.

Who knows what dolls will turn up in the future? As more and more people become aware of the value of dolls and their importance in telling us more about our technology, history and culture, dolls that are found in attics and tucked away in drawers will be brought out and scrutinized, instead of being tossed in the scrap heap.

The dolls in this book are not even half of the dolls produced in Canada in the last 85 years! Where are all the rest? It is up to collectors to find and preserve them for future generations.

Evelyn Robson Strahlendorf

INTRODUCTION

THE PURPOSE OF THIS BOOK

Is a price guide for Canadian dolls ever really necessary? There are many reasons for selling a doll, and unless you are a dealer who is aware of the market and what collectors are willing to pay for a certain doll, you are not going to know what to charge. If you bought the doll 20 years ago for ten dollars, it may be worth a great deal more today. A price guide is only a guide, but it will give you a better idea of your doll's value.

For those who are not collectors and have a doll they would like to sell, it is important to remember that the condition of the doll is sometimes more important than its age. It is a mistake to remove the original outfit and replace it with a dress of modern fabrics. It is better to leave the original mohair wig on than to put a modern wig on the doll. A doll collector will pay more for a doll with the original wig and costume then for one with a brand new dress and wig.

There is a standard for grading composition dolls, a standard for grading vinyl and hard plastic dolls and a standard for grading Eaton's Beauty Dolls.

Compare your doll with the appropriate standard for that type of doll. If the paint on your doll is crazed and some of the hair is missing, you cannot ask for the mint price. The listed mint price is one you will rarely pay for dolls made before 1940, because dolls in perfect condition, with hang tags and complete costume, are very seldom found. Make use of the standards; they are a valuable tool whether buying or selling.

The values listed here are not the prices you will pay if you buy from a garage sale or from a neighbour who wants to get rid of the dolls in her basement. These are the values you will pay at a shop or doll show because the dealer must pay the expenses involved in running a business.

If you are shopping for a special doll, find out what she is worth in mint condition and what you would have to pay if she is only in good condition, and decide for yourself how much you are willing to pay. Prepare yourself with knowledge and you will be happier with your selection, knowing that you bought the best doll at the best price.

STANDARDS FOR GRADING COMPOSITION DOLLS

MINT CONDITION (Mint)

Composition in perfect condition, no flaking or cracks.
Hair still in original set.
Eyes in perfect condition, eyelashes intact.
Original clothing and accessories all there.
Original tags.
Cloth body in perfect condition.

EXCELLENT CONDITION (Ex.)

Composition in very good condition but could have small wear spot, no crazing or cracks.
All hair present, clean and combed in original style.
Eyes in working order, eyelashes intact. If painted eyes, all eye paint intact.
Has most of original clothing but shoes may be replaced with similar style.
Cloth body clean and intact.

GOOD CONDITION (G.)

Composition could be slightly crazed but not bubbled.
Most hair present.
Teeth may be missing.
Eyes in working order but some lashes may be missing.
Should have main piece of original clothing. Some items may be missing.
Clothing may be replaced with exact copy of original clothing or vintage clothing of a similar style.
Cloth body may have small repairs.
May have a missing finger.

FAIR CONDITION (F.)

Composition may be crazed or bubbled.
Some hair present.
Eyes present but could be damaged, some lashes missing.
May have missing fingers or toes.
May not have any original clothing.
May be suitably redressed.
Cloth body may be soiled or repaired.
May be repainted.

STANDARDS FOR GRADING VINYL AND HARD PLASTIC DOLLS

MINT CONDITION (Mint)

Face and body in perfect condition.
Hair still in original set.
Eyes and lashes in perfect condition.
Has all the original clothing and accessories.
Has original tags.
Cloth body in perfect condition.
In perfect working order if mechanical.
Accessories complete.

EXCELLENT CONDITION (Ex.)

Face and body in very good condition but may
have very tiny spots. May be lightly faded. Ears may
be discoloured from earrings.
All hair present, clean and combed in original style.
Eyes in working order, lashes or paint intact.
Has most original clothing but shoes or hat may be
missing but not both.
Shoes may be replaced with similar style.
Cloth body clean and intact.
Complete with important accessories.

GOOD CONDITION (G.)

Face vinyl may have blemished paint. May have marks
on the body.
If from the 1950s the face may be discoloured.
Most hair present and not cut.
Eyes in working order but some lashes may be missing.
Should have main piece of original clothing.
Some items may be missing.
Clothing may be replaced with exact copies of
original clothing or appropriate vintage clothing.
Plastic body may have marks, cloth body may have
small repairs.
Battery box may need cleaning. Key may be missing.

FAIR CONDITION (F.)

Vinyl face blemished and may have small stains.
Some hair present
Eyes may be damaged, some lashes missing.
May not have any original clothing but dressed
in suitable clothing.
Cloth body may be soiled and repaired.
Mechanisms no longer working.

A doll may easily fall between two categories, having some points from a higher category and some from a lower. In this case a price is decided between the two conditions.

USING THIS BOOK

Dolls in this price guide are divided according to their manufacturers and then listed chronologically. Most dolls are marked by the manufacturer on the back of the head or the nape of the neck. This will help you to readily locate the doll in this price guide. However, because the Eaton's Beauty Dolls and the celebrity and working dolls were manufactured by various companies, they are not listed by companies but only chronologically.

We have included a short description of each doll and its markings. The pictures are to identify the dolls but the prices are based on the standards. There is an index for dolls' names and an index for reference numbers.

Before looking at the prices, read the standards for the type of doll in which you are interested. Know what we mean when we give a price for a mint doll or for a doll in fair condition. After reading the standards, apply them to the doll that you are interested in pricing. If it is a composition doll and the hair has been played with, it is no longer in mint condition. If the composition is crazed, it is not in excellent condition. Talking dolls are not in excellent condition if they no longer talk.

If you are selling your doll, compare your doll with the standards. Sometimes the condition of the doll will not fit perfectly into one category, so you will have to price it a little higher or a little lower than the category it is closest to. Start with the category closest to the condition of the doll and reduce the price slightly for each defect. Keep in mind that the condition of the doll is strongly reflected in the price of the doll. Just as real estate people say the three things that count when selling a house are location, location, and location, with dolls it is condition, condition, and condition. If you are buying a doll, compare the doll with the standards for that type of doll. When you find the category the doll is closest to, compare the price asked with the price listed for that particular doll. Remember that if the price for a doll in mint condition seems very high to you, it is because such dolls are rare and they command top dollar.

Also, take into consideration that the dealer usually knows how much demand there is for a doll and that a doll in demand commands a higher price. This book is only a guide and in the end each collector must decide whether a doll is a good buy or not. If you really want a doll, you will probably be willing to pay a little more to get it.

PRICING CANADIAN DOLLS

The prices listed in this book are those normally charged at a doll show or in a store. These are not the prices paid to an owner by a dealer. If you are selling your doll to a dealer, expect to get from 40 to 50 percent less than book value, as the dealer has expenses involved in selling dolls and must make a profit in order to stay in business.

Five factors determine the price of a doll: condition, age, rarity, manufacturer and size. As a general rule, an older doll will be worth more than a similar doll made 20 years later. A doll that was made for only one year will be harder to find than a doll from a common mould that was used for many years. Dolls made by one of the early companies are in more demand from serious collectors because of their historical importance. Dee an Cee dolls are popular with collectors because of their quality and detailed costuming. Pullan dolls are often unusual and are therefore attractive to collectors.

Carefully examine a doll that is claimed to be mint before you decide to buy at the top price, as many dolls are called mint, but are really only excellent or good. A mint composition doll is a doll that was boxed and left on a shelf and never exposed to heat, cold, sunlight or dampness.

Dolls that are "Mint In the box" (MIB) are about 10 to 15 percent higher for vinyl dolls and 40 to 50 percent higher for composition dolls. Composition dolls in their original boxes are much rarer. To be in the MIB category, the box should be labelled with the manufacturer's name and possibly the name of the doll. A cardboard box with nothing printed on it has very little value, if any.

Unusual dolls — such as those with a mechanical action, advertising or celebrity dolls, characters or dolls in costumes, such as Mounties or Scottish dolls, and black dolls — always command a higher price than dolly-faced dolls.

The fashion dolls from the late fifties and early sixties seem to be gaining in favour with doll collectors who appreciate their quality and detailed costuming. Many of the dolls from those years have very thick rooted hair that has been sewn into the vinyl with a very fine needle. In later years the thickness of the needle increased and the rows of hair were rooted further apart, giving a much thinner head of hair.

Since the era of producing play dolls in Canada is over, and there is a limited number of dolls and an ever increasing number of collectors, Canadian dolls will probably increase in value over the next 20 years.

REGIONAL DIFFERENCES

During the last four years, since the second edition of this price guide was published, the economy has been extremely weak for luxury items. Collectables are not classified as necessities, and generally speaking, there has been a drop in the prices for common dolls. However, the price differences among the regions have remained basically the same.

With a population of over ten million, Ontario remains the area of strongest demand and, therefore, has the highest prices, particularly for the more expensive dolls.

Alberta, Saskatchewan and Manitoba collectors seemingly will pay more for Eaton's Beauties and also more for large bisque antique dolls than Ontario and Quebec collectors. It is not uncommon for dealers from the Prairies to buy at Ontario auctions for dolls to sell at home.

For Canadian-made play dolls, prices in Ontario are roughly 10 to 15 percent higher than in the Atlantic provinces and in the Prairies, but for unusual dolls or characters, the differences are closer to 30 percent. In British Columbia prices are only a little less than those in Ontario.

Collectors seem to be more knowledgable than in the past and know what they are looking for and how much they are willing to pay. The reason for that change has been due to the fact that they now have the *Charlton Standard Catalogue of Canadian Dolls* in their hands.

In more heavily populated areas the demand for good dolls pushes the prices up. There does seem to be some leveling off, but with a country the size of Canada, we will never have all regions paying exactly the same price for the same doll.

COLLECTING CANADIAN DOLLS

In the last few years there has been a great deal said about "unity" and the "shared values" of Canadians. Exactly what does that mean? What it means to me is that no matter where I go in Canada, other doll collectors have similar memories and experiences, and we are able to talk as though we had known one another for years.

When I was a child and cut up old Eaton's catalogues to make paper dolls, I thought that I was the only child who had that idea. As I met other collectors from across our broad land, I found that there were hundreds of others who shared that memory of their childhood with me.

At a doll show, where the vendors and artists come from different areas of the country, there is often instant rapport with others who share the same problems and interests of other Canadians.

Anywhere in Canada thousands of collectors know exactly what you mean by a Barbara Ann Scott doll, and that is something only Canadians know. It may not be a wonderful bisque Jumeau, but it is ours. The Barabara Ann Scott doll has become a Canadian icon to thousands of collectors who remember the young woman who represented excellence in her field to many young girls who admired her. Thousands of women have memories of studying the Eaton's Beauty picture in the catalogue and hoping to receive one for Christmas. These shared memories unite us from coast to coast.

The "Maggie Muggins" doll was created to personify the little girl in Mary Grannan's Just Mary stories on CBC radio and on television and in her many books. The hundreds of thousands of children who loved her have now grown up and share their memories of "Maggie Muggins" with other Canadians.

Many other dolls such as the "Marilyn Bell" doll, and the "Karen Magnussen" doll, and the wartime dolls representing our armed forces are known only to Canadian collectors.

Regal's Kimmie was sold by the thousands as a Canadian souvenir. Kimmie frequently wore clothing to represent Inuit or Indian clothing and was also available in a Mountie outfit and a kilt. Kimmie wasn't an expensive doll, but it was cute, and it represented a wholesome Canada to tourists.

Collectors search for the early dolls made by small struggling companies who sought to replace the European dolls during the first World War and later, to survive in a competitive industry. Today, there are no more companies in Canada making toy dolls.

Dolls are an integral part of our culture, and they are indigenous to Canada, as both Inuit and Indian cultures were making dolls long before the Europeans arrived. Our culture is not just music and books and art, it is how we live in Canada, and our shared values and memories make us what we are.

The doll prices given in this book are intended as value guides rather than arbitrarily set prices. Each price recorded here is actually a compilation. The retail prices in this book are recorded as accurately as possible, but in the case of errors, typographical, clerical or otherwise, the author and publisher assume no responsibility for any loss incurred by users of this book.

INUIT DOLLS

From prehistoric times to the present, dolls were made by the Inuit for reasons other than as playthings. Hunters leaving camp by boat would attach a small doll to the boat for good luck. There are also ancient dolls which appear to have been used for religious purposes by the shaman.

Inuit dolls today are mostly made for collectors while Inuit children play with modern commercially made dolls. Some of the dolls made recently for the collector market are larger and authentically dressed, with several layers of clothing and in greater detail. These dolls have jumped in price due to a larger demand and are now selling at $400.00 to 500.00

The more authentic the doll, the more it increases in value. Dolls with heads carved from soapstone, ivory or wood tend to be more valuable than dolls with leather or cloth heads. The older, authentic dolls are becoming increasingly difficult to find and are more expensive.

Like the clothing on the Inuit themselves, the doll clothing varies from one geographical area to another.

INUIT WOMAN - 15 1/4 in.

Date Unknown. 15 1/4 in. (39 cm). Cloth body. Wooden head with carved features and carved tattoo marks on cheeks. Carved hair. Mark: on foot, 784. Original fur and leather clothing. Large hood to accommodate a baby.

Ref.No.: D of C, AR22, p. 9

Range: $250.00 - 325.00

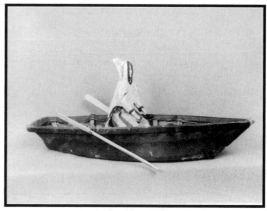

WOMAN POWER

Date Unknown. Height: sitting, 8 1/4 in. (21 cm). Leather body in a sitting position; carved ivory hands. Ivory carved head; eyes painted black. Mark: label, CANADIAN ESKIMO ART; COMMUNITY 757/DNA FRSB./FROBISHER BAY/E564. Authentic sealskin clothing. Umiak is 22 3/4 in. (58 cm) long with a wooden frame covered in sealskin and includes oars.

Ref.No.: D of C, AZ25, p. 9

Range: $800.00 - 950.00

INUIT MAN - 17 in.

Date unknown. 17 in. (43 cm). Cloth body. Wooden head with carved features. Authentic sealskin clothing; well made leather mitts and boots.

Ref.No.: D of C, AR19, p. 10

Range: $250.00 - 350.00

INUIT WOMAN - 8 1/4 in.

Date unknown. 8 1/4 in. (21 cm). Leather body. Soapstone head; carved features and hair. Mark: label, ESKIMO ART, MADE BY AN INUIT AT ESKIMO POINT. Doeskin and sealskin clothing.

Ref.No.: D of C, AZ32, p. 11

Range: $260.00 - 325.00

INUIT MAN - 19 3/4 in.

Date unknown. 19 3/4 in. (50 cm). Cloth body. Wooden head; carved features. Unmarked. Dressed in a woollen hooded parka with fur trim, woollen pants, leather and fur mukluks.

Ref.No.: D of C, AR20, p. 11

Range: $170.00 - 210.00

INUIT WOMAN - 10 in.

Date unknown. 10 in. (25.5 cm). Cloth body. Soapstone head with carved features and hair. Mark: label, #1073, MADE BY DALACIA KASUDLUCK AT DNOUCDJOVCK. Handmade sealskin pants and parka with large hood to accommodate a baby; leather gloves and boots.

Ref.No.: D of C, AE14, p. 11

Range: $260.00 - 325.00

INUGUGULIAJUIT
(THE LITTLE PEOPLE)

Date unknown. 4 in. (10 cm). Leather body. Leather head with painted features. Leather and fur clothing are part of doll. Mark: on label, LA FEDERATION DES COOPERATIVE DU NOUVEAU, QUE. LEVIS, QUE., CANADA.

Ref. No.: D of C, BX32, p. 12

Range: $30.00 - 50.00

INUIT MAN - 9 3/4 in.

Date unknown. 9 3/4 in. (24.5 cm). Cloth body; soapstone mitts and boots. Soapstone head with carved features. Mark: label, ESKIMO/MADE BY AN INUIT AT POND INLET. Dressed in a hooded wool parka trimmed in fur; black pants.

Ref.No.: D of C, AZ33, p. 12

Range: $235.00 - 300.00

INUIT MAN - 7 in.

Date unknown. 7 in. (17 cm). Cloth body. Plastic shoulderhead; painted eyes; moulded black painted hair. Mark: on foot, LABRADOR. Dressed in a sealskin hooded jacket, cotton pants, leather mukluks and mitts. Made in Labrador.

Ref.No.: D of C, BH7, p. 12

Range: $60.00 - 85.00

INUIT MAN - 6 in.

Date unknown. 6 in. (15 cm). Leather body, leather head, no features. Dressed in leather and fur. May have been made by a young person.

Ref.No.: 2R18

Range: $75.00 - 100.00

INUIT MAN - YUKON

Date unknown. 10 1/2 in. (27 cm). Leather body. Leather head; ink-drawn features. Black plush hair. Dressed in fur and leather.
Ref.No.: 2Q4
Range: $90.00 - 130.00

INUIT WOMAN - YUKON

Date unknown. 10 1/2 in. (27 cm). Canvas body. Leather head, ink-drawn features. Fringed fur parka and hood, leather belt with YUKON in bead-work at the back, leather mitts and leather boots with bead trim.
Ref.No.: 2Y9
Range: $80.00 - 120.00

INUIT WOMAN - 11 in.

Date unknown. 11 in. (28 cm). Cloth body. Leather head, embroidered features, stockinette fabric hair. Dressed in slip, parka and fur-trimmed hood, cotton print overdress, leather and fur moccasins and mittens.
Ref.No.: 2J20
Range: $200.00 - 300.00

INUIT GIRL - 7 1/2 in.

ca.1950. 7 1/2 in. (19 cm). Brown hard plastic body, jointed hips, shoulders and neck. Hard plastic head; brown sleep eyes, moulded lashes; closed mouth. Probably made by Reliable. Dressed in white and black fur parka and hood, leather boots. Probably dressed by a native.
Ref.No.: 2R29
Range: $40.00 - 60.00

INUIT MOTHER AND BABY - 13 in.

ca.1950. 13 in. (33 cm). Cloth body. Head; knit fabric over moulded head; embroidered black eyes; hair is crocheted wool cap. Dressed in embroidered felt parka and hood with fur lining and yarn belt. Print dress, leather and fur mukluks and soapstone fish.

Ref.No.: 2C20

Range: $250.00 - 350.00

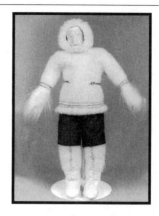

INUIT MAN - 11 in.

ca.1966. 11 in. (28 cm). Cloth body. Bone head with carved features. Unmarked. Dressed in an embroidered white parka trimmed around hood with white fur cloth, wolverine mitts, navy blue sailcloth pants, leather mukluks. Made by an Inuit on Baffin Island.

Ref.No.: D of C, CB15, p. 13

Range: $225.00 - 275.00

INUIT MOTHER AND BABY - 6 in.

1967. Great Whale River. 6 in. (15 cm). Cloth body. Cloth head; embroidered features; wool hair. Dressed in parka and hood, seal skin mittens and mukluks.

Ref.No.: 2K0

Range: $125.00 - 175.00

CLYDE RIVER INUIT

ca.1970. 16 in. (40.5 cm). One-piece cloth body. Cloth head with attached nose; painted features. Completely dressed in baby sealskin and leather boots. Mark: label, ESKIMO ART, handmade by OOTOOVAH TIGULLARAQ FROM CLYDE RIVER.

Ref.No.: D of C, AB1A, p. 13

Range: $275.00 - 400.00

BONE PLAY DOLLS

1970. 3 1/2 in. (9 cm), 4.75 in. (12 cm), 5.25 in. (13.5 cm). Holes drilled in the bone, arms, and legs; attached with strong thread. Largest doll has been carved to suggest clothing.

Ref.No.: D of C, BC7, p. 13

Left: $10.00 ; Centre: $ 12.00 ; Right: $22.00

INUIT WOMAN - 16 in.

ca.1970. Coppermine, N.W.T. 16 in. (41 cm). Cloth body. Suede leather head; embroidered features; yarn hair. Dressed in cotton print overdress with pleated skirt, bias and rick-rack trim, fur-trimmed hood. Lambswool mitts on wool cord. Underdress of green felt with lambswool trim; print slip, cotton panties, purple nylon stockings, brown leather boots with beaded trim.

Ref.No.: 2F4

Range: $225.00 - 325.00

INUIT HUSBAND AND WIFE - 16 and 17 in.

ca.1970. 16 and 17 in. (41-43 cm). Cloth bodies. Cloth heads; embroidered features, applied fabric nose. Authentic clothing. Wife wears long gabardine tights, a cotton undershirt, and a long-sleeved heavy wool garment trimmed with fur at the hemline and wrists. Topped by a cotton dress with an attached fur-trimmed parka. Moccasins have felt uppers and leather feet. Mittens have applied thumbs. Husband wears a colourful cotton undershirt, a fur-trimmed gabardine shirt and a gabardine parka. His leggings and moccasins are similar to his wife's.

Ref.No.: 2P8

Range: $210.00 - 275.00 each

INUIT WOMAN - 15 in.

1974. Alice Evagluk, Coppermine, N.W.T. 15 in. (38 cm). Cloth body. Soapstone carved head. Clothing is patterned after those worn prior to the arrival of Europeans except that the clothing would have been made of fur and leather. The purpose of the distinctive styling was to allow access to sanitation while providing warmth. Navy wool melton cloth hooded jacket with long tail at the back, mitts, leggings with sewn on boots, long underpants with pink and white embroidery, white trim on top.

Ref.No.: 2F8 - 2F7

Range: $250.00 - 275.00

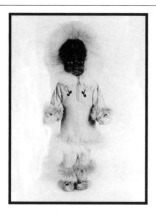

INUIT GIRL - 18 in.

ca.1975. 18 in. (46 cm). Brown plastic body, jointed hips, shoulders and neck. Vinyl head; brown sleep eyes, lashes; rooted straight black hair; closed mouth. Doll made by Regal but probably dressed by a native. Wearing a fur-trimmed wool flannel parka and hood with embroidered front and mittens. Leather moccasins.

Ref.No.: 2R4

Range: **$45.00 - 65.00**

MOUNTIE

ca.1975. 14 in. (35.5 cm). Cloth body and face. White face. Navy jacket with gold trim and fur-trimmed hood, beige leather mitts, brown fur hat, navy trousers and multi-coloured leather boots.

Ref.No.: 3P1

Range: **$225.00 - 275.00**

INUIT MAN - 13 in.

ca.1976. 13 in. (33 cm). Cotton head with embroidered features; wool hair. Felt hands. Authentic fur and leather clothing, felt and fur boots, and leather mitts. Handmade by Allikie Eeshieiut A-K from Frobisher Bay.

Ref.No.: D of C, BH5, p. 14

Range: **$250.00 - 325.00**

INUIT MAN - 13 in.

1976. 13 in. (33 cm). Cloth body; soapstone head with carved features. Clothing made of caribou turned inside out and trimmed with rick-rack. Mark: label, MADE BY ESAU ULAYOK FROM ESKIMO POINT.

Ref.No.: D of C, CP29, p. 14

Range: **$260.00 - 300.00**

INUIT MAN - 5 3/4 in.

1977. 5 3/4 in. (15 cm). Cloth body. Leather head; no features; wool hair. Mark: label, NOLEEANT OF SPENCE BAY/63Y9210. Handmade leather clothing; fur-trimmed hood.

Ref.No.: D of C, AR18, p. 14

Range: $75.00 - 90.00

INUIT MAN - 12 in.

1977. 12 in. (30.5 cm). Whalebone body. Stone head and carved features. Mark: label, JIMMY JACOBSON FROM TUKTOYAKTUK, N.W.T. Dressed in fox, seal, and rabbit furs.

Ref.No.: D of C, BZ13, p. 15

Range: $250.00 - 325.00

INUIT WOMAN - 13 in.

1977. 13 in. (33 cm). Cloth body. Canvas head, embroidered features; black wool hair. Mark: label, MADE BY EMILY KATIAK FROM COPPERMINE, N.W.T. Cotton print overdress, felt underskirt, trimmed with rabbit fur, dark red satin pants, navy felt mukluks with rawhide bottoms, fur mitts, fastened by a braided and tasselled holder, and hood with wolf fur trim.

Ref.No.: D of C, CE2, p. 15

Range: $200.00 - 300.00

INUIT HUSBAND AND WIFE - 12 1/2 in.

ca.1978. 12 1/2 in. (32 cm). Wife's head in embroidered sealskin. Husband's head is embroidered chamois. Dressed in authentic seal skin and wolf fur parkas, pants, mukluks and mittens. Tuk-Tik, the artist, is from the N.W.T.

Ref.No.: HX16

Range: $280.00 - 300.00 each

INUIT WOMAN - 14 in.

1981. Unknown artist, Sachs Harbour, N.W.T. 14 in. (36 cm). Cloth body, leather head, ink-drawn features. Dressed in cotton print overdress, fur-trimmed parka with fox fur trimmed hood, seal skin muk-luks.

Ref.No.: 2P24

Range: $200.00 - 275.00

CAMBRIDGE BAY, N.W.T., DOLL

1986. Cloth body, head, embroidered features and tattoo marks. Fur hair and trim

Ref.No.: ES55

Range: $200.00 - 275.00

INDIAN DOLLS

Indian dolls have been made from prehistoric times to the present. Few Indian dolls survive from the last century because most were not made of durable materials. A few dolls of wood or bone can be found in museums, but since most dolls were made of leather or corn husks and used as playthings, only a few survive.

Some of the dolls shown were commercially produced and were dressed and decorated by Canadian Indians. Many were made by doll artists who were trained by elders in a long tradition of a centuries old art. The criteria we use to define an Indian doll is simply that it must be made or dressed by an Indian artist.

INDIAN MAIDEN
Cloth Body - 7 1/2 in.

Date unknown. 7 1/2 in. (19 cm). Cloth body. Leather head, painted features, black knit fabric hair. Leather fringed dress with bead trim.

Ref.No.: 2R17

Range: $60.00 - 75.00

PLAINS INDIAN - 19 in.

1939. 19 in. (48.5 cm). Cloth body. Leather head; beaded eyes; horsehair braids; beaded mouth. Unmarked. Dressed in handmade buckskin clothing trimmed with beaded patterns, feather headdress, beaded leather shoes.

Ref.No.: D of C, BZ14, p. 21

Range: $165.00 - 250.00

INDIAN TODDLER

ca.1940. 22 in. (56 cm). Cloth body and legs. Composition shoulderhead and forearms. Doll made by Reliable. Painted blue eyes and open-closed mouth. Black yarn wig with braids over moulded hair. Soft leather fringed dress, laced together and beaded. Fringed and beaded leather bib over the dress. Fringed leather leggings. Leather head-dress simulated feathers.

Ref.No.: PGM14

Range: $125.00 - 160.00

SIX NATIONS INDIAN - 6 1/4 in.

1947. 6 1/4 in. (16 cm). Cloth body. Cloth head; features drawn in ink; black human hair braids. Unmarked. Handmade leather clothing.

Ref.No.: D of C, BM30, p. 21

Range: $65.00 - 85.00

STONEY INDIAN DOLL

Georgina Two Young Men. ca.1948. 10 in. (26 cm). Flesh coloured stockinette body, buckskin head, painted features. Braided black yarn hair. Unmarked. All original and hand-made. Blanket hand woven and hand-dyed using natural dyes and traditional Stoney colours of black, red, white and yellow. Doll artist is a well-known medicine woman.

Ref.No.: 2N11

Range: $140.00 - 200.00

INDIAN FAMILY

Katie Scow. ca.1950. Father, 11 in. (28 cm); mother, 9 in. 23 cm); boy, 8 in. (20.5 cm); girl, 7 in, (17 cm). Cloth bodies and heads; embroidered features; wool hair. Mark: on mother's cape, K.C.

Ref.No.: D of C, BZ12, p. 22.

Range: $335.00 - 395.00 group

INDIAN MAIDEN FROM SASKATCHEWAN

ca.1951. 10 1/2 in. (27 cm). Brown hard plastic, one-piece body and legs. Hard plastic head, brown sleep eyes, lashes, black mohair braids. Doll probably made by Reliable. Dressed in fringed white leather dress with turquoise trim and beading. Leather headband with feathers.

Ref.No.: 2F 26

Range: $65.00 - $ 85.00

INDIAN MAIDEN
Plastic Body - 7 1/2 in.

ca.1951. 7 1/2 in. (19 cm). Brown hard plastic body and head. Side glancing sleep eyes, black synthetic hair, closed mouth. Doll made by Reliable. Dressed in a felt dress and boots with intricate hand beading.

Ref.No.: 2K1

Range: $50.00 - $ 75.00

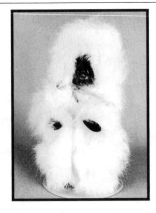

INDIAN CHILD
ca. 1953 - 8 in.

ca.1953. 8 in. (20 cm). Brown hard plastic body and head; brown sleep eyes, moulded lashes; open-closed mouth. Doll made by Reliable. Tag: WHETUNG OJIBWA CRAFTS, CURVE LAKE RESERVE, PETERBORO, ONTARIO. Dressed in white fur. Fur varies, depending on availability.

Ref.No.: 2R27

Range: $30.00 - $ 60.00

BROKEN NOSE

Owa'nyudane' and Gana'gweya'hon. 1960. 7 in. (17 cm). Cornhusk body. Carved wooden mask over face; long grey hair. Mark: on the bottom, IROQRAFTS/SIX NATION RESERVE. Dressed in wool and leather, with bead trim clothing.

Ref.No.: D of C, AZ36, p. 22

Range: $55.00 - 75.00

EAGLE DANCER

Six Nations Indian. 1960. 4 in. (10 cm). Cornhusk body. Head is that of a bird, arms are covered by the wings, eyes are beads. Unmarked.

Ref.No.: D of C, BC55, p. 22

Range: $75.00 - 110.00

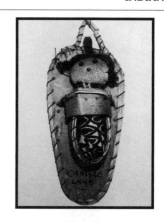

CARLYLE LAKE BABY

ca.1965. 4 in. (10 cm). Nylon over quilt batting body. Nylon over quilt head; blue beads for eyes; white bead for nose; black yarn hair. Birchbark carrier. Mark: CARLYLE LAKE.

Ref.No.: DR32

Mint: $10.00

Note: The name of Carlyle Lake, Saskatchewan, was changed in 1968 to White Bear Lake.

INDIAN MAIDEN
Plastic body - 7 1/2 in.

ca.1967. 7 1/2 in. (19 cm). Brown hard plastic teen body, jointed shoulders and neck. Hard plastic head; brown sleep eyes, moulded lashes; black yarn hair; closed mouth. Unmarked. Dressed by Indians in leather and fur.

Ref.No.: D of C, BP14, p. 25

Range: $20.00 - 30.00

INDIAN MAIDEN
Plastic body - 7 3/4 in.

ca.1970. 7 3/4 in. (19.5 cm). Brown hard plastic teen body, jointed shoulders and neck. Hard plastic head; brown sleep eyes, moulded lashes; black mohair braids; closed mouth. Unmarked. Dressed in beaded leather suit by Indians. Wears feather headdress and carries a bow.

Ref.No.: D of C, BP11, p. 23

Range: $20.00 - 35.00

INDIAN CHILD
ca. 1970 - 12 in.

ca.1970. 12 in. (31 cm). Brown plastic body, jointed hips, shoulders and neck. Vinyl head; black painted eyes; rooted black hair; open-closed mouth. Doll made by Reliable. Tag: OJIBWA ARTS & CRAFTS OF MANITOULIN ISLAND. Original brown leather jacket, pants and hat with white fur trim.

Ref.No.: 2F11

Range: $30.00 - $ 50.00

IROQUOIS WARRIORS

Six Nations Indians. 1970. Height: 5 1/2 in x 22 1/2 in, (14 cm x 57 cm). Cornhusk bodies; no features; synthetic black hair. Unmarked. Dressed in wool, leather, and beads.

Ref.No.: D of C, AZ27, p. 24

Range: $125.00 - 175.00

INDIAN MAIDEN - 16 in.

1972. 16 in. (41 cm). Brown plastic body, jointed hips, shoulders and neck. Vinyl head; brown stencilled eyes, painted uppers; black synthetic hair in braids; open-closed mouth. Doll made by Regal. Dressed in beaded and fringed leather dress and cape.

Ref.No.: 2K14

Range: $30.00 - $ 60.00

BLACKFOOT MEDICINE MAN

Indian. 1974. 10 in. (25.5 cm). Cloth body with wire armature. Leather head; beaded eyes and mouth; black braids. Unmarked. Dressed in handmade beaded leather clothing, fur headdress and carrying leather medicine bag.

Ref.No.: D of C, BX31, p. 24

Range: $100.00 - 150.00

HOOP DANCER

Rhea Skye. 1975. 8 in. (20.5 cm). Cornhusk body and head; no features; black wool braids. Mark: label, RHEA SKYE/MOHAWK INDIAN/RICE LAKE RESERVE. Dressed in leather trimmed with beads.

Ref.No.: D of C, AZ34, p. 24

Range: $70.00 - 85.00

GASESA

Date unknown. Owa'nyudane and Ginada'y'asas. (One of the host of supernaturals dedicated to the healing of certain illnesses). 7 1/2 in. (18 cm). Cornhusk body. Face covered with a cornhusk mask. Mark: on bottom, IROQRAFTS/SIX NATION RESERVE. Original label. Dressed in wool and beaded leather, carrying stick.

Ref.No.: D of C, AZ36A, p. 25

Range: $55.00 - 75.00

MOHAWK INDIAN

1975. 9 in. (23 cm). Cornhusk body and head; no features; black wool braids. Unmarked. Dressed in beaded leather, carrying shield and spear. Made at the Rice Lake Reserve, Ontario.

Ref.No.: D of C, AZ35, p. 25

Range: $65.00 - 85.00

BLACKFOOT INDIAN MAID

ca.1975. 16 in. (41 cm). Brown plastic body, jointed hips, shoulders and neck. Vinyl head; brown sleep eyes, lashes; black rooted hair; closed mouth. Doll made by Regal. Handmade white buckskin fringed dress. Beaded belt, earrings and headband. Necklace of shells and beads. Leather boots.

Ref.No.: 2R3

Range: $45.00 - $ 80.00

FALSE FACE SOCIETY DOLL

Six Nations Indian. 1977. 3 1/4 in. x 5 1/4 in. (8 cm x 13 cm). Cornhusk body. Black mask face with carved features, red painted mouth; black hair possibly dyed moss. Unmarked.

Ref.No.: D of C, BY6, p. 26.

Range: $50.00 - 75.00

LACROSSE PLAYER

Owa'ny udani' and Negi'yend'gowa. Date unknown. 7 in. (17 cm). Cornhusk body and head; no features on the face; black hair. Mark: on bottom, IROQRAFTS/SIX NATION RESERVE. Original label. Dressed in wool, leather, and beads and carrying a lacrosse racquet.

Ref.No.: D of C, BC3, p. 26

Range: $45.00 - 65.00

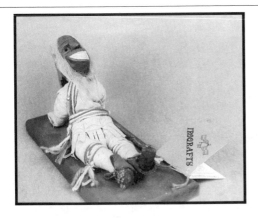

SIX NATIONS INDIAN - 4 in.

Date unknown. Height: 4 in. (10 cm). Cornhusk body. Carved wooden mask; long grey hair. Mark: label. Dressed in leather and wool.

Ref.No.: D of C, BC4, p. 26

Range: $45.00 - 65.00

CREE INDIAN

1978. 6 in. (15 cm). Leather body and head. Embroidered features, yarn hair. Tag: CREE INDIAN/EDMONTON, ALTA./ CANADIANA GIFTS/EDMONTON. Dressed in embroidered white buckskin.

Ref.No.: 2J19

Range: $65.00 - $ 85.00

SALICH BUTTON BLANKET DOLL

Joyce Willie. 1980. 18 in. (45.5 cm). Cloth body. Cloth head; embroidered features; black wool hair. Unmarked. Southern Kwagiutl button blanket and headdress.

Ref.No.: D of C, CA39, p. 28

Range: $250.00 - 300.00

PLAINS INDIAN - 31 in.

Regal. ca.1980. 31 in. (79 cm). Plastic body, jointed hips, shoulders, and neck. Vinyl head; brown sleep eyes, lashes, painted lower lashes; rooted dark brown curls; closed mouth. Mark: on head, REGAL TOY LTD./MADE IN CANADA. Dressed in a white buckskin dress, beaded belt, earrings and headband by a Canadian Indian, Muriel Cuthbert of Wetaskiwin, Alberta. She carryies a beaded leather bag.

Ref.No.: D of C, CO27A, p. 29

Range: $125.00 - 150.00

SIX NATIONS INDIAN
1980 - 6 1/2"

1980. 6 1/2 in. (16.5 cm). Cornhusk body. Apple head; eyes look like seeds; wool hair. Unmarked. Doll is sitting on a stump which bears a label, KEN AND RYE SKYE/SIX NATION INDIAN/INDIANS A. Handmade leather clothing, trimmed with beads.

Ref.No.: D of C, BM28, p. 27

Range: $60.00 - 75.00

CORNHUSK DANCER

Ontario Ojibwa Indian. 1983. 8 in. (20.5 cm). Dancing figure made of cornhusk; black wool braids. Mark: label, ONTARIO OJIBWA/CORN-HUSK DANCER. Dressed in wool and leather with leather shoes, carrying axe.

Ref.No.: D of C, CM6, p. 29

Range: $45.00 - 65.00

INDIAN MAN AND WOMAN

Elizabeth Harry, Sliammon Reservation, Powell River, B.C. Ca.1984. 9 1/2 in. (24 cm). Hand woven of dried grasses. Black hair, white feathers.

Ref.No.: ES30

Price: $600.00 pair

COWICHAN DOLL

Reliable. 1985. 18 in. (45.5 cm). Brown plastic body, jointed hips, shoulders, and neck. Vinyl head; brown sleep eyes, lashes, painted lower lashes; rooted straight black hair; closed mouth. Mark: on head RELIABLE TOYS CO. LTD./C MADE IN CANADA; on body, RELIABLE (in script); label, Handknit Cowichan Indian sweater by S. Betts.

Ref.No.: D of C, CM7, p. 31

Range: $60.00 - 90.00

MOHAWK WARRIOR

Cindy and Isabelle Skye. 1986. 23 in. (58.5 cm). Cornhusk one-piece body, fingers individually wrapped in tiny strips of cornhusk. Cornhusk head, no features. Synthetic black hair in braids. Unmarked. Dressed in leather pants, fringed and beaded; leather apron, bead trim; leather vest, shell trimmed; cotton shirt; leather moccasins, beaded and fur trimmed.

Ref.No.: D of C, CT1, p. 31

Range: $225.00 - 275.00

ENSIP

Margaret L. Cardinal. (Mallard Duck). 1986. 15 1/2 in. (39 cm). All leather one-piece body stuffed with hair. Tucks in the face give the illusion of eyes, mouth and nose. Black hair wig. Unmarked. Dressed in a cotton dress, trimmed with ribbon and wearing a beaded necklace and matching moccasins.

Ref.No.: 2E13

Range: $140.00 - $190.00

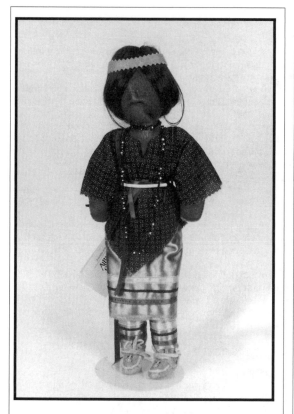

INDIAN MAIDEN
Leather body - 15 1/2 in.

Margaret Louise Cardinal. Ahyikis (Frog). 1986. 15 1/2 in. (39 cm). All leather one-piece body stuffed with hair. Tucks in the face give the illusion of eyes, mouth and nose. Brown hair wig. Unmarked. Dress made of cotton and satin, trimmed with ribbon and beads. Matching moccasins and bead necklace.

Ref.No.: 2E12

Range: $140.00 - $190.00

CREE DOLL

Margaret Louise Cardinal. 1989. 16 in. (41 cm). Deerskin body and head. Tucks in the face to give the illusion of a nose. Black horsehair braids. Unmarked. Dressed in blue print blouse and shawl, blue velvet skirt and leggings with satin ribbon trim. Beaded deerskin moccasins and leggings (under velvet leggings), headband and feather.

Ref.No.: 2O25

Range: $150.00 - $190.00

EATON'S BEAUTY DOLLS

The Eaton's Beauty dolls are not priced based on the condition of the doll in the photograph but on the standards for Eaton's Beauties. For a doll to be mint, it must have the original ribbon. A replacement ribbon has no value, although it may look nice in your collection. The original ribbon increases the value of the doll by approximately $100.00.

April Katz and Dorothy Churchill's dolls must have been bought at Eaton's to be considered of any value. The value of Eaton's Beauty dolls by these two artists is because they are part of a series. These dolls were sold as limited editions and so there are few of them and they are hard to obtain.

The Eaton's Beauty doll of 1989, made by April Katz, was the first of the series created as a lady doll. Generally, collectors disliked this change, as the dolls in the series had always been little girls. Unfortunately, collectors reacted by not buying the doll and Eaton's was left to sell the dolls for just $80.00 each. All the bargain-priced dolls have been sold, and eventually the 1989 doll will increase in value as an integral part of the series. There was no doll issued for 1990.

In 1991 Eaton's had the Eaton's Beauty dolls made by Dynasty Doll Co. of the U.S.A. It was an edition of 500 pieces, which was much larger than usual. However, the price was much less due to the dolls being manufactured in Korea, where labour costs are much lower. The dolls are very pretty and well-made and in keeping with the traditions of the Eaton's Beauty doll.

In 1992 Charlotte Rose, the Eaton's Beauty, was designed by Canadian doll artist Yvonne Richardson and made by the Dynasty Doll Co. in a limited edition of 400 dolls. It was once again a lady doll and sold at half price in 1993. Victoria Jane was the 20-inch Eaton's Beauty in 1993, and in 1994 Emily Anne was designed by Anne Dolan of Dynasty Dolls as the 21-inch Eaton's Beauty.

To celebrate Eaton's 125th anniversary in 1994, a special edition of 125 dolls, called Emily, was available for $750 each. In 1995 the Eaton's Beauty was called Sarah Margaret and was issued in the spring instead of autumn, and a new series, called the 1st Eaton Christmas Beauty, was launched in the autumn with a doll called Ivy Marie.

The Eaton's Beauty issued in the spring of 1996 was called Annabelle, and the second Eaton Christmas Beauty in the new series was available in the autumn.

GRADING STANDARDS FOR EATON'S BEAUTY DOLLS

MINT
Includes the original printed ribbon.
Has original underwear, socks and shoes.
Hair in the original set.
Head in perfect condition, no flakes, chips, cracks.
Body in perfect condition.
Eyes in good working order.
May have appropriate old clothing.

EXCELLENT
Has original underwear, socks and shoes.
Hair may be combed but not thin.
Bisque head not cracked or chipped.
Painted bisque head may have minor worn spots.
Body may show signs of wear, but not broken.
If kid body, no replaced parts, may be mended.
Eyes in working order.

GOOD
Underwear, or socks and shoes may be missing.
Bisque head may have a tiny hairline crack.
Painted bisque may be dirty and worn.
Hair may be worn or replaced with mohair
or human hair wig. Synthetic wigs not acceptable.
May need restringing.
Eyes may need resetting.
Kid body may have replaced arms but body
not completely replaced.

FAIR
Has no original clothing.
Eyes may be broken and need replacing.
Bisque head may have hairline cracks or chips.
Body in need of repair.
Needs new wig.
May have broken fingers.
Teeth may be missing.

"Eaton's Beauty" label

The end label on an "Eaton's Beauty" box for the period 1912-13. See page no. 24 for the Armand Marseille doll that would have been sold under this label

ARMAND MARSEILLE
ca.1900 - 24 in.

ca.1900. 24 in. (62 cm). Kid leather body, upper arms and upper legs, bisque forearms, papier-mâché ball-jointed lower legs. Bisque shoulderhead; blue glass sleep eyes, lashes, painted upper and lower lashes; blond mohair wig; open mouth showing teeth. Mark: on head, 370/AM 3 DEP. Redressed. Replaced ribbon.

Ref.No.: D of C, CF2, p. 67

Mint $750.00 **Ex.** $550.00 **G.** $400.00 **F.** $350.00

Note: Regional price differences.

CUNO & OTTO DRESSEL
1901 - 17 in.

1901. 17 in. (43 cm). Papier-mâché fully ball-jointed body. Bisque head; blue glass sleep eyes, painted upper and lower lashes; light brown mohair wig; open mouth showing four teeth. Mark: on head, Made in Germany/C/1. Original cotton half slip and drawers, socks and shoes and blue hair ribbon. Old cotton dress with original Eaton's Beauty ribbon.

Mint $650.00 **Ex.** $525.00 **G.** $350.00 **F.** $275.00

Note: 1901 was the only year prior to World War II that 17-inch Eaton's Beauty dolls were sold.

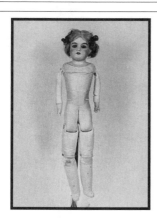

ARMAND MARSEILLE
ca.1902 - 25 in.

ca.1902. 25 in. (64 cm). Leather body, forearms bisque, riveted hips and knees. Bisque turned shoulderhead; grey glass sleep eyes; blond mohair wig; open mouth. Mark: on head, 370/AM 3/DEP. Original cotton half slip not shown. Five different size dolls were offered.

Ref.No.: 2G21

Mint $750.00 **Ex.** $550.00 **G.** $400.00 **F.** $350.00

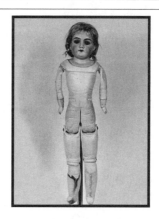

ARMAND MARSEILLE
ca.1902 - 22 in.

ca.1902. 22 in. (56 cm). Leather body, bisque forearms. Bisque shoulderhead; brown glass sleep eyes, painted upper and lower lashes; blond mohair wig; open mouth showing teeth. Mark: on head, 370/AM2 1/2/DEP/MADE IN GERMANY. Seven different size dolls were offered.

Ref.No.: 2G20

Mint $725.00 **Ex.** $525.00 **G.** $380.00 **F.** $325.00

J.D. KESTNER

1905. 26 in. (66 cm). Kid leather body, gusset hip and knee joints, bisque forearms, kid upper arms. Bisque head; blue glass sleep eyes, eyelashes, painted upper and lower lashes; dark brown wig; open mouth showing two teeth. Mark: on head, DEP 15413.

Ref.No. D of C, CH22, p. 68

Mint $1,000.00   Ex. $850.00   G. $575.00   F. $450.00

Note: Regional price differences.

ARMAND MARSEILLE
1908 - 21 1/2 in.

1908. 21 1/2 in. (55 cm). Papier-mâché bodies, wooden stick upper arms and upper legs, composition forearms and lower legs, ball-jointed; bisque socket heads, brown glass sleep eyes, lashes, painted upper and lower lashes; blond mohair wigs in ringlets; open mouth showing four teeth. Mark: on head, ARMAND MARSEILLE/MADE IN GERMANY/390/A8M.

Ref.No.: D of C, CW6, p. 69

Mint $625.00   Ex. $500.00   G. $400.00   F. $325.00

SCHOENAU & HOFFMEISTER
1909 - 18 in.

1909. 18 in. (45.5 cm). Papier-mâché fully ball-jointed body with wooden forearms. Bisque head with a slight sheen; blue glass sleep eyes, lashes, painted upper and lower lashes; brown mohair wig; open mouth showing teeth. Mark: on head, S (a star with PB in the centre) H/1909/1 1/2/GERMANY/.

Ref.No.: D of C, BS2A, p. 69

Mint $800.00   Ex. $625.00   G. $450.00   F. $350.00

SCHOENAU & HOFFMEISTER
1909 - 21 in.

1909. 21 in. (53.5 cm). Papier-mâché fully ball-jointed body. Bisque head; glass sleep eyes, lashes, painted upper and lower lashes; brown human hair wig; open mouth showing two teeth. Mark: on head, S (star with PB in centre) H/ 1909 /3 1/2 / GERMANY.

Ref.No.: D of C, CH18, p. 70

Mint $825.00   Ex. $650.00   G. $475.00   F. $375.00

Note: Regional price differences.

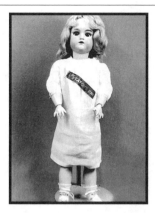

CUNO & OTTO DRESSEL
1909 - 21 in.

1909-10. 21 in. (53.5 cm). Papier-mâché fully ball-jointed body. Bisque head; brown glass sleep eyes, lashes, painted upper and lower lashes; long blond wig with bangs; open mouth showing two teeth. Mark: on head, C/4; oval hole in the back of head.

Ref.No.: D of C, CH26, p. 71

Mint **$750.00** **Ex.** **$650.00** **G.** **$525.00** **F. $425.00**

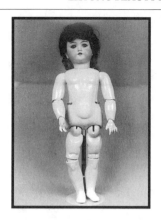

CUNO & OTTO DRESSEL
1909/10 - 19 3/4 in.

1909-10. 19 3/4 in. (50 cm). Papier-mâché fully ball-jointed body with red Holtz Masse stamp. Bisque head; blue glass sleep eyes, eyelashes, painted upper and lower lashes; brown mohair wig with curled bangs; open mouth, showing teeth. Mark: on head, C/3.

Ref.No.: D of C, BT17, p. 70

Mint **$700.00** **Ex.** **$600.00** **G.** **$475.00** **F. $395.00**

Note: Regional price differences.

CUNO & OTTO DRESSEL
1910 - 20 in.

1910. 20 in. (51 cm). Papier-mâché fully ball-jointed body. Bisque head, dimpled chin; blue glass sleep eyes, painted upper and lower lashes; blond mohair wig; open mouth showing teeth. Mark: on head, C/3, two small holes above mark, hole above each ear; on body, red Holtz Masse mark. Original shoes and socks, undershirt, pantalettes and slip.

Ref.No.: D of C, XH16, 72

Mint **$700.00** **Ex.** **$600.00** **G.** **$525.00** **F. $425.00**

Note: Photograph courtesy of Brooks-Kennedy Studio, St. Catharines, Ont.

CUNO AND OTTO DRESSEL
1911 - 19 1/2 in.

1911. 19 1/2 in. (49.5 cm). Fully ball-jointed papier-mâché body. Bisque head, dimpled chin; blue glass sleep eyes, painted upper and lower lashes; blond mohair wig; open mouth showing four teeth. Mark: head, GERMANY/C/3.

Ref.No.: D of C, BH25, p. 70

Mint **$700.00** **Ex.** **$600.00** **G.** **$525.00** **F. $425.00**

Note: Regional price differences.

CUNO & OTTO DRESSEL
1911/12 - 19 in.

1911-12. 19 in. (48.5 cm). Papier-mâché fully ball-jointed body. Bisque head; stationary brown glass eyes; light brown wig; open mouth showing four teeth. Mark: on head, GERMANY/C/3.

Ref.No.: D of C, CH31, p. 72

Mint $700.00 **Ex.** $600.00 **G.** $525.00 **F.** $425.00

ARMAND MARSEILLE
1912/13 - 19 1 /4 in.

1912-13. 19 3/4 in. (50 cm). Composition fully ball-jointed body. Bisque head, dimpled chin; brown glass sleep eyes, lashes, painted upper and lower lashes; long light brown mohair wig; open mouth showing teeth. Mark: on head, ARMAND MARSEILLE/GERMANY/390/A4M.

Ref.No.: D of C, BT8A, p. 73

Mint $625.00 **Ex.** $450.00 **G.** $350.00 **F.** $325.00

ARMAND MARSEILLE
1912/13 - 21 in.

1912-13. 21 in. (53 cm). Composition fully ball-jointed body. Bisque head; brown glass sleep eyes, lashes, painted upper and lower lashes; brown mohair wig; open mouth showing four teeth. Mark: on head, ARMAND MARSEILLE/GERMANY/390./A4M. Original chemise, ribbon, socks and shoes. Original box.

Mint $675.00 **Ex.** $525.00 **G.** $425.00 **F.** $350.00

Note: Regional price differences. Original box increases the value above mint value. For a picture of the label appearing on the box see page no. 20.

ARMAND MARSEILLE
1913/14 - 21 1/2 in.

1913-14. 21 1/2 in. (54 cm). Fully ball-jointed composition body. Bisque head; blue glass sleep eyes, lashes, painted upper and lower lashes; brown mohair wig; open mouth showing teeth. Mark: on head, ARMAND MARSEILLE/MADE IN GERMANY/390/A4M. Old white cotton dress, and undies. Original shoes and socks. Original ribbon.

Mint $675.00 **Ex.** $525.00 **G.** $425.00 **F.** $350.00

Note: Regional price differences. Higher prices in the Prairies and B.C.

ARMAND MARSEILLE
1914/15 - 25 in.

1914-15. 25 in. (63.5 cm). Composition fully ball-jointed body. Bisque head, dimpled chin; blue glass sleep eyes, lashes, painted upper and lower lashes; replaced human hair wig, original was brown mohair; open mouth, showing four teeth. Mark: MADE IN GERMANY/ARMAND MARSEILLE/390/A 8 M.

Ref.No.: D of C, CJ19, p. 73.

Mint $750.00 **Ex.** $575.00 **G.** $450.00 **F.** $375.00

ARMAND MARSEILLE
1914 - 22 1/2 in.

1914. 22 1/2 in. (57 cm). Papier-mâché fully ball-jointed body. Bisque head; Blue glass sleep eyes, painted upper and lower lashes; light brown mohair wig; open mouth showing four teeth. Mark: on head, ARMAND MARSEILLE/MADE IN GERMANY/390/A4M.

Ref.No.: D of C, BP19, p. 73.

Mint $675.00 **Ex.** $550.00 **G.** $425.00 **F.** $350.00

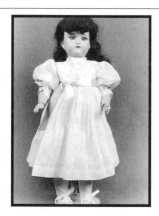

DOMINION TOY

1915. 20 in. (50.5 cm). Composition hands, trunk and legs, wooden arms, fully ball-jointed. Composition head, open crown; light blue tin sleep eyes, painted lashes, red dots in eye corners, nostril dots; original mohair wig, closed mouth. Mark: on body, MADE IN CANADA (in an arch over) DTMC.

Ref.No.: D of C, CL22, p. 74

Mint $450.00 **Ex.** $350.00 **G.** $250.00 **F.** $175.00

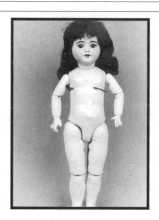

S.F.B.J.
ca.1922 - 20 in.

ca.1922. Eaton Special Doll (not an Eaton's Beauty) 20 in. (51 cm). Papier-mâché body, fully-jointed, wooden arms with French joints, composition hands, composition legs with French joints. Bisque head; all black glass sleep eyes, painted upper and lower lashes; dark brown human hair wig; open mouth showing four porcelain teeth. Mark: on head, S.F.B.J./60/PARIS.

Ref.No.: D of C, CW5, p. 74

Mint $875.00 **Ex.** $800.00 **G.** $675.00 **F.** $500.00

S.F.B.J.
1922/23 - 19 in.

1922-23. Eaton Special Doll (not an Eaton's Beauty). 19 in. (48.5 cm). Composition fully-jointed French body marked with the S.F.B.J. mark. Bisque head; blue glass sleep eyes, lashes; light brown human hair wig; open mouth, four moulded porcelain teeth. Mark: on head, 22/D/S.F.B.J./60/PARIS/3.

Ref.No.: D of C, BH26, p. 75

Mint $875.00 **Ex.** $800.00 **G.** $675.00 **F.** $550.00

ARMAND MARSEILLE
1924 - 21 in.

1924. 21 in. (53.5 cm). Composition fully ball-jointed body. Bisque head; brown glass sleep eyes, eyelashes, painted upper and lower lashes; replaced blond wig; open mouth, showing two teeth. Mark: on head, ARMAND MARSEILLE/390N/GERMANY/A 6 M. Replaced ribbon.

Ref.No.: D of C, AP31, p. 75

Mint $675.00 **Ex.** $525.00 **G.** $425.00 **F.** $325.00

ARMAND MARSEILLE
1924 - 21 1/4 in.

1924. 21 1/4 in. (54 cm). Composition fully ball-jointed body. Bisque head; blue glass sleep eyes, lashes, painted upper and lower lashes; blond mohair wig; open mouth showing teeth. Mark: on head, ARMAND MARSEILLE/GERMANY/ 390/A4M.

Ref.No.: D of C, BQ24A, p. 75

Mint $675.00 **Ex.** $525.00 **G.** $425.00 **F.** $325.00

Note: Photograph neg. no. 79-1624 courtesy of National Museum of Canada, National Museum of Man.

ARMAND MARSEILLE
1925 - 19 in.

1925. 19 in. (48.5 cm). Composition fully ball-jointed body. Bisque head; brown glass sleep eyes, painted upper and lower lashes; long blond mohair wig with bangs; open mouth showing four teeth. Mark: on head, MADE IN GERMANY/390/ A 2 1/2 M.

Ref.No.: D of C, BH27, p. 76

Mint $625.00 **Ex.** $500.00 **G.** $400.00 **F.** 325.00

ARMAND MARSEILLE
1927 - 22 in.

1927. 22 in. (56 cm). Composition fully ball-jointed body. Bisque head; blue glass sleep eyes, painted uppers and lowers; brown mohair wig; open mouth showing four teeth. Mark: on head, ARMAND MARSEILLE/GERMANY/390/A 4 M.

Ref.No.: D of C, CE34, p. 76

Mint $675.00 **Ex.** $550.00 **G.** $425.00 **F.** $325.00

ARMAND MARSEILLE
1927 - 22 in.

1927. 22 in (56 cm). Composition fully ball-jointed body. Bisque head, very rosy cheeks; brown glass sleep eyes, painted upper and lower lashes; blond mohair wig; open mouth, showing four teeth. Mark: on head, 390/A4M. Rest of the marking probably under the wig. Original cotton chemise, trimmed with two red ribbon rosettes, original ribbon, shoes and socks.

Ref.No.: 2H27

Mint $675.00 **Ex.** $550.00 **G.** $425.00 **F.** $325.00

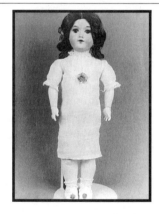

ARMAND MARSEILLE
1927 - 28 in.

1927-28. Fully-jointed doll (not an Eaton's Beauty). 19 1/2 in. (49.5 cm). Composition fully ball-jointed body. Bisque head; blue glass sleep eyes, lashes, painted upper and lower lashes; brown mohair wig; open mouth showing four teeth. Mark: on head, ARMAND MARSEILLE/GERMANY/390/A 3 M.

Ref.No.: D of C, BY14, p. 76

Mint $500.00 **Ex.** $425.00 **G.** $325.00 **F.** $300.00

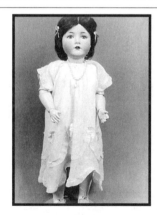

BIG SISTER

Cuno & Otto Dressel. 1927. 29 in. (74 cm). Composition fully ball-jointed body. Bisque head, highly coloured; blue glass sleep eyes, lashes, painted upper and lower lashes; brown human hair wig; open mouth showing four teeth and felt tongue. Mark: on head, CUNO & OTTO DRESSEL/GERMANY.

Ref.No.: D of C, CH32, p. 77

Mint $1,050.00 **Ex.** $925.00 **G.** $725.00 **F.** $525.00

Note: Regional price differences. Higher prices in the Prairies and B.C.

CUNO & OTTO DRESSEL
1929/30 - 25 in.

1929-30. 25 in. (63.5 cm). Composition fully ball-jointed body. Bisque head; grey-blue glass sleep eyes, lashes, painted upper and lower lashes; original brown wig; open mouth showing four teeth. Mark: on head, 6/CUNO & OTTO DRESSEL/GERMANY.

Ref.No.: D of C, CA18, p. 78

Mint $850.00   Ex. $750.00   G. $650.00   F. $500.00

Note: Regional price differences. Original box increases the value above mint.

ARMAND MARSEILLE
1933 - 21 in.

1933. 21 in. (53 cm). Composition fully ball-jointed body. Bisque head; blue glass sleep eyes, lashes, painted upper and lower lashes; blond mohair wig; open mouth, showing teeth. Mark: on head, 390/A3 1/2 M.

Ref.No.: 2017

Mint $625.00   Ex. $525.00   G. $400.00   F. $325.00

ARMAND MARSEILLE
1933 - 20 1/2 in.

1933. 20 1/2 in. (52 cm). Composition body, fully jointed. Bisque head; brown sleep eyes, lashes, painted upper and lower lashes; brown hair; open mouth showing teeth. Mark: on head, ARMAND MARSEILLE/GERMANY/A.4.M. Originally wore a princess slip and ribbon.

Mint $625.00   Ex. $500.00   G. $400.00   F. $325.00

Note: The mint price for this doll with the princess slip and no ribbon is $525.00.

ARMAND MARSEILLE
1934 - 20 in.

1934. 20 in. (50.5 cm). Papier-mâché, straight limbed, jointed hips, shoulders, and neck. Painted bisque head; blue glass sleep eyes, lashes, eyeshadow above eyes; blond mohair wig. Mark: on head, ARMAND MARSEILLE in an arch over 390/A 2 1/2 M.

Ref.No.: D of C, CJ17, p. 78

Mint $500.00   Ex. $375.00   G. $300.00   F. $250.00

Note: Regional price differences. Painted-bisque dolls are not popular with collectors.

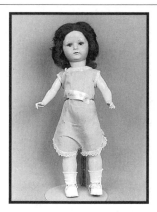

ARMAND MARSEILLE
1935/36 - 19 in.

1935-36. 19 in. (51 cm). Papier-mâché, straight limbed, jointed hips, shoulders, and neck. Painted bisque head; brown glass sleep eyes, lashes, eyeshadow above the eyes; brown mohair wig; closed mouth. Mark: on head, A 449 M/GERMANY/0 1/2. Replaced ribbon.

Ref.No.: D of C, BH23, p. 79

Mint $475.00 **Ex.** $375.00 **G.** $300.00 **F.** $250.00

Note: Painted bisque is less costly than bisque that has been kiln dried.

ARMAND MARSEILLE
1935/36 - 20 in.

1935-36. 20 in. (50.5 cm). Papier-mâché, straight limbed, jointed hips, shoulders, and neck. Painted bisque head; blue glass sleep eyes, lashes, eyeshadow above and below the eyes; blond mohair wig, blue hair-ribbon; closed mouth. Mark: on head, A 449 M/GERMANY/0 1/2. Original Eaton's Beauty ribbon.

Ref.No.: D of C, CH24, p. 79

Mint $475.00 **Ex.** $375.00 **G.** $300.00 **F.** $250.00

ARMAND MARSEILLE
1936/37 - 19 in.

1936-37. 19 in. (43.5 cm). Papier-mâché, straight limbed, jointed hips, shoulders, and head. Painted bisque head; brown glass sleep eyes, lashes, painted upper lashes; brown mohair wig; open mouth showing four teeth. Mark: on head, ARMAND MARSEILLE/GERMANY/390/A 2 1/2 M.

Ref.No.: D of C, BH24, p. 80

Mint $475.00 **Ex.** $375.00 **G.** $300.00 **F.** $250.00

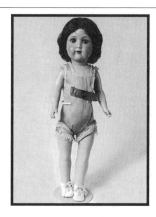

ARMAND MARSEILLE
ca.1938/39 - 18 in.

ca.1938-39. 18 in. (45.5 cm). Papier-mâché body, jointed hips, shoulders and neck. Painted bisque head; brown glass sleep eyes, lashes; brown mohair wig; open mouth showing teeth. Mark: on head, ARMAND MARSEILLE/GERMANY/390/A 2 1/2 M. Original princess slip and shoes. Original Eaton's Beauty ribbon.

Ref.No.: 2Z17

Mint $475.00 **Ex.** $375.00 **G.** $300.00 **F.** $250.00

OLD FASHIONED BEAUTY

Armand Marseille. 1939-40. (Not an Eaton's Beauty). 16 in. (40.5 cm). Composition (cardboard and plaster, painted), straight limbed, jointed hips, shoulders, and neck. Painted bisque head; brown glass sleep eyes, lashes, eyeshadow above eyes; blond mohair wig in ringlets; open mouth showing four teeth. Mark: on head, GERMANY/390/A 2 1/2 M.

Ref.No.: D of C, CJ20, p. 80

Mint $400.00   Ex. $300.00   G. $250.00   F. $200.00

RELIABLE
1940/41 - 18 in.

1940-41. 18 in. (45.5 cm). Composition, straight limbed, jointed hips, shoulders, and neck. Composition head; blue lithographed metal sleep eyes, lashes; light brown mohair wig; open mouth showing teeth. Mark: on head, RELIABLE/MADE IN CANADA.

Ref.No.: D of C, CR18, p. 81

Mint $400.00   Ex. $300.00   G. $250.00   F. $175.00

RELIABLE
1941/42 - 18 1/2 in.

1941-42. 18 1/2 in. (47 cm). Composition straight limbed, jointed hips, shoulders, and neck. Composition head; blue lithographed metal sleep eyes, lashes; blond mohair wig; open mouth showing teeth. Mark: on head, RELIABLE/MADE IN CANADA.

Ref.No.: D of C, CP2, p. 81

Mint $425.00   Ex. $315.00   G. $250.00   F. $175.00

RELIABLE
1942/43 - 19 in.

1942-43. 19 in. (48 cm). Composition, straight limbed, jointed hips, shoulders, and neck. Composition head; blue lithographed metal sleep eyes, lashes; light brown mohair wig; open mouth showing teeth. Mark: on head, RELIABLE/MADE IN CANADA.

Ref.No.: D of C, BC13, p. 81

Mint $425.00   Ex. $315.00   G. $250.00   F. $175.00

RODDY

1953-54. Feature Value Doll (not an Eaton's Beauty). 13 in. (33 cm). Hard plastic walking doll, jointed hips, shoulders, and neck. Hard plastic head; blue sleep eyes, moulded lashes; auburn synthetic wig with bangs; closed mouth. Mark: on body, RODDY/MADE IN ENGLAND.

Ref.No.: D of C, BS10, p. 82

Mint **$100.00** **Ex.** **$75.00** **G.** **$50.00** **F.** **$35.00**

DEE AN CEE
1954 - 18 in.

1954. 18 in. (45.5 cm). Latex body, auburn hair. Original pink, black and white striped dress and red ribbon (hat missing).

Ref.No.: ES56

Mint **$75.00** **Ex.** **$50.00** **G.** **$25.00** **F.** **$20.00**

DEE AN CEE
1957 - 8 in.

1957. 8 in. (20 cm). One-piece, Flexee-vinyl body. Vinyl head; sleep eyes; rooted hair; closed mouth. All original. No Eaton's Beauty ribbon, but box is labelled "Eaton's Beauty." Originally sold for $2.98.

MIB **$125.00** **Ex.** **$80.00** **G.** **$40.00** **F.** **$30.00**
Mint **$25.00** **Ex.** **20.00** **G.** **15.00** **F.** **10.00**
(without identification)

Note: It was also available in 18- and 23-inch sizes. Six outfits were sold for her. The same doll was sold without the Eaton's Beauty box and called Cindy-Petite.

DEE AN CEE
1960 - 18 in.

1960. 18 in. (46 cm). Plastic toddler, jointed hips, shoulders, and neck. Vinyl head; brown sleep eyes, lashes, painted lower lashes; rooted brown curly hair; open mouth nurser. Mark: on head, 1960/EATON BEAUTY BY DEE & CEE; on body, 2. Originally dressed in flowered stiff taffeta, fitted bodice, Peter Pan collar, pinstripe nylon pinafore over dress, velvet tie, silk panties, socks, black plastic strap shoes.

Ref.No.: D of C, CA29, p. 82

Mint **$185.00** **Ex.** **$150.00** **G.** **$85.00** **F.** **$55.00**

REGAL
1962 - 21 in.

1962. 21 in. (53 cm). Plastic body, jointed hips, shoulders, and neck. Vinyl head; blue sleep eyes, lashes; rooted honey blond hair; open mouth with four moulded painted teeth. Mark: on head, 15P / EEGEE; on body, REGAL / CANADA. Original dress with pink nylon bodice, flocked white nylon skirt, trimmed with black velvet. Replaced ribbon.

Ref.No.: 2K25

Mint $175.00 **Ex.** $110.00 **G.** $75.00 **F.** $50.00

Note: The same doll was also sold in different costumes with other names.

REGAL
1963 - 21 in.

1963. 21 in. (53.5 cm). Plastic body, jointed hips, shoulders, and neck. Vinyl head, blue sleep eyes, lashes, painted lower lashes, rooted blond saran curly hair, open mouth nurser. Mark: on head, REGAL / MADE IN CANADA. Redressed. Original dress was white and pink sheer material with lace trimmed overskirt. Extra clothing was available.

Ref.No.: D of C, CP4, p. 82

Mint $150.00 **Ex.** $100.00 **G.** $50.00 **F.** $30.00

REGAL
1964 - 21 in.

1964. 21 in. (53 cm). Plastic body, jointed hips, shoulders, and neck. Vinyl head; blue sleep eyes, lashes, painted lower lashes; rooted brown curls; open mouth nurser. Mark: on head, REGAL, on body, REGAL. Original dress with white skirt and red velveteen bodice, lace trim.

Ref.No.: D of C, BQ11, p. 83

Mint $150.00 **Ex.** $100.00 **G.** $50.00 **F.** $30.00

Note: Original box raises the value above the mint value. The same doll was available in 1965.

RELIABLE
1965 - 18 in.

1965. 18 in. (45.5 cm). One-piece vinyl-flex stuffed body. Vinyl head; blue plastic sleep eyes, lashes, painted lower lashes; rooted brown saran hair; closed watermelon mouth. Mark: on head, RELIABLE / MADE IN CANADA. Original corduroy play suit with heart shaped card with Eaton Beauty on it.

Ref.No.: D of C, BZ15, p. 83.

Mint $130.00 **Ex.** $85.00 **G.** $50.00 **F.** $30.00

Note: Four different Eaton's Beauty dolls were offered.

TWISTY PIXIE

Reliable. 1966. 14 in. (36 cm). Stuffed cloth body with wire armature so the doll can hold any position, vinyl hands. Vinyl head; blue sleep eyes, lashes; brown straight rooted hair; closed mouth. Mark: on head, RELIABLE/ MADE IN CANADA. Original red and white flannelette pyjamas. No badge.

Ref.No.: 2KA20

Mint $100.00 **Ex.** $75.00 **G.** $40.00 **F.** $25.00

Note: Five different dolls were offered as the Eaton Beauty family.

DOROTHY CHURCHILL
1978 - 18 in.

1978. 18 in. (45.5 cm). Fully jointed composition body. Bisque head; blue stationary eyes, lashes, painted upper and lower lashes; brown wig; open mouth showing teeth and tongue. Mark: on head, 47 of 100/ E (inside a diamond) DOROTHY CHURCHILL. Original blue velvet suit, matching hat, white ruffled shirt. Original white ribbon with gold print.

Ref.No.: D of C, CV12, p. 83

Mint $450.00 **Ex.** $350.00 **G.** $200.00 **F.** $150.00

DOROTHY CHURCHILL
1980 - 20 in.

1980. 20 in. (51 cm). Fully jointed composition body. Bisque head; stationary blue eyes, lashes, painted upper and lower lashes; long brown hair wig; open mouth, showing teeth and tongue. Mark: on head, DOROTHY 1980/CHURCHILL E (inside a diamond) 162. Original gown and matching hat. Original white ribbon with gold print.

Ref.No.: D of C, CV10, p. 84

Mint $475.00 **Ex.** $375.00 **G.** $225.00 **F.** $175.00

DOROTHY CHURCHILL
1981 - 18 in.

1981. 18 in. (45.5 cm). Ball-jointed composition body. Bisque head; stationary brown glass eyes, lashes and painted upper and lower lashes; human hair wig in ringlets; closed mouth. Mark: on head, DOROTHY CHURCHILL, a capital E inside a diamond, 79/1981. Original velvet coat with Eaton Beauty label inside. Matching hat, fur muff. Limited edition of 200.

Ref.No.: D of C, CG35, p. 84

Mint $475.00 **Ex.** $375.00 **G.** $225.00 **F.** $175.00

GAIL KAREN

April Katz. 1983. 17 in. (43 cm). All bisque, jointed hips, shoulders, and neck. Bisque head; stationary brown eyes, painted upper and lower lashes. Blond wig in long ringlets; closed mouth. Mark: on head, APRIL KATZ #60/CANADA/1983; card bearing artist's signature. Original mauve moire coat, taffeta dress, slip and pantalettes, matching hat. Limited edition of 200.

Ref.No.: D of C, AP5, p. 85

Mint $450.00   Ex. $350.00   G. $200.00   F. $150.00

APRIL KATZ
1984 - 17 in.

1984. 17 in. (43 cm). All bisque body, jointed hips, shoulders, and neck. Bisque head; brown glass stationary eyes, painted upper and lower lashes; long black hair in ringlets; closed mouth. Mark: on head, 1984 EATON BEAUTY/APRIL KATZ (in script) #250. Made from Steiner mould, SGDG/Paris. Original velvet coat and matching hat, silk dress, slip and pantalettes, fur muff, ice skates and boots. Limited Edition of 250.

Ref.No.: D of C, CY1, p. 85

Mint $450.00   Ex. $350.00   G. $200.00   F. $150.00

APRIL KATZ
1986 - 16 in.

1986. 16 in. (41 cm). Porcelain body, jointed hips, shoulders and neck. Bisque head; blue glass stationary eyes, painted upper and lower lashes; long brown hair wig; open mouth showing teeth. Mark: on head, 1986 EATON'S BEAUTY/BY APRIL KATZ/#7. Original green taffeta dress trimmed with lace, petticoat, pantalettes, shoes and stockings. Matching hairbow. Limited edition of 100.

Ref.No.: 2C25

Mint $400.00   Ex. $325.00   G. $200.00   F. $150.00

APRIL KATZ
1987 - 16 in.

1987. 16 in. (41 cm). Porcelain body, jointed hips, shoulders and neck. Bisque head; blue glass stationary eyes, painted upper and lower lashes; Honey blond wig in ringlets and curled bangs; closed mouth. Mark: on head, 1987 EATON BEAUTY (IN SCRIPT)/BY APRIL KATZ/ #70. Original pink taffeta dress trimmed with ecru lace, petticoat, pantalettes, matching hat, stocking and shoes. Limited edition of 125.

Ref.No.: 2C24

Mint $400.00   Ex. $325.00   G. $200.00   F. $150.00

LOUISETTE

April Katz. 1989. 16 in. (41 cm). Cloth body, porcelain arms, legs and shoulderplate. Bisque head; stationary blue glass eyes, painted upper and lower lashes. Dark brown upswept wig; closed mouth. Mark: on head, APRIL KATZ/1989/134 OF 250. On Tag: LOUISETTE/1989/EATON BEAUTY/LIMITED EDITION/250/APRIL KATZ. Original white and pink taffeta gown.

Ref.No.: PGE1

Mint $300.00 Ex. $225.00 G. $175.00 F. $125.00

JOYCE MARIE

Dynasty Doll Co. 1991. 19 in. (48 cm). Cloth body, porcelain forearms and half legs. Bisque head; blue stationary eyes, lashes, painted lowers; blond wig in ringlets; closed mouth. Mark: on head, Circle ringed with painted leaves, EATON/BEAUTY/BY/DYNASTY. #57/480; hang tag, EATON BEAUTY/BY DYNASTY. Original pink dress with lace and blue ribbon trim. Tiny pearls sewn on net bodice of shirred pink. Crinoline, pantalettes, white stockings and shoes, matching hat with flower trim. Certificate of authenticity. Limited edition of 480 pieces.

Ref.No.: PGB 9

Mint $300.00 Ex. $275.00 G. $200.00 F. $150.00

CHARLOTTE ROSE

Yvonne Richardson. 1992. Dynasty Doll Co. 20 in. (50.5 cm). Cloth body, porcelain forearms and half legs. Bisque shoulder head; blue stationary eyes, lashes, painted lowers; brown wig pulled back; closed mouth. Mark: on head, #/400, incised 718A. Limited edition of 400. Comes with hang tag and wooden stand with name engraved on a metal plate. Original lace-trimmed drawers, petticoat, lined skirt, white lace-trimmed blouse, print jacket, hat and parasol.

Ref.No.: ES57

Mint $400.00 Ex. $325.00 G. $275.00 F. $225.00

EMILY ANNE

1994. Dynasty Doll Co. 21 in. (53 cm). Cloth body with porcelain forearms and half legs. Bisque head; blue stationary eyes, lashes, painted lowers, blue eye-shadow; blond wig; closed mouth. Mark: on head, printed circle with EATON BEAUTY and DYNASTY inside, # over 400 beside the circle. Original costume, satin drawers and crinoline, deep pink satin lace-trimmed dress and matching hat. White ribbon with gold print: EATON BEAUTY DOLL 1994. Limited edition of 400.

Ref.No.: ES58

Mint $250.00 Ex. $225.00 G. $200.00 F. $150.00

SARAH MARGARET

1995. Dynasty Doll Co. 20 in. (50.5 cm). Cloth body with porcelain hands and feet. Bisque head; blue stationary eyes; blond hair. Original baby blue satin dress with over-dress of ivory lace and matching hat. Ivory ribbon with gold print: EATON BEAUTY DOLL. Limited edition of 450. Includes wooden stand.

Mint $250.00 **Ex.** $225.00 **G.** $200.00 **F.** $150.00

IVY MARIE

1995. 20 in. (50.5 cm). Cloth lady body with porcelain hands and feet. Bisque shoulder head; blue stationary eyes, lashes and painted lowers; closed mouth; honey-blond upswept wig. Mark: on head: EATON CHRISTMAS BEAUTY DOLL stamped in ink and a hand lettered #/450 on the shoulder plate. Limited edition of 450. Brass engraved nametag: 1ST EATON CHRISTMAS BEAUTY DOLL IVY MARIE, 1995. Burgundy satin gown with lace and pearl trim, matching hat and parasol and carrying a tiny gift.

Ref.No.: ES60

Mint $325.00 **Ex.** $275.00 **G.** 225.00 **F.** $200.00

ANNABELLE

1996. 20 in. (50.5 cm). Cloth lady body with porcelain hands and feet. Bisque head; blue stationary eyes, lashes and painted lowers; open mouth; dark brown shoulder-length curled wig. Mark: on head: #/450. Limited edition of 450. Original gown of ivory silk pongee with lace and orchid chiffon and satin trim and matching hat. White ribbon with gold print: EATON BEAUTY DOLL.

Mint $250.00 **Ex.** $225.00 **G.** $200.00 **F.** $150.00

CANADIAN BEAUTY DOLL

A very interesting doll has surfaced wearing an original red ribbon and gold print with "Canadian Beauty" on it. An early 20th century advertisement by the Hudson's Bay Company showed a Western Beauty doll, which was similar to the Eaton's Beauty. It is possible that the Canadian Beauty was also originally sold by the Hudson's Bay Company, about 1928.

ARMAND MARSEILLE

ca.1928. 30 in. (76 cm). Composition fully ball-jointed body. Bisque head, highly coloured; celluloid blue sleep eyes, lashes and painted upper and lower lashes; blond mohair wig; open mouth showing four teeth. Mark: on head, ARMAND MARSEILLE/390/A12M. Appropriately redressed in silk dress and velvet coat and bonnet. Original Canadian Beauty ribbon. *Ref.No.: 2A26*

Mint $900.00 **Ex.** $750.00 **G.** $600.00 **F.** $400.00

CANADIAN CELEBRITY DOLLS

A Canadian celebrity doll is one made to represent a well-known Canadian figure, such as a sportsperson or an historic character. The doll does not have to be manufactured in Canada; the criteria is that the person represented be Canadian.

We are very short of celebrity dolls, not because we are short of celebrities but because there are not enough doll collectors in Canada to make such a doll profitable to produce.

Those we do have, however, are much appreciated and are sought after in the collectables market.

DIONNE QUINTUPLETS

Madame Alexander. 1934. 10 in. (25.5 cm). Composition bent-limb baby body, jointed hips, shoulders, and neck. Composition head; brown sleep eyes, lashes, painted lower lashes; brown moulded hair; closed mouth. Mark: on head, DIONNE/ALEXANDER; on body, MADAME ALEXANDER. Made in the U.S.A.

Ref.No.: D of C, BT1A, p. 86

Mint set $2,000.00 - 2,300.00
Ex. sold separately $325.00 - 350.00

DIONNE QUINTUPLETS

Superior. c.1934. Babies, 7 in. (18 cm); nurse, 10 in. (25.5 cm). Composition bent-limb baby bodies, jointed hips, shoulders, and neck. Nurse, straight limbed. Composition heads; babies, brown painted side-glancing eyes; nurse, black painted side-glancing eyes; light brown moulded hair; closed mouths. Mark: babies, on head, SUPERIOR; nurse, unmarked.

Ref.No.: D of C, CE21, p. 87

Mint set $1,200.00

DIONNE QUINTUPLETS

Madame Alexander. 1935. 7 1/2 in. (19 cm). Composition bent-limb baby bodies, jointed hips, shoulders, and neck. Composition head; brown painted side-glancing eyes, painted upper lashes; brown moulded hair; closed mouth. Each doll wears a metal nametag. Mark: on head, ALEXANDER; on back, ALEXANDER. Made in the U.S.A.

Ref.No.: D of C, BW11, p. 89

Mint set, teeter-totter and box $3,500.00
Ex. sold separately $250.00 - 300.00

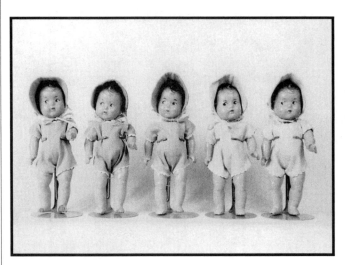

DIONNE QUINTUPLETS

Madame Alexander. 1935. 7 1/2 in. (19 cm). Composition bodies, jointed hips, shoulders, and neck. Composition head; brown painted side-glancing eyes, painted upper lashes; brown moulded hair; closed mouth. Mark: on head, ALEXANDER; on body, ALEXANDER. Made in the U.S.A.

Ref.No.: D of C, AB2, p. 90

Ex. set $1,500.00
Ex. sold separately $225.00 - 275.00

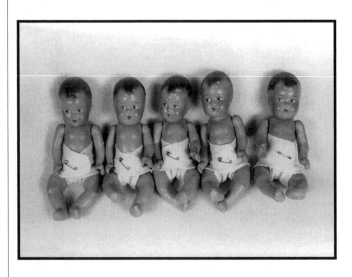

QUINTUPLET DOLLS

ca. 1936. 7 in. (19 cm). All composition bodies, jointed hips, shoulders and necks. Composition heads; side-glancing painted blue eyes; brown moulded hair, closed mouth. Dressed in diapers. Unmarked.

Ref.No.: 2U21

Mint	$350.00	Ex.	$275.00 set
G.	$150.00	F.	$100.00 set

DIONNE QUINTUPLETS

Madame Alexander. 1936. 16 in. (40.5 cm). Composition bodies, jointed hips, shoulders, and neck. Composition head; brown glassene eyes, lashes, painted lower lashes; brown human hair wigs; closed mouth. Mark: on body, ALEXANDER. Made in the U.S.A.

Ref.No.: D of C, BW8, p. 89

Mint set $4,000.00 - 5,000.00
Ex. sold separately $560.00 - 700.00

Note: This set is rarely seen.

BARBARA ANN SCOTT
1948

Reliable. 1948. 15 in. (38 cm). Composition body, jointed hips, shoulders, and neck. Composition head; blue sleep eyes, lashes; painted lower lashes and brows; honey blond mohair wig; open smiling mouth showing teeth. Mark: on head, RELIABLE/MADE IN CANADA. Original lace costume. Simulated pearl head-dress, ice-skates. Originally included a pair of shoes.

Ref.No.: D of C, AM24, p. 90

Mint **$450.00** **Ex.** **$350.00** **G.** **$180.00** **F.** **$80.00**

Note: Regional price differences.

BARBARA ANN SCOTT
1949

Reliable. 1949. 15 in. (38 cm). Composition body, jointed hips, shoulders, and neck. Composition head; blue sleep eyes, lashes, painted lower lashes, brows painted in separate strokes; blond mohair wig; open smiling mouth showing teeth. Mark: on head, RELIABLE/MADE IN CANADA. Blue skating costume trimmed in marabou, ice-skates.

Ref.No.: D of C, AP8, p. 91

Mint **$450.00** **Ex.** **$350.00** **G.** **$180.00** **F.** **$80.00**

BARBARA ANN SCOTT
1950

Reliable. 1950. 15 in. (38 cm). Composition body, jointed hips, shoulders, and neck. Composition head; blue sleep eyes, lashes, painted lower lashes and brows; honey blond saran wig; open smiling mouth showing teeth. Mark: on head, RELIABLE/MADE IN CANADA. Original tag. Velveteen skating costume trimmed with marabou, ice-skates. Some dolls were sold with large velveteen hats trimmed with marabou.

Ref.No.: D of C, AW21, p. 91

Mint **$450.00** **Ex.** **$350.00** **G.** **$180.00** **F.** **$80.00**

BARBARA ANN SCOTT
1951

Reliable. 1951. 15 in. (38 cm). Composition body, jointed hips, shoulders, and neck. Composition head; blue sleep eyes, lashes, painted brows; honey blond mohair wig; open smiling mouth showing teeth. Mark: on head, RELIABLE/MADE IN CANADA. Blue skating costume with tiny gold bows and dots on the fabric, marabou trim, ice-skates.

Ref.No.: D of C, CA23, p. 92

Mint **$450.00** **Ex.** **$350.00** **G.** **$180.00** **F.** **$80.00**

BARBARA ANN SCOTT
1952

1952. 15 in. (38 cm). Composition body; jointed hips, shoulders and neck. Composition head; blue sleep eyes, lashes, painted brows; honey blond wig; open smiling mouth showing teeth. Mark: on head, RELIABLE/MADE IN CANADA. Blue nylon skating costume with pink floral embroidery, matching head-dress and ice-skates.

Ref.No.: GK26

Mint $450.00   Ex. $350.00   G. $180.00   F. $80.00

BARBARA ANN SCOTT
1953

1953. 15 in. (38 cm). Composition body, jointed hips shoulders and neck. Composition head; blue sleep eyes, lashes, painted brows; honey blond saran hair; open smiling mouth showing teeth. Mark: on head, RELIABLE/MADE IN CANADA. Original pink embossed satin skating costume with marabou trim, ice-skates. Original hat had a large brim trimmed with marabou.

Mint $450.00   Ex. $350.00   G. $180.00   F. $80.00

Note: The Barbara Ann Scott doll for 1954 wore a velveteen skating costume and had saran hair.

MARILYN BELL

Dee an Cee. 1954. 16 in. (40.5 cm). One-piece Skintex body. Vinyl head; blue sleep eyes, lashes, painted lower lashes; rooted blond curls; open-closed smiling mouth showing painted teeth. Mark: on head, MARILYN BELL/D&C TOY CO./1954. Swimsuit and robe.

Ref.No.: D of C, AP29A, p. 93

Mint $175.00   Ex. $125.00   G. $75.00   F. $45.00

Note: The head was designed by American Bernard Lipfert. Few dolls are available due to the deterioration of the rubber bodies.

ANNE HEGGTVEIT

Reliable. 1961. 16 in. (40.5 cm). Plastic body and legs, vinyl arms, jointed hips, shoulders, and neck. Vinyl head; blue sleep eyes, lashes, painted lower lashes; rooted blond saran hair; closed mouth. Mark: on body, RELIABLE/CANADA. Original tag, CANADIAN OLYMPIC SKI CHAMPION/ANNE HEGGTVEIT DOLL. MADE BY/RELIABLE IN CANADA.

Ref.No.: D of C, BQ1, p. 92

Mint $145.00   Ex. $95.00   G. $40.00   F. $25.00

Note: Without the identifying costume, this is a common doll.

ANNE HEGGTVEIT

1961. 16 in. (40.5 cm). Plastic body and legs, vinyl arms, jointed hips, shoulders and neck. Vinyl head; blue sleep eyes, lashes, painted lower lashes; rooted blond saran hair; closed mouth. Mark: on body, RELIABLE/CANADA. Original red print zippered ski jacket, ski mitts, town and country ski slacks. Missing ski boots, sunglasses and miniature skis.

Ref.No.: 2M1

Mint **$145.00** **Ex.** **$95.00** **G.** **$40.00** **F.** **$25.00**

KAREN MAGNUSSEN
1974

Regal. 1974. 18 in. (45.5 cm). Plastic body, jointed hips, shoulders, and neck. Vinyl head; blue sleep eyes, lashes, eyeshadow; rooted blond curls; closed mouth. Mark: on head, REGAL TOY/MADE IN CANADA; on body, REGAL/CANADA/PAT. PEND.; dress tag, KAREN MAGNUSSEN, MADE BY REGAL TOY LTD. CANADA. Original black cotton print jumper with lace sleeved skating dress, net pantyhose, ice-skates.

Ref.No.: D of C, CD16, p. 93

Mint **$100.00** **Ex.** **$75.00** **G.** **$40.00** **F.** **$25.00**

KAREN MAGNUSSEN
1975

1975. 18 in. (45.5 cm). Plastic body, jointed hips, shoulders and neck. Vinyl head; blue sleep eyes, lashes, eyeshadow; rooted blond curls; closed mouth. Mark: on head REGAL TOY/MADE IN CANADA; on body, REGAL/CANADA/PAT.PEND. Original lace skating costume, net pantyhose, skates.

Ref.No.: GK15

Mint **$115.00** **Ex.** **$85.00** **G.** **$40.00** **F.** **$25.00**

Note: The 1975 Karen Magnussen doll is harder to find as fewer were sold.

BOBBY ORR
Open Mouth

Regal. 1975. 12 in. (30.5 cm). Plastic body, jointed hips, waist, shoulders, and neck. Vinyl head; blue painted eyes; brown moulded hair; open-closed mouth smiling, showing painted teeth. Mark: on body, MADE IN/HONG KONG. Original Boston Bruins uniform.

Ref.No.: D of C, CF16, p. 94

Mint **$150.00** **Ex.** **$100.00** **G.** **$75.00** **F.** **$50.00**

Note: Bobby Orr dolls have increased in price due to demand by male collectors.

BOBBY ORR
Closed Mouth

ca.1975. 12 in. (30.5 cm). Plastic body, jointed hips, waist, shoulders and neck. Vinyl head; painted eyes with white highlights; brown moulded hair; closed mouth. Unmarked. Original Boston Bruins hockey costume.

Ref.No.: 2E6

Mint **$150.00** **Ex.** **$100.00** **G.** **$75.00** **F.** **$50.00**

THE GREAT GRETZKY

Mattel. 1983. 12 in. (30.5 cm). Plastic body, jointed hips, waist, shoulders, and neck. Vinyl head; painted blue eyes; blond moulded hair; open-closed mouth showing teeth. Mark: on body, MATTEL INC. 1983/TAIWAN.

Ref.No.: D of C, CS14A, p. 95

Mint **$150.00** **Ex.** **$100.00** **G.** **$75.00** **F.** **$50.00**

Note: The market is volatile due to increased demand by hockey fans.

ELIZABETH MANLEY
1989 - 17 in.

Wis-Ton and D.D.C. 1989. 17 in (43 cm). Plastic body, jointed hips, shoulders and neck. Vinyl head; golden brown sleep eyes, lashes; rooted short blond hair; open-closed mouth showing teeth. Mark: on head, ELIZABETH MANLEY/1989/STAR DOLL. Original shocking pink skating costume, white cowboy hat and skates. Head mould was taken from the original sculpture by Jeanne Venton.

Ref.No.: PGA19

Mint **$60.00** **Ex.** **$45.00** **G.** **$30.00** **F.** **$25.00**

ELIZABETH MANLEY
1991 - 17 in.

Wis-Ton and D.D.C. 1991. 17 in. (43 cm). Plastic body, jointed hips, shoulders and neck. Vinyl head; golden brown sleep eyes, lashes; rooted blond hair in pony-tail and bangs; open-closed mouth. Mark: on head, ELIZABETH MANLEY/1989/STAR DOLL. Original white skating costume with gold trim and feathers on the shoulders, skates.

Ref.No.: WW2

Mint **$60.00** **Ex.** **$45.00** **G.** **$30.00** **F.** **$25.00**

THE FORGIE FIVE GO SHOPPING

Distinctive Dolls of Canada. 1990. 12 in. (30.5 cm). Plastic bodies, jointed hips, shoulders and neck. Vinyl heads; sleep eyes, lashes, rooted hair; open-closed mouths. Anya has brown eyes and brown hair; Kiza has brown eyes and brown hair with a small top-knot; Zuri has blue eyes and red hair; Kipp has brown eyes and golden blond hair and Rhys has brown eyes and honey blond hair. The girls wear cotton dresses in their own colours, socks and shoes and a shopping bag with their names on it. The boys wear cotton coveralls in their colours and carry a matching shopping bag. Mark: on heads, STAR DOLL.

Ref.No.: FF1

Mint	**$135.00**	**Ex.**	**$100.00**
G.	**$60.00**	**F.**	**$40.00**

THE FORGIE FIVE AT BEDTIME

Distinctive Dolls of Canada. 1990. 12 in. (30.5 cm). Plastic bodies, jointed hips, shoulders and neck. Vinyl heads; sleep eyes, lashes; rooted hair; open-closed mouths. Mark: on head, STAR DOLL. Original print sleepers for the girls and blue sleepers for the boys. Each doll carries a blanket and a teddy bear. The dolls wear a button with their names in their colours.

Ref.No.: FF2

Mint	**$135.00**	**Ex.**	**$100.00**
G.	**$60.00**	**F.**	**$40.00**

THE FORGIE FIVE GO DANCING

Distinctive Dolls of Canada. 1991. 12 in. (30.5 cm). Plastic bodies, jointed hips, shoulders and neck. Vinyl heads; sleep eyes, lashes; rooted hair; open-closed mouths. Mark: on head, STAR DOLL. Zuri and Kiza have two ponytails, Anya has one. Dressed in original ballet body suits in their colours. Girls wear net tutus and the boys wear leg warmers.

Ref.No.: FF3

Mint $135.00 **Ex.** $100.00 **G.** $60.00 **F.** $40.00

THE WORKING DOLL

A working doll is one that has a purpose other than just a toy, such as an advertising doll, a display doll or one that represents an organization or a Canadian literary character. Since the costume often creates the character, the clothing is very important.

Most of the dolls in this category were made in Canada, however, we have included a few, such as the Barbie dolls or the Anne of Green Gables dolls, that were made in other countries. The criteria here is that the doll represent Canada or something Canadian.

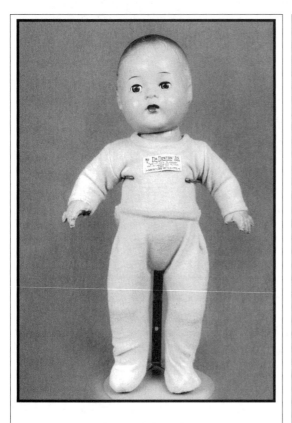

DR. DENTON DOLL

Unknown. ca.1938. 17 in. (43 cm). Composition body, jointed hips, shoulders, and neck. Composition head; brown sleep eyes, lashes, painted lower lashes; brown moulded hair, closed mouth. Unmarked. Original two piece blue sleepers with label marked, No./5/DR. DENTON 34/INCH/TWO-PIECE SLEEPER/Pat. IN CANADA DEC.8,1925/MADE BY/MERCURY MILLS LTD.

Ref.No.: D of C, CD24, p. 101

Mint **$100.00** **Ex.** **$75.00** **G.** **$50.00** **F.** **$35.00**

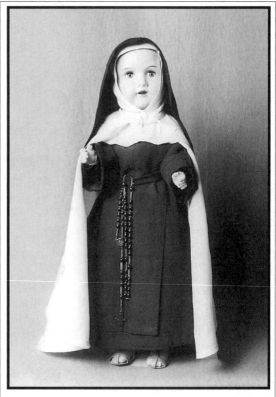

NUN
1942 - 19 in.

Reliable. ca.1942. 19 in. (45.5 cm). Composition body, jointed hips, shoulders, and neck. Composition head; blue stencilled metal eyes, lashes; no hair; open mouth showing teeth. Mark: on head, RELIABLE/MADE IN CANADA. Original nun's costume, fine brown wool habit, cream linen cape, cotton wimple, leather sandals. Wearing a tiny rosary made in France.

Ref.No.: D of C, BO1, p. 103

Mint **$300.00** **Ex.** **$250.00** **G.** **$200.00** **F.$150.00**

MOUNTIE DOLL

ca.1946. 8 1/2 in. (22 cm). Celluloid body, jointed hips, shoulders and neck. Celluloid head; brown painted eyes; moulded brown hair; closed mouth. Original hang tag, NATIVE HANDICRAFT/OF CANADA. Original felt red and navy uniform, black boots, belt and holster and tiny metal gun. Hat missing. Doll not made in Canada.

Ref.No.: 2Z6

Mint $40.00 **Ex.** $30.00 **G.** $25.00 **F** $20.00

SANTA CLAUS BANK

1947. 7 in. (18 cm). Composition body painted appropriately. Mark: RD 1947/A DEE AN CEE PRODUCT/SANTA CLAUS BANK/TORONTO, CANADA.

Ref.No.: GK10

Mint $30.00 **Ex.** $25.00 **G.** $15.00 **F.** $10.00

BLUE BONNET MARGARINE DOLL

ca.1951. 7 1/2 in. (19 cm). Hard plastic body, jointed hips, shoulders and neck. Hard plastic head; side-glancing, black painted eyes, eyelashes; blond mohair wig. Mark: on body, RELIABLE/MADE IN CANADA; on arms, 229-4, 229-3. Original gown and bonnet, painted shoes.

Ref.No.: 2G3

Mint $30.00 **Ex.** $25.00 **G.** $20.00 **F.** $15.00

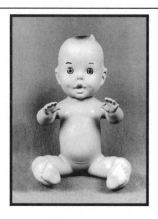

GERBER BABY

Viceroy. 1955. 12 in. (30.5 cm). All rubber bent-limb baby body, jointed hips, shoulders and neck. Rubber head with dimples; inset blue plastic eyes; detailed moulded hair; open-mouth nurser. Mark: on body, A VICEROY/SUNRUCO DOLL/MADE IN CANADA/Patent Pending.

Ref.No.: D of C, BN4, p. 100

Mint $100.00 **Ex.** $75.00 **G.** $45.00 **F.** $30.00

Note: This is a rare doll as it was made for only one year. The Canadian verion had much curlier hair

ANNE OF GREEN GABLES
ca.1955

ca.1955. 8 in. (20 cm). Hard plastic body, jointed hips, shoulders and neck. Hard plastic head; painted eyes; red braid wig; closed mouth. Mark: original hand tag, A PEGGY NISBET MODEL/S7528/ANNE OF GREEN GABLES/MADE IN ENGLAND. Original grey dress, hat and bag.

Ref.No.: 2R9

Mint $90.00 **Ex.** $75.00 **G.** $45.00 **F.** $30.00

CAMPBELL SOUP KID
ca.1955

Reliable. ca.1955. 10 in. (25.5 cm). One-piece vinyl body, jointed neck. Vinyl head; black painted side-glancing eyes, painted upper lashes; light brown moulded hair; closed watermelon mouth. Mark: on head,, CAMPBELLS. Original red and white dress.

Ref.No.: D of C, BM33, p. 99

Mint $75.00 **Ex.** $50.00 **G.** $25.00 **F.** $20.00

DOMINION FOOD STORE
ca.1955 - 8 in.

ca.1955. 8 in. (20 cm). Hard plastic, jointed body. Side-glancing sleep eyes; brown mohair wig. Red cape, trimmed with gold, white dress with gold dots. Made especially for the Dominion Food Store. Costume not shown in catalogue.

Ref.No.: SP2

Mint $35.00 **Ex.** $25.00 **G.** $15.00 **F.** $10.00

DOMINION FOOD STORE
ca.1955 - 13 in.

ca.1955. 13 in. (33 cm). Hard plastic, jointed body. Blue sleep eyes; light brown mohair wig. Red cape, trimmed in white, white dress with gold and lace trim. Made especially for the Dominion Food Store. Costume not shown in catalogue.

Ref.No.: SP3

Mint $200.00 **Ex.** $150.00 **G.** $90.00 **F.** $30.00

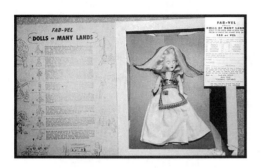

DUTCH DOLL

ca.1955. 6 in. (15 cm). Hard plastic body, jointed shoulders and neck. Sleep eyes; blond mohair wig. By Fab-Vel Dolls, Toronto, for Fab Detergent, a product of Colgate-Palmolive. Part of the Dolls of the World series of eight dolls.

Ref.No.: PS7

Mint $75.00 **Ex.** $50.00 **G.** $25.00 **F.** $20.00

MOUSEKETEER

Reliable. ca.1955. 11 in. (28 cm). Vinyl body, jointed hips, shoulders, and neck. Vinyl head with mouse ears and bow moulded to the head; inset blue plastic side-glancing eyes, painted upper lashes; brown moulded hair; open-closed smiling mouth. Mark: on head, RELIABLE.

Ref.No.: D of C, CH5, p. 102

Mint $65.00 **Ex.** $45.00 **G.** $35.00 **F.** $25.00

CAMPBELL SOUP KID
1956

ca.1956. 10 in. (25.5 cm). One-piece vinyl body. Vinyl head; painted side-glancing eyes; moulded brown hair; closed watermelon mouth. Mark: on head, CAMPBELLS; on body, RELIABLE. Original dress and cape.

Ref.No.: 2J15

Mint $75.00 **Ex.** $50.00 **G.** $25.00 **F.** $20.00

YOUNG OLYMPIANS OF CANADA

Reliable. 1958. 11 in. (28 cm). Hard plastic teen body, jointed shoulders and neck. Hard plastic head; blue sleep eyes, moulded lashes; blond mohair wig; closed mouth. Mark: on back, RELIABLE/PAT. 1958. Original ski suit with label on the chest, skis and poles. Original medal, YOUNG OLYMPIANS OF CANADA. JEUNES OLYMPIENS DU CANADA.

Ref.No.: D of C, BN9, p. 103

Mint $40.00 **Ex.** $30.00 **G.** $20.00 **F.** $15.00

MISS LUCKY GREEN

1960. 15 in. (38 cm). Plastic body, jointed hips, shoulders and neck. Vinyl head; blue sleep eyes, lashes, painted lowers; rooted honey blond hair in pony-tail and bangs; closed mouth. Mark: on head, PULLAN. Original green cotton dress with white, lace-trimmed pinafore.

Ref.No.: E11 12

Mint   **$85.00**   **Ex.**   **$55.00**   **G.**   **$40.00**   **F.**   **$30.00**

PEPSI-COLA MISS CANADA

ca.1960. 17 in. (43 cm). Plastic body, jointed hips, shoulders and neck. Vinyl head; blue sleep eyes, lashes, painted lowers; rooted platinum blond hair; closed mouth. Mark: on body, RELIABLE (in script). Original costume of white brocade taffeta strapless evening gown with fingerless gloves, red taffeta cape with white lining and fake fur collar, pearl earrings and tiara. Ribbon with Pepsi-Cola Miss Canada printed on.

Ref.No.: 2K36

Mint   **$125.00**   **Ex.**   **$75.00**   **G.**   **$35.00**   **F.**   **$25.00**

BARBARA ANNE BROWNIE

1961. 16 in. (41 cm.). Plastic body, jointed hips, shoulders and neck. Vinyl head; blue sleep eyes, lashes; rooted curly auburn hair; closed mouth. Mark: on head, RELIABLE; on body, RELIABLE (in script)/CANADA.Original brown cotton Brownie dress. Originally the uniform included a felt beret, belt, tie and white socks.

Ref.No.: 2KA11

Mint   **$75.00**   **Ex.**   **$55.00**   **G.**   **$30.00**   **F.**   **$20.00**

MISS CURITY

ca. 1962. 15 in. (38 cm). Plastic body, jointed hips, shoulders and neck. Vinyl head; blue sleep eyes, lashes; rooted blond curls; closed mouth. Mark; on head, RELIABLE; on body, RELIABLE (in script)/CANADA. Original white cotton uniform and cap, replaced shoes. Cap says "Miss Curity."

Ref.No.: 2M5

Mint   **$65.00**   **Ex.**   **$40.00**   **G.**   **$25.00**   **F.**   **$15.00**

SHARRON, SIMPSON'S ATHLETIC CLUB DOLL

ca.1965. 11 1/2 in. (29 cm). Plastic body, jointed hips, shoulders, waist and neck. Vinyl head; side-glancing blue eyes; rooted long blond hair; open-closed mouth showing teeth. Mark: on T shirt, SIMPSON'S / ATHLETIC / CLUB / ATHLETIQUE / SIMPSONS. Original sweat suit.

Ref.No.: 2R30

Mint $40.00 **Ex.** $30.00 **G.** $20.00 **F.** $10.00

DENISE FASHION DOLL

ca.1965. 11 1/2 in. (29 cm). Plastic body, jointed hips, shoulders and neck. Vinyl head; painted side-glancing eyes; rooted brown hair; closed mouth. This was an advertising doll for a textile company. Mark: on head, HONG KONG; on body, MADE IN HONG KONG; on box, BY L. DAVIS TEXTILES CO. LIMITED. Original red bathing suit, black shoes, includes stand.

Ref.No.: 2R21

Mint $45.00 **Ex.** $30.00 **G.** $20.00 **F.** $10.00

CAMPBELL SOUP CHEF KID

Reliable. 1966. 10 in. (25.5 cm). One-piece vinyl body, jointed at neck. Vinyl head; black painted side-glancing eyes, painted upper lashes; brown moulded hair; closed watermelon mouth. Mark: on head, CAMPBELL / RELIABLE / MADE IN CANADA / 10. Original red and white chef's costume including socks. Did not come with shoes.

Ref.No.: D of C, CF8, p.99

Mint $75.00 **Ex.** $55.00 **G.** $35.00 **F.** $20.00

EXPO HOSTESS

1967. 11 1/2 in. (29 cm). Plastic body, jointed hips, shoulders and neck. Vinyl head; blue side-glancing eyes; rooted platinum blond hair; closed mouth. Unmarked. Original blue suedine suit, white blouse, red underwear and hat of blue, navy and white. Black shoulder bag and high-heeled shoes. Dressed like the Hostess guides at Montreal's Centennial Expo.

Ref.No.: E11 11

Mint $65.00 **Ex.** $40.00 **G.** $25.00 **F.** $15.00

YOUNG SASQUATCH

1968. 8 in. (20 cm). One-piece plastic body covered with furry material. Vinyl head; painted blue eyes; long brown straight hair; closed watermelon mouth. Mark; on head, JAPAN. Original booklet with the Sasquatch story on a string around his neck, WESTCOAST SASQUATCH DISTRIBUTORS, LANGLEY, B.C. Original gold stretchy fake fur pants. On stand, Souvenir of B.C.

Ref.No.: 2C0

Mint $30.00   **Ex.** $25.00   **G.** $20.00   **F.** $15.00

MISS TEENAGE CANADA

ca.1968. 11 1/2 in. (29 cm). Plastic body, jointed hips, shoulders and neck. Vinyl head; blue side-glancing eyes; rooted brown hair; closed mouth. Mark: on head, REGAL TOY/MADE IN CANADA. Original red knit dress with white sash and orange lettering.

Ref.No.: 2D5

Mint $50.00   **Ex.** $30.00   **G.** $20.00   **F.** $15.00

KATIE-CURAD

Reliable. ca.1970. 17 in. (43 cm). Plastic teen body, jointed hips, shoulders, and neck. Vinyl head; sleep eyes, lashes, painted lower lashes; rooted blond curls; closed mouth. Mark: on head, RELIABLE (in script); on body, RELIABLE (in script) /MADE IN CANADA. Original white cotton pant suit and cap with name on it.

Ref.No.: D of C, BH19, p. 101

Mint $75.00   **Ex.** $45.00   **G.** $25.00   **F.** $20.00

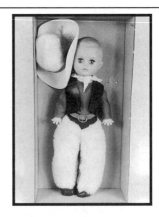

STAMPEDE SLIM, CALGARY STAMPEDE DOLL

ca.1970. 18 1/2 in. (47 cm). Plastic body, jointed hips, shoulders and neck. Vinyl head; sleep eyes, lashes; moulded light brown hair; closed mouth. Mark: on head, REGAL; on box, CALGARY STAMPEDE, THE GREATEST OUTDOOR SHOW ON EARTH. Original red cotton shirt, brown vinyl vest, vinyl cowboy boots, fur chaps and white felt cowboy hat.

Ref.No.: 2J7, 2J8

Mint $115.00   **Ex.** $80.00   **G.** $40.00   **F.** $25.00

Note: This doll was not available in eastern Canada.

CAMPBELL SOUP DOLL

Regal. ca.1975. 18 in. (45.5 cm). Plastic body, jointed hips, shoulders, and neck. Vinyl head; brown sleep eyes, lashes, three painted upper lashes; rooted black hair in braids and bangs; closed smiling mouth. Mark: on head, REGAL TOY LTD./MADE IN CANADA/166 E.

Ref.No.: D of C, BX11, p. 100

Mint $75.00 **Ex.** $50.00 **G.** $30.00 **F.** $20.00

MISS WESTON

Reliable. ca.1975. 14 in. (35.5 cm). Plastic body and legs, vinyl arms, jointed hips, shoulders, and neck. Vinyl head; blue sleep eyes, lashes, painted lower lashes; rooted blond hair in ponytail and bangs; open-mouth nurser. Mark: on head, RELIABLE/MADE IN CANADA. Original costume.

Ref.No.: D of C, CA16, p. 101

Mint $55.00 **Ex.** $40.00 **G.** $25.00 **F.** $15.00

OILERS DOLL

ca.1975. 19 in. (48 cm). Cloth body, arms and legs with vinyl hocky gloves and skates glued on. Vinyl head, permantly covered with vinyl helmet; blue sleep eyes, lashes; closed mouth. Original hockey pants and shirt with "Oilers" printed on the front. Original box, N.H.L. HOCKEY KIDS.

Ref.No.: 2Z27

Mint $40.00 **Ex.** $30.00 **G.** $25.00 **F.** $20.00

TORONTO MAPLE LEAF DOLL

ca.1975. 19 in. (48 cm). Cloth body, arms and legs with hockey gloves and skates glued on. Vinyl head, permanently covered with vinyl helmet; blue sleep eyes, lashes; closed mouth. Mark: on box, N.H.L. HOCKEY KIDS. Original blue hockey pants and shirt with "Toronto Maple Leafs" printed on front.

Ref.No.: PGM11

Mint $40.00 **Ex.** $30.00 **G.** $25.00 **F.** $20.00

CANADIAN OLYMPIC FLAG BEARER

1976. 11 in. (28 cm). Brown plastic body, jointed hips, shoulders and neck. Vinyl head; side-glancing painted black eyes; rooted straight black hair; closed mouth. Mark: on head, C1967/RELIABLE; on back, RELIABLE/CANADA. Original sheepskin snowsuit and hat trimmed with suede, suede belt. Includes Olympic flag.

Ref.No.: 2B20

Mint   **$45.00**   **Ex.**   **$30.00**   **G.**   **$20.00**   **F.**   **$15.00**

BROWNIE DOLL

1978. 12 in. (30 cm). Cloth body, arms and legs. Cloth head; embroidered brown eyes; yellow yarn hair in braids; embroidered closed mouth. Mark: paper tag on dress, MADE IN PHILIPPINES. Original brown cotton uniform and tam, scarf with maple leaves on it. Original "Owl" tee-shirt.

Ref.No.: 2O0

Mint   **$30.00**   **Ex.**   **$25.00**   **G.**   **$15.00**   **F.**   **$10.00**

Note: A similar doll dressed as a Sparks child came out in 1990 and was dressed in pink to represent the new group.

CANADIAN GIRL GUIDE

Beau Sol. 1980. 12 in. (30.5 cm). Cloth body and head. Embroidered features; wool hair. Unmarked. Original blue cotton uniform, tam and neck scarf.

Ref.No.: D of C, BN19, p. 104

Mint   **$30.00**   **Ex.**   **$25.00**   **G.**   **$15.00**   **F.**   **$8.00**

Note: The doll is no longer available, however a Guide uniform is available to change the doll from a Brownie into a Guide.

CANADIAN PATHFINDER DOLL

1980. 12 in. (30 cm). Cloth body and head. Embroidered features; wool hair. Original navy cotton skirt, white blouse, navy panties, scarf with green maple leaves.

Ref.No.: Z31

Mint   **$30.00**   **Ex.**   **$25.00**   **G.**   **$15.00**   **F.**   **$8.00**

Note: New dolls are available in dark or light fabric, dressed in underwear, for $7.95. Different uniforms available separately.

ESKIMO BARBIE

1982. 11 1/2 in. (29 cm). Light brown plastic body, jointed hips, shoulders and neck. Light brown vinyl head; ethnic features, brown eyes; rooted dark brown hair; closed mouth. Mark: on head, CMATTEL INC. 1980; on body, MATTEL INC. 1966/TAIWAN. Original white parka and hood with grey artificial fur trim, plastic boots. 1st ed. box no. 3898.

Ref.No.: PGM4

MIB $125.00   **Ex.** $60.00   **G.** $20.00   **F.** $10.00

Note: With Barbie dolls "mint in the box" (MIB) is very important as the box often contains accessories, information and extras that increase the value of the doll. The first edition of the Eskimo Barbie doll suffered some discolouration from the dark lining of the box. There was a second edition in 1991, box number 9844, which sells for about $40.00.

GAS GENIE

ca.1985. 19 in. (48 cm). Wis-Ton. Vinyl face, fur fabric body in blue, red and white. Advertised North Western Utilities Ltd.

Ref.No.: ES19

MIB $25.00   **Ex.** $20.00   **G.** $15.00   **F.** $10.00

Note: The Gas Genie was the creation of ex-Disney cartoonist Gene Hazelton of San Diego. It was licensed to utility companies in the U.S. and Canada. A similar doll was first used by North Western in 1959.

CANADIAN BARBIE

1988. 11 1/2 in. (29 cm). Plastic body, jointed hips, shoulders and neck. Vinyl head; blue eyes; rooted blond hair in a pony-tail; open-closed mouth showing teeth. Made by Mattel. Original R.C.M.P. uniform, black pants with a yellow stripe; red suedine jacket, plastic belt, black boots, felt hat. Original box, CANADIAN BARBIE; map and information about Canada on the back.

Ref.No.: HX13

MIB $100.00   **Ex.** $50.00   **G.** $20.00   **F.** $10.00

Note: Not originally available in Canada, but later a few were available from Woolco stores.

SKATING STAR BARBIE

1988. 11 1/2 in. (29 cm). Plastic body, jointed hips, shoulders and neck. Vinyl head; blue eyes, painted lashes; rooted blond hair; open-closed mouth. Original white skating costume, pantyhose, silver head piece, earrings, pink flowers, skates and hairbrush. Made by Mattel. Original box, "CALGARY 1988/OLYMPIC WINTER GAMES." OFFICIAL LICENSED PRODUCT.

Ref.No.: HX14

MIB $75.00   **Ex.** $30.00   **G.** $20.00   **F.** $10.00

Note: Only 70,000 dolls were made, which is a small edition for a Barbie.

CAMPBELL SOUP KID
1989

1989. 10 in. (26 cm). Plastic body, jointed hips, shoulders and neck. Vinyl head; side-glancing black eyes; moulded brown hair; closed watermelon mouth. Unmarked. Original red sweat-suit and hat, white socks and shoes. Shirt has picture of a pair of figure-skaters printed on the front. Sold at the Professional World Cup Figure Skating Competition, December, 1989.

Ref.No.: 2PGE23

Mint $35.00   **Ex.** $25.00   **G.** $20.00   **F.** $15.00

ANNE OF GREEN GABLES
1990 - 13 1/2 in.

1990. 13 1/2 in. (35 cm). Plastic body, jointed hips, shoulders and neck. Vinyl head; blue sleep eyes, lashes, painted lowers; rooted red braids and bangs; closed mouth. Mark: on head, ALEXANDER/19c65; hang tag, MADAME ALEXANDER/ANNE OF GREEN GABLES. Original dress with white lace trimmed blouse, plaid taffeta skirt, blue velveteen jacket, straw hat with pink bow, white stockings and boots.

Ref.No.: 2Z28

Mint $150.00   **Ex.** $95.00   **G.** $75.00   **F.** $45.00

SCOTT DOLL

1990. 12 in. (30 cm). Cloth body, arms and legs. Cloth head; blue printed eyes; yellow yarn hair; printed watermelon mouth. Mark: label on body, SCOTT. Original red and white cotton dress, black suedine shoes sewn on.

Ref.No.: 2Z10

Mint $30.00   **Ex.**   20.00   **G.** $15.00   **F.** $10.00

Note: Inside the plastic bag the doll comes in, Scott Paper Products states that it uses the money from the sale of dolls to help disadvantaged children.

COMMERCIAL DOLLS OF THE TWENTIETH CENTURY

ANGELO STUDIOS REG'D.
Quebec City, Quebec
ca.1938 -

This is a company that buys dolls and then dresses them in extremely well-made and authentic nun's clothing. The fabrics used for the clothing are very good quality, and each doll wears authentic beads and an imported crucifix.

Angelo Studios may also have dressed the Reliable composition nun doll, reference number BO1, which appears as a working doll.

Since only three dolls have turned up over a period of 25 years, it is possible that the dolls were dressed by a religious order using the tongue-in-cheek name Angelo Studios. Whoever dressed these three dolls was very familiar with the proper attire of religious orders.

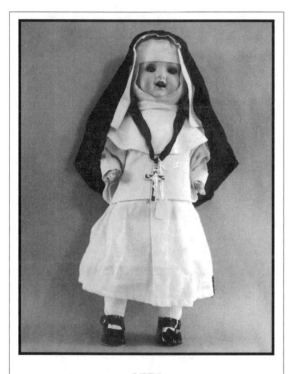

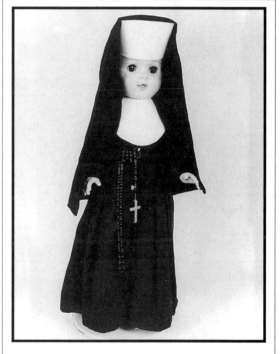

NUN
1938 - 12 in.

ca.1938. 12 in. (30.5 cm). Composition body, jointed hips shoulders and neck. Bisque head; brown sleep eyes, lashes, eyeshadow; open mouth with two teeth. Mark: on head, 931+/GERMANY/9/0C; on clothing, ORIGINAL/NUN DOLLS/BY/ANGELO STUDIOS REG'D/Quebec City, Canada. Original nun's clothing, crucifix.

Ref.No.: GK6

Mint $300.00 **Ex.** $250.00 **G.** $195.00 **F.** $150.00

NUN
1960 - 22 in.

1960. 22 in. (56 cm). Plastic body, jointed hips, shoulders and neck. Vinyl head; brown sleep eyes, lashes; rooted brown hair; open-closed mouth. Mark: on head, D&C; on body, DEE AN CEE. Doll is made by Dee an Cee but it was not dressed by them. The costume is very well-made and includes beads and a crucifix. It may have been dressed by the Angelo Studio but until more information turns up, we can't be sure.

Ref.No.: 2K24

Mint $110.00 **Ex.** $75.00 **G.** $40.00 **F.** $25.00

AVONLEA TRADITIONS
Richmond Hill, Ontario
1988 -

In 1988 Avonlea Traditions was granted licensing rights from L. M. Montgomery's family to produce dolls based on the "Anne of Green Gables" story. The original moulds were created by Yvonne Richardson and the dolls were produced by Springfield Farm Studio. Twenty-five artists' proof dolls of "Arriving at the Station," "Puffed Sleeves" and "School Days," plus ten of Diana Barry were personally finished by Yvonne Richardson. These dolls were numbered AP__/25 and AP__/10.

The first 25 of all four dolls in the regular production run were personally painted and finished by Sue Hagedon of Springfield Farm Studio. Each doll is numbered and comes with a certificate of authenticity.

ANNE OF GREEN GABLES
1989 - 14 in.

1989. 14 in. (36 cm). Stuffed cloth body and head, red yarn braids. All original.

Ref.No.: GK18

Mint $36.00   **Ex.** $25.00   **G.** $20.00   **F.** $10.00

Note: This doll was originally available in 20 in. size selling for $45.00. Now available only in a 16 in. size for $40.00 Also available in kits.

ANNE OF GREEN GABLES
"Arriving at the Station"
1989 - 16 in.

1989. 16 in. (41 cm). Cloth body, porcelain hands and feet. Porcelain head; stationary green eyes; red wig in braids; closed mouth. Dolls are numbered and come with a certificate of authenticity. Mark: a sequential number. Designed by Yvonne Richardson.

Price: $260.00

Artist's Proof: $525.00

Note: A 14-inch size of this doll is also available from the artist.

ANNE OF GREEN GABLES
"Puffed Sleeves"

1990. 16 in. (40.5 cm). Cloth body, porcelain hands and feet. Porcelain head; stationary green eyes; red wig in braids; closed mouth. Dolls are numbered and come with a certificate of authenticity. Mark: a sequential number preceded with the letter P.

Price: $260.00

Artist's Proof: $525.00

ANNE OF GREEN GABLES
"Arriving at the Station"
1990 - 19 in.

1990. 19 in. (48.5 cm). Cloth body, vinyl head, hands and feet, set-in eyes, rooted red hair. Designed by Yvonne Richardson; made by Irwin Toy. Mark: on head, R.&D. MACDONALD/YVONNE RICHARDSON/c1989/ANNE OF/GREEN GABLES.

Price: $35.00

ANNE OF GREEN GABLES
"School Days"

1991. 16 in. (40.5 cm). Cloth body, porcelain hands and feet. Porcelain head; stationary green eyes; red wig in braids; closed mouth. Dolls are numbered and come with a certificate of authenticity. Mark: a sequential number preceded by the letter S.

Price: $260.00

Artist's Proof: $525.00

DIANA BARRY

1991. 16 in. (40.5 cm). Cloth body, porcelain hands and feet. Porcelain head: stationary eyes; black wig; closed mouth. Dolls are numbered and come with a numbered certificate of authenticity. Mark: a sequential number preceded with the letter D. Designed by Yvonne Richardson.

Ref.No.: Z4

Price: $260.00

Artist's Proof: $525.00

BEAVER DOLL AND TOY CO.
1917 -

No information is available on the Beaver Doll and Toy Co. at this time.

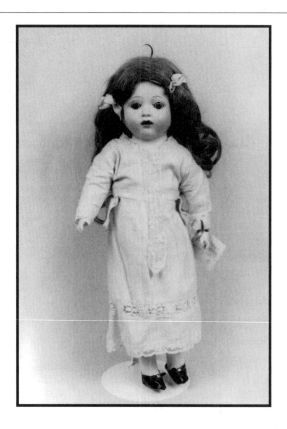

BEAVER
1917 - 18 in.

ca.1917. 18 in. (45.5 cm). Excelsior stuffed body and legs, composition forearms. Composition shoulderhead; blue sleep eyes, painted upper and lower lashes; human hair wig over moulded hair; open mouth with two teeth. Unmarked. Original box: BEAVER DOLL AND TOY CO. A rare doll.

Ref.No.: D of C, CX10, p. 121.

Mint $275.00 **Ex.** $200.00 **G.** $150.00 **F.** 125.00

BEAVER DOLL COMPANY
ca.1950 -

One small doll has been found in its original box, labelled Beaver Doll Company, Canada. The doll is of a hard plastic with side-glancing eyes, such as those made by Reliable around 1950. The doll has a blond mohair wig and is dressed as a bride. No picture is available.

BERT PERLMAN INC. (KEHAGIAS)
1985 - 1986

The Bert Perlman Inc. Co. of the United States sold dolls under the name Kehagias, although the dolls were made on contract by Reliable in Toronto. The contract with Reliable has ended and Kehagias dolls are no longer available in Canada.

ARTIST

1985. 9 1/2 in. (24 cm). Plastic body, vinyl arms and legs, jointed hips, shoulders and neck. Vinyl head; blue sleep eyes, lashes; long black rooted hair; closed mouth. Mark: on body, KEHAGIAS/MADE IN/CANADA. Wrist label KEHAGIAS/RELIABLE TOY CO. LTD.

Ref.No.: D of C, CN7, p. 122

Mint $40.00   **Ex.** $35.00   **G.** $25.00   **F.** $20.00

BEAUTY QUEEN

1985. 9 1/2 in. (24 cm). Plastic body, vinyl arms and legs, jointed hips, shoulders and neck. Vinyl head; blue sleep eyes, lashes; long blond rooted curly hair; closed mouth. Mark: on body, KEHAGIAS/MADE IN/CANADA. Wrist label, KEHAGIAS/RELIABLE TOY CO./TORONTO, CANADA.

Ref.No.: D of C, CN3A, p. 122

Mint $40.00   **Ex.** $35.00   **G.** $30.00   **F.** $20.00

HEATHER
1985 - 21 in.

1985. 21 in. (53.5 cm). Cloth body, vinyl arms and legs. Vinyl head; blue sleep eyes, lashes; slightly moulded light brown hair; closed mouth. Mark: on head, RELIABLE (in script)/MADE IN CANADA; tag on body, MADE BY ONT. REG. NO. 63A 3438/RELIABLE TOY CO. LTD. TORONTO, CANADA; tag on arm, KEHAGIAS/ RELIABLE TOY CO. LTD/LTEE/TORONTO, CANADA.

Ref.No.: D of C, XH24, p. 123

Mint   **$50.00**   **Ex.**   **$40.00**   **G.**   **$30.00**   **F.**   **$20.00**

ADAM

1985. 21 in. (53.5 cm). Cloth body, vinyl arms and legs. Vinyl head; blue sleep eyes, lashes; slightly moulded light brown hair; closed mouth. Mark: on head, RELIABLE (in script)/MADE IN CANADA; tag on body, MADE BY ONT. REG. NO. 63A 3438/RELIABLE TOY CO. LTD. TORONTO, CANADA; tag on arm, KEHAGIAS /RELIABLE TOY CO. LTD/LTEE /TORONTO, CANADA.

Ref.No.: D of C, XH23, p. 123

Mint   **$50.00**   **Ex.**   **$40.00**   **G.**   **$30.00**   **F.**   **$20.00**

KEHAGIAS

1985. 12 in. (30.5 cm). Vinyl one-piece bent-limb baby body. Vinyl head; blue painted side-glancing eyes; light brown moulded hair; open mouth nurser. Unmarked. Original box, KEHAGIAS/RELIABLE TOY CO./MADE IN CANADA.

Ref.No.: D of C, CS15A, p. 123.

Mint   **$25.00**   **Ex.**   **$20.00**   **G.**   **$15.00**   **F.**   **$10.00**

BRIDESMAID

1986. 13 in. (34 cm). Plastic body, jointed hips, shoulders and neck. Vinyl head; blue sleep eyes, lashes; long dark brown rooted hair; closed mouth. Unmarked. Original hang tag, RELIABLE-KEHAGIAS; Reliable doll-stand. Original pink dress with white collar, ribbon and lace trim, flowers in her hair, white stockings, panties and shoes.

Ref.No.: 2KA4

Mint   **$45.00**   **Ex.**   **$35.00**   **G.**   **$25.00**   **F.**   **$15.00**

BRIDE
1986 - 14 in.

1986. 14 in. (36 cm). Plastic body, jointed hips, shoulders and neck. Vinyl head; blue sleep eyes, lashes; rooted long black hair; closed mouth. Original brides lace and net gown with matching head-dress and veil.

Ref.No.: DH11

Mint $45.00 **Ex.** $35.00 **G.** $25.00 **F.** $20.00

POOR CINDERELLA

1986. 9 1/2 in. (24 cm). Plastic body, jointed hips, shoulders and neck. Vinyl head; blue sleep eyes, lashes; long blond rooted hair; closed mouth. Mark: on body, KEHAGIAS/MADE IN/CANADA; original hang tag, RELIABLE-KEHAGIAS, Reliable doll-stand. Original brown cotton dress with yellow apron, brown head scarf, black shoes, white panties, carrying broom.

Ref.No.: 2KA5

Mint $40.00 **Ex.** $35.00 **G.** $25.00 **F.** $20.00

CINDERELLA
1986 - 9 1/2 in.

1986. 9 1/2 in. (24 cm). Plastic body, jointed hips, shoulders and neck. Vinyl head; blue sleep eyes, lashes; long blond rooted hair; closed mouth. Mark: on body, KEHAGIAS/MADE IN/CANADA; original hang tag, RELIABLE-KEHAGIAS, Reliable doll-stand. Includes ball gown, petticoat, white stockings, lace trimmed panties, white shoes and a crown.

Ref.No.: 2J29

Mint $45.00 **Ex.** $40.00 **G.** $25.00 **F.** $20.00

NURSE
1986 - 9 1/2 in.

1986. 9 1/2 in. (24 cm). Plastic body, jointed hips, shoulders and neck. Vinyl head; blue sleep eyes, lashes; rooted dark brown hair; closed mouth. Original nurses' uniform; original Kehagias-Reliable hang tag. Comes with a Reliable stand.

Ref.No.: GK22

Mint $40.00 **Ex.** $35.00 **G.** $25.00 **F.** $20.00

BEST-MADE TOYS LTD.
Toronto, Ontario
ca.1959 -

KOWEEKA STUFFED DOLL

ca.1959. 14 in. (36 cm). Stuffed yellow pile snowsuit with light brown simulated fur on hands and feet. Hard vinyl mask face with black mohair showing beneath hood. Open-closed smiling mouth. Probably made for the Hudson's Bay Co.

Ref.No.: 2R22

Mint $60.00 **Ex.** $50.00 **G.** $35.00 **F.** $25.00

KOWEEKA BABY

ca.1959. 10 1/2 in. (26.5 cm). Stuffed cloth body in a sitting position. Vinyl face from the "Koweeka" mould; painted black eyes; black synthetic hair; open-closed smiling mouth, showing teeth. Unmarked.

Ref.No. D of C; BU3, p. 141

Mint $50.00 **Ex.** $40.00 **G.** $30.00 **F.** $20.00

BABY TOY

Date unknown. 10.5 in. (26.5 cm). Stuffed yellow and white pile snowsuit forms the body. Vinyl face; painted blue eyes; open-closed mouth. Label: BEST-MADE TOYS.

Ref.No.: ES101

Mint   **$25.00**   **Ex.**   **$20.00**   **G.**   **$15.00**   **F.**   **$10.00**

THE BISCO DOLL CO.
1917 - 1920

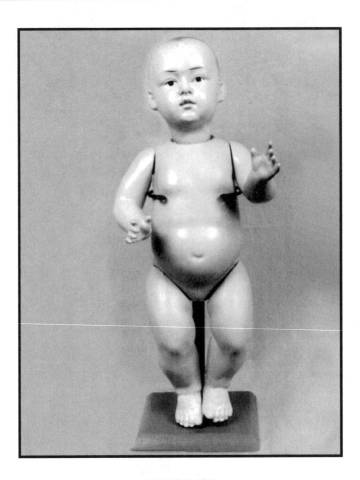

BISCO BABY
1918 - 16 1/2 in.

1918. 16 1/2 in. (42 cm). All painted bisque, bent-limb body, jointed hips, shoulders and neck. Painted bisque socket head, blue painted intaglio eyes with highlights, black line over eye; nostril dots; light brown moulded hair; open-closed mouth painted soft pink with fine outline in dark pink. Mark: on head and body. The Bisco Baby is a rare Canadian doll.

Ref.No.: D of C, CW9, p. 124

Mint $475.00   Ex. $400.00   G. $250.00   F. $185.00

BOMA MFG.
North Vancouver, B.C.
1980 -

CANADIANA TRADING
ca.1970 -

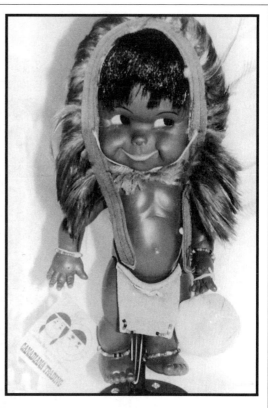

COWICHAN

1987. 12 in. (30.5 cm). Brown plastic body, jointed hips, shoulders and neck. Vinyl head; brown sleep eyes, lashes; rooted black hair; open-closed mouth. Mark: on head, STAR DOLL. Original hand-knit sweater and tuque, jeans and leather boots. The dolls are made by Star Doll Division of Wis-Ton Toy Mfg. Co. Ltd. in Etobicoke and dressed by BOMA.

Ref.No.: 2B6

Mint $60.00 **Ex.** $45.00 **G.** $25.00 **F.** $15.00

INDIAN DOLL

ca.1975. 12 in. (30.5 cm). Brown plastic body, jointed hips, shoulders and neck. Vinyl head; three-dimensional side-glancing black eyes; rooted black hair; watermelon mouth. Mark: on head, REGAL; on tag, Canadiana TRADING. Original costume.

Ref.No.: HX2

Mint $45.00 **Ex.** $40.00 **G.** $30.00 **F.** $25.00

CARLSON DOLLS (CANADA) LTD.

INDIAN GIRL WITH PAPOOSE

ca.1985. 11 in. (28 cm). Brown plastic body, jointed hips, shoulders and neck. Brown vinyl head; brown sleep eyes, lashes; long black hair; open-closed mouth. Mark: on tag, HANDCRAFTED BY CARLSON DOLLS (CANADA) LTD/ DISTRIBUTED EXCLUSIVELY BY I.P.S. (HANDICAFTS)/BURLINGTON, CANADA. Original purple leather fringed and beaded dress, boots and headband.

Ref.No.: 2N25

Mint $40.00   **Ex.** $35.00   **G.** $25.00   **F.** $15.00

CHEERIO TOY COMPANY
1939 - 1966

CHEERIO
1947 - 6 in.

ca.1947. 6 in. (15 cm). One-piece hard plastic body and head, jointed shoulders. Painted side-glancing eyes; moulded hair; closed mouth. Moulded shoes and socks. Mark: on back, CHEERIO/MADE IN CANADA.

Ref.No.: 2R24

Mint $20.00 **Ex.** $15.00 **G.** $10.00 **F.** $5.00

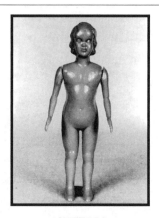

CHEERIO
1948 - 4 1/2 in.

ca.1948. 4 1/2 in. (12 cm). One-piece hard plastic body and head, jointed shoulders. Moulded features and hair. Mark: on back, CHEERIO (in a circle)/MADE IN CANADA.

Ref.No.: 2R25

Mint $25.00 **Ex.** $20.00 **G.** $15.00 **F.** $10.00

CHEERIO
1950 - 8 in.

ca.1950. 8 in. (20.5 cm). One-piece hard plastic doll. Blue painted side-glancing eyes, light brown moulded hair; closed mouth. Mark: on body, CHEERIO/MADE IN CANADA.

Ref.No.: D of C, BW20, p. 125

Mint $35.00 **Ex.** $30.00 **G.** $20.00 **F.** $15.00

CLS
Toronto, Ontario

 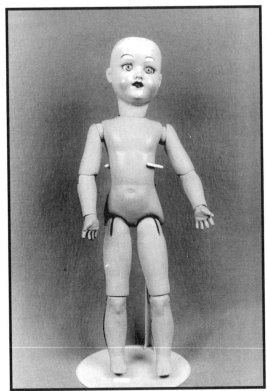

CLS

Date unknown. 19 1/2 in. (49.5 cm). Composition body, forearms, hands and lower legs; wooden upper arms and upper legs. French knee joints, German ball-jointed elbows. Painted bisque head; blue glass sleep eyes; painted upper and lower lashes; brown horsehair wig; open mouth showing four teeth. Mark: on head, incised, CLS trademark with TORONTO/CANADA. A rare doll.

Ref.No.: D of C, CP22, CP28, p. 126, 127

Mint **$550.00** **Ex.** **$475.00** **G.** **$350.00** **F.** **$250.00**

COMMERCIAL TOY CO.
Toronto, Ontario
1917

This company was in business for only one year.

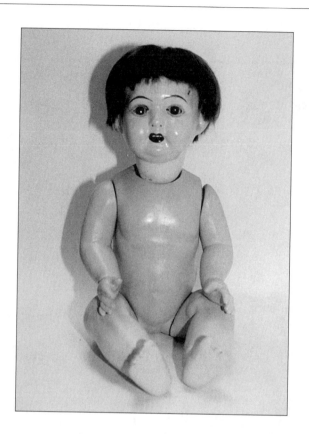

COMMERCIAL TOY

1917. 20 in. (50.5 cm). Five-piece composition body. Head is a clay-like composition, not as fine as bisque. Original paint on head; body has been repainted to match face colour. Celluloid sleep eyes, painted lashes; open mouth; four teeth; reddish mohair wig of excellent quality.

Mint $300.00   Ex. $250.00   G. $150.00   F. $80.00

C & W NOVELTY CORP.
Toronto, Ontario
1954 — ca.1960

This is not the same company as the C & W Pottery (1919).

The dolls made by C & W Novelty appear to be more like prototypes created before going into production. The style of the bodies is similar to those of blow moulded plastic dolls manufactured in the sixties. They appear to be too well-made to be priced as children's toys. Hopefully, more information will be found to explain the mystery.

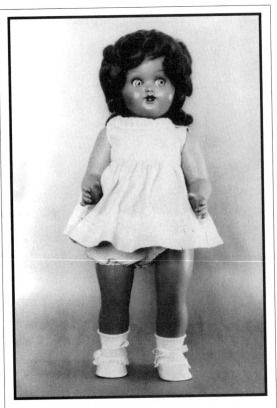

C & W
1960 - 18 in.

ca.1960. 18 in. (46 cm). Plaster and cardboard composition body, jointed hips, shoulders and neck. Plaster composition head; blue flirty tin sleep eyes; brown mohair wig; closed mouth. Mark: on back, C & W / TORONTO / CANADA. A rare doll.

Ref.No.: DF1

Mint $200.00 Ex. $175.00 G. $125.00 F. $75.00

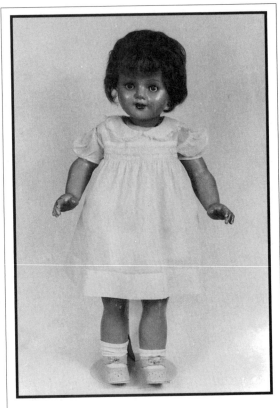

C & W
1960 - 28 in.

ca.1960. 28 in. (71 cm). Plaster and cardboard composition body, jointed hips, shoulders and neck, wooden joints. Plaster composition head; flirty blue glass sleep eyes, lashes, painted lowers; blond mohair wig; open mouth with four teeth. Redressed. A rare doll.

Ref.No.: 2J11 and 2J12

Mint $250.00 Ex. $200.00 G. $150.00 F. $90.00

DEE AN CEE TOY COMPANY LTD.
1938 - 1964

Dee an Cee was owned by Max Diamond and Morris Cone. In 1939, Arthur Cone, son of Morris joined the firm. Arthur Cone became president of the company when his father died in 1957.

The company motto was "Quality above all," and truly Dee an Cee dolls are known among collectors as very well-made dolls that are unusually well-dressed. Dee an Cee was the first Canadian doll company to advertise on television. Dee an Cee was sold to Mattel in 1962 and manufacturing in Canada was gradually discontinued. The name was no longer used after 1964.

BETTY
1938 - 15 in.

ca.1938. 15 in. (38 cm). Cloth body, upper arms and legs, composition forearms. Composition shoulderhead; blue painted eyes; moulded hair, painted reddish blond; closed mouth. Unmarked. Original dress and bonnet.

Ref.No. D of C; BN15 p. 131

Mint $110.00 **Ex.** $75.00 **G.** $40.00 **F.** $25.00

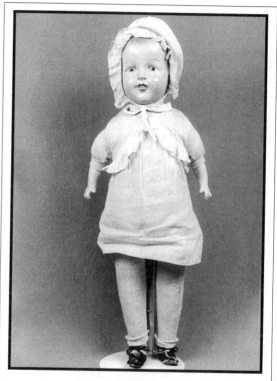

DEE AN CEE
1938 - 27 1/2 in.

ca.1938. 27 1/2 in. (70 cm). Excelsior stuffed cloth body, legs and upper arms; composition forearms. Composition shoulderhead, painted blue eyes, long painted upper lashes; moulded hair painted brown; open-closed mouth showing two painted teeth. Mark: on shoulderplate, DEE AN CEE/MADE IN CANADA. Original pink and blue cotton dress.

Ref.No.D of C; BF36 p. 131

Mint $200.00 **Ex.** $165.00 **G.** $85.00 **F.** $45.00

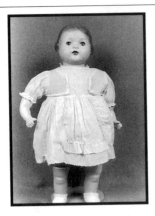

DEE AN CEE
1938 - 24 in.

ca.1938. 24 in. (61 cm). Cloth body, composition arms and legs. Composition shoulderhead; blue sleep eyes, lashes; moulded hair, light brown; closed mouth. Mark: on shoulderplate, A/DEE & CEE TOY. Original costume.

Ref.No. D of C; CE8 p. 131

Mint **$235.00** **Ex.** **$185.00** **G.** **$120.00** **F.** **$65.00**

NORA

1938. 15 in. (38 cm). Cloth body and legs, composition forearms. Composition shoulderhead; painted brown side-glancing eyes; moulded short brown hair; closed mouth. Mark: on shoulderplate, DEE AN CEE/MADE IN/CANADA. (The N in AN and IN are backward). Originally wore a cotton-print dress.

Ref.No. D of C; AM19 p. 132

Mint **$100.00** **Ex.** **$75.00** **G.** **$40.00** **F.** **$30.00**

DEE AN CEE
Moulded Hair

ca.1939. 17 in. (43 cm). Cloth body, composition forearms and bent-limb legs. Composition shoulderhead; blue tin sleep eyes, painted upper lashes; moulded hair; closed mouth. Mark: on shoulderplate, DEE & CEE TOY CO./MADE IN CANADA. Redressed.

Ref.No. D of C; CW25 p. 132

Mint **$95.00** **Ex.** **$75.00** **G.** **$40.00** **F.** **$25.00**

SWEETUMS
1939 - 24 in.

1939. 24 in. (61 cm). Cloth body, composition arms and legs. Composition shoulderhead; blue celluloid sleep eyes, lashes, painted lower lashes, eye shadow; blond mohair wig over moulded hair; closed mouth. Mark: shoulderplate, A DEE & CEE TOY. Original dress in yellow organdy, with mauve bolero effect, apron effect on skirt, lace, pink and blue rayon trim, with matching bonnet.

Ref.No.: 2E20

Mint **$250.00** **Ex.** **$195.00** **G.** **$130.00** **F.** **$65.00**

DEE AN CEE
Brown Mohair Wig

ca.1939. 17 in. (43 cm). All composition body, jointed hips, shoulders and neck. Composition head; brown tin sleep eyes, lashes; brown mohair wig; open mouth, two teeth and tongue. Mark: on body DEE AN CEE. Pink dress, may be original.

Ref.No.: DF 3.

Mint $175.00　　Ex. $125.00　G. $65.00　F. $40.00

SNUGGLES
1939 - 23 in.

ca.1939. 23 in (58.5 cm). Cloth body, composition forearms and straight legs. Composition shoulderhead; blue metal sleep eyes, lashes, painted lower lashes; reddish brown moulded hair, closed mouth. Mark: label on the dress, SNUGGLES/DEE AN CEE TOY/MADE IN CANADA. Original pink organdy dress and bonnet.

Ref.No. D of C; CN23 p. 132

Mint　$210.00　Ex.　$175.00　G.　$135.00　F.　$55.00

SNUGGLES
1940 - Closed Mouth

ca.1940. 22 in. (56 cm). Cloth body, composition forearms and straight legs. Composition shoulderhead; blue tin sleep eyes, lashes, painted lower lashes; blond mohair wig; closed mouth. Original white dress bearing the doll's name.

Ref.No. D of C; BJ4 p. 133

Mint　$250.00　Ex.　$195.00　G.　$115.00　F.　$60.00

DEE AN CEE
1940 - 11 1/2 in.

ca.1940. 11 1/2 in. (29.5 cm). Dark brown composition bent-limb baby, head and trunk one-piece, jointed hip and shoulders. Painted side-glancing black eyes, moulded black hair plus wool top-knots, closed mouth. Mark: on back, DEE AN CEE/CANADA.

Ref.No. D of C; CC14 p. 133

Mint　$125.00　Ex.　$95.00　G.　$55.00　F.　$35.00

DEE AN CEE
1940 - 24 in.

ca.1940. 24 in. (61 cm). Excelsior stuffed cloth body and legs, composition arms. Composition shoulderhead; blue painted eyes; reddish blond moulded hair; closed mouth. Original pink organdy dress and matching bonnet.

Ref.No. D of C; CT16 p. 133

Mint **$145.00** **Ex.** **$110.00** **G.** **$60.00** **F.** **$40.00**

SWEETUMS
1940 - 19 in.

ca.1940. 19 in. (48 cm). All composition body, jointed hips, shoulders and neck. Composition head; brown sleep eyes, lashes, painted lowers; brown moulded hair; open mouth, two teeth. Unmarked, original tag. Original, lace trimmed, pink organdy dress, matching bonnet, socks and shoes.

Ref.No.: 2T1.

Mint $160.00 **Ex.** **$125.00** **G.** **$65.00** **F.** **$45.00**

DEE AN CEE
1941 - 20 in

ca.1941. 20 in. (50 cm.). All composition, jointed hips, shoulders and neck. Composition head; brown painted eyes; moulded brown hair; closed mouth. Mark: on body; DEE AN CEE. Original, lace-trimmed white batiste dress with matching bonnet.

Ref.No.: 2C23

Mint $165.00 **Ex.** **$130.00** **G.** **$70.00** **F.** **$45.00**

SWEETUMS
1941 - 24 in.

ca.1941. 24 in. (61 cm.). Composition shoulderhead, arms, lower legs; cloth body. Mohair wig, blue sleep eyes, lashes, closed mouth, crier. Redressed. Mark: on shoulder plate, A DEE & CEE TOY.

Ref.No.: ES25

Mint **$250.00** **Ex.** **$195.00** **G.** **$125.00** **F.** **$60.00**

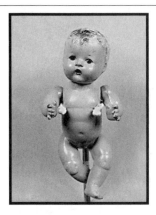

DRINKING BABY

ca.1941. 12 in. (30.5 cm). Composition bent-limb body, jointed hips, shoulders, and neck. Composition head; brown painted eyes, black line over eye; moulded brown hair; metal mouth nurser. Mark: on body, DEE AN CEE/CANADA.

Ref.No. D of C; DA1 p. 134

Mint **$85.00** **Ex.** **$65.00** **G.** **$40.00** **F.** **$25.00**

SNUGGLES
1942 - Open Mouth

ca.1942. 22 in. (56 cm). Cloth body, composition forearms and straight legs. Composition shoulderhead; blue tin sleep eyes, lashes, painted lower lashes; moulded black hair; open mouth showing two inset teeth and red tongue. Original dress, bonnet and shoes.

Ref.No. D of C; BJ3 p. 134

Mint **$225.00** **Ex.** **$175.00** **G.** **$100.00** **F.** **$60.00**

DEE AN CEE
1942 - 17 in.

ca.1942. 17 in. (43 cm.). All composition body, jointed hips, shoulders and neck. Composition head; painted brown eyes; black moulded hair; closed mouth. Mark: on body, DEE AN CEE. Redressed.

Ref.No.: 2G28

Mint **$135.00** **Ex.** **$100.00 G.** **$60.00** **F.** **$35.00**

CRYING BABY

1944. 21 in. (53.5 cm). Cloth body, with crier, composition forearms and straight legs. Composition head; blue painted eyes, long painted upper lashes; brown moulded hair; open-closed mouth showing two painted teeth. Unmarked. Original dotted dress and bonnet, socks and shoes.

Ref.No. BJ10 p. 135

Mint **$235.00** **Ex.** **$195.00** **G.** **$115.00** **F.** **$60.00**

LITTLE DARLING
Blue Tin Eyes

ca.1944. 24 in. (61 cm). Cloth body, composition forearms and straight legs. Composition head; blue tin sleep eyes, lashes, painted lower lashes; moulded brown hair; open mouth showing two teeth. Mark: on shoulderplate, DEE CEE TOY/MADE IN CANADA. Original pink cotton dress, bonnet and bloomers.

Ref.No. D of C; CI15 p. 135

Mint $240.00 **Ex.** $200.00 **G.** $120.00 **F.** $65.00

LITTLE DARLING
Blue Sleep Eyes

ca.1945. 24 in. (61 cm). Cloth body, composition forearms and straight legs. Composition head; blue sleep eyes, lashes, painted lower lashes; moulded brown hair; open mouth showing two teeth. Mark: on shoulderplate, DEE & CEE TOY CO./MADE IN CANADA. Original ruffled pink cotton dress and matching frilled bonnet.

Ref.No. D of C; BF31 p. 136

Mint $250.00 **Ex.** $200.00 **G.** $125.00 **F.** $65.00

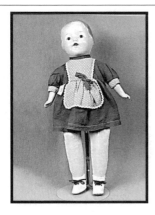

BETTY
1945 - 23 in.

ca.1945. 23 in. (58 cm). Excelsior stuffed cloth body, legs, and upper arms; composition forearms. Composition shoulderhead; painted brown eyes; moulded strawberry blond hair. Unmarked. Original navy dress with name on label.

Ref.No. D of C; BC18 p. 136

Mint $125.00 **Ex.** $90.00 **G.** $50.00 **F.** $30.00

DEE AN CEE
1946 - 14 in.

ca.1946. 14 in. (35.5 cm). Composition body, jointed hips, shoulders, and neck. Composition head; blue sleep eyes, lashes, painted lower lashes; blond mohair wig; closed rosebud mouth. Mark: on back, DEE AN CEE/CANADA. Redressed.

Ref.No. D of C; CE31 p. 136

Mint $140.00 **Ex.** $95.00 **G.** $65.00 **F.** $40.00

DEE AN CEE
1947 - 14 in.

ca.1947. 14 in. (35.5 cm). Composition body, jointed hips, shoulders and neck. Composition head; blue sleep eyes, lashes, painted lower lashes; blond mohair wig; closed mouth. Mark: on body, DEE AN CEE/CANADA. Original red and white cotton dress, replaced shoes and socks.

Ref.No.: 2G30

Mint $140.00 **Ex.** $95.00 **G.** $65.00 **F.** $40.00

SNUGGLES
1947 - 18 in.

ca.1947. 18 in. (45.5 cm). Cloth body, composition hands and straight legs. Composition head; brown sleep eyes, lashes, painted lower lashes; moulded brown hair; closed mouth. Mark: on head, DEE & CEE DOLL. Original printed cotton dress and matching bonnet.

Ref.No. D of C; CI4 p. 137

Mint $160.00 **Ex.** $120.00 **G.** $75.00 **F.** $50.00

SWEETUMS
1948 - 14 in.

1948. 14 in. (35.5 cm). Cloth body with crier, Skintex arms and legs. Composition shoulderhead. Eyes painted blue. Moulded hair, painted strawberry blond. Closed mouth. Original organdy dress and bonnet.

Ref.No. D of C; BC19 p. 137

Mint $70.00 **Ex.** $55.00 **G.** $35.00 **F.** $25.00

CHERUB SMILE-N-CRY DOLL

1948. 13 1/2 in. (34.5 cm). Cloth body, legs and upper arms, composition forearms. Composition two-face head, one face smiling and one crying; painted blue side-glancing eyes; bald head; closed mouth on one face, open-closed mouth on the other. Original red and white checked dress and matching bonnet.

Ref.No. D of C; CC11 p. 138

Mint $260.00 **Ex.** $190.00 **G.** $125.00 **F.** $60.00

Note: Regional price differences.

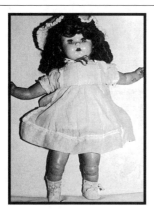

SWEETUMS
1949 - 19 in.

1949. 19 in. (48.5 cm). Cloth body, Composition head, Skintex arms and legs; blue sleep eyes, lashes; closed mouth; replaced brown wig, originally mohair. Original yellow organdy dress with white lace trim and matching bonnet.

Ref.No.: DR18

Mint $75.00 **Ex.** $60.00 **G.** $45.00 **F.** $25.00

BUNKY

1949. 15 in. (38 cm.). Cloth body. Composition head, painted blue eyes, moulded reddish hair, Open-closed mouth. Original name tag.

Ref.No.: 2KA18

Mint $35.00 **Ex.** $25.00 **G.** $15.00 **F.** $10.00

SNUGGLES
1949 - 22 in.

ca.1949. 22 in. (56 cm). Cloth body, composition forearms and straight legs. Composition shoulderhead; blue tin sleep eyes, lashes, eyeshadow, painted lower lashes; blond mohair wig; open mouth showing two teeth and tongue. Original pink and white costume.

Ref.No. D of C; CX18 p. 139

Mint $260.00 **Ex.** $200.00 **G.** $130.00 **F.** $75.00

SNUGGLES
1949 - 24 in.

1949. 24 in. (61 cm). Cloth body, composition forearms and straight legs. Composition shoulderhead; blue tin sleep eyes, lashes, eyeshadow, lower lashes painted grey; blond mohair wig; open-closed mouth. Unmarked. Original white batiste dress and matching bonnet, trimmed with pink ribbon, replaced socks and shoes.

Ref.No.: 2Q5

Mint $285.00 **Ex.** $230.00 **G.** $130.00 **F.** $80.00

BETTY
1949 - 18 in.

1949. 18 in. (45.5 cm). Excelsior stuffed cloth body, legs and upper arms, composition forearms. Composition shoulderhead; blue painted eyes; moulded reddish-brown hair; closed mouth. Mark: on shoulderplate, A/DEE & CEE TOY. Original dress.

Ref.No. D of C; CE29 p. 139

Mint $150.00 **Ex.** $95.00 **G.** $55.00 **F.** $40.00

DEE AN CEE
1950 - 14 in.

ca.1950. 14 in. (35 cm). All composition, jointed hips, shoulders and neck. Composition head; blue sleep eyes, lashes, painted lowers; blond saran wig over moulded hair; closed mouth. Mark: on body, DEE AN CEE/CANADA. Original red and white checked cotton dress.

Ref.No.: 2Q31

Mint $140.00 **Ex.** $125.00 **G.** $75.00 **F.** $40.00

DEE AN CEE
1950 - 26 in.

ca.1950. 26 in. (66 cm). One-piece Skintex body, swivel neck. Vinyl head; blue sleep eyes, lashes; light brown moulded hair; open-closed mouth, moulded tongue. Mark: on head, DEE & CEE. Redressed.

Ref.No. D of C; CB21 p. 139

Mint $60.00 **Ex.** $50.00 **G.** $40.00 **F.** $20.00

DEE AN CEE
1951 - 14 in.

ca.1951. 14 in. (36 cm). One-piece Skintex body. Vinyl head; set-in brown eyes; moulded black hair; open-closed mouth, two upper teeth. Mark: on head, DEE AN CEE. Original black and white fur fabric snowsuit, felt boots.

Ref.No.: HX18

Mint $75.00 **Ex.** $60.00 **G.** $35.00 **F.** $25.00

CAROL
ca.1952 - 25 in.

ca.1952. 25 in. (63.5 cm). One-piece Skintex body. Vinyl head; blue sleep eyes, lashes, painted lower lashes; rooted blond saran hair with bangs; closed mouth. Mark: on head, DC. Original mauve printed taffeta dress with lace trim, black velvet ribbons, shoes and socks.

Ref.No. D of C; CF12 p. 140

Mint $70.00 **Ex.** $60.00 **G.** $40.00 **F.** $20.00

SNUGGLES
ca.1952 - 22 in.

ca.1952. 22 in. (56 cm). Composition shoulderhead, cloth body, composition arms and legs. Blue sleep eyes, lashes, painted lowers; grey eye-shadow; closed mouth; blond saran wig. Redressed.

Ref.No.: ES53

Mint $260.00 **Ex.** $185.00 **G.** $130.00 **F.** $75.00

DREAM BABY
1953 - 16 in.

ca.1953. 16 in. (40 cm). One-piece Skintex body. Stuffed vinyl head; inset blue plastic eyes; rooted blond saran hair; open-closed mouth. Unmarked. Original printed taffeta dress.

Ref.No.: 2B12

Mint $50.00 **Ex.** $40.00 **G.** $25.00 **F** $15.00

Note: Dolls made with a rubber skin (Skintex) do not appreciate in value.

SWEETUMS
1953 - 17 in.

1953. 17 in. (43 cm). Composition shoulderhead. Cloth body with crier. Originally had Magic Skin arms and legs, but now replaced with cloth. Blond mohair wig; blue sleep eyes with lashes. Original pink and blue organza dress and hat; original shoes, socks and dress label.

Ref.No.: ES11

With Magic Skin arms and legs:
Mint $70.00 **Ex.** $60.00 **G.** $40.00 **F** $20.00
With replaced Compo arms & legs:
Mint $95.00 **Ex.** $75.00 **G.** $50.00 **F** $30.00

HONEY BEA
ca.1954 - 15 in.

ca.1954. 15 in. (38 cm). One-piece Flexee-vinyl body, dimpled knees. Vinyl head; brown sleep eyes, lashes, painted lower lashes; rooted saran ponytail and bangs; closed mouth. Mark: on head, DEE & CEE. Wearing roller-skates. Original red and white checked dress.

Ref.No. D of C; CB32 p. 140

Mint   **$55.00**   **Ex.**   **$45.00**   **G.**   **$25.00 F.**   **$15.00**

WILLY-WHISTLE

1954. 12 in. (30 cm). Vinyl body, jointed at shoulders and neck. Moulded vinyl head with moulded brown hair and yeat hat with red feather; painted side-glancing eyes; mouth open to whistle, coo voice. Mark: on head, DEE & CEE. Original blue shorts and red shirt.

Ref.No.: 2GK19

Mint   **$55.00**   **Ex.**   **$40.00**   **G.**   **$30.00 F.**   **$20.00**

HEIDI
1954 - 13 in.

1954. 13 in. (33 cm). One-piece stuffed Skintex body. Vinyl head; inset plastic eyes; moulded hair in braids, painted yellow with red barretts; open-closed mouth, painted teeth. Mark: on head, DEE CEE. Redressed.

Ref.No. D of C; CG23 p. 140

Mint   **$55.00**   **Ex.**   **$45.00**   **G.**   **$35.00 F.**   **$25.00**

CHERUB

1954. 24 in. (61 cm). Skintex body. Vinyl head; blue sleep eyes; moulded blond hair. Original pale blue dress with inset of blue, white and yellow print.

Ref.No.: ES20

Mint   **$80.00**   **Ex.**   **$60.00**   **G.**   **$40.00 F.**   **$20.00**

SWEETUMS
1954 - 17 in.

1954. 17 in. (43 cm). Cloth body and legs, composition forearms. Composition head; tin blue sleep eyes, lashes; moulded brown hair; open mouth showing felt tongue. Unmarked. Original white organdy gown with pink matching bonnet.

Ref.No.: 2B10.

Mint $160.00 **Ex.** $125.00 **G.** $55.00 **F.** $35.00

SNUGGLES
1954 - 22 in.

1954. 22 in. (58 cm). Cloth body, composition arms and legs. Composition shoulderhead; blue tin sleep eyes, lashes and grey painted lowers; brown mohair wig; closed mouth. Unmarked. Original blue and white cotton skirt, white blouse and a matching hat.

Ref.No.: 2R15

Mint $185.00 **Ex.** $135.00 **G.** $75.00 **F.** $40.00

BRIDE DOLL
1955 - 17 in.

1955. 17 in. (43.5 cm). One-piece Flexee-vinyl body. Vinyl head; blue sleep eyes, lashes, painted lower lashes; rooted blond saran hair; closed mouth. Unmarked.

Ref.No.: D of C; CI10 p. 141

Mint $65.00 **Ex.** $55.00 **G.** $40.00 **F.** $20.00

HEIDI
1955 - 14 in.

1955. 14 in. (35.5 cm). One-piece Flexee-vinyl body. Set-in blue plastic eyes; moulded yellow hair. Clothing a copy of original. Blue dress, white sleeves, white apron with red trim, red bows.

Ref.No.: ES10

Mint $55.00 **Ex.** $45.00 **G.** $35.00 **F.** $25.00

BUTTERCUP
1956 - 13 in.

1956. 13 in. (33 cm). One-piece stuffed vinyl body. Vinyl head; blue plastic sleep eyes; moulded hair; open-closed mouth. Unmarked. Paper tag on doll. Original blue satin sleeper, trimmed with pink braid, matching bonnet with white fur fabric trim.

Ref.No.: 2N26

Mint $65.00 **Ex.** $50.00 **G.** $25.00 **F.** $15.00

MANDY
1956 - 14 in.

1956. 14 in. (35.5 cm). One-piece stuffed Skintex brown body. Vinyl head; black painted eyes, ethnic features; heavily detailed moulded hair in braids at the back and painted black; open-closed mouth, painted teeth. Mark: on head, DEE & CEE. Original costume.

Ref.No. D of C; CF31 p. 141

Mint $75.00 **Ex.** $60.00 **G.** $40.00 **F.** $20.00

NINA BRIDE
1956 - 19 in.

1956. 19 in. (48 cm). One-piece stuffed vinyl body. Vinyl head; blue sleep eyes, lashes, painted lowers; rooted blond hair; closed mouth. Mark: on head, D&C. Original taffeta, net and lace bridal gown and cap.

Ref.No.: 2K37

Mint $55.00 **Ex.** $40.00 **G.** $25.00 **F.** $15.00

NANETTE BRIDESMAID
1956 - 19 1/2 in.

1956. 19 1/2 in. (49.5 cm). One-piece, stuffed vinyl body. Vinyl head; honey blond rooted hair; blue sleep eyes. Mark: on head, D & C. Original pink taffeta, lace and net dress and cap, pink vinyl high-heels, bouquet of flowers.

Ref.No.: ES49

Mint $60.00 **Ex.** $40.00 **G.** $25.00 **F.** $15.00

CAROL
1957 - 25 in.

1957. 25 in. (63.5 cm). One-piece stuffed Flexee-vinyl body. Vinyl head; blue sleep eyes, lashes, painted lower lashes; rooted honey blond saran hair; closed mouth. Mark: on head, DC. Original pink and white check dress and bonnet.

Ref.No. D of C; BC15 p. 142

Mint **$65.00** **Ex.** **$55.00** **G.** **$40.00 F.** **$30.00**

TONI
1958 - 10 1/2 in.

1958. 10 1/2 in. (27 cm). Vinyl body, jointed hips, shoulders, waist and neck. Vinyl head; blue sleep eyes, moulded lashes; rooted brown hair; closed mouth. Mark: on head, D&C; on body, DEE AN CEE. Original black lace undies, black high-heeled shoes. Many different outfits were sold separately

Ref.No.: 2M15

Mint **$85.00** **Ex.** **$60.00** **G.** **$30.00** **F.** **$20.00**

Note: This is not the same doll as Toni by Reliable.

HONEY BEE
1958 - 15 in

1958. 15 in. (38 cm). Flexee vinyl, one-piece body. Vinyl head; rooted blond hair. Original printed taffeta dress.

Ref.No.: ES9

Mint **$50.00** **Ex.** **$40.00** **G.** **$30.00** **F.** **$20.00**

NINA BRIDE
1958 - 24 in.

1958. 24 in. (61 cm). Flexee-vinyl one-piece body. Vinyl head; brown sleep eyes, lashes; rooted brown hair; closed mouth. Mark: on head, AMC. Original tag. Original three-tier net and lace gown, taffeta underskirt, net veil with lace trim, lily of valley bouquet.

Ref.No.: 2C12

Mint **$90.00** **Ex.** **$60.00** **G.** **$30.00** **F.** **$20.00**

TINY TEARS
1958 - 13 in.

1958. 13 in. (33 cm). Vinyl bent-limb baby, jointed hips, shoulders and neck; with crier. Vinyl head; brown sleep eyes, eyelashes; rooted brown curls. Open mouth nurser. Unmarked. Originally came with suitcase and layette.

Ref.No. D of C; BF30 p. 142

Mint $115.00 **Ex.** $85.00 **G.** $50.00 **F.** $25.00

Note: A variation of this doll has moulded hair. Mint and Ex. prices include suitcase and layette.

LYNN

1958. 17 in. (43 cm). One-piece, vinyl-skin body. Vinyl head; blue inset eyes; deeply moulded light brown curls; closed mouth. Original white pique dress with red-and-white striped polished cotton frills. Mandarin hat and high heels. Red bow at waist missing.

Ref.No.: DR19

Mint $75.00 **Ex.** $60.00 **G.** $35.00 **F.** $25.00

SWEET SUE IN HER
EVENING ENSEMBLE

1958. 17 in. (43 cm). Vinyl body, jointed hips, shoulders, waist and neck. Vinyl head; blue sleep eyes, lashes; rooted blond curls; closed mouth. Mark: on head, DEE & CEE; on back, DEE AN CEE. Original gown of blue nylon skirt, taffeta lame bodice, lame hooded cloak with satin lining, white crinoline, blue panties, high-heeled shoes, earrings and ring.

Ref.No.: 2C14

Mint $100.00 **Ex.** $75.00 **G.** $45.00 **F.** $25.00

NINA BRIDE
1958 - 18 in.

1958. 18 in. (46 cm). Vinyl body, jointed at hips, shoulders, waist and neck. Vinyl head; blue sleep eyes, lashes, painted lowers; red rooted saran hair; closed mouth. Mark: on body, B18. Original net gown, white slip, white net veil, pearl earrings; original box.

Ref.No.: 2N15

Mint $75.00 **Ex.** $60.00 **G.** $35.00 **F.** $25.00

CINDY IN HER SUNDAY BEST

1958. 17 in. (43.5 cm). Plastic body, jointed hips, waist, shoulders, and neck. Vinyl head; blue sleep eyes, lashes, painted lower lashes; rooted honey blond saran curls; closed mouth. Mark: on head, D & C; on body, DEE AN CEE. Original costume.

Ref.No. D of C; CF30 p. 143

Mint $60.00 **Ex.** $40.00 **G.** $25.00 **F.** $20.00

DEE AN CEE
1958 - 22 in.

ca.1958. 22 in. (56 cm). Hard plastic body, jointed hips, shoulders, and neck. Hard plastic head; blue sleep eyes, lashes, painted lower lashes; moulded hair, painted light brown; open mouth showing two inset teeth and tongue. Mark: on body, D&C. Original pink cotton eyelet dress and matching bonnet, bootees.

Ref.No. D of C; BY16 p. 144

Mint $200.00 **Ex.** $175.00 **G.** $95.00 **F.** $75.00

Note: This doll appeared on a commemorative postage stamp issued June 8, 1990.

OUR LOVABLE FAMILY, CINDY,
PENNY AND BABY SISTER

1959. CINDY has a plastic body with jointed hips, waist, shoulders, and neck. Vinyl head, sleep eyes, lashes and painted lower lashes; rooted blond hair; closed mouth. PENNY has a vinyl body; jointed hips, shoulders, and neck. Vinyl head; sleep eyes, lashes; rooted Buster Brown hair; closed mouth. BABY SISTER has one-piece vinyl body. Original costumes.

Ref.No. D of C; CX19 p. 143

Mint $175.00 **Ex.** $125.00 **G.** $75.00 **F.** $55.00

CINDY
1959 - 17 in.

ca.1959. 17 in. (43 cm). Vinyl body, jointed hips, shoulders, waist and neck. Vinyl head; blue sleep eyes, lashes; rooted blond hair; closed mouth. Mark: on head, DEE AN CEE, on body DEE AN CEE. Original dress with white satin top, navy and light blue striped skirt.

Ref.No.: 2DH12

Mint $60.00 **Ex.** $45.00 **G.** $30.00 **F.** $25.00

CINDY BRIDE
1959 - 23 in.

ca.1959. 23 in. (58 cm). Vinyl body, jointed hips, shoulders and neck. Vinyl head; blue sleep eyes, lashes, painted lowers; rooted auburn hair; closed mouth. Unmarked. Original bridal gown with silver thread in the fabric, veil, high-heeled shoes.

Ref.No.: 2G27

Mint $75.00 **Ex.** $60.00 **G.** $35.00 **F.** $25.00

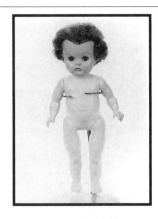

DREAM BABY
1959 - 16 in.

1959. 16 in. (40.5 cm). Plastic body, jointed hips, shoulders, and neck. Vinyl head; blue sleep eyes, lashes, painted lower lashes; rooted short curly brown hair; closed mouth. Mark: on head, DEE CEE; on body, DEE AN CEE. Originally wore pin dotted polished cotton dress with white sheer nylon sleeves, collar and pinafore trimmed with lace and tied at the sides with white satin ribbons. Stiff white net bonnet edged to match the dress with soft net frill under the brim. Included feeding bottle.

Ref.No. D of C; AE10 p. 143

Mint $55.00 **Ex.** $35.00 **G.** $25.00 **F.** $15.00

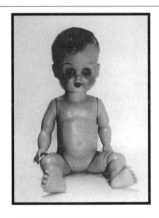

DRINK AND WET BABY
1959 - 14 in.

1959. 14 in. (35.5 cm). Five-piece plastic body. Vinyl head; blue sleep eyes; moulded blond hair; open mouth nurser. Mark: on head, D&C.

Mint $20.00 **Ex.** $15.00 **G.** $10.00 **F.** $5.00

KELLY IN PIGTAILS

1959. 16 in. (40.5 cm). Plastic body, jointed hips, shoulders, and neck. Vinyl head; blue sleep eyes, lashes, painted lower lashes; rooted blond saran hair in pigtails with bangs; closed mouth. Mark: on head, 3; on body, D&C.

Ref.No. D of C; CR10 p. 144

Mint $55.00 **Ex.** $45.00 **G.** $35.00 **F.** $20.00

BUTTERCUP
ca.1959 - 18 in.

ca.1959. 18 in. (45.5 cm). Fully jointed, vinyl head and arms, plastic body and legs. Blond rooted hair; blue sleep eyes; open-closed mouth. Redressed. Mark: on head, DEE & CEE /MADE IN CANADA.

Mint $35.00 **Ex.** $25.00 **G.** $20.00 **F.** $15.00

NANETTE BRIDESMAID
1959 - 19 in.

1959. 19 in. (48.5 cm). Hard plastic teen body, jointed hips, waist, shoulders, and neck. Vinyl head; brown sleep eyes, lashes, painted lower lashes; rooted brown saran curls; closed mouth. Unmarked. Original pink net and lace gown, original tag.

Ref.No. D of C; BQ15 p. 147

Mint $60.00 **Ex.** $50.00 **G.** $35.00 **F.** $25.00

BABY SUE
1959 - 24 in.

1959. 24 in. (61 cm). Plastic baby body, jointed hips, shoulders, and neck. Vinyl head; brown sleep eyes, lashes, painted lower lashes; rooted auburn short curls; open mouth nurser. Mark: on body, DEE AN CEE. Redressed similar to the original.

Ref.No. D of C; BX5 p. 144

Mint $70.00 **Ex.** $55.00 **G.** $40.00 **F.** $25.00

KELLY
1959 - 15 in.

l959. 15 in. (38 cm). Plastic body, jointed hips, shoulders, and neck. Vinyl head; blue sleep eyes, lashes, painted lower lashes; rooted blond saran curls; closed mouth. Mark: on head, MADE IN CANADA/DEE AN CEE. Original pink and white striped dress with matching panties. Originally wore a "camel-hair" double-breasted coat with simulated brass buttons over dress with striped jersey head-scarf, black shoes and white socks.

Ref.No.: D of C; CB14 p. 145

Mint $55.00 **Ex.** $40.00 **G.** $20.00 **F.** $15.00

DREAM BABY
1959 - 18 in.

1959. 18 in. (46 cm). Plastic body, jointed hips, shoulders, and neck. Vinyl head; blue sleep eyes, lashes, painted lower lashes; rooted curly brown hair; closed mouth. Mark: on head, DEE AN CEE. Made with a very thick heavy plastic. Redressed.

Ref.No. D of C; AM23 p. 145

Mint $60.00 **Ex.** $45.00 **G.** $35.00 **F.** $25.00

Note: Originally wore same costume as described in reference number AE10, page 91.

HONEY BEA
1959 - 18 in.

1959. 18 in. (45.5 cm). Plastic body, jointed hips, shoulders, and neck. Vinyl head; brown sleep eyes, lashes, painted lower lashes; rooted, saran, brown ponytail and bangs; closed mouth. Mark: on head, DEE AN CEE. Original lace trimmed nylon party dress over matching slip and panties. Satin ribbon trim matches hair ribbon. Vinyl button up shoes.

Ref.No. D of C; BS12 p. 146

Mint $90.00 **Ex.** $75.00 **G.** $45.00 **F.** $25.00

HONEY BEA
1959 - 25 in.

1959. 25 in. (63.5 cm). One-piece, stuffed Flexee-vinyl body. Vinyl head; blue sleep eyes, lashes, painted lowers; rooted blond hair in ponytail; closed mouth. Original flocked nylon dress, white socks and white shoes.

Mint $65.00 **Ex.** $55.00 **G.** $40.00 **F.** $25.00

Note: This doll also came in 21- and 18-inch sizes.

BONNIE
1959 - 19 in.

1959. 19 in. (48.5 cm). One-piece stuffed Flexee-vinyl. Vinyl head; blue sleep eyes, lashes; rooted blond saran hair; closed mouth. Mark: on head, DEE AN CEE. Original Scottish dress.

Ref.No.: D of C; CF29 p. 145

Mint $55.00 **Ex.** $45.00 **G.** $30.00 **F.** $20.00

BONNIE
1959 - 17 in.

1959. 17 in. (43 cm). One-piece stuffed vinyl body. Vinyl head; inset blue eyes; deeply moulded hair; closed mouth. Mark: on head, DEE & CEE. Originally wore Scottish dress with tartan skirt and black brushed rayon long sleeved bodice with lace ruffles at neck and wrists, tartan shawl with slide shoulder buckle, black brushed rayon tam with feather, high-heeled black shoes.

Ref.No. D of C; CW31 p. 146

Mint $70.00 **Ex.** $50.00 **G.** $30.00 **F.** $20.00

ALICE IN WONDERLAND
1959 - 18 in.

1959. 18 in. (45.5 cm). Vinyl body, jointed hips, shoulders and neck. Vinyl head; blue sleep eyes, lashes, painted lowers; rooted blond hair; closed mouth. Mark: on head, DEE AN CEE; on body, D&C. Original pink flocked dotted net over matching taffeta, styled in tiers with fitted bodice and baby velvet ribbon sash.

Ref.No.: 2K27

Mint $100.00 **Ex.** $75.00 **G.** $40.00 **F.** $20.00

SWEET SUE FORMAL

1959. 18 in. (45.5 cm). Plastic body, jointed waist, hips, shoulders, and neck. Vinyl head; blue sleep eyes, lashes, painted lower lashes; rooted saran hair in a ponytail with bangs; closed mouth. Mark: on head, DEE CEE. Original lace trimmed gown and simulated fur stole.

Ref.No. D of C; BZ28 p. 147

Mint $75.00 **Ex.** $60.00 **G.** $40.00 **F.** $25.00

CINDY NURSE

1959. 16 in. (40.5 cm). Vinyl body, jointed hips, shoulders and neck. Vinyl head; blue sleep eyes, lashes, painted lowers; rooted blond hair; closed mouth. Unmarked. Original striped uniform and apron. Original costume included a cap and cape. Complete set included a vinyl baby carriage and an 8 1/2 in. baby wearing a bunting suit.

Ref.No.: 2N28

Mint $110.00 Ex. $75.00 G. $30.00 F. $15.00

Note: Mint and Ex. prices include carriage and baby.

CINDY BRIDE
1959 - 17 in.

1959. 17 in. (43 cm). Plastic body, jointed hips, waist, shoulders, and neck, wearing nail polish. Vinyl head; pierced ears and pearl earrings; blue sleep eyes, lashes, painted lower lashes; rooted short blond saran hair; closed mouth. Mark: on head, D&C; on body, DEE AN CEE.

Ref.No. D of C; BX16 p. 148

Mint $65.00 Ex. $50.00 G. $35.00 F. $25.00

CINDY BRIDE
1959 - 18 in

1959. 18 in. (46 cm). Vinyl body, jointed hips, shoulders and neck. Vinyl head; blue sleep eyes, lashes, painted lowers; rooted blond hair; closed mouth. Mark: on head, D&C; on body, DEE AN CEE. Originally dressed in bridal gown, pearl earrings, solitaire ring, carrying a bouquet. Came with white and gold travelling case containing outfit doll is wearing, mirror and comb.

Ref.No.: 2Z 28

Mint $85.00 Ex. $75.00 G. $35.00 F. $25.00

Note: Mint price includes travelling case.

MARGO
1959 - 27 in.

1959. 27 in. (68.5 cm). One-piece Flexee vinyl body. Vinyl head; blue sleep eyes, lashes, painted lowers; rooted brown hair; open-closed mouth. Mark: DC. Original flocked nylon dress and matching bonnet, socks and shoes.

Ref.No.: 2P13

Mint $75.00 Ex. $55.00 G. $30.00 F. $25.00

Note: Also came in a 24-inch size.

DEE AN CEE
1959 - 16 in.

ca.1959. 16 in. (41 cm). Vinyl body, jointed hips, shoulders and neck. Vinyl head; blue sleep eyes, lashes; rooted blond hair; closed mouth. Mark: on head, DEE AN CEE; on body, D&C. Original pink gown adn net underskirt.

Ref.No.: 2DF2

Mint $55.00 **Ex.** $40.00 **G.** $30.00 **F.** $15.00

PENNY BALLERINA

1960. 14 in. (35.5 cm). Plastic body, jointed hips, shoulders and neck. Vinyl head; bright green sleep eyes, lashes; freckled face; closed mouth; rooted red straight hair. Redressed. Originally wore a green taffeta ballet dress with triple pink net underskirt, matching taffeta panties, ballet slippers and velvet flowered headband. Mark: on head, DEE CEE; on body, D&C.

Ref.No.: 2A24

Mint $80.00 **Ex.** $60.00 **G.** $35.00 **F.** $25.00

Note: A very unusual doll as few vinyl dolls have green eyes.

KOWEEKA
1960 - 15 in.

ca.1960. 15 in. (38 cm). Brown plastic body, jointed hips, shoulders, and neck. Vinyl head; painted black eyes; rooted straight black hair; open-closed mouth, smiling and showing painted teeth. Mark: on head, KOWEEKA [c]/HUDSONS BAY CO.; on body, MADE IN CANADA/DEE AND CEE. Original parka, hood and pants.

Ref.No. D of C; CX14 p. 149

Mint $125.00 **Ex.** $85.00 **G.** $65.00 **F.** $45.00

BABY SUE
1960 - 16 in.

1960. 16 in. (40.5 cm). Plastic body, bent-limb doll; jointed hips, shoulders and neck; crier. Vinyl head; blue sleep eyes, lashes, painted lowers; open nurser mouth; rooted short, curly reddish hair. Original pink taffeta dress with printed nylon pinafore, pink shoes and hat. Mark: on head, DEE CEE.

Ref.No.: ES40

Mint $40.00 **Ex.** $35.00 **G.** $25.00 **F.** $20.00

SWEET SUE

1960. 18 in. (45.5 cm). Plastic body, jointed hips, shoulders, waist and neck. Vinyl head; blue sleep eyes, lashes, painted lowers; closed mouth; rooted black pony-tail hairdo. Mark: on head, DEE&CEE; on body, DEE AN CEE. Original sheer printed floral skirt, black velvet top, trimmed with flowers, pink petticoat, pearls, nylons, high-heels, grey stole.

Ref.No.: 2C27

Mint $65.00 **Ex.** $55.00 **G.** $40.00 **F.** $25.00

POLLYANNA

1960. 31 in. (79 cm). Plastic teen-aged girl, jointed hips, shoulders, and neck. Vinyl head; blue sleep eyes, lashes, distinctive black lashes painted at outside of upper eyelids; rooted blond saran hair with bangs; open-closed mouth, smiling and showing painted teeth. Mark: on head, WALT DISNEY/PROD./MFR. BY DEE AN CEE/NF; on body, DEE AN CEE. Redressed similar to the original.

Ref.No. D of C; CS22A p. 150

Mint $155.00 **Ex.** $125.00 **G.** $85.00 **F.** $55.00

Note: Modelled from actress Hayley Mills.

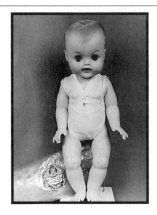

DRINK 'N WET BABY
Moulded Hair

1960. 19 in. (48 cm). Plastic baby body, jointed hips, shoulders, and neck. Vinyl head; blue sleep eyes, lashes, painted lower lashes; moulded light brown hair; open mouth nurser. Mark: on head, DEE CEE. Original underwear.

Ref.No. D of C; CD8 p. 148

Mint $30.00 **Ex.** $25.00 **G.** $20.00 **F.** $15.00

DRINK 'N WET BABY
Saran Hair

1960. 19 in. (48 cm). Plastic baby body, jointed hips, shoulders, and neck. Vinyl head; blue sleep eyes, lashes, painted lower lashes; brown rooted saran curly hair; open mouth nurser. Mark: on head, DEE CEE. Redressed. Originally dressed in pinafore style sundress of checked cotton with matching pants and bonnet, white bootees and a feeding bottle.

Ref.No. D of C; CG19 p. 149

Mint $50.00 **Ex.** $35.00 **G.** $30.00 **F.** $20.00

BABY SUE DRINK 'N WET

1960. 16 in. (40.5 cm). Plastic body, jointed hips, shoulders and neck. Vinyl head; blue sleep eyes, lashes, painted lower lashes; rooted blond curly hair; open-mouth nurser. Mark: on back, DEE AN CEE. Original white dress and bonnet with red and white trim and white shoes and socks.

Mint **$55.00** **Ex.** **$45.00** **G.** **$30.00** **F.** **$20.00**

Note: This doll is also available in 14- and 13-inch sizes.

BABY SUE
ca.1960 - 18 in.

ca.1960. 18 in. (45.5 cm). Plastic body, jointed hips, shoulders and neck. Vinyl head; brown sleep eyes, lashes, painted lowers; open mouth nurser; rooted red hair. Mark: DEE CEE. Original pink coat and matching hat, flowered print dress. Bottle missing.

Ref.No.: 2J10

Mint **$60.00** **Ex.** **$45.00** **G.** **$35.00** **F.** **$20.00**

KELLY
1960 - 18 in.

1960. 18 in. (45.5 cm). Plastic body, jointed hips, shoulders, and neck. Vinyl head; blue sleep eyes, lashes and painted lower lashes; rooted blond saran hair; closed mouth. Mark: on head, DEE AN CEE. Original embroidered pink nylon dress, socks and shoes.

Ref.No. D of C; CI9 p. 151

Mint **$65.00** **Ex.** **$45.00** **G.** **$35.00** **F.** **$25.00**

BRIDE
ca.1960 - 19 in.

ca.1960. 19 in. (48 cm). Plastic body, jointed hips, shoulders and neck. Vinyl head; blue sleep eyes, lashes, painted lowers; open-closed mouth; rooted blond hair. Mark: on head, DEE AN CEE. Original lace trimmed bridal gown and veil.

Ref.No.: 2P14

Mint **$75.00** **Ex.** **$55.00** **G.** **$35.00** **F.** **$20.00**

WILLY

1960. 16 in. (40.5 cm). Plastic body, jointed hips, shoulders, and neck. Vinyl head; blue sleep eyes, lashes, painted lower lashes; well defined moulded hair, painted black; closed mouth. Mark on body, DEE AN CEE. Original black wool suit and white shirt, black shoes.

Ref.No. D of C; CW22 p. 153

Mint $65.00 **Ex.** $50.00 **G.** $35.00 **F.** $25.00

KELLY
1960 - 16 in.

1960. 16 in. (40.5 cm). Plastic body, jointed hips, shoulders, and neck. Vinyl head; brown sleep eyes, lashes, painted lower lashes; rooted short curly brown saran hair; closed mouth. Mark: on head, D&C/3; on body, 165-5/D&C. Original sunsuit.

Ref.No. D of C; AM21 p. 151

Mint $55.00 **Ex.** $40.00 **G.** $30.00 **F.** $25.00

CALYPSO JILL
1960 - 14 in.

1960. 14 in. (35.5 cm). Plastic body, jointed hips, shoulders, and neck. Vinyl head; moulded eyes painted black; black moulded hair in pigtails and bangs; mouth open-closed. Mark: on head, DEECEE.

Red.No.: D of C; CR21 p. 148

Mint $115.00 **Ex.** $85.00 **G.** $70.00 **F.** $50.00

Note: This doll appeared on a commemorative postage stamp issued June 8th, 1990, which adds to its value.

MARGO RED RIVER GIRL

1960. 16 in. (40.5 cm). Plastic body, jointed hips, shoulders and neck. Vinyl head, sleeps eyes, lashes, rooted saran hair, closed mouth. Navy coat, fully lined in red, double breasted with six buttons and attached hood. Tallesed cap, mitts, pants and vinyl button shoes to match.

Mint $70.00 **Ex.** $50.00 **G.** $35.00 **F.** $25.00

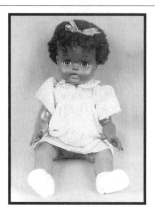

DRINK 'N WET
COLOURED BABY
Rooted curly hair

1961. 20 in. (50.5 cm). Brown plastic body, jointed hips, shoulders, and neck. Vinyl head; brown sleep eyes, lashes, painted lower lashes; rooted short curly hair; open mouth nurser. Mark: on body, 20-638. Redressed. Originally came with a bottle and wore a red and white polka dot sunsuit.

Ref.No.: D of C; CJ4 p. 153

Mint   **$60.00**   **Ex.**   **$45.00**   **G.**   **$40.00**   **F.**   **$30.00**

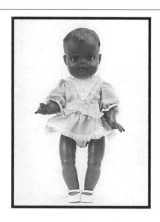

DRINK 'N WET
COLOURED BABY
Moulded black hair

1961. 20 in. (50.5 cm). Brown plastic body, jointed hips, shoulders, and neck. Vinyl head; brown sleep eyes, lashes; moulded black hair; open mouth nurser. Mark: on head, DEE CEE. Redressed. Originally dressed in shirt and diaper and came with a plastic bottle.

Mint   **$50.00**   **Ex.**   **$35.00**   **G.**   **$25.00**   **F.**   **$20.00**

BABY SUE
ca.1961 - 20 in.

ca.1961. 20 in. (50.5 cm). Plastic body, jointed hips, shoulders and neck. Vinyl head; blue sleep eyes, lashes, painted lowers; rooted blond straight hair; open mouth nurser. Mark: on head, D&C; on body, DEE AN CEE. Original dress.

Ref.No.: PGC2

Mint   **$60.00**   **Ex.**   **$45.00**   **G.**   **$35.00**   **F.**   **$25.00**

BABY JANE

1961. 13 1/2 in. (35.0 cm). Soft cloth body, vinyl legs and arms. Vinyl head; green sleep eyes, plastic lashes; brown rooted hair over moulded sides of head; open-closed mouth. Mark: on head, DEE AN CEE © 1961. Originally wore a lace trimmed cotton dress and came with a plastic bottle.

Mint   **$55.00**   **Ex.**   **$45.00**   **G.**   **$35.00**   **F.**   **$25.00**

Note: This doll also came with a 5-piece plastic body.

CALYPSO BILL
1961 - 16 in.

1961. 16 in. (40.5 cm). Brown plastic body, jointed hips, shoulders, and neck. Vinyl head; painted black eyes; moulded black curly hair; open-closed mouth showing six painted teeth. Mark: DEE CEE. Original costume and straw hat.

Ref.No.: D of C; CD19 p. 154

Mint $125.00 **Ex.** $90.00 **G.** $75.00 **F.** $55.00

CALYPSO JILL
1961 - 16 in.

1961. 16 in. (40.5 cm). Brown plastic body, jointed hips, shoulders and neck. Vinyl head; painted black eyes; well defined moulded hair with bangs and pigtails in black; open-closed mouth, smiling and showing painted teeth. Mark: on body, DEE AN CEE. Original costume including, necklace and bracelets.

Ref.No.: D of C; CS9 p. 154

Mint $125.00 **Ex.** $90.00 **G.** $75.00 **F.** $55.00

PRETTY BABY
1961 - 12 in.

1961. 12 in. (30 cm). Vinyl body, jointed hips, shoulders and neck. Vinyl head; brown sleep eyes, lashes, painted lowers; rooted brown hair over moulded hair; open mouth nurser. Mark: DEE CEE/12RD. Original pink gingham dress and matching hat.

Ref.No.: 2J34

Mint $45.00 **Ex.** $35.00 **G.** $20.00 **F.** $15.00

KELLY
1961 - 16 in.

1961. 16 in. (41 cm). Plastic body, jointed hips, shoulders and neck. Vinyl head; brown sleep eyes, lashes, painted lowers; orange rooted upswept hair; closed mouth. Mark: on head, DEECEE; on body, DEE AN CEE. Original white evening gown with green taffeta stole, original tag.

Ref.No.: 2C19

Mint $60.00 **Ex.** $50.00 **G.** $35.00 **F.** $25.00

LULUBELLE
1961 - 20 in.

1961. 20 in. (51 cm). Brown plastic body, jointed hips, shoulders and neck. Vinyl head; golden brown sleep eyes, lashes; rooted black curly hair; open mouth nurser. Mark: on head, DEE AN CEE; on body, DEE AN CEE. Originally wore high waisted gingham polka-dot dress trimmed with lace, socks, shoes and bottle.

Ref.No.: D of C; CW22A p. 154

Mint $65.00   **Ex.** $50.00   **G.** $40.00   **F.** $30.00

DREAM BABY
1961 - 17 in.

1961. 17 in. (43 cm). Cloth body, vinyl bent-limb arms and legs. Vinyl head; chubby face, blue sleep eyes, lashes, rooted straight blond hair over moulded hair; open-closed mouth. Mark: on head, DEE AN CEE. Original embroidered nylon dress and panties.

Ref.No.: D of C; BN32 p. 155.

Mint $50.00   **Ex.** $45.00   **G.** $35.00   **F.** $25.00

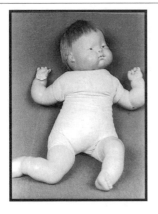

DREAM BABY
1961 - 18 in.

1961. 18 in. (45.5 cm). Cloth body, vinyl bent-limb arms and legs. Vinyl head; painted blue eyes; rooted straight saran hair; closed mouth. Mark: on head, DEE CEE. Originally wore flannelette baby doll pyjamas and was wrapped in a blanket.

Ref.No.: D of C; CW10 p. 155

Mint $50.00   **Ex.** $40.00   **G.** $35.00   **F.** $25.00

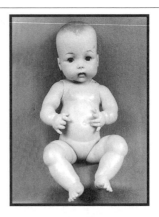

DREAM BABY
1961 - Brown Moulded Hair

1961. 19 in. (48 cm). Vinyl bent-limb baby body, jointed hips, shoulders, and neck. Vinyl head; blue sleep eyes, lashes and painted lower lashes; reddish brown moulded hair; open mouth nurser. Mark: on head, DEE CEE/1961; on body, DC. Originally came with a shirt, diaper, blanket and bottle.

Ref.No.: D of C; BX6 p. 155

Mint $75.00   **Ex.** $60.00   **G.** $45.00   **F.** $35.00

KELLY IN PARTY DRESS
1961 - 16 in.

1961. 16 in. (40.5 cm). Five-piece plastic body. Vinyl head; blue sleep eyes; rooted brown pony tail; closed mouth. Original peach taffeta party dress and attached panties. Lace-trimmed apron missing.

Ref.No.: PS3

Mint $55.00 **Ex.** $40.00 **G.** $30.00 **F.** $25.00

CINDY
1961 - 17 in.

1961. 17 in. (43 cm). Plastic teen body, jointed hips, waist, shoulders, and neck. Vinyl head; brown sleep eyes, lashes, painted lower lashes; rooted brown hair; closed mouth. Redressed. Originally came in three different high fashion outfits that included hats and high-heeled shoes.

Ref.No. D of C; CT23 p. 157

Mint $70.00 **Ex.** $55.00 **G.** $35.00 **F.** $25.00

Note: This doll is hard to find in her original costume.

DREAM BABY
1961 - Brown Straight Hair

1961. 18 in. (45.5 cm). Vinyl bent-limb baby body, jointed hips, shoulders, and head. Vinyl head; blue sleep eyes, lashes, painted lower lashes; rooted brown straight hair over moulded hair; open mouth nurser. Mark: on head, DEE CEE; on body, DEE CEE. Redressed in dress and bonnet similar to the original.

Ref.No. D of C; CA36 p. 156

Mint $85.00 **Ex.** $65.00 **G.** $50.00 **F.** $40.00

MOON BABY
1961 - 18 in.

1961. 18 in. (45.5 cm). Plastic body vinyl bent-limb arms and legs, jointed hips, shoulders, and neck. Vinyl head; large blue sleep eyes, long dark lashes; rooted blond saran hair; open mouth nurser. Mark: on head, DEE CEE. Original sunsuit, bonnet and bottle.

Ref.No. D of C; CD3 p. 156

Mint $75.00 **Ex.** $65.00 **G.** $50.00 **F.** $35.00

MARYBEL THE GET WELL DOLL

1961. 15 in. (38 cm). Plastic body and legs, vinyl arms. Vinyl head; blue sleep eyes, lashes, painted lower lashes; rooted brown saran hair; open mouth nurser. Mark: on head, DEE CEE; on body, D&C.

Ref.No. D of C; CF32 p. 158

Mint $115.00   **Ex.** $75.00   **G.** $40.00   **F.** $20.00

Note: Mint price requires original crutches, arm and leg casts.

WILLY THE SAILOR

1961. 16 in. (40.5 cm). Plastic body, jointed hips, shoulders, and neck. Vinyl head; blue sleep eyes, lashes, painted lower lashes; moulded hair, painted black; closed mouth. Original label, DEE AND CEE/QUALITY ABOVE ALL. Original costume.

Ref.No. D of C; BQ6 p. 157

Mint $80.00   **Ex.** $65.00   **G.** $35.00   **F.** $20.00

WILLY THE MOUNTIE

1961. 16 in. (40.5 cm). Plastic body, jointed hips, shoulders and neck. Vinyl head; blue sleep eyes, lashes, painted lower lashes; moulded black hair; closed mouth. Original costume. Hat missing.

Ref.No. D of C; BQ21 p. 158

Mint $90.00   **Ex.** $70.00   **G.** $35.00   **F.** $20.00

MOON BABY
1961 - 28 in.

1961. 28 in. (71 cm). Plastic bent-limb baby body, jointed hips, shoulders and neck, with a crier in the body. Vinyl head; blue sleep eyes, lashes, painted lower lashes; rooted saran black hair in a baby feather cut; open mouth nurser. Mark: on head, DEE CEE. Original embroidered nylon dress and matching bonnet. Missing knitted bootees.

Ref.No. D of C; BZ21 p. 157

Mint $90.00   **Ex.** $75.00   **G.** $60.00   **F.** $45.00

NINA BRIDE
1961 - 16 in.

1961. 16 in. (40.5 cm). Plastic body, jointed hips, shoulders and neck. Vinyl head; blue sleep eyes, lashes, painted lowers; rooted blond hair; closed mouth. Mark: on head, DEE CEE/3; on body, DEEANCEE. Original white satin wedding gown with net overskirt, veil and flowers, original tag.

Ref.No.: 2B3

Mint $60.00 **Ex.** $45.00 **G.** $35.00 **F.** $20.00

KELLY
1961 - 22 in.

1961. 22 in. (56 cm). Plastic body, jointed hips, shoulders, and neck. Vinyl head. Brown sleep eyes, eyelashes; painted lower lashes. Rooted dark brown short curls. Open-closed mouth. Mark: on head, D&C. Original costume.

Ref.No. D of C; BS32 p. 158

Mint $65.00 **Ex.** $50.00 **G.** $35.00 **F.** $25.00

ANNETTE FROM BABES IN TOYLAND

1961. 20 in. (50.5 cm). Vinyl body, jointed hips, shoulders, neck, arms, legs and waist. Vinyl head. Brown sleep eyes, rooted eyelashes, painted lower lashes; long brown rooted hair; closed pale orange mouth. All original green skirt and vest overlaid with black lace, white blouse, black lace veil, red flowers. Mark: on label, ANNETTE DOLL/INSPIRED BY/WALT DISNEY'S BABES IN TOYLAND/MADE IN CANADA BY DEE AN CEE TOY CO. LTD. © COPYRIGHT 1961 WALT DISNEY PRODUCTIONS.

Mint $175.00 **Ex.** $130.00 **G.** $75.00 **F.** $40.00

DEE AN CEE
1961 - 16 in.

ca.1961. 16 in. (41 cm). Vinyl body, jointed hips, shoulders and neck. Vinyl head; blue sleep eyes, lashes; rooted brown hair; open mouth nurser. Mark: on head, DEECEE. Original pink and white dress and bootees, matching floral wreath in her hair.

Ref.No.: HX8.

Mint $55.00 **Ex.** $45.00 **G.** $35.00 **F.** $15.00

CHATTY BABY

1961. 18 in. (46 cm). Plastic body, jointed hips, shoulders and neck. Vinyl head; blue sleep eyes, lashes; rooted blond straight hair; open-closed mouth. Original red cotton dress tagged CHATTY BABY/1962 MATTEL INC/MADE IN CANADA/BY DEE AN CEE. Mark: on body, CHATTY CATHY/C1960/CHATTY BABY/C1961/BY MATTEL INC./ U.S. PAT.

Ref.No.: 2C11

Mint $115.00 **Ex.** $80.00 **G.** $45.00 **F.** $30.00

Note: Mint and Ex. prices are for talking dolls.

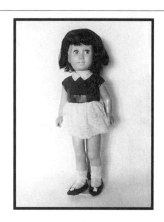

CHATTY CATHY

1961. 20 in. (50 cm). Hard plastic body, jointed hips, shoulders, and neck; holes in the front for speaker and pullring in the back to operate talking device. Vinyl head; blue sleep eyes, lashes, freckles; rooted blond saran hair with bangs; open-closed mouth showing two teeth. Mark: on body, CHATTY CATHY/c1961 CHATTY BABY/c1961/BY MATTEL INC./U.S. PAT. 3,017,187/OTHER U.S. &/FOREIGN PATS. PEND./PAT. IN CANADA 1962. Original dress with red velveteen bodice and lace skirt, red shoes and white socks.

Ref.No. D of C; BU5 p. 159

Mint $140.00 **Ex.** $90.00 **G.** $60.00 **F.** $40.00

PRETTY BABY
1961 - 14 in.

1961. 14 in. (35.5 cm). Plastic body, jointed hips, shoulders and neck. Vinyl head; blue sleep eyes, lashes; rooted blond hair; open mouth nurser. Mark: on head, DEE CEE/14. Original blue nylon dress and matching bonnet, panties. Replaced socks and shoes.

Ref.No.: 2DH5

Mint $40.00 **Ex.** $30.00 **G.** $20.00 **F.** $15.00

GINA BEATNIK

1961. 21 in. (53 cm). Plastic body, jointed hips, shoulders and neck. Vinyl head; brown sleep eyes, lashes, heavy eye makeup; rooted brown straight hair; closed mouth. Mark; on head, DEECEEc. Original purple fake fur sweater, straight black felt skirt, black tights, black felt shoes with gold elastic trim.

Ref.No.: 2GK3

Mint $115.00 **Ex.** $80.00 **G.** $50.00 **F.** $40.00

KELLY SUNDAY BEST

1961. 19 in (48 cm). Plastic body, jointed hips, shoulders and neck. Vinyl head; blue sleep eyes, lashes, painted lowers; long straight brown rooted hair; closed mouth. Mark: on head, DEE AN CEE; on body, DC. Original white high waisted nylon dress, trimmed with striped nylon and lace over a white taffeta slip. Long silk stockings, vinyl shoes. White straw hat is missing.

Ref.No.: 2X12

Mint $70.00 **Ex.** $60.00 **G.** $35.00 **F.** $25.00

WALKER

ca.1961. 23 in. (58.5 cm). Plastic body, jointed hips, shoulders and neck. Vinyl head; sleep eyes, lashes, painted lowers; rooted honey blond hair; open-closed mouth, Original dress, leotights and shoes. Mark: on head, DEE AND CEE; original ribbon, HOLD MY LEFT HAND UP AND I WILL WALK WITH YOU. MADE IN CANADA BY DEE AN CEE.

Ref.No.: 2J13

Mint $65.00 **Ex.** $50.00 **G.** $30.00 **F.** $25.00

KELLY
1961 - 30 in.

1961. 30 in. (76 cm). Plastic body, jointed hips, shoulders and neck. Vinyl head; brown sleep eyes, lashes, painted lowers; rooted brown hair; closed mouth. Mark: on head, D&C/5. Original pink cotton dress with black ribbon trim. Original "Walk with Me" ribbon. Replaced shoes.

Ref.No.: 2K19

Mint $75.00 **Ex.** $60.00 **G.** $40.00 **F.** $30.00

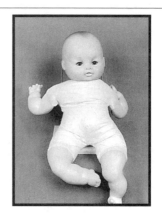

DREAM BABY
Moulded Hair

ca.1962. 18 in. (45.5 cm). Cloth body, vinyl bent-limb arms and legs. Vinyl head; blue sleep eyes, lashes; light-brown slightly moulded hair; open-closed mouth. Mark: on head, DEE AN CEE/MADE IN CANADA.

Ref.No. D of C; CD25 p. 159

Mint $55.00 **Ex.** $45.00 **G.** $35.00 **F.** $25.00

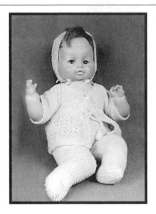

DREAM BABY
Rooted Blond Hair

ca.1962. 18 in. (45.5 cm). Pink cloth body, vinyl bent-limb arms and legs, swivel neck. Vinyl head; blue sleep eyes, lashes; rooted blond straight hair; open-closed mouth, moulded tongue. Mark: on head, DEE AN CEE/MADE IN CANADA.

Ref.No. D of C; CB17 p. 159

Mint $60.00 **Ex.** $50.00 **G.** $40.00 **F.** $30.00

TINY CHATTY BABY

1962. 15 in. (38 cm). Plastic body, jointed hips, shoulders and neck, pullring at shoulder. Vinyl head; blue sleep eyes, lashes; rooted straight brown hair; open-closed mouth showing two moulded teeth.

Ref.No. D of C; CX16 p. 160

Mint $110.00 **Ex.** $85.00 **G.** $40.00 **F.** $30.00

Note: Mint and Ex. prices are for talking dolls.

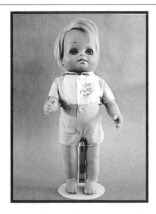

TINY CHATTY BROTHER

1962. 15 in. (38 cm). Plastic body, jointed hips, shoulders and neck. Pull ring at shoulder. Vinyl head; blue sleep eyes, lashes; rooted straight blond hair; open-closed mouth. Mark: on body, TINY CHATTY BABY TM/TINY CHATTY BROTHER TM/C1962 MATTEL INC/HAWTHORNE, CALIF. U.S.A./U.S. PAT. 3,017,187/AND FOREIGN PATENTS PENDING/PATENTED IN CANADA 1962. Original blue and white suit tagged MATTEL'S TINY CHATTY BROTHER TM/C1962. MADE IN CANADA BY DEE & CEE TOY CO. LTD.

Ref.No.: 2PGGK14

Mint $125.00 **Ex.** $95.00 **G.** $50.00 **F.** $30.00

CHARMIN CHATTY

1962. 25 in. (63 cm). Plastic body, jointed hips, shoulders and neck; opening at waist to slide in records and turn on. Vinyl head; blue side-glancing sleep eyes, lashes; rooted straight blond hair; watermelon mouth. Mark: on body, CHARMIN CHATTY/C1961/ MATTEL INC. Original middy blouse sailor suit dress, red socks, saddle shoes, black glasses. Doll also came with several plastic records allowing her to have a large repertoire of conversations.

Ref.No.: PGM15

Mint $160.00 **Ex.** $110.00 **G.** $75.00 **F.** $50.00

CINDY BRIDE
ca.1962 - 17 in.

ca.1962. 17 in. (43 cm). Plastic teen body, jointed hips, shoulders and neck. Vinyl head, holes for earrings; brown sleep eyes, lashes, painted lower lashes; rooted blond saran hair; closed mouth. Mark: D & C. Original costume.

Ref.No. D of C; CF21 p. 161

Mint $65.00 **Ex.** $55.00 **G.** $35.00 **F.** $25.00

DREAM BABY
ca.1962 - 18 in.

ca.1962. 18 in. (45.5 cm). Five-piece plastic body. Vinyl head; sleep eyes; rooted blond hair. Original pink and white dress and hang tag.

Ref.No.: ES31

Mint $60.00 **Ex.** $40.00 **G.** $30.00 **F.** $20.00

DEE AN CEE
1962 - 19 in.

ca.1962. 19 in. (48 cm). Plastic bent-limb baby body, jointed hips, shoulders, and neck. Blue sleep eyes, lashes; light brown moulded hair; open mouth nurser. Mark: on head, DEE AN CEE.

Ref.No. D of C; CP5 p. 160

Mint $60.00 **Ex.** $50.00 **G.** $40.00 **F.** $30.00

SUNTAN WALKER

1962. 30 in. (76 cm). Plastic body, jointed hips, shoulders and neck. Vinyl head; green sleep eyes, lashes; rooted short dark brown hair; dark complexion. Mark: on head, D & C 2. Redressed

Ref.No.: ES42

Mint $65.00 **Ex.** $55.00 **G.** $40.00 **F.** $30.00

BABY ELISA

ca.1962. 8 in. (20 cm). Cloth body, vinyl arms and legs. Vinyl head; grey sleep eyes, lashes; rooted straight brown hair over moulded hair; open-closed mouth. Mark: tag sewn into body, BABY ELISA R/MADE IN CANADA BY/DEE & CEE TOY CO. LTD. Original pink cotton top, white eyelet skirt with rosebud trim.

Ref.No.: 2E18

Mint $35.00 **Ex.** $30.00 **G.** $25.00 **F.** $15.00

DEE AN CEE
1962 - 17 in.

ca.1962. 17 in. (43 cm). Plastic teen body, jointed hips, shoulders, and neck. Vinyl head; blue sleep eyes, lashes; rooted blond saran hair; closed mouth. Mark: D & C. Original gown.

Ref.No. D of C; CF25 p. 161

Mint $60.00 **Ex.** $45.00 **G.** $35.00 **F.** $25.00

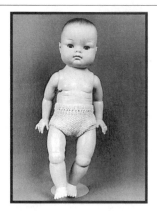

DEE AN CEE
1963 - 19 in.

ca.1963. 19 in. (48 cm). Plastic body, jointed hips, shoulders and neck. Vinyl head; blue sleep eyes, lashes; light brown slightly moulded hair; closed mouth. Mark: on head, DEE AN CEE CANADA; on body, MADE IN CANADA DEE AN CEE.

Ref.No. D of C; CD9 p. 160

Mint $55.00 **Ex.** $45.00 **G.** $30.00 **F.** $20.00

DEE AN CEE
1963 - 20 in.

ca.1963. 20 in. (51 cm). Plastic body, jointed hips, shoulders and neck. Vinyl head; blue sleep eyes, lashes; rooted brown saran curly hair; closed mouth. Mark: on head, DEE CEE/CANADA/20; on body, MADE IN CANADA/DEE AN CEE.

Ref.No. D of C; CL26 p. 162

Mint $60.00 **Ex.** $50.00 **G.** $35.00 **F.** $20.00

KOOKIE

ca.1963. 25 in. (63.5 cm). Black cloth body, legs and upper arms, pink cloth forearms. Vinyl head; brown sleep eyes, lashes, eyeshadow and extra heavy upper lashes, painted lower lashes; rooted long black hair; open-closed mouth. Mark: on head, DEE CEE. Original burlap shift.

Ref.No. D of C; BU17 p. 161

Mint $65.00 **Ex.** $50.00 **G.** $35.00 **F.** $30.00

MARY McCLARY

ca.1963. 17 in. (43 cm). Plastic teen body, jointed hips, waist, shoulders and neck. Vinyl head; blue sleep eyes, lashes, tiny painted lower lashes, three long upper lashes at outside edges of eyes; rooted brown saran hair with blond streak at the front; closed mouth. Mark: on head, DEE & CEE; on body, DEE AN CEE. Original lace gown and high-heeled shoes. It was given as a premium when McClary appliances were purchased.

Ref.No. D of C; BX13 p. 162

Mint $140.00 **Ex.** $85.00 **G.** $45.00 **F.** $30.00

Note: An extremely well made and detailed doll. Probably not more than a thousand were made as a special order.

BABY PATTABURP

ca.1963. 17 in. (43 cm). Cloth body, vinyl arms and legs. Vinyl head; blue sleep eyes, lashes; rooted straight blond hair; open-closed mouth. Mark: on head, DEE AN CEE; label on body, MATTEL.

Ref.No.: D of C; DH6 p. 162

Mint $55.00 **Ex.** $40.00 **G.** $30.00 **F.** $15.00

DEE AN CEE
Brown Plastic Body- 1963 - 12 in.

ca.1963. 12 in. (30 cm). Brown plastic body and legs, vinyl arms, upturned hands. Brown vinyl head; inset brown plastic eyes, moulded lashes, painted lower lashes; rooted light brown hair; open-closed mouth. Mark: on head, DEE CEE/MADE IN CANADA. Original costume.

Ref.No. D of C; CJ11 p. 163

Mint $40.00 **Ex.** $30.00 **G.** $25.00 **F.** $15.00

DEE AN CEE
1963 - 11 1/2 in

ca.1963. 11 1/2 in. (29 cm). Brown plastic body, vinyl arms, upturned hands, jointed hips, shoulders and neck. Vinyl head; fixed brown eyes, plastic lashes, painted lower lashes; rooted straight black hair; open-closed mouth. Mark: on head, DEE CEE/MADE IN CANADA; on body, DEE & CEE/MADE IN CANADA. Original parka, hood and pants.

Ref.No. D of C; BU31 p. 163

Mint $45.00 **Ex.** $35.00 **G.** $25.00 **F.** $15.00

DEE AN CEE
1963 - 12 in.

ca.1963. 12 in. (30 cm). Plastic body, jointed hips, shoulders, and neck. Vinyl head; fixed blue plastic eyes, moulded lashes; rooted blond braids; open-closed mouth. Mark: on head, DEE CEE/MADE IN/CANADA. Original red cotton skirt, organdy pinafore and kerchief.

Ref.No. D of C; CJ10 p. 163

Mint $40.00 **Ex.** $30.00 **G.** $25.00 **F.** $15.00

KICHI'MA
(Great Chief)

1963. 15 in. (38 cm). Plastic body, jointed hips shoulders and neck. Vinyl head; black painted eyes; rooted black hair in braids; watermelon mouth. Original suedine suit with braid and rick-rack trim, leather mocassins. Original tag. MADE EXCLUSIVELY FOR THE HUDSON'S BAY CO. Mark: on head, c1963/HUDSON BAY CO.; on body, MADE IN CANADA/DEEANCEE.

Ref.No.: 2D6

Mint $150.00 **Ex.** $100.00 **G.** $60.00 **F.** $45.00

Note: An unusual doll and hard to find.

DEE AN CEE
1963 - 23 in.

ca.1963. 23 in. (58.5 cm). Plastic body, jointed hips, shoulders and neck. Vinyl head; blue sleep eyes, lashes; rooted light brown hair; open mouth showing two upper and two lower teeth. Mark: lower back, DEE AN CEE. Redressed.

Ref.No.: 2I6

Mint $65.00 **Ex.** $55.00 **G.** $35.00 **F.** $30.00

DEE AN CEE
Long Blond Hair

1964. 15 in. (38 cm). Plastic body, jointed hips, shoulders and neck. Vinyl head; blue side-glancing sleep eyes, lashes; rooted long blond hair; closed pouty mouth. Mark: on head, DEE & CEE/MADE IN CANADA/1964. Original dress.

Ref.No. D of C; BX10 p. 164

Mint $55.00 **Ex.** $40.00 **G.** $30.00 **F.** $20.00

DEE AN CEE
Platinum Blond Hair

1964. 15 in. (38 cm). Plastic body and legs, vinyl arms, jointed hips, shoulders and neck. Vinyl head; blue side-glancing sleep eyes, lashes; rooted platinum blond saran hair; closed pouty mouth. Mark: on head, DEE & CEE/MADE IN CANADA/COPYRIGHT 1964. Original costume.

Ref.No. D of C; AN5 p. 164

Mint $55.00 **Ex.** $40.00 **G.** $30.00 **F.** $20.00

BRIDE
1964 - 16 in.

1964. 16 in. (41 cm). Plastic body, jointed hips, shoulders and neck. Vinyl head; blue side-glancing sleep eyes, lashes; rooted long dark brown hair; closed mouth. Mark: on head, DEE AND CEE/MADE IN CANADA/19C64. Original white lace bridal gown.

Ref.No.: 2I4

Mint $60.00 **Ex.** $40.00 **G.** $25.00 **F.** $20.00

BEANY

ca.1964. 18 in. (46 cm). Cloth body, vinyl hands and feet. Vinyl head; side-glancing eyes, painted blue; open-closed mouth. Mark: on head, DEECEE/MADE IN CANADA. Stuffed clothing forms the body. Missing propeller on top of cap.

Ref.No.: 2Q29

Mint $65.00 **Ex.** $55.00 **G.** $35.00 **F.** $25.00

DISTINCTIVE DOLLS OF CANADA LTD.
1987 - 1992

D.D.C. was established to provide a line of collectable Canadian-made dolls. In 1988 the Sir John A. Macdonald doll was produced in vinyl from an original mould. The doll was designed by Yvonne Richardson of West Hill, Ontario.

In 1989 Wis-Ton and D.D.C. co-produced a vinyl Elizabeth Manley doll dressed in shocking pink, and in 1991 a smaller edition of Elizabeth was manufactured wearing a white and gold skating costume. The original head mould was made from a design by Jeanne Venton of Victoria, B.C.

D.D.C. produced three editions of the Forgie quintuplet dolls in 1990 and in 1991.

The company also promoted porcelain dolls sculpted by original Canadian doll artists, since many Canadian doll collectors are unaware of the talented artists living in Canada. Since most collectors buy doll magazines from the United States, the American doll artists are often better known here than the Canadian artists.

TEMPERAMENTAL TAMMY

1987. 17 in. (43 cm). Cloth body, vinyl arms and legs. Vinyl head with three faces and a knob on top to turn the head. Original lace trimmed cotton dress with matching panties, brushed knit jacket and hood, socks and shoes. A small edition of less than 100.

Ref.No.: Z5

Mint $50.00   **Ex.** $35.00   **G.** $25.00   **F.** $20.00

SIR JOHN A. MACDONALD

1988. 18 in. (46 cm). Vinyl body, jointed hips, shoulders and neck. Vinyl head; blue painted eyes; grey moulded curly hair; closed mouth. Mark: on head, MACDONALD/YVONNE RICHARDSON/1987 CANADA; on back, MACDONALD/YVONNE RICHARDSON/1987 CANADA/DISTINCTIVE DOLLS/ OF CANADA LTD/logo. Dressed in white cotton shirt, lined cream wool pants and vest, black wool coat, tie, moulded boots and pocket watch. Includes medallion with the company logo and tag on his wrist.

Ref.No.: DM6 and DM 7

Mint $180.00 Ex. $150.00 G. $100.00 F. $80.00

ELIZABETH MANLEY
1989 - 16 in.

1989. Celebrity Series #2. 16 in. (41 cm). All porcelain body, jointed hips, shoulders and neck. Porcelain head; golden brown glass eyes, painted lashes; blond short wig; open-closed mouth showing teeth. Mark: on head in script, ELIZABETH MANLEY/BY JEANNE VENTON/FOR/ DISTINCTIVE DOLLS OF/CANADA, 1989/#30. Limited edition of 32 and sold out. Blue Spandex costume with sheer over-skirt, silver sequin trim, hand-made leather skates, sterling silver medal on a vertically striped ribbon.

Ref.No.: AD36

Mint $550.00

BARBARA ANN SCOTT - 1991

1991. Celebrity Series #3. 14 1/2 in. (37 cm). Cloth body, porcelain arms and legs. Porcelain head; blue glass eyes, painted lashes; honey blond wig; smiling open-closed mouth, showing teeth. Mark: on head, BARBARA ANN SCOTT/c1991/BY HEATHER BROWNING MACIAK/NUMBER 1 OUT OF 99/H.B. MACIAK. Shimmer satin skating costume with marabou trim, matching panties and marabou trimmed bonnet, hand-made leather skates. Hand-made by Heather Browning Maciak of Calgary. Limited edition of 99.

Ref.No.: Z7

Mint $495.00

PRINCE HENRY

1991. 14 in. (35.5 cm). All porcelain body, jointed hips, shoulders and neck. Porcelain head; stationary blue eyes, painted upper and lower lashes; blond wig; closed mouth. Mark: on head, PRINCE HENRY/BY JEANNE VENTON/1991C/2/200. Original blue cotton sailor suit with black braid trim and red ribbon tie, matching sailor hat, black shoes. The head of Prince Henry is an original sculpture by Jeanne Venton. The dolls were made for D.D.C. by Meggan's Doll House.

Ref.No.: Z6

Mint $200.00

MEGGAN JOAN

1991. Canadian Child Series. 22 in. (56 cm). Cloth body, porcelain shoulderplate, arms and legs. Bisque head; blue stationary eyes, painted lashes; blond wig; closed mouth. Doll designed by Jeanne Venton and made for D.D.C. by Ann Marie Porcelain Production in N.B. Original pale pink lace-trimmed cotton dress, cotton petticoat and bloomers, white lace stockings and leather shoes. Includes a porcelain name pendant.

Ref.No.: Z9

Mint $400.00

SNOW BIRD

1991. Canadian Child Series. 22 in. (56 cm). Cloth body, light brown porcelain shoulderplate, arms and legs. Light brown bisque head; dark brown stationary eyes, painted lashes; black wig; closed mouth. Doll designed by Jeanne Venton and made for D.D.C. by Ann Marie Porcelain Productions. Original white leather fringed dress, leather mocassins, cotton bloomers and a beaded necklace and headband. Includes a porcelain name pendant.

Ref.No.: Z10

Mint $425.00

KIRSTEN APRIL

1991. Canadian Child Series. 22 in. (56 cm). Cloth body, porcelain shoulderplate, arms and legs. Bisque head; stationary green eyes, painted lashes; light brown wig; open-closed mouth showing teeth. Doll designed by Jeanne Venton and made for D.D.C. by Ann Marie Porcelain Productions. Original blue cotton print dress, white pinafore, cotton petticoat and bloomers, white socks, leather shoes and a floral head wreath. Includes porcelain name pendant (not shown).

Ref.No.: 2Y19

Mint $375.00

MELISSA ROSE 1880

1991. 14 in. (35.5 cm). Porcelain body, arms and legs. Bisque head; stationary blue eyes, painted lashes; auburn wig; open-closed mouth showing teeth. Head designed by Jeanne Venton. Doll made for D.D.C. by Meggan's Doll House. Original blue taffeta, lace-trimmed dress in Victorian style, matching bonnet trimmed with a feather, white boots and stockings.

Ref.No.: Z11

Mint $200.00

DOMINION TOY MANUFACTURING COMPANY LIMITED
1911 - 1932

Dominion was the first commercial doll company in Canada and was established by Aaron Cone and his son Morris. Both men were talented doll designers and created many faces with natural child-like charm.

Very little documentation about this company has survived, and it is often difficult to determine the exact year a doll was made. Much can be determined by studying the changing technology as they progressed to an ever better product and by comparing the dolls whose owners are sure of the date they received them. Dominion dolls are truly antique dolls, as they were made 65 to 85 years ago.

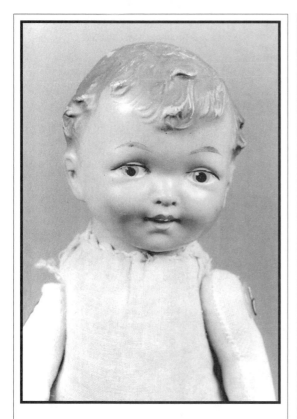

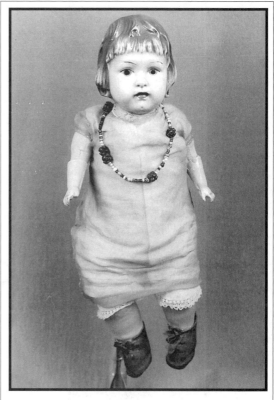

DOMINION
1911 - 19 in.

ca.1911. 19 in. (48 cm). Excelsior stuffed cloth body, legs and upper arms; composition forearms. Composition head; painted blue eyes with highlights and a fine black line over the eye; deeply moulded hair, painted light brown; open-closed mouth showing two moulded teeth. Unmarked.

Ref.No.: D of C, BW34, p. 166

Mint $250.00 **Ex.** $200.00 **G.** $135.00 **F.** $75.00

DOMINION
1911 - 16 1/2 in.

ca.1911. 16 1/2 in. (42 cm). Excelsior stuffed cloth body, legs and upper arms; composition gauntlet hands. Composition shoulderhead with small round shoulderplate; eyes painted blue with a fine black line over each eye; deeply moulded hair, painted brown; closed mouth. Unmarked.

Ref.No.: D of C, BX34, p. 167

Mint $235.00 **Ex.** $185.00 **G.** $140.00 **F.** $75.00

DOMINON
ca. 1911 - 9 in.

ca.1911. 9 in. (23 cm). Excelsior stuffed cloth body, legs and arms, jointed hips and shoulders with metal discs; one arm is longer than the other. Blue side-glancing painted eyes, black line over eye; light brown moulded hair with moulded headband; closed mouth. Mark: Original label with the Dominion shield marked, DOMINION/BRAND/DOLLS & TOYS/MADE IN CANADA.

Ref.No.: D of C, CN19, p. 167

Mint **$150.00** **Ex.** **$125.00** **G.** **$80.00** **F.** **$60.00**

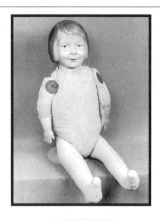

DOMINON
ca. 1912 - 29 in.

ca.1912. 29 in. (73.5 cm). Excelsior stuffed cloth body and legs, composition gauntlet hands, jointed hips and shoulders with metal discs. Composition flange head; blue intaglio eyes, fine black line over eye; deeply moulded light brown hair; closed smiling mouth. Unmarked.

Ref.No.: D of C, CB24, p. 167

Mint **$285.00** **Ex.** **$250.00** **G.** **$175.00** **F.** **$100.00**

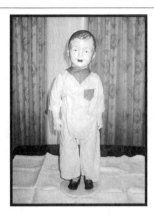

BOY SCOUT DOLL

ca.1912. 31 in. (79 cm). Excelsior stuffed cloth body and legs, composition arms. Composition head; painted blue intaglio eyes, fine black line over eye; moulded reddish brown hair; closed mouth. Original Boy Scout costume with insignia on pocket.

Ref.No.: 2X5

Mint **$285.00** **Ex.** **$250.00** **G.** **$175.00** **F.** **$100.00**

DOMINION
ca. 1913 - 17 in.

ca.1913. 17 in. (43 cm). Excelsior stuffed cloth body, legs and upper arms; composition gauntlet hands. Composition head; painted blue side-glancing eyes; moulded hair with moulded hole for a ribbon, painted brown; closed mouth. Unmarked.

Ref.No.: D of C, CI8, p. 168

Mint **$145.00** **Ex.** **$115.00** **G.** **$70.00** **F.** **$60.00**

DOMINION
ca. 1914 - 13 in.

ca.1914. 13 in. (33 cm). Cloth body, composition arms, attached by nails through the body, cloth legs with composition black boots glued on. Legs attached with nails and metal disks. Composition head; blue painted eyes, moulded light brown hair, closed mouth. Redressed in old cotton fabric dress of the period.

Ref.No.: 2Z16

Mint $160.00 **Ex.** $130.00 **G.** $75.00 **F.** $55.00

DOMINION
ca. 1915 - 13 3/4 in.

ca.1915. 13 3/4 in. (35 cm). Excelsior stuffed cloth body, legs and forearms; composition lower arms; feet are stitched on black fabric. Composition shoulderhead; painted eyes; moulded hair, painted strawberry blond; closed mouth, painted orange-red. Unmarked. Label on original dress.

Ref.No.: D of C, BF5, p. 169

Mint $195.00 **Ex.** $150.00 **G.** $95.00 **F.** $60.00

TIPPERARY TOMMY

ca.1915. 14 in. (35.5 cm). Cloth body with composition hands and boots. Composition head; painted blue eyes with a fine black line over each eye; moulded hair, painted light brown; closed mouth, painted red. Unmarked.

Ref.No.: D of C, AP9, p. 168

Mint $220.00 **Ex.** $160.00 **G.** $110.00 **F.** $85.00

NAUGHTY MARIETTA

ca.1915. 15 in. (38 cm). Cloth body, composition gauntlet hands, cloth legs, composition white moulded boots with original socks. Arms and legs attached by nails and metal disks. Composition head; side-glancing painted blue eyes; heavily moulded blond hair with moulded head-band; open-closed mouth showing painted teeth. "Naughty Marietta" was designed by Aaron Cone and made first in the United States by Ideal of New York.

Ref.No.: 2Z15

Mint $225.00 **Ex.** $175.00 **G.** $95.00 **F.** $65.00

DOMINION
Open Mouth with Teeth

ca.1915. 20 in. (50.5 cm). Fully ball-jointed composition body. Composition head; sleep eyes, painted lashes; open mouth with teeth; original mohair wig. Mark: on body, shield with D.T.M.C. with MADE IN CANADA inside. Redressed.

Ref.No.: ES50

Mint $325.00 **Ex.** $275.00 **G.** $185.00 **F.** $140.00

DOMINION
Open-closed Mouth, Four Painted Teeth

ca.1915. 20 in. (50.5 cm). Fully ball-jointed composition body. Composition head; sleep eyes, painted lashes; open-closed mouth, four painted teeth; replaced mohair wig. Mark: on body, shield with D.T.M.C. MADE IN CANADA. Redressed.

Ref.No.: ES51

Mint $325.00 **Ex.** $275.00 **G.** $185.00 **F.** $140.00

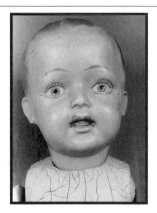

DOMINION BOY
ca. 1916 - 25 in.

ca.1916. 25 in. (63.5 cm). All composition bent-limb baby. Composition head; painted blue eyes with a fine black line over the eye, and painted lashes; moulded hair. Open-closed mouth with two painted teeth. Unmarked.

Ref.No.: D of C, CD7, p. 169

Mint $325.00 **Ex.** $275.00 **G.** $175.00 **F.** $125.00

Note: This doll has a lovely moulded face. Dolls of this era are worth restoring.

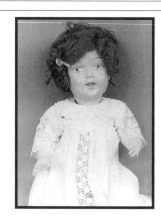

DOMINION GIRL
ca. 1916 - 23in.

ca.1916. 23 in. (58.5 cm). All composition bent-limb baby. Composition head; painted blue eyes, fine black line over the eye, and painted lashes; original brown mohair wig; open-closed mouth with two painted teeth. Mark: a shield on the body with D.T.M.C. in it.

Ref.No.: D of C, CF5, p. 169

Mint $350.00 **Ex.** $290.00 **G.** $185.00 **F.** $135.00

DOMINION
ca.1916 - 14in.

ca.1916. 14 in. (35.5 cm). All composition bent-limb baby. Painted eyes; two painted teeth. Mark: on body, MADE IN CANADA D.T.M.Co.

Mint **$185.00** **Ex.** **$160.00** **G.** **$100.00** **F.** **$75.00**

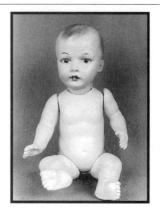

DOMINION
ca.1917 - 14 in.

ca.1917. 14 in. (35.5 cm). All composition bent-limb baby. Composition head; painted intaglio violet eyes with a fine black line over each eye, and painted lashes; moulded light brown hair; closed mouth. Mark: a shield on the body with D.T.M.C./MADE IN CANADA in it.
Ref.No.: D of C, CL6, p. 171

Mint **$200.00** **Ex.** **$175.00** **G.** **$105.00** **F.** **$75.00**

DUTCH BOY

ca.1917. 17 in. (43 cm). Excelsior-stuffed cloth body and legs, composition gauntlet hands. Composition shoulderhead; painted blue eyes with fine black line over the eye and painted upper lashes; blond mohair wig; closed mouth. Mark: on shoulderplate, D.T.C. Original blue and white cotton Dutch Boy suit. Replaced shoes.
Ref.No.: DB1

Mint **$190.00** **Ex.** **$140.00** **G.** **$110.00** **F.** **$80.00**

Note: This doll appeared on a commemorative postage stamp issued June 8, 1990.

DOMINION
ca.1917 - 17 in.

ca.1917. 17 in. (43 cm). All composition, bent-limb baby body; five piece. Eyes intaglio, painted violet; open-closed mouth with two painted teeth.

Mint **$300.00** **Ex.** **$275.00** **G.** **$200.00** **F.** **$150.00**

Note: This doll appeared on a commemorative postage stamp issued June 8, 1990.

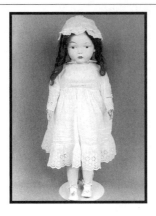

DOLLY WALKER

ca.1918. 28 in. (71 cm). Cardboard body with composition forearms, wooden upper arms and wooden legs, jointed with hinges. Composition shoulderhead; painted blue eyes; fine black line over the eye; nostril dots; moulded hair, painted light brown plus a human hair wig which is not attached to the head. Closed mouth. Mark: D.T.M.C./MADE IN CANADA. Original white cotton dress and matching hat.

Ref.No.: D of C, CA8, p. 170

Mint **$700.00** **Ex.** **$400.00** **G.** **$275.00** **F. $175.00**

DOMINION
ca.1919 - 14 in.

ca.1919. 14 in. (35.5 cm). Cloth body, legs and forearms; composition lower arms. Composition shoulder head; painted blue eyes; painted long upper lashes; moulded hair painted light brown; closed mouth painted red. Mark: on shoulderplate, D.T.CO. .

Ref.No.: D of C, BH32, p.171

Mint **$150.00** **Ex.** **$120.00** **G.** **$95.00** **F.** **$55.00**

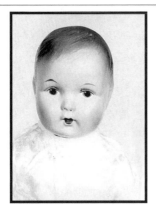

DOMINION
ca.1919 - 20 in.

ca.1919. 20 in. (51 cm). Cloth body and legs, composition forearms. Composition shoulderhead; mauve painted eyes, black line over eye, painted upper lashes; moulded brown hair; closed mouth. Mark: on shoulderplate, D.T.Co. Redressed.

Ref.No.: 2R13

Mint **$155.00** **Ex.** **$125.00** **G.** **$95.00** **F.** **$50.00**

DOMINION
ca.1920 - 19 in.

ca.1920. 19 in. (48 cm). Excelsior stuffed cloth body and upper arms; bent-limb legs; composition gauntlet hands. Composition head with open crown and wooden pate; grey tin sleep eyes, painted lashes; original blond mohair wig; open mouth. Mark: MADE IN CANADA/D.T.M.C. on the body. Originally had pink shoes and white socks.

Ref.No.: D of C, CL27, p. 172

Mint **$250.00** **Ex.** **$215.00** **G.** **$175.00** **F.** **$130.00**

DOMINION
ca.1920 - 19 1/2 in.

ca.1920. 19 1/2 in. (49.5 cm). Cloth body, legs and forearms; composition lower arms. Composition shoulder head; painted blue eyes, painted long upper lashes; original blond wig; closed mouth painted red. Mark: D.T.C. on shoulderplate. Original rompers, replaced hat and shoes.

Ref.No. : D of C, AP19, p. 172

Mint $250.00   Ex. $215.00   G. $150.00   F. $95.00

DOMINION
ca.1920 - 17 in.

ca.1920. 17 in. (43 cm). Cloth body and legs. Composition shoulderhead and hands. Painted blue eyes with highlights; closed mouth; moulded blond hair with loop for hair bow. Unmarked. Hang tag: DOLLS & TOYS/OF QUALITY/DOMINION TOY CO LIMITED/DOMINION BRAND/MADE IN CANADA. Original blue print dress, yellow-green bows and black shoes.

Mint $250.00   Ex. $215.00   G. $150.00   F. $95.00

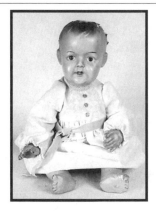

DOMINION
ca.1920 - 14 1/2 in.

ca.1920. 14 1/2 in. (37 cm). All composition, bent-limb baby, jointed hips, shoulders and neck. Composition head; blue painted eyes, upper and lower lashes; moulded brown hair; open-closed mouth with two painted teeth. Mark: D.T.C. Redressed.

Ref.No.: 2Q23

Mint $185.00   Ex. $160.00   G. $105.00   F. $75.00

METAL HEAD DOLL

ca.1920. 19 in. (48 cm). Cloth body, composition gauntlet hands. Metal head, with dimples; painted blue eyes; moulded blond hair; closed mouth. Mark: on neck, MADE IN CANADA (in an arch over)/ DTMC. Redressed.

Ref.No.: 2Z1

Mint $180.00   Ex. $140.00   G. $95.00   F. $60.00

Note: This is the only metal head doll we have ever discovered that was made in Canada. A rare doll.

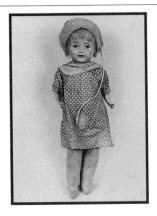

DOMINION
ca.1921 - 22 in.

ca.1921. 22 in. (56 cm). Cloth body and legs, composition forearms. Composition shoulderhead; blue painted eyes, painted upper lashes; blond mohair wig; open-closed mouth. Unmarked. Original blue and white cotton dress and bonnet.

Ref.No.: 2P29

Mint **$200.00** **Ex.** **$150.00** **G.** **$115.00** **F.** **$75.00**

ALICE

ca.1922. 20 in. (51 cm). Excelsior stuffed cloth body and legs, composition gauntlet hands. Composition shoulderhead; blue painted eyes, long painted upper lashes; blond mohair wig over moulded hair; closed mouth. Mark: on head, D.T.C.

Ref.No.: D of C, CN27, p. 172

Mint **$195.00** **Ex.** **$150.00** **G.** **$115.00** **F.** **$75.00**

DOMINION
ca.1922 - 18 in.

ca.1922. 18 in. (46 cm). Excelsior stuffed cloth body and legs, composition arms. Composition shoulderhead; tin sleep eyes; blond mohair wig; closed mouth. Mark: on head D.T.M.C. MADE IN CANADA (inside shield). Original white cotton dress with pink flowers, blue border around bottom.

Ref.No.: 2KA13

Mint **$180.00** **Ex.** **$150.00** **G.** **$115.00** **F.** **$75.00**

DOMINION
ca.1922 - 20 in.

ca.1922. 20 in. (51 cm). Fully ball-jointed composition body, jointed knees, hips, shoulders, elbows, wrists and neck. Composition head; blue tin sleep eyes, lashes, painted upper and lower lashes; blond mohair wig; open mouth, two teeth. Mark: on body, DOMINION SHIELD. Original white cotton homemade dress, replaced shoes, sash and hat.

Ref.No.: DF4

Mint **$325.00** **Ex.** **$275.00** **G.** **$185.00** **F.** **$140.00**

DOMINION
ca.1923 - 20 1/2 in.

ca.1923. 20 1/2 in. (52 cm). Fully ball-jointed composition body with wooden arms. Composition head; light green celluloid sleep eyes; painted upper and lower lashes with red dots in the corners; open-closed mouth with four painted teeth. Mark: on the body, MADE IN CANADA/D.T.M.C.

Ref.No.: D of C, CA31, p. 173

Mint **$325.00** **Ex.** **$275.00** **G.** **$185.00** **F.** **$140.00**

DOMINION
1923 - 20 in.

1923. 20 in. (51 cm). Fully ball-jointed composition body, wooden arms, jointed knees, hips, shoulders, elbows, wrists and neck. Composition head; green celluloid sleep eyes, painted upper and lower lashes; black mohair wig, styled in original braids; open-closed mouth showing four painted teeth. Mark: on body, MADE IN CANADA/DTMC. Dressed in ivory silk dress, dark green wool coat and matching hat, trimmed with lighter green rayon on cuffs, collar and hat bows.

Ref.No.: 2N20

Mint **$325.00** **Ex.** **$275.00** **G.** **$185.00** **F.** **$140.00**

DOMINION
ca.1924 - 19 in.

ca.1924. 19 in. (48 cm). Fully ball-jointed composition body with wooden arms and composition legs. Composition head; grey-blue celluloid sleep eyes, painted upper and lower lashes; original brown mohair wig; open mouth with teeth missing. Mark: on the body; within a shield D.T.M.C./MADE IN CANADA.

Ref.No.: D of C, CC8, p. 173

Mint **$300.00** **Ex.** **$260.00** **G.** **180.00** **F.** **140.00**

KUDLEE BABY

ca.1924. 18 in. (45.5 cm). Kapok stuffed cloth body and legs, composition gauntlet hands. Composition shoulderhead; celluloid sleep eyes; moulded hair; open-closed mouth, tongue painted darker than the lips. Mark: on shoulderplate, DTMCO.; original label, KUDLEE/BABY/KAPOK FILLED/MADE IN CANADA/BY/DOMINION TOY CO. LTD./TORONTO.

Ref.No.: D of C, CN28, p. 174

Mint **$275.00** **Ex.** **$250.00** **G.** **$195.00** **F.** **$130.00**

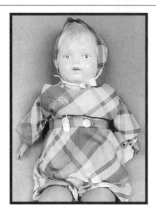

DOMINION
ca.1924 - 21 in.

ca.1924. 21 in. (53.5 cm). Excelsior stuffed body, legs and upper arms, composition forearms, crier in the body. Composition shoulderhead; painted blue eyes with fine black line over each eye, painted upper lashes; blond mohair wig; closed mouth. Mark: D.T.C. on shoulderplate.

Ref.No.: D of C, CF4, p. 174

Mint $195.00 **Ex.** $150.00 **G.** $125.00 **F** $75.00

DOMINION
ca.1925 - 16 in.

ca.1925. 16 in. (40.5 cm). Composition fully ball-jointed body. Composition head; grey celluloid sleep eyes, painted upper and lower lashes; replaced mohair wig; open mouth showing teeth. Mark: on body, DOMINION SHIELD. Redressed in old fabric dress.

Ref.No.: 2S2

Mint $225.00 **Ex.** $150.00 **G.** $105.00 **F.** $65.00

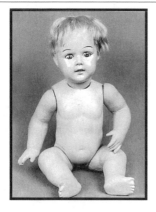

DOMINION
ca.1926 - 14 in.

ca.1926. 14 in. (35.5 cm). All composition bent-limb baby. Composition open crown head; blue celluloid sleep eyes with painted lashes; blond mohair wig; open-closed mouth showing two painted teeth. Mark: MADE IN CANADA/D.T.M.C. on the body.

Ref.No.: D of C, CD33, p.175

Mint $200.00 **Ex.** $160.00 **G.** $125.00 **F.** $85.00

BED DOLL
ca.1926 - 27 in.

ca.1926. 27 in. (68.5 cm). Cloth body very long and slender. Composition head; brown painted side-glancing eyes with highlights; a fine black line around the eye with painted upper and lower lashes; grey eye shadow and a fine black line above the eye; brows are a series of separate strokes; closed mouth and nostril dots; black synthetic wig. Mark: D.T.C.

Ref.No.: D of C, CC5, p. 175

Mint $250.00 **Ex.** $210.00 **G.** $150.00 **F.** $75.00

BED DOLL
ca.1926 - 26 in.

ca.1926. 26 in. (66 cm). Long slender cloth body. Composition head; black painted eyes with black eyeliner; light brown synthetic hair; closed mouth. Mark: on head, D.T.C.

Ref.No.: D of C, CQ12, p. 175

Mint $250.00 **Ex.** $210.00 **G.** $160.00 **F.** $75.00

DOMINION
ca.1926 - 20 in.

ca.1926. 20 in. (51 cm). Excelsior stuffed cloth body, legs and upper arms; composition forearms. Composition shoulderhead; painted blue eyes; painted upper lashes; blond mohair wig; open mouth with two teeth. Mark: D.T. CO. on shoulderplate.

Ref.No.: D of C, BZ7, p. 176

Mint $200.00 **Ex.** $160.00 **G.** $115.00 **F.** $75.00

DOMINION
ca.1926 - 23 in.

ca.1926. 23 in. (58.5 cm). Excelsior stuffed cloth body, legs, and upper arms; composition three-quarter arms. The cloth on the legs is pink. Composition shoulderhead; blue celluloid sleep eyes; lashes; painted upper and lower lashes; blond mohair wig; open mouth showing two inset teeth and tongue. Mark: D.T.M.C. on shoulderplate.

Ref.No.: D of C, CL25, p. 176

Mint $225.00 **Ex.** $175.00 **G.** $140.00 **F.** $90.00

BED DOLL
ca.1927 - 26 in.

ca.1927. 26 in. (66 cm). Long cloth body, arms and legs. Composition head; painted black eyes, eye shadow; dark brown mohair wig; closed mouth. Mark: on head D.T.C. Original pink gown with sheer blue underskirt, lace trimmed, matching hat, blue satin shoes with silver high-heeled shoes.

Ref.No.: 2Q33

Mint $250.00 **Ex.** $210.00 **G.** $150.00 **F.** $75.00

DOMINION
ca.1927 - 26 in.

ca.1927. 20 in. (51 cm). Excelsior stuffed cloth body, legs and upper arms; composition forearms. Composition shoulderhead; blue tin sleep eyes, lashes, painted lower lashes; original mohair wig; open mouth showing teeth and tongue. Unmarked.

Ref.No.: D of C, CM8, p. 176

Mint $175.00 Ex. $150.00 G. $125.00 G. $75.00

BED DOLL
ca.1927 - 27 in.

ca.1927. 27 in. (68.5 cm). Cloth body; very long and slender. Composition head; painted black eyes with highlights; grey eyeshadow and a black line outlining the eye; brown mohair wig; closed mouth. Mark: D.T.C. on head.

Ref.No.: D of C, CC6, p. 177.

Mint $250.00 Ex. $210.00 G. $150.00 F. $75.00

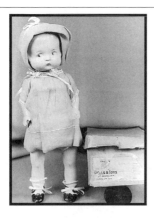

PANSY

ca.1928. 14 1/2 in. (37 cm). Excelsior stuffed cloth body, composition arms and legs that are attached to the body by a heavy wire. Composition shoulderhead; painted blue side-glancing eyes; painted upper lashes; fine black line over the eye; moulded reddish gold hair; closed mouth. Unmarked.

Ref.No.: D of C, CM9, p. 177

Mint $225.00 Ex. $195.00 G. $140.00 F. $75.00

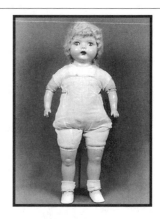

DOMINION
ca.1928 - 27 1/2 in.

ca.1928. 27 1/2 in. (70 cm). Cloth body, upper arms and upper legs; composition forearms and long straight lower legs; crier in the body. Composition shoulder head; blue sleep celluloid eyes, painted upper and lower lashes; blond mohair wig with bangs; open mouth showing teeth and tongue. Mark: D.T.C. on shoulderplate.

Ref.No.: D of C, BT24, p. 177

Mint $275.00 Ex. $225.00 G. $175.00 F. $110.00

DOMINION
ca.1929 - 19 in.

ca.1929. 19 in. (48 cm). Cloth body and legs, composition forearms. Composition shoulderhead; sleep eyes, replaced wig; open mouth, two teeth and tongue. Original navy and white dress, white hat and teddy, blue slippers with fur trim.

Ref.No.: GK4

Mint $160.00 **Ex.** $130.00 **G.** $105.00 **F.** $65.00

DOMINION
ca.1929 - 17 in.

ca.1929. 17 in. (43 cm). Cloth body, upper arms and upper legs, composition bent-limb arms and straight legs. Composition shoulderhead with dimpled cheeks; blue celluloid sleep eyes; lashes; painted upper lashes; moulded hair painted blond; open mouth showing two inset teeth and tongue. Mark: on shoulderplate D.T.M.C.

Ref.No: D of C, BY12, p. 178

Mint $215.00 **Ex.** $175.00 **G.** $140.00 **F.** $75.00

DOMINION
ca.1930 - 28 in.

ca.1930. 28 in. (71 cm). Cloth body and legs, composition arms. Composition shoulderhead; painted blue eyes, painted upper lashes; brown human hair wig; open-closed mouth. Mark: on shoulderplate, D.T.C.; on tag, shield with DOMINION/BRAND/DOLLS & TOYS/OF QUALITY/ DOMINION TOY CO./LIMITED. Original lace-trimmed yellow cotton dress and matching bonnet. Replaced shoes

Ref.No.: 2Q26

Mint $250.00 **Ex.** $195.00 **G.** $130.00 **F.** $85.00

 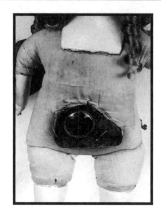 

TALKING DOLL

1932. 27 in. (69 cm). Cloth body, composition arms and legs, talking mechanism in the body, metal handle on side to wind victrola. Composition shoulderhead; blue celluloid eyes, lashes; wig; open mouth. Mark: on shoulderplate, D.T.C. Clothing replaced in original style. Includes a box of 5 wax record cylinders which play: 1. Now I lay me down to sleep; 2+3. London bridge; 4. Little Boy Blue; 5. One, two, buckle your shoe.

Ref.No.: 2R36, 2Q19-20

Mint. $450.00 Ex. $375.00 G. $295.00 F. $130.00

Note: This doll demonstrates the superb quality and technological advancement of the Dominion Toy Company. It is a fine Canadian historical artifact. Unfortunately it has been repainted and the wig replaced with a modern one, which reduces the value considerably.

EARLE PULLAN COMPANY LIMITED
1945 - 1967

The Earle Pullan Company began operations in 1945, and at first they made plush animals and games. In 1947 they began producing composition dolls and then changed to manufacturing dolls with a stuffed rubber skin in 1952. By 1954 they were making dolls with vinyl heads and, a few years later, made plastic dolls with jointed arms and legs.

Pullan dolls were well made and very nicely dressed. Many were unusual and innovative. In some cases, such as the Pitiful Pearl doll, Pullan was the only manufacturer in Canada. Since Pitiful Pearl was not popular at the time, few were made, and the doll is presently very hard to find.

BIRTH CERTIFICATE DOLL

1947. 20 in. (51 cm.). All composition baby, jointed hips, shoulders and neck. Composition head; blue sleep eyes, lashes, painted upper lashes; blond wig; closed mouth. Unmarked. Original silk rayon gown and matching bonnet with pastel ribbon trim.

Ref.No.: D of C, PU13, p. 183

Mint $200.00 **Ex.** $145.00 **G.** $85.00 **F.** $50.00

PULLAN
1947 - 19 in.

1947. 19 in. (48 cm). All composition, jointed hips, shoulders and neck. Composition head; blue sleep eyes, lashes, painted lower lashes; original light brown mohair wig with bangs; closed painted rosebud mouth. Mark: on head, PULLAN on body, PULLAN. Original pink, blue and white cotton dress and bonnet, shoes and socks.

Ref.No.: D of C, BH16, p. 183

Mint $200.00 **Ex.** $145.00 **G.** $85.00 **F.** $50.00

BABY JASPER

1948. 10 in. (25 cm). All composition dark brown bent-limb baby, jointed hips, shoulders and neck. Composition head; side-glancing eyes painted black; moulded hair painted black; closed mouth painted red. Mark: on body, A PULLAN DOLL. Originally wore a two-tone sunsuit.

Ref.No.: D of C, BM35, p. 184

Mint $95.00 **Ex.** $75.00 **G.** $50.00 **F.** $35.00

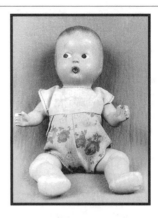

DINKY DRINKY

1948. 10 in. (25 cm). All composition baby, jointed hips and shoulders. Composition one-piece head and body; side-glancing eyes painted black; moulded hair painted reddish brown; metal ring in mouth painted red. Mark: on body, PULLAN DOLL. Original cotton play-suit.

Ref.No.: D of C, BW28, p. 184

Mint $65.00 **Ex.** $45.00 **G.** $30.00 **F.** $20.00

BABY PULLAN

1948. 10 in. (25 cm). All composition baby, jointed hips and shoulders. Composition one-piece head and body; painted blue eyes, side-glancing; moulded hair painted reddish brown; closed mouth painted red. Mark: on body, PULLAN DOLL. Original cotton play-suit.

Ref.No.: D of C, BW27, p. 185

Mint $55.00 **Ex.** $40.00 **G.** $30.00 **F.** $20.00

BABY TWINKLE

1948. 14 1/2 in. (37 cm). All composition, jointed hips, shoulders and neck. Composition head; sleep eyes, lashes, painted upper lashes; knee-length blond wig; closed mouth. Original bathrobe and diaper.

Ref.No.: D of C, PU12, p. 184

Mint $150.00 **Ex.** $105.00 **G.** $60.00 **F.** $40.00

Note: This is a rare doll.

MISS PULLAN

1948. 20 in. (51 cm). All composition, jointed hips, shoulders and neck. Composition head; sleep eyes, lashes; mohair wig; closed mouth. Unmarked. Original tailored woollen coat and hat, shoulder-strap purse, romper dress, shoes and socks.

Ref.No.: D of C, PU11, p. 185

Mint $240.00   Ex. $185.00   G. $95.00   F. $60.00

LITTLE LULU
Cloth Body

1949. 14 in. (35.5 cm). Cloth body. Swivel type cloth head; black painted eyes; black wig with red hairbow; watermelon mouth. Unmarked. Original red cotton dress.

Ref.No.: D of C, PU10, p. 185

Mint $235.00   Ex. $175.00   G. $120.00   F. $75.00

Note: A cartoon character, Little Lulu is very collectable.

SHIRLEY

1949. 14 in. (35.5 cm). All composition toddler, jointed hips, shoulders and neck. Composition head; brown sleep eyes, lashes, lowers painted reddish brown; original blond wig in braids; closed rosebud mouth. Mark: on head, PULLAN DOLL; on body, PULLAN DOLL. Original cotton blue and white checked dress and bonnet, blue shoes and white socks.

Ref.No.: D of C, CA35, p. 186

Mint $145.00   Ex. $105.00   G. $60.00   F. $35.00

BETTY
1949 - 20 in.

1949. 20 in. (51 cm). All composition toddler, jointed hips, shoulders and neck. Composition head; blue painted eyes, painted upper lashes; moulded hair painted light brown; closed mouth. Mark: on head, PULLAN. Original cotton print dress and tam.

Ref.No.: D of C, CG12, p. 186

Mint $125.00   Ex. $90.00   G. $60.00   F. $35.00

JACK AND JILL

1950. 14 in. (35.5 cm). All composition, jointed hips, shoulders and neck. Composition head; sleep eyes, lashes, painted lower lashes; moulded light brown hair; closed mouth. Unmarked. Original matching tailored cotton outfits.

Ref.No.: D of C, PL32, p. 187

JACK
Mint $95.00   **Ex.** $75.00   **G.** $50.00   **F.** $35.00
JILL
Mint $95.00   **Ex.** $75.00   **G.** $50.00   **F.** $35.00

SKATING QUEEN

1950. 18 in. (45.5 cm). All composition jointed hips, shoulders, and neck. Composition head; sleep eyes, lashes, painted lower lashes; blond wig; closed mouth. Unmarked. Original red felt skating costume with white fringe trim, hat and roller-skates.

Ref.No.: D of C, PU5, p. 187

Mint $165.00   **Ex.** $140.00   **G.** $75.00   **F.** $55.00

WEDDING DOLL

1950. 20 in. (51 cm). All composition, jointed hips, shoulders and neck. Composition head; sleep eyes, lashes, painted lower lashes; brown wig; closed mouth. Unmarked. Original satin gown trimmed with lace, net veil, flowered head-dress, and bouquet.

Ref.No.: D of C, PL31, p. 186

Mint $160.00   **Ex.** $120.00   **G.** $75.00   **F.** $45.00

WALKING DOLL
1951 - 20 in.

1951. 20 in. (50.5 cm). All composition child, jointed hips, shoulders and neck. Composition head; brown sleep eyes, lashes; blond mohair wig; closed mouth painted red. Mark: on body, PULLAN. Original blue angel-skin dress and matching bonnet, shoes and socks.

Ref.No.: D of C, AZ4, p. 188

Mint $225.00   **Ex.** $170.00   **G.** $90.00   **F.** $60.00

LITTLE LULU
Composition Body

1951. 14 in. (35.5 cm). All composition, jointed hips, shoulders and neck. Composition head; oval eyes painted all black; moulded hair painted black, red ribbon stapled on head; watermelon mouth painted red. Mark: on head, PULLAN DOLL. Original red cotton dress, black socks and shoes.

Ref.No.: D of C, AW28, p. 189

Mint $275.00 **Ex.** $210.00 **G.** $120.00 **F.** $75.00

ALICE IN WONDERLAND
1951 - 17 in.

1951. 17 in. (43 cm). All composition, jointed hips, shoulders and neck. Composition head; sleep eyes, lashes, painted lower lashes; long blond hair; open mouth showing teeth. Unmarked. Original costume.

Ref.No.: D of C, PU8, p. 188

Mint $175.00 **Ex.** $140.00 **G.** $75.00 **F.** $55.00

LOIS
1951 - 17 in.

1951. 17 in. (43 cm). All composition, jointed hips, shoulders and neck. Composition head; sleep eyes, lashes, painted lower lashes; blond saran wig; closed mouth. Unmarked. Satin lace trimmed party frock, socks and shoes.

Ref.No.: D of C, PU7, p. 187

Mint $155.00 **Ex.** $140.00 **G.** $75.00 **F.** $55.00

SWEETIE

1951. 17 in. and 21 in. (43 cm and 53.5 cm). Cloth body, crier, stuffed rubber arms and legs. Composition head; sleep eyes, lashes; curled wig; closed mouth. Unmarked. Original organdy dress and matching bonnet.

Ref.No.: D of C, PU6, p. 188

Mint $115.00 **Ex.** $75.00 **G.** $45.00 **F.** $25.00

Note: Few of the rubber-skin dolls have survived. The above prices are for the 21-inch doll

CINDERELLA
1952 - 17 in.

1952. 17 in. (43 cm). All composition, jointed hips, shoulders and neck. Composition head; brown sleep eyes, lashes, painted red lower lashes; blond mohair wig; closed mouth, painted red. Unmarked; original hang tag. Original blue taffeta gown with net overskirt with flowers. Net headdress with sequins.

Ref.No.: E11-24

Mint $175.00 **Ex.** $140.00 **G.** $75.00 **F.** $55.00

GIANT SQUEEZE ME DOLLS

1952. 28 in. (71 cm). One-piece rubber latex stuffed with foam rubber. Hard plastic head; sleep eyes, lashes, painted lowers; moulded hair; open mouth, inset plastic teeth.

Ref.No.: D of C, PU4 & PU3, p. 189

GIRL
Mint $125.00 **Ex.** $85.00 **G.** $60.00 **F.** $35.00
BOY
Mint $125.00 **Ex.** $85.00 **G.** $60.00 **F.** $35.00

ESKIMO
1953 - 14 in.

1953. 14 in. (35.5 cm). All composition, jointed hips, shoulders and neck. Composition head; painted black eyes; moulded black hair; open-closed mouth showing two teeth. Mark: on head, PULLAN DOLL. Original black and white fur fabric snowsuit and felt boots.

Ref.No.: HX19.

Mint $140.00 **Ex.** $95.00 **G.** $70.00 **F.** $45.00

BABY LOVIE

1953. 25 in. (63.5 cm). Cloth body, crier, stuffed rubber arms and legs. Composition head; sleep eyes, lashes; curled mohair wig; closed mouth. Unmarked. Original costume.

Ref.No.: D of C, PU1, p. 190

Mint $120.00 **Ex.** $85.00 **G.** $55.00 **F.** $35.00

CORONATION DOLL

1953. 17 in. (43 cm) All composition, jointed hips, shoulders and neck. Composition head; sleep eyes, lashes; brown wig; open mouth showing teeth. Unmarked.

Ref.No.: D of C, PU2, p. 189

Mint $275.00   **Ex.** $210.00   **G.** $105.00   **F.** $45.00

LUCILLE

1954. 17 in., 19 in. and 23 in. (43 cm, 48.5 cm and 58.5 cm). Cloth body with crier, stuffed rubber arms and legs. Vinyl head; sleep eyes, lashes; deeply moulded blond hair; open-closed mouth. Unmarked. Original embroidered ninon dress.

Ref.No.: D of C, PL36, p. 190

Mint $90.00   **Ex.** $60.00   **G.** $40.00   **F.** $30.00

Note: The above prices are for the 23-inch doll.

SUNSHINE TWIN
Closed Mouth

1954. 25 in. (63.5 cm). One-piece stuffed rubber body, with cryer. Vinyl head; sleep eyes, lashes; deeply moulded light brown hair; closed mouth. Unmarked.

Ref.No.: D of C, PL37, p. 191

Mint $75.00   **Ex.** $55.00   **G.** $45.00   **F.** $25.00

SUNSHINE TWIN
Open-Closed Mouth

1954. 25 in. (63.5 cm). One-piece stuffed rubber body, squeeze voice. Vinyl head; sleep eyes, lashes; deeply moulded light brown hair; open-closed mouth. Unmarked.

Ref.No.: D of C, PU0, p. 191

Mint $75.00   **Ex.** $55.00   **G.** $45.00   **F.** $25.00

BILLY
1954 - 20 in.

1954. 20 in. (51 cm). One-piece latex rubber body. Vinyl head with dimples; hazel sleep eyes with lashes and painted lower lashes; deeply moulded hair with a curl in the front, light brown; open-closed mouth. Mark: on head, PULLAN. Redressed.

Ref.No.: D of C, CW8, p. 190

Mint **$65.00** **Ex.** **$50.00** **G.** **$35.00** **F.** **$20.00**

BEDTIME BUNTING

1955. 20 in. and 22 in. (51 cm and 56 cm). Latex body with squeeze voice. Vinyl head; sleep eyes, lashes; moulded light brown hair; open-closed mouth. Unmarked. Original printed flannelette pyjamas with matching bootees and hat.

Ref.No.: D of C, PL34, p. 191

Mint **$75.00** **Ex.** **$55.00** **G.** **$35.00** **F.** **$20.00**

OVERALLS BABY

1955. 20 in. (51 cm). Latex body and legs, squeeze voice, vinyl arms. Vinyl head; sleep eyes, lashes; moulded light brown hair; open-closed mouth. Unmarked. Original overalls, matching hat, knitted jersey shirt, with teddy bear wearing matching overalls.

Ref.No.: D of C, PL35, p. 191

Mint **$75.00** **Ex.** **$55.00** **G.** **$35.00** **F.** **$20.00**

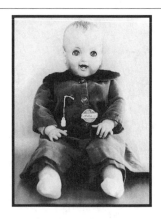

BABY BUNTING
1956 - 20 in.

1956. 20 in. (51 cm). Cloth body, vinyl hands and legs. Vinyl head; blue sleep eyes, lashes, Moulded brown hair; open-closed mouth, two painted lower teeth. Mark: on head, PULLAN. Original hang tag.

Ref.No.: DH13.

Mint **$75.00** **Ex.** **$65.00** **G.** **$55.00** **F.** **$35.00**

Note: The doll shown in the catalogue was dressed in a fleece bunting suit. It was also made with a latex body.

CANDY
1956 - 17 in.

1956. 17 in. (43 cm). One-piece vinyl skin body with wire armature inside to enable the doll to assume any position. Vinyl head; sleep eyes, lashes, painted lower lashes; brown rooted saran hair; mouth open-closed. Unmarked. Original striped pyjamas and hat.

Ref.No.: D of C, PL28, p. 192

Mint $45.00 **Ex.** $35.00 **G.** $25.00 **F.** $20.00

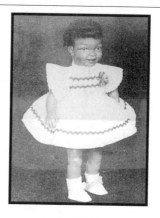

MINDY
1957 - 15 in.

1957. 15 in. (38 cm). One-piece doll with brown vinyl skin with flexiwire armature. Brown vinyl head; painted eyes; black heavily detailed moulded hair in braids; open-closed mouth. Unmarked. Original white ninon dress with red rick-rack trim.

Ref.No.: D of C, PL30, p. 192

Mint $125.00 **Ex.** $95.00 **G.** $65.00 **F.** $40.00

PULLAN
1956 - 15 in.

1956. 15 in. (38 cm). One-piece vinyl body, jointed neck. Vinyl head; blue sleep eyes, lashes, painted lower lashes; very detailed moulded hair painted brown; open-closed mouth. Mark: on head, PULLAN.

Ref.No.: D of C, BN25, p. 192

Mint $40.00 **Ex.** $30.00 **G.** $25.00 **F.** $15.00

SKISUIT DOLL

1957. 17 in. and 24 in. (43 cm and 61 cm). One-piece vinyl body with flexiwire, squeeze voice. Vinyl head; sleep eyes, lashes; rooted curly saran hair; open-closed mouth. Unmarked. Original zippered white fleece ski-suit with red braid trim, white bonnet with red pom-pom and red mitts.

Ref.No.: D of C, PL24, p. 193

17 in. Size
Mint $50.00 **Ex.** $40.00 **G.** $30.00 **F.** $15.00
24 in. Size
Mint $65.00 **Ex.** $50.00 **G.** $35.00 **F.** $20.00

BABY BUNTING
1957 - 22 in.

1957. 22 in. (56 cm). Vinyl body with flexiwire, squeeze voice. Vinyl head; sleep eyes, lashes; rooted curly saran hair; open-closed mouth. Unmarked. Wearing lace trimmed fleece bunting suit with matching bonnet.

Ref.No.: D of C, PL25, p. 193

Mint $55.00 **Ex.** $45.00 **G.** $30.00 **F.** $20.00

BABY TEARS

1957. 14 in. and 16 in. (35.5cm and 40.5 cm). Plastic body, jointed hips, shoulders and neck. Vinyl head; sleep eyes, lashes, moulded hair, open mouth nurser. Unmarked.

Ref.No.: D of C, PL27, p. 193

Moulded Hair:
Mint $45.00 **Ex.** $35.00 **G.** $20.00 **F.** $15.00

Rooted Hair:
Mint $50.00 **Ex.** $40.00 **G.** $20.00 **F.** $15.00

Note: The prices above are for the 14-inch doll.

BALLERINA
1957 - 17 in.

1957. 17 in. (43 cm). Vinyl body with wire in the legs to allow the doll to assume any position. Vinyl head; sleep eyes, lashes; rooted saran hair in chignon style; closed mouth. Unmarked. Dressed in sheer silver net skirt and sparkling bodice, ballet stockings and ballet slippers.

Ref.No.: D of C, PL29, p. 194

Mint $80.00 **Ex.** $55.00 **G.** $35.00 **F.** $20.00

CINDY
1957 - 14 in.

1957. 14 in. (35.5 cm). One-piece doll with brown vinyl skin, jointed neck. Vinyl head; brown sleep eyes, lashes, painted lower lashes; very curly rooted black hair; closed mouth. Mark: on head, PULLAN 2; on body, A; on foot, V-15-2. Redressed.

Ref.No.: D of C, CH9, p. 194

Mint $50.00 **Ex.** $40.00 **G.** $30.00 **F.** $20.00

BABS

1957. 15 in. (38 cm). One-piece vinyl body. Vinyl head; fixed brown eyes; deeply moulded hair in a ponytail; closed mouth. Mark: on head, PULLAN. Redressed. Originally wore Knee length checkered dress.

Ref.No.: D of C, CO20, p. 195

Mint $40.00 **Ex.** $35.00 **G.** $30.00 **F.** $15.00

CURLY DIMPLES

1958. 18 in. (46 cm). Plastic body, jointed hips, shoulders and neck. Vinyl head; blue flirty sleep eyes, lashes; rooted saran blond curls; open-closed mouth showing teeth. Mark: on head, PULLAN. Original lace-trimmed, pink ninon party dress, lace-trimmed petticoat, panties, shoes and socks. Originally her hair was curled in the style of Shirley Temple's.

Ref.No.: 2X15

Mint $110.00 **Ex.** $75.00 **G.** $45.00 **F.** $35.00

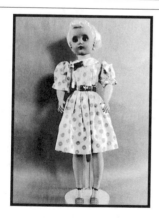

MARIE

1958. 22 in. (56 cm). One-piece stuffed vinyl body. Vinyl head; blue sleep eyes, lashes; rooted platinum blond hair; closed mouth. Mark: on head, PULLAN. Original cotton print dress with plastic belt.

Ref.No.: GK24.

Mint $65.00 **Ex.** $50.00 **G.** $35.00 **F.** $20.00

BRIDE
1958 - 17 in.

1958. 17 in. (43 cm). Plastic teen body, jointed hips, shoulders, and neck. Vinyl head, earrings; blue sleep eyes, lashes; rooted saran blond hair; closed mouth. Mark: PULLAN. Redressed. Originally wore embossed satin wedding gown, trimmed in lace, with waist length veil trimmed with lace, and carried a lilies of the valley bouquet.

Ref.No.: D of C, CT21, p. 194

Mint $55.00 **Ex.** $45.00 **G.** $35.00 **F.** $20.00

MOTHER AND FAMILY

1958. Mother, 21 in. (53.5 cm), daughter, 12 in. (30.5 cm), son, 10 in. (25.5 cm), baby, 8 in. (20.5 cm). Mother: vinyl body, jointed shoulders and neck. Vinyl head; sleep eyes, lashes; rooted saran curls; closed mouth. Daughter: vinyl body; vinyl head; glassine eyes; rooted hair; closed mouth. Son: vinyl body and head with freckles; painted side-glancing eyes; moulded hair; closed smiling mouth. Baby: vinyl body and head; painted eyes; moulded hair. Unmarked. Original costumes.

Ref.No.: D of C, PL26, p. 196

Mint **$225.00** **Ex.** **$180.00** **G.** **$95.00** **F.** **$75.00**

Note: The prices above are for the complete set.

LORETTA

1958. 14 in. (35.5 cm). One-piece stuffed vinyl body. Vinyl head: blue sleep eyes, lashes; rooted brown hair; closed mouth. Mark: on head, PULLAN. Original yellow taffeta dress, red plastic belt, replaced shoes.

Ref.No.: 2KA9

Mint **$45.00** **Ex.** **$35.00** **G.** **$25.00** **F.** **$15.00**

DREAM DOLL

1958. 16 in. (40.5 cm). One-piece body, soft vinyl skin stuffed with foam, jointed neck. Vinyl head; blue sleep eyes, lashes, painted lower lashes; rooted blond saran hair; closed mouth painted red. Mark: on head, PULLAN. Replaced clothing similar to the original.

Ref.No.: D of C, BH14, p. 197

Mint **$50.00** **Ex.** **$40.00** **G.** **30.00** **F.** **$20.00**

ORIENTAL PRINCESS

1958. 20 in. (50.5 cm). Plastic teen doll, jointed at waist, elbows, knees, hips, shoulders and ankles. Vinyl head with pierced ears, earrings; blue sleep eyes, lashes, painted lower lashes; rooted long black saran hair worn up in a roll; closed mouth. Mark: on head, PULLAN. Original white synthetic long sleeved body suit with matching long pants. Overtop is a long sleeveless vest with oriental fan print, bordered with white grosgrain, white high-heeled shoes.

Ref.No.: D of C, CG17, p. 196

Mint **$110.00** **Ex.** **$75.00** **G.** **$45.00** **F.** **$25.00**

RAGS TO RICHES DOLL

1958. 21 in. (53.5 cm). Plastic teen body and legs, vinyl arms, jointed shoulders and neck. Vinyl head; blue sleep eyes, lashes; rooted reddish-brown long saran hair with bangs and originally worn in a ponytail; closed mouth painted red. Mark: on neck, PULLAN; on back, A; sole of left foot 16; sole of right foot VH3-21. Original taffeta gown which reverses to a cotton peasant dress.

Ref.No.: D of C, BF33, p. 196

Mint **$75.00** **Ex.** **$55.00** **G.** **$35.00** **F.** **$20.00**

PULLAN
1959 - 12 1/2 in.

1959. 12 1/2 in. (32 cm). Plastic body, jointed hips, shoulders and neck. Vinyl head; blue inset eyes; rooted reddish-blond straight hair; closed mouth painted red. Mark: on head, PULLAN. Original dotted pink dress and bonnet.

Ref.No.: D of C, BJ23, p. 197

Mint $60.00   **Ex.** $50.00   **G.** $35.00   **F.** $25.00

BRIDE
1959 - 15 in.

1959. 15 in. (38 cm). Plastic body, jointed hips, shoulders, and neck. Vinyl head; blue sleep eyes, lashes, painted lower lashes; rooted brown curled hair; closed mouth. Mark: on head, PULLAN; original label. Original white satin gown with silver net overlay and lace trimming. Matching net veil streaked with silver, carrying bouquet.

Ref.No.: D of C, BX8, p. 198.

Mint $55.00   **Ex.** $45.00   **G.** $30.00   **F.** $20.00

MADEMOISELLE

1959. 21 in. (53.5 cm). Plastic body, jointed hips, shoulders and neck. Vinyl head: blue sleep eyes, lashes; rooted blond hair; closed mouth. Mark: on head; PULLAN. Original cotton print dress, straw hat, gloves, purse, earrings and high-heeled shoes.

Ref.No.: 2D7.

Mint $60.00   **Ex.** $50.00   **G.** $30.00   **F.** $20.00

Note: Costume shown in the catalogue is a skirt of taffeta and velveteen with a sheer white blouse.

BABY PRINCESS

1959. 23 in. (58.5 cm). Plastic baby body, jointed hips, shoulders and neck. Vinyl head; sleep eyes, lashes; rooted blond saran curls with long forehead curl; open mouth nurser. Unmarked. Original striped nylon dress with a coloured lace yoke.

Ref.No.: D of C, PL2, p. 197

Mint $65.00   **Ex.** $45.00   **G.** $35.00   **F.** $25.00

ANNETTE
1959 - 15 in.

1959. 15 in. (38 cm). Plastic body, jointed hips, shoulders and head. Vinyl head; blue sleep eyes, lashes, three painted upper lashes; rooted short blond hair with bangs; closed mouth. Mark: on head, PULLAN. Original black and white striped denim coat and matching hat with red cotton dress.

Ref.No.: D of C, BZ23, p. 198

Mint $70.00 **Ex.** $55.00 **G.** $30.00 **F.** $20.00

CINDY
1959 - 15 in.

1959. 15 in. (38 cm). Vinyl body, jointed hips, shoulders and neck. Vinyl head; blue sleep eyes, lashes, painted lowers; rooted blond hair; closed mouth. Mark: on head, PULLAN. Blue and white cotton checked skirt and white blouse.

Ref.No.: 2K3

Mint $65.00 **Ex.** $55.00 **G.** $45.00 **F.** $25.00

NURSE
1959 - 17 in.

1959. 17 in. (43 cm). Plastic body, jointed hips, shoulders and neck. Vinyl head: blue sleep eyes, lashes; rooted brown hair; closed mouth. Mark: on head, PULLAN. Original blue and white cotton nurse's uniform, cotton panties, replaced shoes and socks.

Ref.No.: 2K34

Mint $65.00 **Ex.** $50.00 **G.** $30.00 **F.** $20.00

I.G.A. DOLL

1959. 29 in. (73.5 cm). One-piece stuffed vinyl. Vinyl head; brown sleep eyes, lashes; rooted red hair; closed mouth. Mark: on head, PULLAN. Original mauve and silver net evening gown and stole, original earrings.

Ref.No.: 2K20

Mint $85.00 **Ex.** $65.00 **G.** $40.00 **F.** $30.00

Note: This is an I.G.A. premium doll, which makes this also a working doll.

BRIDE
1959 - 21 in.

1959. 21 in. (53 cm). Vinyl body, joined hips, shoulders and neck. Vinyl head; blue sleep eyes, lashes; rooted blond hair; closed mouth. Mark: on head, PULLAN. Original white bridal gown.

Ref.No.: 2E1

Mint   **$60.00**   **Ex.**   **$45.00**   **G.**   **$30.00**   **F.**   **$20.00**

MISS LUCKY GREEN
Rooted Honey Blond Hair

1960. 15 in. (38 cm). Plastic body, jointed hips, shoulders, and neck. Vinyl head; blue sleep eyes, lashes, painted lower lashes; rooted honey blond saran hair in ponytail and bangs; closed mouth. Mark: on head, PULLAN.

Ref.No.: D of C, CP20, p. 199

Mint   **$80.00**   **Ex.**   **$65.00**   **G.**   **$45.00**   **F.**   **$30.00**

Note: Miss Lucky Green is also a working doll.

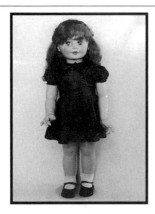

MISS LUCKY GREEN
Closed Mouth

1960. 35 in. (89 cm). Plastic body, jointed hips, shoulders and neck. Vinyl head; blue sleep eyes, lashes; rooted red-gold hair; closed mouth. Mark: on body, 35 - 5/PULLAN. Original dark green dress, socks and shoes. White apron is missing.

Ref.No.: 2A13

Mint   **$160.00**   **Ex.**   **$125.00**   **G.**   **$95.00**   **F.**   **$50.00**

MISS LUCKY GREEN
Open-closed Mouth

1960. 35 in. (89 cm). Plastic body, jointed hips, shoulders and neck. Vinyl head; blue sleep eyes, lashes; rooted short curly honey blond hair; open-closed mouth, smiling and showing upper and lower teeth. Unmarked. Original dark green dress, white apron and socks and shoes.

Ref.No.: Z29

Mint   **$170.00**   **Ex.**   **$135.00**   **G.**   **$100.00**   **F.**   **$60.00**

ANNETTE
1960 - 15 in.

1960. 15 in. (38 cm). Plastic body, jointed hips, shoulders and neck. Vinyl head; blue sleep eyes, lashes; rooted dark blond hair; closed mouth. Mark: on head PULLAN; on body, PULLAN/15-5. Doll originally wore a print dress, corduroy coat lined with the dress fabric and trimmed with fur fabric collar, hat and muff.

Ref.No.: 2G10

Mint $70.00 **Ex.** $55.00 **G.** $30.00 **F.** $20.00

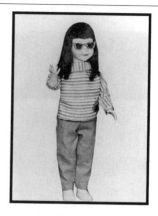

BEATNIK DOLL

1960. 21 in. (53.5 cm). Plastic, jointed hips, shoulders and neck. Vinyl head. Sleep eyes. Rooted long straight black saran hair. Mouth closed, smiling. Unmarked. Original striped denim shirt and matching slacks, sunglasses.

Ref.No.: D of C, PL6, p. 198

Mint $120.00 **Ex.** $90.00 **G.** $65.00 **F.** $35.00

ROSANNE

1960. 22 in. (56 cm). Plastic body, jointed hips, shoulders and neck. Vinyl head; blue sleep eyes, lashes, painted lowers; rooted brown curls; open-mouth nurser. Mark: on head, PULLAN. Original blue nylon dress.

Ref.No.: 2P21

Mint $65.00 **Ex.** $55.00 **G.** $40.00 **F.** $30.00

WENDY ANN
1960 - 35 in.

1960. 35 in. (89 cm). Plastic body, jointed hips, shoulders and neck. Vinyl head; sleep eyes, lashes; rooted curly saran hair; closed mouth. Unmarked. Original polished cotton pinafore and blouse.

Ref.No.: D of C, PL4, p. 199

Mint $125.00 **Ex.** $95.00 **G.** $60.00 **F.** $40.00

BOBBY
1961 - 20 in.

1961. 20 in. (51 cm). Plastic body, jointed hips, shoulders and neck. Vinyl head; sleep eyes, lashes; moulded light brown hair; closed mouth. Unmarked. Original costume.

Ref.No.: D of C, PL16, p. 200

Mint $65.00 **Ex.** $50.00 **G.** $40.00 **F.** $25.00

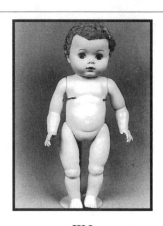

JILL

1961. 20 in. (51 cm). Plastic toddler, jointed hips, shoulders and neck; vinyl head; blue plastic sleep eyes, lashes, painted lower lashes; rooted light brown curls; open mouth nurser. Mark: on head, PULLAN; on body, PULLAN. Originally wore flocked taffeta dress with velvet ribbon trim.

Ref.No.: D of C, CW14, p. 199

Mint $60.00 **Ex.** $45.00 **G.** $35.00 **F.** $25.00

EVELYN

1961. 30 in. (76 cm). Plastic body, jointed hips, shoulders and neck. Vinyl head; blue sleep eyes, lashes, painted lowers; rooted honey blond curls; closed mouth. Mark: on head, PULLAN. Original cotton dress in red print and white apron with red rick-rack trim, socks and shoes.

Ref.No.: 2K4.

Mint $75.00 **Ex.** $65.00 **G.** $45.00 **F.** $30.00

LOIS
1961 - 32 in.

1961. 32 in. (81 cm). Plastic body, jointed hips, shoulders and neck. Vinyl head; sleep eyes, lashes, rooted curly saran hair; closed mouth. Unmarked. Original lined and tailored cordette coat and matching hat, print dress, socks and shoes.

Ref.No.: D of C, PL15, p. 200

Mint $120.00 **Ex.** $85.00 **G.** $55.00 **F.** $45.00

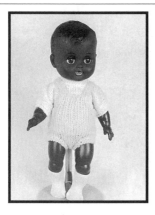

BABY ROSEBUD

1961. 11 in. (28 cm). Brown plastic body, jointed hips, shoulder and neck. Brown vinyl head; brown sleep eyes, lashes; moulded black hair; open-mouth nurser. Mark: on head, PULLAN; on body, 12-5. Drinks and wets. Redressed. Originally wore flannelette shirt and diaper plus bottle.

Ref.No.: 2G34

Mint $40.00   **Ex.** $35.00   **G.** $30.00   **F.** $20.00

BOBBY
1961 - 15 in.

1961. l5 in. (38 cm). Plastic body, jointed hips, shoulders, and neck. Hard vinyl head; blue sleep eyes, lashes, painted lower lashes; well-defined moulded hair painted light brown; closed mouth. Mark: on head, PULLAN; on body, PULLAN. Original short pants and sweater.

Ref.No.: D of C, BN30, p. 202

Mint $55.00   **Ex.** $45.00   **G.** $30.00   **F.** $20.00

LITTLE MISTER BAD BOY
1961 - 16 in.

1961. 16 in. (40.5 cm). Plastic body, vinyl arms, jointed hips, shoulders and neck. Hard vinyl head; blue sleep eyes, lashes, painted lower lashes; well defined moulded hair painted brown; closed mouth painted red. Mark: on head, PULLAN. Original cotton striped two-piece suit. Hat missing.

Ref.No.: D of C, BN26, p. 200

Mint $75.00   **Ex.** $55.00   **G.** $40.00   **F.** $20.00

LITTLE MISTER BAD BOY
1961 - 30 in.

1961. 30 in. (76 cm). Plastic body, jointed hips, shoulders and head. Hard vinyl head; blue sleep eyes, lashes; moulded light brown hair; closed mouth. Mark: on head, PULLAN. Original striped suit. Hat missing.

Ref.No.: D of C; BZ19 p. 201

Mint $150.00   **Ex.** $105.00   **G.** $70.00   **F.** $50.00

BILLY
1961 - 13 in.

1961. 13 in. (33 cm). Plastic body, jointed hips, shoulders and neck. Vinyl head; inset grey stationary eyes; Moulded light brown curls; closed mouth. Mark: on head, A PULLAN DOLL. Redressed. Originally wore flannelette overalls, shirt and socks.

Ref.No.: 2G35

Mint $45.00   **Ex.** $30.00   **G.** $20.00   **F.** $10.00

DOLLY POP

1961. 15 1/2 in. (39.5 cm). Plastic toddler, jointed hips, shoulders and neck; spring in the right hand to bring a lollipop to her mouth. Vinyl head; blue sleep eyes, lashes, painted lower lashes; rooted straight blond hair over moulded hair; open mouth nurser. Mark: on head, PULLAN. Original cotton romper dress.

Ref.No.: D of C, BQ20, p. 20

Mint $65.00   **Ex.** $55.00   **G.** $35.00   **F.** $25.00

Note: Mint and Ex. prices are for dolls in working order.

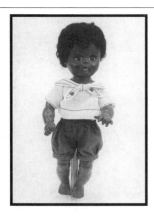

MINDY

1961. 16 in. (40 cm). Brown plastic body, jointed hips, shoulders and neck. Brown vinyl head; brown sleep eyes, lashes, painted lower lashes; rooted black curly hair; open mouth nurser. Mark: on head, PULLAN. Originally dressed in lace trimmed cotton dress and came with a plastic bottle.

Mint $45.00   **Ex.** $35.00   **G.** $40.00   **F.** $25.00

Note: This doll also came in 12-inch size.

CINDY
1961 - 20 in.

1961. 20 in. (50.5 cm). Brown plastic body, jointed hips, shoulders and neck. Brown vinyl head; brown sleep eyes, lashes; rooted black curly hair; open mouth nurser. Unmarked.

Ref.No.: D of C, PL17, p. 201

Mint $65.00   **Ex.** $55.00   **G.** $45.00   **F.** $35.00

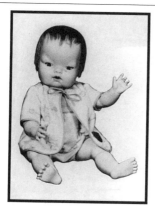

BABY TALKS

1961. 20 in. (50.5 cm). Vinyl body, jointed hips, shoulders and neck. Vinyl head; inset plastic eyes; rooted saran hair; open mouth. "Baby Talks" has a special six read voice mechanism that allows her to chuckle, goo, and giggle by squeezing her tummy and moving her to and fro. Unmarked.

Ref.No.: D of C, PL14, p. 201

Mint $70.00 **Ex.** $60.00 **G.** $40.00 **F.** $30.00

PRETTY PENNY
1962 - 31 in.

1962. 31 in. (79 cm). Plastic body, jointed hips, shoulders and neck. Vinyl head; blue sleep eyes, lashes; rooted straight honey blond hair; closed mouth. Mark: PULLAN WALKING DOLL on hang tag. Original rayon dress with striped skirt, socks and shoes.

Ref.No.: 2P11.

Mint $70.00 **Ex.** $60.00 **G.** $45.00 **F.** $30.00

PRETTY PENNY
1962 - 36 in.

1962. 36 in. (91.5 cm). Plastic body, jointed hips, shoulders and neck. Vinyl head; blue sleep eyes, lashes; rooted blond curls; closed mouth. Mark: on head, PULLAN. Original pink taffeta dress with white apron, socks and shoes.

Ref.No.: DH15.

Mint $135.00 **Ex.** $95.00 **G.** $60.00 **F.** $40.00

WENDY ANN
1962 - 36 in.

1962. 36 in. (91.5 cm). Plastic body, jointed hips, shoulders and neck. Vinyl head; blue sleep eyes, lashes, painted lower lashes; honey blond saran curly hair with bangs; closed mouth. Unmarked.

Ref.No.: D of C, CZ10, p. 203

Mint $135.00 **Ex.** $95.00 **G.** $60.00 **F.** $40.00

ANGEL FACE

1962. 14 in. (35.5 cm). Plastic toddler, jointed hips, shoulders and neck. Vinyl head; blue sleep eyes, lashes; rooted brown curls with bangs; open mouth nurser. Mark: on head, PULLAN. Original ninon party dress. Replaced socks and shoes.

Ref.No.: D of C, BN16, p. 203

Mint $45.00   **Ex.** $35.00   **G.** $25.00   **F.** $15.00

PATSY BONNETHEAD

1962. 14 in. (35.5 cm). Plastic body, jointed hips, shoulders and neck. Vinyl head; inset blue plastic eyes; moulded light brown hair with moulded blue bonnet on head; open-closed mouth with painted teeth and tongue. Mark; on hat, PULLAN. Redressed. Originally wore blue checked cotton dress with white trim.

Ref.No.: 212

Mint $55.00   **Ex.** $45.00   **G.** $30.00   **F.** $20.00

CLEOPATRA

1962. 22 in. (56 cm). Plastic, jointed hips, shoulders and neck. Vinyl head; painted eyes with eyeshadow and eyeliner; rooted extra long black saran hair; closed mouth. Unmarked. Original costume.

Ref.No.: D of C, PL8, p. 202.

Mint $135.00   **Ex.** $95.00   **G.** $65.00   **F.** $45.00

Note: This is a scarce doll.

VALERIE
1962 - 23 in.

1962. 23 in. (58 cm). Plastic body, jointed hips, shoulders and neck. Vinyl head; blue sleep eyes, lashes, painted lower lashes; rooted short blond hair; closed mouth. Mark: on head, PULLAN/MADE IN CANADA. Original pink and white play-suit.

Ref.No.: D of C, AM34, p. 203

Mint $50.00   **Ex.** $40.00   **G.** $30.00   **F.** $20.00

ESKIMO
1962 - 16 in.

1962. 16 in. (40.5 cm). Plastic body and legs, vinyl arms, jointed hips, shoulders and neck. Vinyl head; inset brown plastic eyes; rooted short straight black hair; closed mouth. Mark: on head, PULLAN. Original parka and hood. Originally wore matching pants.

Ref.No.: D of C, BZ32, p. 204

Mint $65.00   **Ex.** $55.00   **G.** $45.00   **F.** $30.00

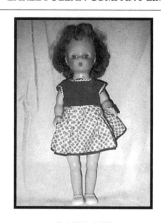

LANA LEE
1962 - 16 in.

1962. 16 in. (40.5 cm). Five-piece plastic body. Vinyl head; sleep eyes; rooted hair; open-closed mouth. Mark: on head, PULLAN/MADE IN CANADA.

Ref.No.: ES36

Mint $45.00   **Ex.** $30.00   **G.** $20.00   **F.** $15.00

WENDY ANN
1963 - 36 in.

1963. 36 in. (91.5 cm). Plastic body, jointed hips, shoulders, and neck. Vinyl head; sleep eyes, lashes; rooted long straight blond hair; closed mouth. Unmarked. Original blue and white cotton dress, socks and shoes.

Ref.No.: D. of C, PL11, p. 204

Mint $135.00   **Ex.** $95.00   **G.** $60.00   **F.** $40.00

FRITZ AND FREDA

1963. 13 in. (33 cm). Plastic bodies, jointed hips, shoulders and neck. Vinyl head; painted eyes; deeply moulded painted hair; closed mouth. Unmarked. Original costumes.

Ref.No.: D. of C, PL13, p 206

SINGLE:
Mint $65.00   **Ex.** $50.00   **G.** $40.00   **F.** $30.00
PAIR:
Mint $145.00   **Ex.** $115.00   **G.** $90.00   **F.** $70.00

PATSY
1963 - 13 in.

1963. 13 in. (33 cm). Plastic body, jointed hips, shoulders and neck. Vinyl head; blue plastic inset eyes; moulded brown hair; closed mouth. Mark: on head, A PULLAN DOLL. Original dress and hang tag.

Ref.No.: DH14

Mint $45.00   **Ex.** $35.00   **G.** $20.00   **F.** $15.00

LANA LEE
1963 - 16 in.

1963. 16 in. (40.5 cm). Plastic body, jointed hips, shoulders and neck. Vinyl head; blue sleep eyes, lashes, painted lashes at outside upper edge of eye; rooted blond hair; watermelon mouth. Mark: on head, PULLAN/MADE IN CANADA. Original pink cotton dress with lace trim.

Ref.No.: D of C, CI6, p. 205

Mint $50.00   **Ex.** $35.00   **G.** $25.00   **F.** $20.00

POOR PITIFUL PEARL

1963. 16 in. (40.5 cm). Plastic body and legs, vinyl arms, jointed hips, shoulders and neck. Vinyl head with freckles; brown sleep eyes, lashes and painted upper lashes; rooted long blond hair; watermelon mouth. Mark: on head, PULLAN. Original one-piece outfit.

Ref.No.: D of C, BF4, p. 205

Mint $75.00   **Ex.** $65.00   **G.** $50.00   **F.** $35.00

Note: Hard to find as few were made.

VALERIE
1962 - 24 in.

1963. 24 in. (61 cm). Plastic body, jointed hips, shoulders and neck. Vinyl head with dimple in her chin; blue sleep eyes, lashes, painted lowers; rooted brown curls; open-closed mouth. Mark: on head, PULLAN. Original cotton blend dress, white with red and blue polka dots, red vest, socks and shoes.

Ref.No.: 2F24

Mint $55.00   **Ex.** $45.00   **G.** $30.00   **F.** $20.00

LOUIE

1963. 12 in. (30.5 cm). Plastic jointed hips, shoulders, and neck. Vinyl head; painted side-glancing eyes; rooted red saran curls; closed watermelon mouth. Unmarked. Original cotton play-suit.

Ref.No.: D of C, PL10, p. 206

Mint $40.00 **Ex.** $35.00 **G.** $25.00 **F.** $15.00

SAMSON
(Beatle) Short black hair

1964. 13 in. (33 cm). Plastic body, jointed hips, shoulders and neck. Vinyl head; inset blue plastic eyes, three long eyelashes on outer sides of eyes; rooted straight black hair; open-closed mouth. Mark; on head, PULLAN. Original red jacket and black pants. Doll officially sold as SAMSON but an obvious takeoff of the BEATLES, undoubtedly due to copyright problems.

Ref.No.: PGL24

Mint $75.00 **Ex.** $60.00 **G.** $35.00 **F.** $15.00

SAMSON
(Beatle) Long black hair

1964. 13 in. (33 cm). Plastic body, jointed hips, shoulders and neck. Vinyl head; inset blue plastic eyes with three painted upper lashes on outer edges of eyes; rooted straight black hair; closed mouth. Mark: on head, PULLAN DOLL. Original deep pink flannel jacket, black pants.

Ref.No.: 2N1

Mint $75.00 **Ex.** $60.00 **G.** $35.00 **F.** $15.00

VALERIE
1964 - 21 in.

ca.1964. 21 in. (53.5 cm). Plastic body, jointed hips, shoulders and neck. Vinyl head; blue sleep eyes, lashes; rooted honey blond curls; open-mouth nurser. Mark: on head PULLAN. Blue cotton skirt with black vest, lace bodice and apron. Replaced shoes.

Ref.No.: PGC6

Mint $55.00 **Ex.** $45.00 **G.** $35.00 **F.** $25.00

MARJIE

1964. 12 in. (30.5 cm). Plastic body, jointed hips, shoulders and neck. Vinyl head; blue painted side-glancing eyes; rooted blond hair; closed mouth. Mark: on head, MARJIE. Original shorts set and shoes.

Ref.No.: 2D4

Mint $40.00   **Ex.** $30.00   **G.** $20.00   **F.** $15.00

PEACHES

1964. 12 in. (30.5 cm). Plastic body and legs, vinyl arms, jointed hips, shoulders and neck. Vinyl head, glassine fixed eyes, moulded lashes; rooted brown hair; open closed mouth. Unmarked. Original costume.

Ref.No.: D of C, PL12, p. 207

Mint $40.00   **Ex.** $30.00   **G.** $20.00   **F.** $10.00

VIC AND VICKY

1964. 10 in. (25.5 cm). Plastic toddlers, vinyl arms, jointed hips, shoulders and neck. Vinyl head; painted side-glancing blue eyes, painted lashes. Boy has rooted strawberry blond hair, girl has rooted blond hair. Open-closed mouth. Mark: on head, PULLAN, MADE IN CANADA.

Ref.No.: D of C, BN14, p. 207

PAIR:
Mint $80.00   **Ex.** $60.00   **G.** $40.00   **F.** $30.00
SINGLE
Mint $35.00   **Ex.** $25.00   **G.** $15.00   **F.** $10.00

CURLIE CUTIE

1964. 17 in. (43 cm). Plastic body, jointed hips, shoulders and neck. Vinyl head; blue sleep eyes, lashes; rooted blond hair, with a "grow" section at back which grows when ring on neck is pulled; closed mouth. Mark: on head, PULLAN/MADE IN CANADA. Originally wore a striped cotton dress, and came with a brush and comb.

Ref.No.: PGC4

Mint $60.00   **Ex.** $45.00   **G.** $35.00   **F.** $20.00

MARLANE

1964. 12 in. (30.5 cm). Plastic teen body and legs, vinyl arms, jointed hips, shoulders and neck. Vinyl head; painted side-glancing eyes, painted upper lashes; rooted straight red saran hair; closed mouth. Mark: on head, PULLAN. Original costume.

Ref.No.: D of C, CF27, p. 208

Mint $35.00 **Ex.** $25.00 **G.** $15.00 **F.** $10.00

BOXER

1965. 12 in. (30.5 cm). Plastic, jointed hips, shoulders and neck. Vinyl head; painted side-glancing eyes with one permanently black eye; rooted light brown hair; closed watermelon mouth. Unmarked.

Ref.No.: D of C, PL23, p. 208

Mint $55.00 **Ex.** $45.00 **G.** $35.00 **F.** $20.00

Note: Not many were made. Doll also sold without the black eye.

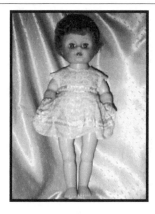

LANA LEE
1965 - 16 in.

1965. 16 in. (40.5 cm). Five-piece plastic body. Vinyl head; sleep eyes; rooted hair; closed mouth. Mark: on head, PULLAN. Original pink and green print dress.

Ref.No.: ES34

Mint $50.00 **Ex.** $35.00 **G.** $25.00 **F.** $20.00

ROSELLA
1965 - 19 in.

1965. 19 in. (48 cm). Plastic body, jointed hips, shoulders and neck. Vinyl head; blue sleep eyes, lashes; rooted long sandy blond hair; closed mouth. Mark: on head, FC; on body, PULLAN/CANADA. Original red slacks and flowered top.

Ref.No.: DF6

Mint $45.00 **Ex.** $35.00 **G.** $25.00 **F.** $15.00

TWINKLE SCOTTIE

1965. 9 in. (23 cm). Five-piece vinyl body. Vinyl head; blue painted eyes; closed mouth; blond rooted hair. Mark: on head, PULLAN/MADE IN CANADA.

Mint $30.00 **Ex.** $20.00 **G.** $15.00 **F.** $10.00

PEACHES SCOTCH LASS

1965. 12 in. (30.5 cm). Plastic body, jointed hips, shoulders and neck. Vinyl head; blue plastic inset eyes, moulded lashes; rooted honey blond hair; open-closed mouth. Mark: on head, PULLAN. Original tartan skirt, white blouse, red velvet jacket and matching hat.

Ref.No.: 2C28

Mint $45.00 **Ex.** $35.00 **G.** $20.00 **F.** $10.00

BABY DARLING

1965. 16 in. (40.5 cm). Plastic body, jointed hips, shoulders and neck. Vinyl head; blue sleep eyes, lashes, painted lowers; rooted blond hair; open-mouth nurser. Mark: on head, PULLAN. Original pink taffeta and lace party dress.

Ref.No.: 2G12

Mint $45.00 **Ex.** $35.00 **G.** $20.00 **F.** $15.00

PRETTY PENNY
1965 - 30 in.

1965. 30 in. (76 cm). Plastic, jointed hips, shoulders and neck. Vinyl head; sleep eyes, lashes, eyeshadow; rooted long straight saran hair with bangs; open-closed mouth. Unmarked. Original simulated leopard coat and hat, blouse and slacks, socks and shoes.

Ref.No.: D of C, PL21, p. 208

Mint $80.00 **Ex.** $70.00 **G.** $45.00 **F.** $30.00

PEANUTS

1965. 11 in. (28 cm). Plastic body, jointed hips, shoulders and neck. Vinyl head; side-glancing blue eyes; rooted red-gold hair; closed mouth. Sunsuit may be original. Doll came with a complete layette.

Ref.No.: 2I23

Mint $35.00 **Ex.** $25.00 **G.** $20.00 **F.** $15.00

MISS MARJIE

1965. 12 in. (30.5 cm). Plastic body, vinyl arms, jointed hips, shoulders and neck. Vinyl head; painted side-glancing eyes; rooted blond curly hair with a "growing" section on top; closed mouth. Mark: on head, MARJIE.

Ref.No.: D of C, BN33, p. 209

Mint $45.00 **Ex.** $35.00 **G.** $25.00 **F.** $20.00

PEACHES INDIAN GIRL

1965. 12 in. (30.5 cm). Brown plastic body and legs, vinyl arms with upturned hands, jointed hips, shoulders and neck. Vinyl head; brown sleep eyes, plastic lashes; incised brows; rooted straight black saran hair; open-closed mouth. Mark: on head, PULLAN/MADE IN CANADA; on body, PULLAN.

Ref.No.: D of C, CH12, p. 209

Mint $40.00 **Ex.** $30.00 **G.** $20.00 **F.** $10.00

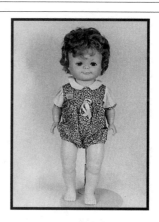

BABY BEAUTY

1965. 21 in. (53.5 cm). Plastic body, jointed hips, shoulders and neck. Vinyl head; blue sleep eyes, lashes; rooted blond curls; watermelon mouth. Mark: on head, PULLAN/CANADA. Redressed. Originally wore print dress with sheer apron, panties, shoes and socks.

Ref.No.: 2I32

Mint $55.00 **Ex.** $45.00 **G.** $35.00 **F.** $25.00

CENTENNIAL DOLL

1966. 4 1/2 in. (11.5 cm). Brown vinyl one-piece body, jointed neck. Brown vinyl head; side-glancing painted black eyes; rooted straight black hair; closed smiling mouth. Original felt cowboy suit with centennial symbol on vest.

Ref.No.: 2C4

Mint $50.00   Ex. $40.00   G. $30.00   F. $20.00

Note: As this doll was not shown in the catalogue, it is considered a special-order doll. It is also a working doll.

TWINKLE ESKIMO

1966. 10 in. (25.5 cm). Vinyl body, jointed hips, shoulders, and neck. Vinyl head; painted black side-glancing eyes; rooted straight black hair; closed mouth. Unmarked.

Ref.No.: D of C, PL20, p. 210

Mint $30.00   Ex. $25.00   G. $15.00   F. $10.00

PROSPECTOR

1966. 14 in. (35.5 cm). Cloth body formed by clothing, vinyl arms, vinyl boots. Cloth head with vinyl face; black painted eyes; grey fake fur hair, beard is rooted into face; smiling watermelon mouth. Mark: tag on body, EARLE PULLAN CO. LTD./TORONTO, CANADA.

Ref.No.: D of C, XH26, p. 209

Mint $40.00   Ex. $30.00   G. $25.00   F. $15.00

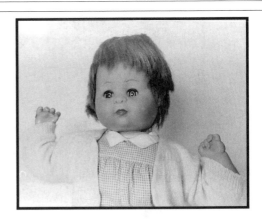

HUGGUMS

1966. 19 in. (48 cm). Cloth body, vinyl bent-limb arms and legs. Vinyl head; blue sleep eyes, lashes; rooted straight dark blond hair; closed mouth. Mark: on head, PULLAN/18. Redressed.

Ref.No.: 2I10

Mint $55.00   Ex. $45.00   G. $30.00   F. $20.00

SUZANNE
Platinum Blond Long Hair

1966. 16 in. (40.5 cm). Plastic body, jointed hips, shoulders and neck. Vinyl head; blue sleep eyes, lashes, painted lower lashes; rooted platinum blond, long straight saran hair; closed mouth. Mark: on head, PULLAN.

Ref.No.: D. of C, CO17, p. 210

Mint $50.00   **Ex.** $40.00   **G.** $30.00   **F.** $20.00

SUZANNE
Red Saran Hair

1966. 17 in. (43 cm). Plastic body with vinyl arms, jointed hips, shoulders and neck. Vinyl head; sleep eyes, lashes; rooted red saran hair; closed mouth. Unmarked. Original dress.

Ref.No.: D of C, PL18, p. 210

Mint $50.00   **Ex.** $40.00   **G.** $30.00   **F.** $20.00

ROSELLA
1966 - 19 in.

1966. 19 in. (48 cm). Plastic body, jointed hips, shoulders and neck. Vinyl head; blue sleep eyes, lashes, painted lowers; rooted blond hair; light pink closed mouth. Mark: on head, PULLAN/MADE IN CANADA; on body, PULLAN/CANADA. Redressed to match the catalogue picture except for a matching beret.

Ref. 2J15

Mint $55.00   **Ex.** $45.00   **G.** $25.00   **F.** $15.00

EASTMAN'S LIMITED
St. Hyacinthe, Quebec
ca. 1946 -

EASTMAN'S
1946 - 24 in.

ca.1946. 24 in. (61 cm). Cloth body, composition arms and legs. Composition head; inset blue plastic eyes over painted whites; moulded brown hair; closed mouth. Unmarked. Original box. Original dotted cotton skirt, white bodice, matching bonnet, white cotton petticoat and drawers, socks and shoes.

Ref.No.: PGM17

Mint $185.00   Ex. $125.00   G. $75.00   F. $45.00

Note: Paint appears to be of a poor quality as it flakes.

F AN B
ca.1948 -

No record can be found of this company in Canada. It may be a branch of the American EffanBee company, which was founded by Bernard E. Fleischaker and Hugo Baum.

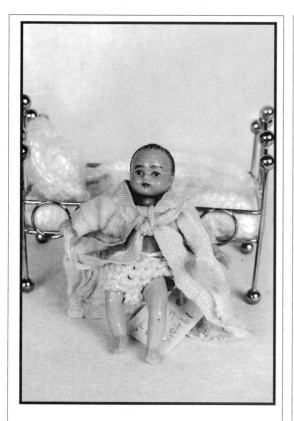

F AN B
ca.1948 - 2 3/4 in.

ca.1948. 2 3/4 in. (7 cm). Hard plastic body and head, jointed hips and shoulders. Painted features. Mark: on back, F AN B/CANADA. Redressed.

Ref.No.: 2J18

Mint $25.00 **Ex.** $20.00 **G.** $15.00 **F.** $10.00

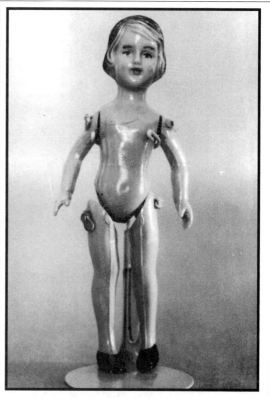

F AN B
ca.1948 - 5 in.

ca.1948. 5 in. (13 cm). Hard plastic body and head, jointed hips and shoulders, wired to trunk. Painted features and moulded hair. Mark: on back, F AN B/MADE/IN/CANADA.

Ref.No.: DH23

Mint $35.00 **Ex.** $30.00 **G.** $25.00 **F.** $20.00

THE FLORENTINE STATUARY COMPANY
1917 - 1932

Florentine made an excellent quality doll. They are very collectable, but hard to find.

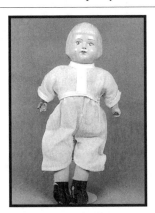

FLORENTINE
ca.1918 - 12 1/2 in.

ca.1918. 12 1/2 in. (31 cm). Cloth body, legs and upper arms, wooden forearms and hands, painted pink. Composition shoulderhead; painted blue eyes with a fine black line over the eyes, painted brows; moulded Buster Brown hair, painted brown; closed mouth painted red, nostril dots. Mark: on shoulderplate, FLORENTINE / TORONTO. Original thin cotton one-piece suit.

Ref.No.: D of C, AM26, p. 211

Mint $150.00   Ex. $135.00   G. $85.00   F. $50.00

INDIAN
ca. 1918 - 17 in.

ca.1918. 17 in. (43 cm). Excelsior stuffed cloth body and legs, composition gauntlet hand. Brown composition shoulderhead; black painted eyes with highlights, black line over eye; black human hair wig; closed mouth. Mark: on shoulderplate, FLORENTINE / TORONTO.

Ref.No.: D of C, CN11, p. 212

Mint $280.00   Ex. $240.00   G. $165.00   F. $75.00

Note: A rare doll.

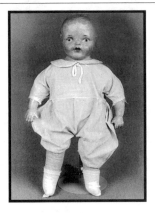

FLORENTINE
ca.1920 - 22 in.

ca.1920. 22 in. (56 cm). Cloth body and legs, composition forearms. Composition shoulderhead; blue painted eyes, black line over eye, upper painted lashes; blond moulded hair; closed mouth. Unmarked.

Ref.No.: D of C, BZ8, p. 213

Mint $195.00   Ex. $150.00   G. $110.00   F. $85.00

FLORENTINE
ca.1925 - 24 in.

ca.1925. 24 in. (61 cm). Cloth body with composition arms and legs. Composition shoulderhead; sleep eyes; open mouth, teeth; mohair wig over moulded hair. Mark: on shoulderplate, FLORENTINE / TORONTO. Redressed.

Mint $285.00   Ex. $225.00   G. $160.00   F. $85.00

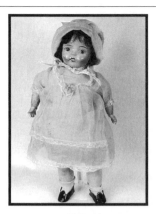

FLORENTINE
ca.1925 - 18 in.

ca.1925. 18 in. (45 cm). Cloth body with composition arms and legs. Composition shoulderhead; blue tin inset eyes, painted upper and lower lashes; brown curly wig with bangs; open mouth showing teeth. Mark: on shoulderplate, FLORENTINE/TORONTO. Original organdy dress, lace and rosette trim, matching bonnet, original lace trimmed combinations, socks and shoes.

Ref.No.: 2E7

Mint $250.00 **Ex.** $200.00 **G.** $150.00 **F.** $85.00

FLORENTINE
ca.1925 - 24 in.

ca.1925. 24 in. (61 cm). Cloth body with composition arms and legs. Composition shoulderhead; blue sleep eyes, painted lashes and brows; blond wig; open mouth, showing teeth and tongue. Mark: on shoulderplate, FLORENTINE/TORONTO.

Ref.No.: D of C, AP21, p. 214

Mint $300.00 **Ex.** $250.00 **G.** $175.00 **F.** $95.00

FLORENTINE
ca.1927 - 18 in.

ca.1927. 18 in. (45.5 cm). Cloth body and legs, composition forearm. Composition shoulderhead; blue painted eyes, black painted upper lashes; moulded hair; open-closed mouth. Mark: on shoulderplate, FLORENTINE/TORONTO.

Ref.No.: D of C, CR16, p. 214

Mint $150.00 **Ex.** $120.00 **G.** $95.00 **F.** $55.00

FLORENTINE
ca.1930 - 27 in.

ca.1930. 27 in. (68.5 cm). Cloth body, composition arms and legs. Composition shoulderhead; painted eyes, painted upper and lower lashes; pale blond wig over moulded hair; open-closed mouth showing teeth. Mark: on shoulderplate, FLORENTINE/TORONTO. Redressed.

Ref.No.: HX17.

Mint. $270.00 **Ex.** $220.00 **G.** $160.00 **F.** $95.00

FREEMAN TOY COMPANY
1943 - 1952

Freeman dolls are hard to find, as few were made and the company was short-lived. Their composition dolls often have a problem with crazing and frequently the surface coat of paint powders away. Freeman dolls are easily identified by their distinctive painting. Before they began making dolls, Freeman produced stuffed animals.

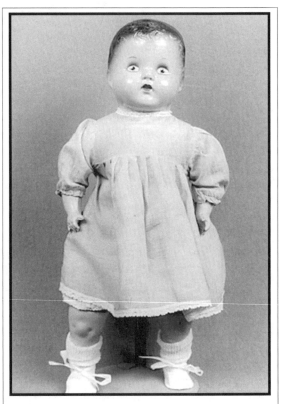

FREEMAN
ca.1943 - 14 in.

ca.1943. 14 in. (35.5 cm). Cloth stuffed body. Cloth stuffed head with moulded face; blue painted eyes; brown yarn hair. Original tag, PRODUCED BY FREEMAN TOY COMPANY/TORONTO. Purple cloth suit with hood forms the body and head.

Ref.No.: DF5

Mint $35.00 **Ex.** $30.00 **G.** $20.00 **F.** $15.00

FREEMAN
ca.1944 - 20 in.

ca.1944. 20 in. (51 cm). Cloth body, composition forearms and straight legs. Composition head; blue painted eyes, painted lower lashes, upper eyeshadow; black moulded hair; closed mouth. Unmarked. Original cotton dress, replaced socks and shoes. Bonnet missing.

Ref.No.: D of C, CL31, p. 216

Mint $150.00 **Ex.** $105.00 **G.** $75.00 **F.** $50.00

DIDY-WET

ca.1945. All composition bent-limb baby, jointed hips, shoulders and neck. Composition head; painted eyes; moulded hair; open-mouth nurser. Unmarked.

Ref.No.: D of C, CZ2, p. 215

Mint $130.00 **Ex.** $70.00 **G.** $50.00 **F.** $30.00

FREEMAN
ca.1946 - 19 in.

ca.1946. 19 in. (48.5 cm). Cloth body, composition forearms and straight legs. Composition head; blue painted eyes, painted lower lashes, upper eyeshadow; brown moulded hair; closed mouth. Unmarked. Original white cotton dress and bonnet with rick-rack trim, shoes and socks.

Ref.No.: D of C, CA27, p. 216

Mint $150.00 **Ex.** $105.00 **G.** $75.00 **F.** $50.00

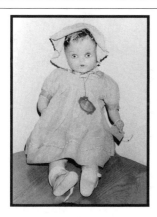

FREEMAN
ca.1946 - 25 in.

ca.1946. 25 in. (63.5 cm). Cloth body, composition arms and legs. Composition head; painted blue eyes, eyeshadow, painted lower lashes; moulded brown hair; closed mouth. Original Tag: A GENUINE FREEMAN DOLL/MADE IN CANADA. Original pink and blue cotton dress, bonnet, socks and shoes.

Ref.No.: D of C, CT20, p.216

Mint $160.00 **Ex.** $115.00 **G.** $90.00 **F.** $60.00

FREEMAN
ca.1947 - 24 in.

ca.1947. 24 in. (61 cm). Cloth body, composition forearms, straight legs. Composition head; blue painted eyes, painted lower lashes, upper eyeshadow; brown moulded hair; closed mouth. Original Tag: A/GENUINE/FREEMAN DOLL (in script)/MADE IN CANADA. Original white and blue cotton dress and bonnet trimmed in rick-rack, socks and shoes.

Ref.No.: D of C, CA33, p. 217

Mint $160.00 **Ex.** $115.00 **G.** $90.00 **F.** $60.00

FREEMAN
ca.1948 - 16 in.

ca.1948. 16 in. (40.5 cm). Composition body, jointed hips, shoulders and neck. Composition head; blue sleep eyes, lashes, painted lower lashes; brown mohair wig in braids with curly bangs; closed mouth. Mark: on body, FREEMAN TOY/TORONTO, CANADA. Original cotton dress, socks and shoes.

Ref.No.: D of C, AP11, p. 217

Mint $175.00 Ex. $130.00 G. $75.00 F. $55.00

FREEMAN
ca.1948 - 16 1/2 in.

ca.1948. 16 1/2 in. (42 cm). Composition body, jointed hips, shoulders and neck. Composition head; blue painted eyes, painted upper lashes; brown mohair wig in braids with curly bangs; closed mouth. Mark: on body, FREEMAN TOY CO./TORONTO,CA. Replaced clothing.

Ref.No.: 2M3

Mint $175.00 Ex. $130.00 G. $75.00 F. $55.00

FREEMAN
ca.1948 - 22 in.

ca.1948. 22 in. (56 cm). Cloth body, composition arms and legs. Composition flange head; painted blue eyes, eyeshadow, painted lower lashes; moulded dark brown hair; closed mouth. Original label: A GENUINE/FREEMAN DOLL/MADE IN CANADA. Original blue and white cotton dress and bonnet. Replaced socks and shoes.

Ref.No.: D of C, CT6, p. 217

Mint $155.00 Ex. $110.00 G. $85.00 F. $60.00

FREEMAN
ca.1950 - 24 in.

ca.1950. 24 in. (61 cm). Cloth body, composition hands and legs. Composition head; blue sleep eyes, lashes, painted lower lashes; blond mohair wig with curly bangs; open mouth showing two teeth and tongue. Original Tag: A FREEMAN/DOLL/MADE IN CANADA/FREEMAN TOY COMPANY/TORONTO. Original lace-trimmed pink organdy dress and bonnet, shoes and socks.

Ref.No.: D of C, AZ5, p. 218

Mint $300.00 Ex. $225.00 G. $105.00 F. $75.00

FREEMAN
ca.1951 - 17 in.

ca.1951. 17 in. (43 cm). Composition body, jointed hips, shoulders and neck. Composition head; blue sleep eyes, lashes, painted lower lashes; blond mohair wig; closed mouth. Mark: on head, FREEMAN TOY/TORONTO. Original label, A FREEMAN DOLL/MADE IN/CANADA/FREEMAN TOY COMPANY/TORONTO. Original pink dress, socks and shoes.

Ref.No.: D of C, CN34, p. 218

Mint $185.00 **Ex.** $140.00 **G.** $95.00 **F.** $65.00

FUNMATE CANADA LTD.
Vancouver, British Columbia

BUNDLE UP BABY

ca.1985. 12 in. (30.5 cm). Soft-sculptured head with room inside head and arms for a child's hand; works like a puppet. Doll made in Taiwan; packaged in Canada. Box: FUNMATE VANCOUVER, B.C.

Ref.No.: ES54

Mint $20.00

GILTOY COMPANY
Montreal, Quebec
ca.1945 - 1952

GILTOY
ca.1945 - 14 in.

ca.1945. 14 in. (35.5 cm). Composition body, jointed hips, shoulders and neck. Composition head; blue painted side-glancing eyes; brown moulded hair; closed mouth. Mark: on body, W.O.L. Original label, GILTOY/OUR TRADEMARK IS/YOUR GUARAN -TEE/FOR QUALITY AND/WORKMANSHIP.

Ref.No.: D of C, CN24, p. 219

Mint $175.00 Ex. $125.00 G. $75.00 F. $50.00

GOODTIME TOYS
1970 - 1977

This was a short-lived company whose dolls cannot be identified without a cloth body label or the box.

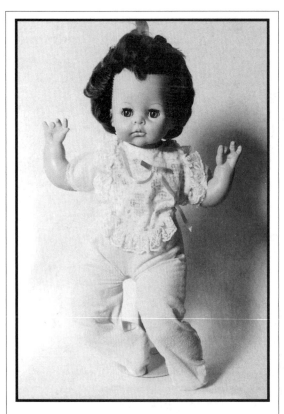

GOODTIME TOYS
ca.1970 - 20 in.

ca.1970. 20 in. (51 cm). Cloth body, stuffed with chipped foam, bent-limb vinyl arms and legs. Vinyl head; grey-blue sleep eyes, lashes; rooted brown curls; closed mouth. Mark: tag on body, GOODTIME TOYS INC. Original yellow flannelette sleepers, yellow flowered bib.

Ref.No.: 2F23

Mint $35.00 **Ex.** $25.00 **G.** $20.00 **F.** $15.00

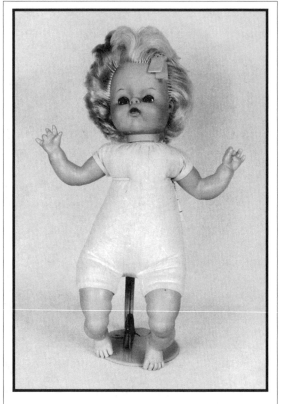

GOODTIME TOYS
ca.1972 - 16 in.

ca.1972. 16 in. (40.5 cm). Cloth body with crier, bent-limb vinyl arms and legs. Vinyl head; blue sleep eyes, lashes; rooted blond hair; open-closed mouth. Mark: on head, STAR DOLL/MADE IN CANADA; on body label, GOODTIME TOYS.

Ref.No.: 2O33

Mint $35.00 **Ex.** $25.00 **G.** $20.00 **F.** $15.00

FASHION DOLL

ca.1975. 20 in. (51 cm). Plastic teen body, jointed hips, shoulders and neck. Vinyl head; blue sleep eyes, lashes, eyeshadow; rooted platinum long hair on the side and short on top; closed mouth. Mark: on head, 14R.

Ref.No.: D of C, BX15, p. 219

Mint **$45.00** **Ex.** **$35.00** **G.** **$25.00** **F.** **$15.00**

BOUDOIR DOLL
ca.1975 - 20 in.

ca.1975. 20 in. (51 cm). Plastic teen body, jointed hips, shoulders and neck. Vinyl head; grey sleep eyes, lashes, eye-shadow; rooted platinum hair, short around face with long ringlets at each side; closed mouth. Original long pink flowered gown with white flocking in the design. Full circle skirt is generously embellished with a double row of 3 in. ivory lace. Includes rose bouquet.

Ref.No.: 2P9

Mint **$50.00** **Ex.** **$40.00** **G.** **$25.00** **F.** **$15.00**

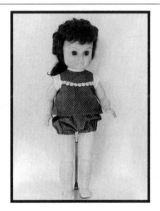

GOODTIME TOYS
ca.1976 - 24 in.

ca.1976. 24 in. (61 cm). Plastic body, jointed hips, shoulders and neck. Vinyl head; blue sleep eyes, lashes; rooted brown hair; closed mouth. Mark: on head, STAR DOLL/C1965 CANADA. Redressed.

Ref.No.: 2I8

Mint **$45.00** **Ex.** **$35.00** **G.** **$25.00** **F.** **$15.00**

Note: Mould originally owned by Star Doll and sold to Goodtime Toys when Star went out of business.

HASSENFELD BROS. INC. (HASBRO)
Cooksville, Ontario
ca.1960 -

G.I. Joes have skyrocketed in value in the last few years. One reason is the 50th anniversary of the end of World War II and another is that the young men who played with them as children are now actively collecting them with great enthusiasm. The prices listed are for an action figure in very good condition with a complete uniform but no box.

G.I. JOE
World War II American Soldier

1964. 11 1/2 in. (29 cm). Hard plastic body, jointed ankles, knees, hips, waist, wrists, elbows, shoulders and neck. Vinyl head; painted blue or brown eyes; blond, red, brown or black painted hair. Combat field jacket, green pants, calf-high boots, green helmet, cartridge belt, M-1 rifle and knapsack. Mark: on right buttock, G.I. JOE REG T.M. / COPYRIGHT 1964 / BY HASBRO ® / PATENT PENDING / MADE IN CANADA.
Mint: $250.00

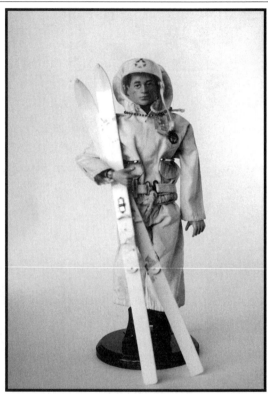

G.I. JOE
Ski Patrol

1966. 11 1/2 in. (29 cm). Hard plastic body, jointed ankles, knees, hips, waist, wrists, elbows, shoulders and neck. Vinyl head; painted blue or brown eyes; blond, red, brown or black painted hair. White parka and pants, white cartridge belt, skis, ski poles (missing), mittens (missing), white helmet, goggles (missing) and white M-1 rifle (missing). Mark: on right buttock, G.I. JOE REG T.M. / COPYRIGHT 1964 / BY HASBRO ® / PATENT PENDING / MADE IN CANADA.
Mint: $250.00

G.I. JOE
Australian Jungle Fighter

1966. 11 1/2 in. (29 cm). Hard plastic body, jointed ankles, knees, hips, waist, wrists, elbows, shoulders and neck. Vinyl head; painted blue eyes; blond painted hair. Khaki bush jacket and shorts, knee-high olive green socks (missing), brown boots, grenades, flamethrower (missing), knife, machete, entrenching tool and the Victoria Cross medal (missing). Mark: on right buttock, G.I. JOE REG T.M. /COPYRIGHT 1964/BY HASBRO®/PATENT PENDING /MADE IN CANADA (MADE IN CANADA sometimes absent). Part of the Action Soldiers of the World series.

Mint: $275.00

G.I. JOE
British Commando

1966. 11 1/2 in. (29 cm). Hard plastic body, jointed ankles, knees, hips, waist, wrists, elbows, shoulders and neck. Vinyl head; painted blue or brown eyes; blond, red, brown or black painted hair. Dark green flannel jacket and pants, brown boots, green helmet, gas mask and bag (missing), Sten Mark 2S submachine gun, canteen and Victoria Cross medal (missing). Mark: on right buttock, G.I. JOE REG T.M. / COPYRIGHT 1964 / BY HASBRO ® / PATENT PENDING / MADE IN CANADA. Part of the Action Soldiers of the World series.

Mint: $325.00

G.I. JOE
German Soldier

1966. 11 1/2 in. (29 cm). Hard plastic body, jointed ankles, knees, hips, waist, wrists, elbows, shoulders and neck. Vinyl head; painted brown eyes; blond painted hair. Dark green flannel jacket and pants, black calf-high boots, grey helmet, Luger pistol and holster, cartridge belt, woolly field pack, 9 mm Schmeisser machine gun, grenades and Iron Cross medal (missing). Mark: on right buttock, G.I. JOE REG T.M. / COPYRIGHT 1964 / BY HASBRO ® / PATENT PENDING / MADE IN CANADA (MADE IN CANADA sometimes absent). Part of the Action Soldiers of the World series.

Mint: $450.00

G.I. JOE
Japanese Imperial Soldier

1966. 11 1/2 in. (29 cm). Hard plastic body, jointed ankles, knees, hips, waist, wrists, elbows, shoulders and neck. Vinyl head; painted brown eyes; black painted hair. Khaki jacket, pants and helmet, brown boots, Nambu pistol, holster (missing), Arisaka rifle with bayonet (missing), field pack, cartridge belt and Order of the Kite medal (missing). Mark: on right buttock, G.I. JOE REG T.M. / COPYRIGHT 1964 / BY HASBRO ® / PATENT PENDING / MADE IN CANADA. Part of the Action Soldiers of the World series.

Mint: $700.00

G.I. JOE
Royal Canadian Mounted Police

1968. 11 1/2 in. (29 cm). Hard plastic body, jointed ankles, knees, hips, waist, wrists, elbows, shoulders and neck. Vinyl head; painted blue or brown eyes; blond, red, brown or black painted hair. Red tunic, navy breeches, RCMP hat with hat band (missing), brown belt with revolver and holster and high brown boots (later replaced with black). Mark: on right buttock, G.I. JOE REG T.M. / COPYRIGHT 1964 / BY HASBRO ® / PATENT PENDING / MADE IN CANADA (MADE IN CANADA sometimes absent). Available in Canada only.

Mint: $300.00

G.I. JOE
Russian Infantry Man

1966. 11 1/2 in. (29 cm). Hard plastic body, jointed ankles, knees, hips, waist, wrists, elbows, shoulders and neck. Vinyl head; painted blue or brown eyes; blond, red, brown or black painted hair. Dark green jacket and pants, fur hat, black calf-high boots, D.P. machine gun, field glasses and case (missing), grenades (missing), ammo box and Order of Lenin medal (missing). Mark: on right buttock, G.I. JOE REG T.M. / COPYRIGHT 1964 / BY HASBRO ® / PATENT PENDING / MADE IN CANADA. Part of the Action Soldiers of the World series.

Mint: $350.00

IDEAL DOLL MFG. CO.
Montreal, Quebec
ca.1948

MARY HAD A LITTLE LAMB
ca.1948 - 12 in.

ca.1948. 12 in. (30.5 cm). Rubber skin body. Vinyl head; inset blue plastic eyes, painted uppers; moulded brown hair; open-closed mouth. Unmarked. Box: IDEAL DOLL MFG. CO., MONTREAL; tag, PUBLIC DOLL CREATION PDC. Original red and white checked dress, white apron, matching bonnet, red and white polka-dot panties, socks and shoes. Set includes a record of "Mary Had a Little Lamb" and a white fur fabric lamb with a vinyl face.

Ref.No.: 2S6

Mint **$125.00** **Ex.** **$75.00** **G.** **$35.00** **F.** **$25.00**

Note: The rubber skin on this doll is rapidly deteriorating, but it is a rare doll. It gives us a record of a company operating in Montreal that was not known before.

INDIEN ART ET ESKIMO DE LA MAURICE INC.
St. Tite, Quebec
1979 -

This company operates out of a small town in northern Quebec. The dolls are not authentically native but are popular souvenir dolls for tourists. The dolls, reference numbers 2F14 and 2Q1, were manufactured by Regal Toy Ltd. and dressed by Indien Art et Eskimo de la Maurice Inc.

INDIAN
ca.1980 - 10 in.

ca.1980. 10 in. (25.5 cm). Brown plastic body, jointed hips, shoulders and neck. Vinyl head, design painted on cheeks; side glancing black eyes; rooted straight black hair; watermelon mouth. Mark: on head, REGAL/MADE IN CANADA; on back, REGAL/CANADA. All original.

Ref.No.: 2F14

Mint $45.00   **Ex.** $35.00   **G.** $25.00   **F.** $15.00

OTTER BELT

1982. 12 in. (30.5 cm). Brown moulded one-piece body made of an unbreakable latex mixture. Painted designs on face and arms. Black painted eyes, wool braids, closed mouth. Mark: on label, INDIEN ART ESKIMO/OTTER BELT.

Ref.No.: D of C, AO22, p. 220

Mint $95.00   **Ex.** $75.00   **G.** $55.00   **F.** $35.00

INDIAN CHILD
1983 - 4 in.

1983. 4 in. (10 cm). Brown one-piece moulded body. Black painted side-glancing eyes, black moulded hair, closed mouth. Mark: label, INDIEN ART ESKIMO.

Ref.No.: D of C, AP4, p. 220

Mint $25.00   **Ex.** $20.00   **G.** $12.00   **F.** $8.00

INDIAN
ca.1983 - 15 in.

ca.1983. 15 in. (38 cm). Brown plastic body, jointed hips, shoulders and neck. Brown vinyl head; brown stencilled eyes; rooted straight black hair; open-closed mouth. Mark: on head, REGAL TOY LTD./MADE IN CANADA/151TPE; tag, CRAFTED BY INDIEN ESKIMO/CANADA. Dressed in a fringed leather suit, moccasins and head-dress.

Ref.No.: 2Q1

Mint $50.00   **Ex.** $40.00   **G.** $30.00   **F.** $20.00

MAISON DE POUPEES INC.
Laval, Quebec
ca.1980-

DOROTHY

1980. 18 in. (46 cm). Cloth body and head. Painted features, floss hair. Mark: tag, MAISON DE POUPEES INC./HANDICRAFT DOLL'S WORKSHOP/LAVAL, QUEBEC. Original striped tricot jumpsuit, hat and shoes.
Ref.No.: 2M2

Mint **$35.00** **Ex.** **$25.00** **G.** **$20.00** **F.** **$15.00**

ANIK

ca. 1981. 18 in. (46 cm). Cloth body and head, needle sculpted nose. Eyes are black glued on circles, four painted lashes, fun-fur hair. Mark: on hang tag, MAISON DE POUPEES INC./ATELIER D'ARTISANT/LAVAL, QUE. Original dark brown fringed jacket and pants with beige fringed collar, headband.
Ref.No.: 2F19

Mint **$30.00** **Ex.** **$25.00** **G.** **$20.00** **F.** **$15.00**

WAPITI

1983. 26 in. (66 cm). Cloth body and head, needle sculpted nose. Eyes are brown felt. Mark: on hang tag, MAISON DE POUPEES INC./HANDICRAFT DOLLS WORKSHOP/LAVAL, QUEBEC. Original brown suede tricot Indian pants and shirt, headband.
Ref.No.: 2K21

Mint **$35.00** **Ex.** **$25.00** **G.** **$20.00** **F.** **$15.00**

MAYFAIR COMPANY
Toronto, Ontario
ca.1950s - 1960

Mayfair imported dolls, made a large wardrobe of clothing for them and boxed them in Canada. Costumes were available separately. Mayfair also made clothes for the major doll companies.

DEBBIE

ca.1960. 8 in. (20 cm). Five-piece vinyl teen body. Vinyl head; sleep eyes, moulded lashes; rooted hair; painted nail polish; high-heel feet. Unmarked.

Mint $75.00   **Ex.** $60.00   **G.** $30.00   **F.** $20.00

Note: Debbie had 36 outfits available, including miniature accessories.

MEGGAN'S DOLL HOUSE
Smiths Falls, Ontario
1972 -

Meggan's Doll House is owned by Heather Anne and Jim Moriarty. Although the business has been established since 1972, it wasn't until 1987 that it really became successful. The factory, which produces over 400 porcelain dolls per month, is located in Smiths Falls, Ontario. The artistic control is in Heather Anne's hands, and the marketing is taken care of by Jim.

Meggan's dolls have a fine, smooth, bisque finish, and the painting is very well done. The workshop employs about 12 people who are very well-trained in their craft.

Walt Disney World in Orlando, Florida, invited Meggan's to show and sell its porcelain dolls at Disney's eight-day World Doll and Teddy Bear Convention in 1989. Meggan's dolls were a sell-out and they were invited back for the 1990 show.

The Japanese government selected Meggan's to participate in a travelling trade show in Japan in 1989 and in 1990 Meggan's attended the famous Nuremburg Toy Fair. Meggan's Doll House is putting Canada on the map as a porcelain doll maker.

The company sells only wholesale, and over 350 stores carry its dolls. Since Heather began sculpting original dolls and producing them in small editions, the dolls are more popular than ever. They are dressed in pastel shades and often include accessories, such as tiny bears, for the dolls to carry.

Meggan's has a line of "Classics," which are in editions of one to 300. The small editions usually sell out quickly.

Meggan's "Collectibles" was a line of 22 dolls, and these were unlimited, however the "Collectibles" line was discontinued in 1991. Today, all of the dolls sold by Meggan's Doll House are created entirely by Heather Anne. Meggan's Doll House produces the entire doll in house from the sculpting through to the design of the limited-edition certificates. It is the first Canadian company to receive multiple nominations for Collectible of the Year, and is the only one to design and produce their nominated dolls.

SANDY

1989. 15 in. (38 cm). All porcelain body, jointed hips, shoulders and neck. Bisque head; blue stationary eyes, painted upper and lower lashes; closed mouth; blond hair dressed in ringlets. Original pink cotton dress, trimmed with white lace and ribbon, white net stockings and white shoes. Limited edition of 100.

Mint: $140.00

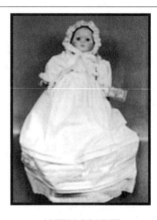

ANITA MARIE

1989. (Original). 17 in. (43.5 cm). Cloth body, porcelain hands and feet. White gown and bonnet. Retired 1991.

Ref.No.: PGA16

Mint: $250.00

GRETCHEN

1989. (Meggan's Collectibles). 17 in. (43.5 cm). All porcelain. Lace trimmed dress, socks and shoes. Retired 1990.

Ref.No.: PGA15

Mint: $140.00

EMILY

1989. (Classic) 20 in. (52 cm). All porcelain. Blue stationary eyes, painted lashes; blond wig. Cotton dress, holding cloth bodied porcelain doll which is a reproduction of a "Tynie Byo-Lo." Also wearing "fuzzy slippers." First issue of Moments of Childhood Series. Limited edition of 300.

Ref.No.: PGA14

Mint: $270.00

VICTORIA ANNE

1989. (Original). 20 in. (51 cm). Cloth body, porcelain hands and feet. Rose dress, flowered apron, socks and shoes. Limited edition of 200. Retired 1991.

Ref.No.: PGA11

Mint: $225.00

SARAH

1989. (Classic) 18 in. (46 cm). Lace trimmed blouse and skirt with matching hat. Carrying a basket. Limited edition of 100. Retired 1990.

Ref.No.: PGA13

Mint: $220.00

FRANNY

1990. 14 in. (36 cm). Cloth body, porcelain hands and feet. Bisque head; stationary blue eyes, painted lashes; honey blond wig; closed mouth. Original pink and white, lace-trimmed dress with flounced skirt, white stockings and pink shoes. Limited edition of 100. An original commemorative doll for the 1990 Walt Disney World Showcase.

Ref.No.: MDH2

Mint: $325.00

SHIRLEY WHO SKATES ON CHOCOLATE LAKE

1990. 14 in. (36 cm). Cloth body, porcelain hands and feet. Bisque head; stationary eyes, painted lashes; brown wig; closed mouth. Original rose velvet long skirt, white lace blouse, blue cape. Limited edition of 100. An original commemorative doll for the 1989 Walt Disney World Showcase.

Ref.No.: MDH1

Mint: $325.00

PATTY

1990. 15 in. (38 cm). Cloth body, porcelain hands and feet. Bisque head; stationary green side-glancing eyes, painted upper and lower lashes; honey blond hair dressed in ringlets. Original peach gown trimmed with cream satin and peach lace frills, cream satin pantaloons trimmed with lace, white socks and cream shoes. Limited edition of 25.

Mint: $330.00

ANGIE

1990. 16 in. (40.5 cm). Cloth body, porcelain hands and feet. Bisque head; blue "googlie" eyes, painted upper lashes; blond hair dressed in ringlets; closed mouth. Original red-brown print dress with blue ribbon trim and matching mob cap, white net stockings and white shoes.

Mint: $150.00

NOELE

1990. (Classic). 19 in. (48 cm). Fully porcelain doll, blue stationary eyes, painted lashes; dark brown wig. Pale pink satin and lace dress, cotton underskirt, and several crinolines. Holding a satin Christmas stocking. Limited edition of 25. Edition sold out.

Mint: $450.00

Note: This was Meggan's Doll House's first Christmas doll.

KATIE

1990. (Classic) 20 in. (52 cm). All porcelain. Blue stationary eyes, painted lashes; blond wig. Cotton eyelet dress, holding teddy, which is wearing matching trim. Second issue of the Moments of Childhood Series. Limited edition of 300.

Mint: $270.00

HEATHER
1990 - 22 in.

1990. (Classic). 22 in. (56 cm). Cloth body, articulated arms and head. Blue stationary eyes, painted lashes; dark brown wig. Satin and lace dress, velvet hat, cape and purse. Limited edition of 7 dolls created to commemorate the 1990 Canadian Art and Collectibles Show. Edition sold out upon release.

Mint: $800.00

ME TOO

1991. 14 in. (36 cm). All porcelain body, jointed hips, shoulders and neck. Bisque head; green stationary eyes, painted lashes; red wig; closed mouth, freckles. Original head mould. Limited edition of 100. Original cotton print dress with eyelet trim, white stockings and shoes. Includes glasses.

Ref.No.: Z13

Mint: $195.00

JUST FOR YOU

1991. 15 in. (38 cm). Cloth body, porcelain hands and feet. Bisque head; stationary eyes, painted lashes; wig ; closed mouth. "Just For You" is made to the customer's order, having the colour eye, hair, and name the new owner chooses. The doll's name is engraved on a pendant around her neck. An original mould but each doll is different.

Ref.No.: MDH3

Mint: $190.00

PEACHES AND CREAM

1991. 15 in. (38 cm). Cloth body, porcelain hands and feet. Bisque head; stationary, side-glancing brown eyes, painted lashes; red wig; closed mouth. Original pink ribbon and lace trimmed white dress, white stockings and shoes. Includes white teddy bear. Original head mould. Limited numbered edition of 150.

Ref.No.: MDH5

Mint: $250.00

Note: Peaches and Cream received a nomination for Collectible of the Year by the readers of *Insight to Collectibles*.

BETSY

1991. 18 in. (46 cm). All porcelain body, jointed hips, shoulders and neck. Bisque head; stationary blue eyes, painted upper and lower lashes; honey blond hair dressed in ringlets; closed mouth. Original red cotton dress trimmed with white lace, red cotton bloomers trimmed with white lace, white net stockings and white shoes. Limited edition of 25.

Mint: $250.00

CHERISH
1991 - 19 in.

1991. (Classic). 19 in. (48 cm). Fully porcelain doll; blue stationary eyes, painted lashes; blond wig. Pale blue satin and lace dress, cotton underskirt, and several crinolines. Limited edition of 40 dolls created to commemorate "Mother's Day" 1991. Edition sold out upon release.

Mint: $350.00

Note: Cherish received a nomination for Collectible of the Year by the readers of *Insight to Collectibles*.

JANIE

1991. (Classic). 20 in. (52 cm). All porcelain. Brown stationary eyes, painted lashes; auburn wig. Cotton dress, holding braided jump rope. Hair decorated with ribbon and flowers. Third issue of Moments of Childhood Series. Limited edition of 300.

Mint: $270.00

HEATHER
1991 - 22 in.

1991. (Classic). 22 in. (56 cm). Cloth body, articulated arms and head. Brown stationary eyes, painted lashes; dark brown wig. Pink satin and lace dress. Holding wooden heart shaped box containing porcelain plate numbered in co-ordination with the doll. Limited edition of 25, created to commemorate the 1991 Canadian Art and Collectibles Show. Sold out upon release.

Mint: $350.00

ZOE AND CRESTA BEAR

1991. 35 in. (85 cm). A One-of-a-kind doll created for the Walt Disney World Showcase of Dolls, sold at auction. Soft bodied construction, with poseable porcelain head and arms; porcelain legs. Dressed in a crushed velvet dress, trimmed in dusty rose velvet ribbons. Cotton broadcloth underdress, two crinolines, and bloomers. Fully lined, velvet cape and hat. Cresta Bear is a one-of-a-kind bear created by bear artist Olive Ashby exclusively for this presentation.

Mint: $1,150.00

Note: From the collection of Linda Holdsclaw, Florida.

KIM

1991. 17 in. (43 cm). All porcelain body, jointed hips, shoulders and neck. Bisque head; brown stationary eyes, lashes; long red curly hair; closed mouth. Original red plaid cotton dress, trimmed in lace and ribbon, white stockings and shoes. Includes a wooden wagon and plush teddy bear. Original head mould. Limited edition of 50.

Ref.No.: Z12

Mint: $270.00

SUGAR AND SPICE

1991. 21 in. (53 cm). Cloth body, porcelain hands and feet. Bisque head; stationary blue eyes, painted lashes; platinum blond wig; closed mouth. Original pale pink gown and overskirt, lavishly trimmed with silver ribbon and lace, matching hair ribbon. Includes teddy bear designed by Olive Ashby. Limited edition of 10. Available only at the 1991 Walt Disney World Showcase of Dolls at Disney World, U.S.A.

Ref.No.: MDH4

Mint: $450.00

ELLIE

1992. (Classic). 20 in. (52 cm). All porcelain; brown stationary eyes, painted lashes; carrot red wig. Cotton dress; holding hand-made blue bird. Fourth issue of the Moments of Childhood Series. Limited edition 300.

Mint: $270.00

MARY HAD A LITTLE LAMB

1994. 14 in. (35.5 cm). All porcelain with jointed shoulders, neck, hips, elbows and wrists. Pale blue glass eyes; slightly open mouth. Original rose-print dress and pink underskirt. Mary holds school books. White plush lamb with pink collar and silver bell. Limited edition of 50.

Mint: $230.00

MIGHTY STAR COMPANY LIMITED
1977 -

Mighty Star is still in operation but no longer manufactures dolls in Canada.

MIGHTY STAR
ca.1978 - 23 in.

ca.1978. 23 in. (58.5 cm). Plastic body, jointed hips, shoulders and neck. Vinyl head; blue sleep eyes, lashes; rooted blond hair with side braids; closed mouth. Mark: on head, DOLL/C1965 CANADA.

Ref.No.: D of C, CG25, p. 221

Mint   **$40.00**   **Ex.**   **$30.00**   **G.**   **$20.00**   **F.**   **$15.00**

MIGHTY STAR
ca.1979 - 32 in.

ca.1979. 32 in. (81 cm.). Plastic body, jointed hips, shoulders and neck. Vinyl head; blue sleep eyes, lashes, painted lowers; rooted long blond hair; closed mouth. Mark: on head, 3/CMIGHTY STAR/CANADA/33W. Original cotton gown.

Ref.No.: 2I18

Mint   **$45.00**   **Ex.**   **$35.00**   **G.**   **$30.00**   **F.**   **$20.00**

MIGHTY STAR
ca.1979 - 32 in.

ca.1979. 32 in. (81 cm). Plastic body, jointed hips, shoulders and neck. Vinyl head; blue sleep eyes, lashes, painted lowers; rooted long blond hair; closed mouth. Mark: on head, MIGHTY STAR/CANADA. Original fur fabric coat and plastic boots, hat missing.
Ref.No.: 2P12

Mint **$45.00** **Ex.** **$35.00** **G.** **$30.00** **F.** **$20.00**

MIGHTY STAR
1980 - 19 in.

1980. 19 in. (48.5 cm). Plastic teen body and legs, jointed hips, shoulders and neck. Vinyl head; blue sleep eyes, lashes; rooted long blond hair with bangs; closed mouth. Mark: on head, 14R.
Ref.No.: D of C, CG6, p. 221

Mint **$40.00** **Ex.** **$35.00** **G.** **$25.00** **F.** **$15.00**

DISCO DOLL

1980. 20 in. (51 cm). Plastic teen body, jointed hips, shoulders and neck. Vinyl head; blue sleep eyes, lashes; rooted platinum blond hair; closed mouth. Original silver and blue outfit, high-heeled shoes.
Ref.No.: 2P26

Mint **$40.00** **Ex.** **$35.00** **G.** **$25.00** **F.** **$15.00**

MIGHTY STAR
1981 - 20 in.

1981. 20 in. (51 cm). Plastic teen body, jointed hips, shoulders and neck. Vinyl head; brown sleep eyes, lashes, painted lower lashes; rooted long brown curls with bangs; closed mouth. Unmarked.
Ref.No.: D of C, AO8, p. 221

Mint **$35.00** **Ex.** **$30.00** **G.** **$25.00** **F.** **$15.00**

COUNTRY CUZZINS

1981. 24 in. (61 cm). Cloth body, arms and legs, vinyl hands. Vinyl head; blue sleep eyes, lashes; rooted long curly blond hair; closed mouth. Mark: on head, 4/MIGHTY STAR/CANADA. Original overalls, shirt and hat.

Ref.No.: D of C, CG7, p. 222

Mint $45.00   **Ex.** $30.00   **G.** $25.00   **F.** $20.00

MIGHTY STAR
ca.1981 - 23 in.

ca.1981. 23 in. (58.5 cm). Cloth body, arms and legs, vinyl hands. Vinyl head; brown sleep eyes, lashes, painted lowers; rooted brown hair; closed smiling mouth. Mark: on head, MIGHTY STAR/CANADA. Original denim skirt and print top, striped arms and legs.

Ref.No.: 2I17

Mint $40.00   **Ex.** $35.00   **G.** $25.00   **F.** $20.00

Note: This is obviously a character like Country Cuzzins, but without a box or label it is hard to tell.

MIGHTY STAR
1981 - 20 in.

1981. 20 in. (51 cm). Plastic teen body, jointed hips, shoulders, and neck. Vinyl head; blue sleep eyes, lashes, painted lower lashes; rooted blond with bangs; closed mouth. Mark: on head, 14R. All original.

Ref.No.: D of C, AO7, p. 222

Mint $35.00   **Ex.** $30.00   **G.** $25.00   **F.** $15.00

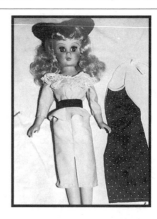

MIGHTY STAR FASHION DOLL

ca.1981. 20 in. (51 cm). Five-piece vinyl body. Vinyl head; blue sleep eyes, lashes; rooted long blond hair; closed mouth. Mark: on head, 14R.

Ref.No.: DR35

Mint $40.00   **Ex.** $35.00   **G.** $25.00   **F.** $15.00

PEBBLES

1981. 12 in. (30.5 cm). Cloth body, vinyl arms and legs. Vinyl head; painted side-glancing black eyes; rooted straight red hair; open-closed mouth. Mark: on head, c1980/HANNA-BARBERA INGS/MIGHTY STAR/HONG KONG/1187; on box, MADE BY MIGHTY STAR DOLL DIVISION, TORONTO. Original two piece playsuit.

Ref.No.: DB5

Mint **$40.00** **Ex.** **$30.00** **G.** **$20.00** **F.** **$15.00**

BUNNY BABY

ca.1981. 11 in. (28 cm). Pink brushed-knit fabric body with bunny tail. Vinyl head; black painted eyes; rooted blond hair around the face only; closed mouth. Mark: on head, MADE IN CANADA; on body tag, MIGHTY STAR LTD. Original matching bunny hood with ears.

Ref.No.: 2M19

Mint **$30.00** **Ex.** **$25.00** **G.** **$20.00** **F.** **$15.00**

MIGHTY STAR
1982 - 18 in.

1982. 18 in. (45.5 cm). Plastic body, jointed hips, shoulders and neck. Vinyl head; blue sleep eyes, lashes, blue eyeshadow; rooted brown curls with bangs; closed mouth. Mark: on head, 5. Original clothing.

Ref.No.: D of C, AP3, p. 222

Mint **$35.00** **Ex.** **$25.00** **G.** **$20.00** **F.** **$15.00**

BABY CRISSIE
1982 - 18 in.

1982. 18 in. (45.5 cm). Cloth body with crier, vinyl arms and legs. Vinyl head; blue sleep eyes, lashes; slightly moulded light brown hair; open-closed mouth. Mark: on head, STAR/09094/PLATED MOULDS INC./C1961.; on body, MADE BY ONT. REG. NO. 71B7816/MIGHTY STAR LTD.-DOLL DIVISION. Original clothing.

Ref.No.: D of C, XH27, p. 223

Mint **$35.00** **Ex.** **$30.00** **G.** **$20.00** **F.** **$15.00**

BABY WETSY

1982. 16 in. (40.5 cm). Plastic body and legs, vinyl arms, jointed hips, shoulders and neck. Vinyl head; blue sleep eyes, lashes; rooted brown curls; open mouth nurser. Unmarked. Original clothing.

Ref.No.: D of C, CG5, p. 223

Mint $25.00 **Ex.** $20.00 **G.** $15.00 **F.** $10.00

MIGHTY STAR
ca.1982 - 32 in.

ca.1982. 32 in. (81 cm). Plastic body, jointed hips, shoulders and neck. Vinyl head; blue sleep eyes, lashes, painted lowers; rooted long blond hair; closed mouth. Mark: on head, 3/MIGHTY STAR/CANADA. Original one-piece dress with white cotton bodice and plaid skirt.

Ref.No.: PGC14

Mint $40.00 **Ex.** $35.00 **G.** $25.00 **F.** $20.00

DENNIS THE MENACE

1983. 13 in. (33 cm). Cloth body, arms and legs, vinyl hands. Vinyl head; black painted eyes; blond moulded hair; watermelon mouth. Mark: on head, KETCHAM INC./C1981; on body, MIGHTY STAR LTD., DOLL DIVISION; on clothing, DENNIS THE MENACE/C1983 KETCHAM INC. ALL RIGHTS RESERVED/BY/PAR/MIGHTY STAR. Original blue and white striped cotton shirt, red cotton overalls, shoes sewn to feet. There appears to be only one Canadian license granted by Hank Ketcham, creator of Dennis, to produce Dennis dolls.

Ref.No.: 2M17

Mint $60.00 **Ex.** $50.00 **G.** $35.00 **F.** $25.00

BABY CRISSIE
1983 - 13 in.

1983. 13 in. (33 cm). Pink cloth body, with vinyl arms and legs. Vinyl head; blue sleep eyes, upper lashes; moulded light brown hair; open-closed mouth. Mark: on head, 21 / M.S. / 1983 / HONG KONG / 31465. Tag: on body, MIGHTY STAR LTD. / DOLL DIVISION. May be original nightie.

Ref.No.: SW1

Mint $25.00 **Ex.** $20.00 **G.** $15.00 **F.** $10.00

SUSIE STEPPS
1983 - 17 in.

1983. 17 in. (43 cm). Plastic body, jointed hips, shoulders and neck. Vinyl head; blue sleep eyes, lashes, painted lowers; rooted straight blond hair; closed mouth. Mark: on head, 6; on box, MIGHTY STAR. Original blue plaid cotton dress and tam, solid blue jacket, panties, shoes and socks.

Ref.No.: 2L23

Mint $35.00   **Ex.** $30.00   **G.** $25.00   **F.** $20.00

CANADA GIRL

1983. 12 in. (30.5 cm). Plastic body, jointed hips, shoulders and neck. Vinyl head; blue sleep eyes, lashes; rooted blond short curls; open-closed mouth. Mark: on head, STAR DOLL. Original clothing.

Ref.No.: D of C, AA18, p. 223

Mint $35.00   **Ex.** $25.00   **G.** $15.00   **F.** $10.00

LIV'N LUV

1984. 26 in. (66 in). Cloth body, vinyl bent limb arms and legs. Vinyl head; brown sleep eyes, lashes; moulded pale brown hair; open-closed mouth showing two lower teeth. Mark: on head, HONG KONG; on box, MADE BY MIGHTY STAR, DOLL DIVISION, TORONTO. According to a company spokesperson, the dolls were assembled and dressed in Canada. Original white quilted sleepers, bootees missing.

Ref.No.: PGM21

Mint $40.00   **Ex.** $35.00   **G.** $30.00   **F.** $20.00

PEACH BLOSSOM

ca.1984. 16 in. (40.5 cm). Cloth body, arms and legs. Vinyl head; painted side-glancing black eyes; rooted blond curls; watermelon mouth. Mark: on head, 13/MIGHTY STAR/CANADA/16AB. Original yellow gingham dress with white cotton apron.

Ref.No.: DH7

Mint $25.00   **Ex.** $20.00   **G.** $15.00   **F.** $10.00

MORMIT PRODUCTS
1945 - 1965

The *British Doll Collectors's News*, issue 10, September 1992, finally solved the mystery of the Mormit doll. The name *Mormit* comes from two names, Mr. F.G. Mitchell and Mr. Morris, who were partners in the English company Morris Mitchell and Co. Ltd. They used a derivation of their surnames, Mormit, as their trademark for their "Dolls of the Future," the first vinyl drink-and-wet dolls that were advertised as being fully bathable.

Their early series of dolls, which began in 1945, was the Marie series. The first two dolls in the series were Marie-Jose and Marie-Valerie after Mr. Mitchell's two daughters. The next dolls were named Marie-Mia, Marie-Lou and Marie-Ann. The patent number on the back of the doll is an English patent number.

The Morris Mitchell Company must have had a small company in Canada in 1946, but so far this is the only Mormit doll that has surfaced, marked Made in Canada.

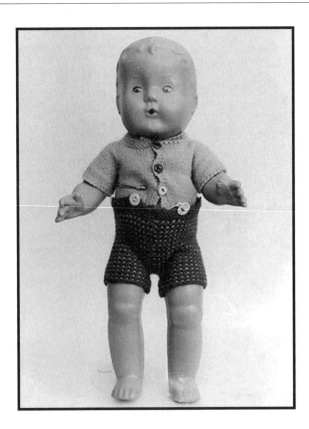

MARIE-LOU

1946. 16 in. (40.5 cm). Heavy rubbery vinyl body, jointed hips, shoulders and neck. Heavy vinyl head; inset plastic eyes; moulded curls, no colour; open-mouth nurser. Mark: on body, MARIE-LOU/PRO PATENT 30189/45/MORMIT PRODUCTS/MADE IN CANADA. Redressed.

Ref.No.: 2N12

Mint $150.00 Ex. $95.00 G. $65.00 F. $45.00

NOMA TOYS LTD.
Owen Sound, Ontario 1945 -

Dolls are unmarked but the boxes identify them as made by Noma, in Owen Sound, Canada.

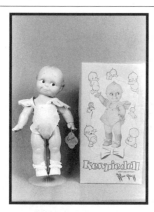

KEWPIE DOLL - 1945

1945. 13 in. (33 cm). Composition body, jointed hips, shoulders and neck. Composition head; black painted side-glancing eyes; distinctive kewpie-style moulded hair; closed watermelon mouth. Unmarked.

Ref.No.: D of C, BF25, p. 224

Mint $300.00 **Ex.** $250.00 **G.** $175.00 **F.** $125.00

KEWPIE DOLL - 1947

1947. 11 in. (28 cm). Composition body, one-piece head and legs, jointed shoulders. Painted black, side-glancing eyes, upper lashes; moulded, painted hair; watermelon mouth. Mark: on chest, original red heart-shaped decal marked, KEWPIE. Original striped shorts and slippers.

Ref.No.: DB15

Mint $200.00 **Ex.** $175.00 **G.** $135.00 **F.** $100.00

SCOOTLES

1947. 13 in. (33 cm). Composition body, jointed hips, shoulders and neck. Composition head dimpled cheeks and chin, nostril dots; blue painted eyes, painted upper lashes; reddish moulded curls; closed watermelon mouth. Unmarked.

Ref.No.: D of C, CD15, p. 224

Mint $400.00 **Ex.** $350.00 **G.** $275.00 **F.** $160.00

NOMA ELECTRONIC DOLL

1950. 28 in. (71 cm). Real human voice sings songs, recites nursery rhymes, laughs and says her prayers. English and French record inside.

Mint $225.00 **Ex.** $175.00 **G.** $75.00 **F.** $55.00

Note: The mint and ex. dolls must be in working condition

OIL PATCH KIDS
Alberta
ca1985

The "Oil Patch Kids" seemed to be available only on the Prairies. Who owned the company, and where it was located could not be discovered. The dolls and pets were made in Hong Kong.

OIL PATCH BOY

1985. 10 in. (25.5 cm). Cloth body. Vinyl head with freckles; blue stencilled eyes; rooted black wool hair; closed watermelon mouth. Unmarked. Original "Well" license. Comes with plastic oil barrel and black velvet Oil Patch Pet with eyes and feet.

Ref.No.: D of C, CR12, p. 225

Mint $35.00 **Ex.** $30.00 **G.** $20.00 **F.** $15.00

OIL PATCH GIRL

1985. 10 in. (25.5 cm). Cloth body. Vinyl head with freckles; blue stencilled eyes; rooted black yarn hair in two pony-tails; watermelon mouth. Mark: label on the body, HONG KONG. Original "Well" license. Original coveralls, turtle neck T shirt, plastic helmet. Includes black velvet Oil Patch Pet, plastic oil can.

Ref.No.: 2N9

Mint $35.00 **Ex.** $30.00 **G.** $20.00 **F.** $15.00

PERFECT DOLL COMPANY
1948

The Perfect Doll Company lasted only one year, which makes their dolls quite rare.

PERFECT
1948 - 12 in.

1948. 12 in. (30.5 cm). Composition bent-limb baby body. Composition head; blue painted eyes with fine black line and highlights; brown moulded hair; closed mouth. Mark: on head, PERFECT / MADE IN CANADA.

Ref.No.: D of C, AP32, p. 225

Mint $160.00   **Ex.** $130.00   **G.** $85.00   **F.** $65.00

Note: This is a rare doll.

REGAL TOY COMPANY
1959 - 1984

The Regal Toy Company was established in 1959 in Toronto by Frank Samuels. The company produced dolls made with blow-moulded plastic bodies and rotational-moulded vinyl heads. Baby dolls were often made with cloth bodies and soft vinyl heads.

Regal dolls often had a Canadian theme, as the company used fabrics such as the Maple Leaf Tartan and cottons with maple leaves to dress their dolls. They also produced a doll which sang in either English or French, depending on which record the child played.

Frank Samuels died in 1973 after producing Canadian dolls, first with Reliable and then with Regal, for 53 years. He was followed as president of the company by his brother Ben Samuels.

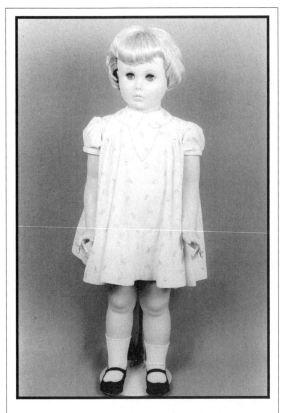

LITTLE PRINCESS WALKER
Blond Saran Hair

1961. 36 in. (91.5 cm). Plastic body, jointed hips, shoulders and neck. Vinyl head; blue sleep eyes, lashes, painted lower lashes; rooted blond saran hair; closed mouth. Unmarked.

Ref.No.: D of C, CS25A, p. 228

Mint **$125.00** **Ex.** **$75.00** **G.** **$50.00** **F.** **$40.00**

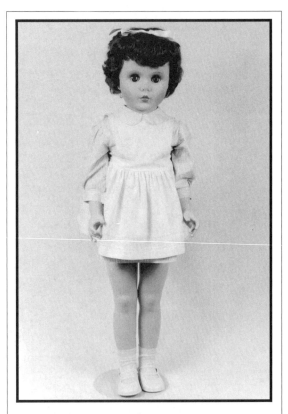

LITTLE PRINCESS WALKER
Brown Curly Hair

1961. 36 in. (91.5 cm). Plastic body, jointed hips, shoulders and neck. Vinyl head; blue sleep eyes, lashes, painted lowers; brown curly hair; closed mouth. Mark: on back, REGAL. Original light green striped dress and white pinafore, socks and shoes, hair ribbon.

Ref.No.: 2A12

Mint. **$125.00** **Ex.** **$75.00** **G.** **$50.00** **F.** **$40.00**

LIZA
Plastic Body

1961. 14 in. (35.5 cm). Plastic body and limbs; jointed neck, shoulders and hips. Brown sleep eyes, lashes; black moulded hair with three tufts of rooted, saran hair. Redressed.

Ref.No.: SP5

Mint. $45.00 **Ex.** $35.00 **G.** $25.00 **F.** $20.00

BABY DEAR
1961 - 20 in.

1961. 20 in. (51 cm). Light plastic body, jointed hips, shoulders and neck. Light plastic head; inset blue eyes; moulded red hair; open-closed mouth. Mark: on body, REGAL. Redressed. Originally wore cotton shirt, diaper, and was wrapped in a blanket tied with a ribbon.

Ref.No.: 2P31

Mint $75.00 **Ex.** $50.00 **G.** $45.00 **F.** $35.00

Note: One of the earliest Regal babies. Feels like celluloid. Rare.

LIZA
Vinyl Body

1961. 14 in. (35.5 cm). Five-piece body. Brown vinyl head; brown sleep eyes, lashes; open mouth nurser; rooted black curls. Original red-checked cotton dress with lace trim, white cotton apron trimmed with lace and red-checked scarf.

Ref.No.: DR10

Mint $40.00 **Ex.** $35.00 **G.** $25.00 **F.** $20.00

DIAPER BABY

ca.1961. 16 in. (40.5 cm). Five-piece vinyl body. Brown sleep eyes; open-mouth nurser. Mark: back of waist, 20-68B. Originally wore a checked sun-suit.

Ref.No.: PS5

Mint $50.00 **Ex.** $40.00 **G.** $30.00 **F.** $20.00

WALKING PLAY PAL
1962 - 23 in.

1962. 23 in. (58.5 cm). Plastic body, jointed hips, shoulders, and neck. Vinyl head; blue sleep eyes, lashes, painted lower lashes; rooted light brown curls over moulded hair; open mouth nurser. Mark: on head, REGAL TOY/CANADA; on body, REGAL (in script)/CANADA.

Ref.No.: D of C, CD17, p. 228

Mint $45.00 **Ex.** $40.00 **G.** $25.00 **F.** $20.00

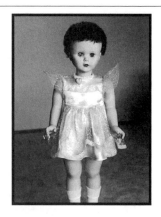

WALKING PLAY PAL
ca.1962 - 30 in.

ca.1962. 30 in. (76 cm). Five-piece plastic body. Vinyl head; blue sleep eyes, lashes, painted lower lashes; rooted curly brown hair; closed mouth. Unmarked. Original white dress.

Ref.No.: ES61

Mint $45.00 **Ex.** $35.00 **G.** $30.00 **F.** $25.00

WALKING PLAY PAL
1962 - 35 in.

1962. 35 in. (89 cm). Plastic body, jointed hips, shoulders and neck. Vinyl head; blue sleep eyes, lashes; rooted saran honey blond curls; closed mouth. Mark: on body, REGAL TOY/CANADA. Original red cotton dress.

Ref.No.: D of C, BZ20, p. 311

Mint $115.00 **Ex.** $75.00 **G.** $40.00 **F.** $30.00

RONNIE

1962. 13 in. (33 cm). Plastic body, jointed hips, shoulders and neck. Vinyl head; blue sleep eyes, lashes; deeply moulded reddish blond hair; closed mouth. Mark: REGAL. Redressed. Originally wore dark short pants, white shirt and a bow-tie, white socks and shoes.

Ref.No.: 2N31

Mint $55.00 **Ex.** $45.00 **G.** $35.00 **F.** $25.00

Note: Made only for one year.

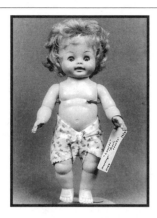

TEAR DROPS
1962 - 12 in.

1962. 12 in. (30.5 cm). Plastic body, jointed hips, shoulders and neck. Vinyl head; blue sleep eyes, lashes, painted lower lashes; rooted saran curls; open mouth nurser. Mark: on head, REGAL TOY/MADE IN CANADA; on body, REGAL/CANADA.

Ref.No.: D of C, CG29, p. 229

Mint $35.00 **Ex.** $30.00 **G.** $20.00 **F.** $10.00

BOUDOIR DOLL
1962 - 15 in.

1962. 15 in. (38 cm). Plastic body and legs, vinyl arms, jointed hips, shoulders and neck. Vinyl head; blue sleep eyes, lashes, painted lower lashes; rooted long grey hair with bangs; closed mouth. Mark: on head, a crown over REGAL TOY/MADE IN CANADA. Original lace-trimmed gown.

Ref.No.: D of C, AP27, p. 229

Mint $35.00 **Ex.** $25.00 **G.** $20.00 **F.** $10.00

PENNY

1962. 17 in. (43 cm). Plastic body, jointed hips, shoulders and neck. Vinyl head; blue sleep eyes, lashes, painted lower lashes; rooted blond curly saran hair; closed mouth. Mark: on head, REGAL TOY. Original blue cotton print dress.

Ref.No.: D of C, CI11, p. 229

Mint $35.00 **Ex.** $25.00 **G.** $20.00 **F** $10.00

GAIL
1962 - 13 in.

1962. 13 in. (33 cm). Plastic body, jointed hips, shoulders and neck. Vinyl head; blue plastic sleep eyes, lashes; rooted dark brown saran curly hair; closed mouth. Mark: on head, a crown over REGAL TOY/MADE IN CANADA; on body, REGAL/ CANADA. Original lace-trimmed dress.

Ref.No.: D of C, CG8, p. 228

Mint $35.00 **Ex.** $30.00 **G.** $20.00 **F.** $10.00

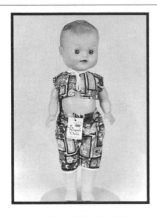

SUN-SUIT BABY

1962. 16 in. (41 cm). Plastic body, jointed hips, shoulders and neck. Vinyl head; inset plastic eyes; moulded red hair; open-mouth nurser. Mark: on head, 14; on back, REGAL/CANADA. Original sun-suit and hang tag.

Ref.No.: 2B22

Mint $30.00 **Ex.** $25.00 **G.** $15.00 **F.** $10.00

SANTA LAMP

ca.1962. 12 in. (30.5 cm). Moulded painted plastic one-piece body. Cord and plug in back so it can be used as a light. Mark: REGAL TOY (under crown)/TORONTO/CANADA.

Ref.No.: GK12

Mint $25.00 **Ex.** $20.00 **G.** $15.00 **F.** $10.00

GAIL
1962 - 16 in.

1962. 16 in. (40.5 cm). Plastic body, jointed hips, shoulders and neck. Vinyl head; blue sleep eyes, lashes, painted lower lashes; rooted blond hair with bangs; closed mouth. Mark: on head, REGAL TOY/MADE IN CANADA.

Ref.No.: D of C, CS7, p. 230

Mint $35.00 **Ex.** $25.00 **G.** $15.00 **F.** $10.00

NURSE
1963 - 14 in.

1963. 14 in. (35.5 cm). Plastic body, jointed hips, shoulders and neck. Vinyl head; blue sleep eyes, lashes; rooted blond hair; closed mouth. Mark: on head, REGAL TOY under crown MADE IN CANADA. Original nurse uniform, cap, socks and shoes.

Ref.No.: PGB18

Mint $40.00 **Ex.** $35.00 **G.** $20.00 **F.** $15.00

BABY DEAR
ca.1963 - 20 in.

ca.1963. 20 in. (51 cm). Plastic bent-limb baby body, jointed hips, shoulders and neck. Vinyl head; blue sleep eyes, lashes; rooted dark brown hair; open mouth nurser. Mark: on head, a crown over REGAL TOY/MADE IN CANADA; same on body. Originally wore a snowsuit.

Ref.No.: D of C, CE7, p. 230

Mint $50.00 **Ex.** $35.00 **G.** $25.00 **F.** $20.00

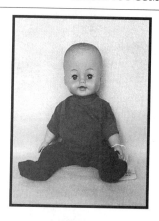

REGAL
ca.1963 - 11 in.

ca.1963. 11 in. (28 cm). Five-piece, plastic body. Vinyl head; brown sleep eyes, moulded lashes, three painted lashes at the side of each eye; open mouth nurser. Mark: on head, REGAL TOY/MADE IN CANADA. Sold in a variety of costumes.

Ref.No.: SW12

Mint $20.00 **Ex.** $15.00 **G.** $10.00 **F.** $8.00

KIMMIE
Rooted Curly Red Hair

ca.1963. 10 in. (25 cm). Vinyl body, jointed hips, shoulders and neck. Vinyl head; side-glancing painted green eyes; rooted curly red hair; watermelon mouth; freckles. Unmarked. Original hang tag. Original jump-suit.

Ref.No.: 2B25

Mint $40.00 **Ex.** $30.00 **G.** $20.00 **F.** $15.00

Note: Kimmies with red hair are more in demand.

KIMMIE
1963 - 12 in.

1963. 12 in. (30.5 cm). Chubby plastic body, jointed hips, shoulders and neck. Vinyl head; black three-dimensional side-glancing eyes; rooted blond hair; watermelon mouth. Mark: on head, and body, REGAL/MADE IN CANADA. Redressed similar to original.

Ref.No.: 2Z14

Mint $45.00 **Ex.** $30.00 **G.** $25.00 **F.** $20.00

Note: The 12-inch Kimmie was usually made in brown plastic and dressed as an Indian or an Inuit.

REGAL
ca.1963 - 21 in.

ca.1963. 21 in. (53.5 cm). Plastic body, jointed hips, shoulders and neck. Vinyl head; brown sleep eyes, lashes; rooted brown curls; open-closed mouth. Mark: on body, REGAL/CANADA. Redressed.

Ref.No.: D of C, CJ13, p. 230

Mint $45.00 **Ex.** $30.00 **G.** $20.00 **F.** $15.00

BABY DEAR
1963 - 20 in.

1963. 20 in. (51 cm). Plastic body, vinyl bent-limb arms and legs, jointed hips, shoulders and neck. Vinyl head; blue sleep eyes, lashes, painted lower lashes; rooted brown curls; open-closed mouth. Mark: on head, REGAL TOY/MADE IN CANADA. Replaced clothing similar to the original.

Ref.No.: D of C, CO1A, p. 231

Mint: $50.00 **Ex.** $40.00 **G.** $25.00 **F.** $20.00

SUSAN SCHOOLGIRL

1963. 22 in. (56 cm). Plastic body, jointed hips, shoulders and neck. Vinyl head; sleep eyes, lashes; rooted curly blond hair; open-closed mouth showing moulded painted teeth. Mark: on head, 15P/EEGEE/[COPYRIGHT]; on body, REGAL/CANADA. Original white blouse and attached navy jumper with Regal name, replaced socks and shoes.

Ref.No.: 2GK23

Mint $90.00 **Ex.** $75.00 **G.** $45.00 **F.** $30.00

KIMMIE
Rooted Black Hair

1963. 10 in. (25 cm). Plastic body, jointed hips, shoulders and neck. Vinyl head; side-glancing painted black eyes; painted lashes; rooted black hair; closed mouth. Mark: on head, REGAL/MADE IN CANADA; on back, REGAL/CANADA. Original hang tag. Original jump-suit.

Mint $40.00 **Ex.** $30.00 **G.** $20.00 **F.** $15.00

KIMMIE
Rooted Curley Red Hair

1964. 11 in. (27 cm). Plastic body and legs. Vinyl head and arms; jointed hips, shoulders and neck; side-glancing painted green eyes; painted lashes; rooted curly red hair; watermelon mouth; freckles. Mark: on head, REGAL/MADE IN CANADA; on back, REGAL/Canada. Original dress.

Ref.No.: 2B25

Mint **$40.00** **Ex.** **$30.00** **G.** **$20.00** **F.** **$15.00**

Note: Kimmies with red hair are more in demand.

KIMMIE ESKIMO

1964. 10 in. (25.5 cm). Brown plastic body, jointed hips, shoulders and neck. Vinyl head; painted black side-glancing eyes, painted upper lashes; rooted straight black hair; closed watermelon mouth. Mark: on head, REGAL/MADE IN CANADA. Original clothing.

Ref.No.: D of C, CW23A, p. 231

Mint **$40.00** **Ex.** **$30.00** **G.** **$20.00** **F.** **$15.00**

BABY KIMMIE ESKIMO

1964. 9 in. (23 cm). Vinyl bent-limb baby body, jointed hips, shoulders and neck. Vinyl head; black painted side-glancing eyes, three painted upper lashes; rooted black straight hair; closed mouth. Mark: on head, REGAL TOY/MADE IN CANADA; on body, REGAL TOY/MADE IN CANADA/9-G. Original Inuit parka, hood and leggings.

Ref.No.: 2N7

Mint **$35.00** **Ex.** **$30.00** **G.** **$20.00** **F.** **$15.00**

BABY KIMMIE
Blue Eyes

1964. 9 in. (23 cm). Vinyl body, jointed hips, shoulders and neck. Vinyl head; blue side-glancing eyes; rooted red-gold curls; smiling closed mouth. Mark: on head, REGAL TOY/MADE IN CANADA. Redressed.

Ref.No.: 2Q36

Mint **$30.00** **Ex.** **$25.00** **G.** **$20.00** **F.** **$15.00**

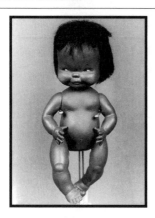

BABY KIMMIE
Black Painted Eyes

1964. 9 in. (23 cm). Vinyl bent-limb baby body, jointed hips, shoulders and neck. Vinyl head; black painted side-glancing eyes, three painted upper lashes; rooted black straight hair; closed mouth. Mark: on head, REGAL TOY/MADE IN CANADA; on body, REGAL TOY/MADE IN CANADA/9-G. Originally wore Inuit parka, hood and leggings.

Ref.No.: D of C, CW20, p. 231

Mint $35.00 **Ex.** $30.00 **G.** $20.00 **F.** $15.00

KIMMIE
ca.1964 - 10 in.

ca.1964. 10 in. (25.5 cm). Vinyl body, jointed hips, shoulders and neck. Vinyl head; green side-glancing eyes; freckles; rooted red hair; watermelon mouth. Mark: on head, REGAL/MADE IN CANADA; on body, REGAL/CANADA. Original turquoise cotton pleated skirt with printed bodice dress, shoes and socks.

Ref.No.: 2F2

Mint $40.00 **Ex.** $30.00 **G.** $20.00 **F.** $15.00

KIMMIE (Beatle)
Marked

1964. 10 in. (25.5 cm). Vinyl body, jointed hips, shoulders and neck. Vinyl head; side-glancing eyes; freckles; rooted brown straight hair; watermelon mouth. Mark: on head, REGAL/MADE IN CANADA. Original plaid jacket and black pants, tie.

Ref.No.: 2J9

Mint $50.00 **Ex.** $40.00 **G.** $20.00 **F.** $15.00

KIMMIE (Beatle)
Unmarked

1964. 10 in. (25.5 cm). Vinyl body, jointed hips, shoulders and neck. Vinyl head; side-glancing green eyes; freckles; rooted dark brown straight hair; watermelon mouth. Unmarked. Original red cotton pants, white shirt with red trim.

Ref.No.: 2F0

Mint $45.00 **Ex.** $35.00 **G.** $20.00 **F.** $15.00

CANDY
1964 - 24 in.

1964. 24 in. (61 cm). Plastic body, jointed hips, shoulders and neck. Vinyl head; brown sleep eyes, lashes, painted lower lashes; rooted long blond nylon hair with bangs; closed mouth. Mark: on head, REGAL TOY/MADE IN CANADA. Original clothing.

Ref.No.: D of C, BM1, p. 232

Mint $65.00 **Ex.** $45.00 **G.** $25.00 **F.** $20.00

CATHY
1964 - 15 in.

1964. 15 in. (38 cm). Five-piece plastic body. Vinyl head; blue sleep eyes, lashes, painted lower lashes; rooted dark blond hair; closed mouth. Mark: on head, REGAL / CANADA. Redressed. Sold in various costumes.

Ref.No.: SW14

Mint $35.00 **Ex.** $25.00 **G.** $20.00 **F.** $15.00

BABY ELLEN
ca.1964 - 21 in.

ca.1964. 21 in. (53 cm). Plastic body, jointed hips, shoulders and neck. Vinyl head; blue sleep eyes, lashes, painted lowers; rooted honey blond curly hair; open-mouth nurser. Mark: on back, REGAL. Original dress with printed taffeta skirt and blue suedine bodice, replaced socks and shoes.

Ref.No.: 2B8

Mint $55.00 **Ex.** $40.00 **G.** $25.00 **F.** $20.00

TEENY TINY TEARS
1964 - 11 in.

1964. 11 in. (28 cm). Vinyl body, jointed hips, shoulders and neck. Vinyl head; blue sleep eyes, lashes, three side lashes painted; rooted brown hair; open-mouth nurser. Mark: on head, REGAL TOY/CANADA. Original pink gingham dress.

Ref.No.: 2E17

Mint $55.00 **Ex.** $45.00 **G.** $25.00 **F.** $20.00

Note: There was also a 9-inch Teeny Weenie Tiny Tears. This doll was advertised as cries real tears, drinks, wets and blows bubbles.

SCOTTISH LASSIE
ca.1964 - 13 in.

ca.1964. 13 in. (33 cm). Plastic body, jointed hips, shoulders and neck. Vinyl head; blue sleep eyes, lashes; rooted blond hair; closed mouth. Mark: on head, a crown. Original tartan skirt, white blouse and velvet jacket, replaced shoes.

Ref.No.: 2N29

Mint $40.00 **Ex.** $35.00 **G.** $25.00 **F.** $15.00

KIMMIE
1965 - 12 in.

1965. 12 in. (30.5 cm). Brown plastic body and legs, vinyl arms, jointed hips, shoulders and neck. Brown vinyl head; moulded black three-dimensional side-glancing eyes; rooted black hair; closed watermelon mouth. Mark: on head, REGAL/MADE IN CANADA. Original leather and fur parka, hood and leggings.

Ref.No.: D of C, CH11, p. 232

Mint $50.00 **Ex.** $40.00 **G.** $30.00 **F.** $20.00

LIZA
1965 - 21 in.

1965. 21 in. (53 cm). Brown plastic body, jointed hips, shoulders and neck. Vinyl head; brown sleep eyes, lashes; rooted curly black hair; open-mouth nurser. Mark: on head, S.T. 17ME; on back, REGAL/CANADA. Original red and white dress.

Ref.No.: 2B23

Mint $65.00 **Ex.** $55.00 **G.** $40.00 **F.** $30.00

TEENY TINY TEARS
1965 - 12 in.

1965. 12 in. (30.5 cm). Plastic body. Drinks, wets and cries tears. Vinyl head; open mouth. Originally came with pacifier in mouth, shampoo, comb and layette. Mark: on head, REGAL CANADA. Redressed.

Mint $60.00 **Ex.** $50.00 **G.** $35.00 **F.** $30.00

SNUGGLES
ca.1965 - 16 in.

ca.1965. 16 in. (40.5 cm). Cloth body and legs with sponge stuffing. Vinyl half arms and head; brown sleep eyes, lashes; rooted brown hair; watermelon mouth. Original orange overalls, orange and cream print blouse.

Ref.No.: GK13

Mint $40.00 **Ex.** $35.00 **G.** $25.00 **F.** $15.00

SNUGGLES
ca.1966 - 18 in.

ca.1966. 18 in. (45.5 cm). Moulded foam plastic on a wire frame, vinyl forearms. Vinyl swivel head; dark brown sleep eyes, three outer lashes; rooted dark brown hair; closed watermelon mouth. Mark: on head, REGAL TOY/MADE IN CANADA.

Ref.No.: D of C, CH7, p. 232

Mint $45.00 **Ex.** $35.00 **G.** $25.00 **F.** $15.00

Note: Very few of these dolls were made, they are hard to find.

POPPI
1966 - 11 in.

1966. 11 in. (28 cm). Plastic body, jointed hips, shoulders and neck. Vinyl head; stencilled eyes with dark eye shadow; rooted dark blond hair; closed mouth. Mark: on head, REGAL/CANADA. Original dress and coat. Matching hat is missing.

Ref.No.: 2R16

Mint $35.00 **Ex.** $30.00 **G.** $20.00 **F.** $15.00

KIMMIE
1966 - 10 in.

1966. 10 in. (25.5 cm). Vinyl body, jointed hips, shoulders and neck. Vinyl head; side-glancing green eyes, freckles; rooted brown hair; watermelon mouth. Mark: on head, REGAL/MADE IN CANADA; on back, REGAL/CANADA. Original Maple Leaf Tartan jumper and matching beret, socks and shoes. Dolls were dressed in Canada's tartan to celebrate the Centennial in 1967.

Ref.No.: 2F3

Mint $40.00 **Ex.** $30.00 **G.** $20.00 **F.** $15.00

WALKING PLAY PAL
1966 - 24 in.

1966. 24 in. (61 cm). Plastic body, jointed hips, shoulders and neck. Vinyl head; blue sleep eyes, lashes; rooted blond curls in original set; closed mouth. Mark: on head, REGAL TOY/MADE IN/CANADA; on back, REGAL/CANADA. Original dress with polka dot skirt, matching hairbow, socks and shoes.

Ref.No.: 2B7

Mint $45.00   **Ex.** $40.00   **G.** $30.00   **F.** $20.00

TRESSY GROW HAIR
With Make-up

1967. 12 in. (30.5 cm). Plastic teen body and legs, vinyl arms, jointed hips, shoulders and neck. Vinyl head; blue painted side-glancing eyes; rooted brown saran hair with "growing" section out of the top of her head with a key supplied to wind it back in; closed mouth. Mark: on head, REGAL. Original dress.

Ref.No.: D of C, BZ30, p. 233.

Mint $45.00   **Ex.** $30.00   **G.** $20.00   **F.** $15.00

Note: Tressy was originally made in 1964 and was produced for several years.

TRESSY GROW HAIR
Without Make-up

1967. 12 in. (30.5 cm). Plastic teen body and legs, vinyl arms, jointed hips, shoulders and neck. Vinyl head. This is the pale-faced version, meant for makeup application, no eyelashes. Blue painted side-glancing eyes; rooted brown hair with "growing" section out of the top of her head, with a key supplied to wind it back in. Mouth closed. Mark: on head, REGAL TOY/MADE IN CANADA. Original dress. Clothes could be bought separately.

Ref.No.: 2P10

Mint $50.00   **Ex.** $35.00   **G.** $25.00   **F.** $15.00

POPPI
1967 - 12 in.

1967. 12 in. (30.5 cm). Plastic body, jointed hips, shoulders and neck. Vinyl head; brown stencilled eyes with heavy eyeshadow; rooted curly blond hair; closed mouth. Mark: on head, REGAL/CANADA. Original Maple Leaf Tartan jumper and matching beret.

Ref.No.: DF11

Mint $45.00   **Ex.** $35.00   **G.** $20.00   **F.** $15.00

BABY JILL
1967 - 18 in.

1967. 18 in. (45.5 cm). Five-piece plastic body. Vinyl head; blue sleep eyes; rooted blond hair; open mouth nurser. Mark: on head, REGAL MADE IN CANADA; on body, REGAL CANADA.

Ref.No.: ES26

Mint $40.00 **Ex.** $30.00 **G.** $20.00 **F.** $15.00

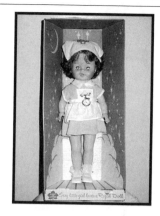

CAROL NURSE

1967. 14 in. (35.5 cm). Five-piece plastic body. Blue eyes; brown hair. Original blue uniform with white apron and head scarf. Original watch.

Ref.No.: ES24

Mint $40.00 **Ex.** $30.00 **G.** $25.00 **F.** $20.00

LIZA
1967 - 12 in.

1967. 12 in. (30.5 cm). Brown plastic body, jointed hips, shoulders and neck. Vinyl head; brown stencilled eyes; rooted black hair in two pony tails; closed mouth. Mark: on head, REGAL/CANADA; on body, REGAL/CANADA. Original pink print dress. Originally wore white socks and shoes.

Ref.No.: GK5

Mint $45.00 **Ex.** $35.00 **G.** $25.00 **F.** $15.00

CANDY WALKER

1967. 25 in. (63.5 cm). Plastic body, jointed hips, shoulders and neck. Vinyl head; blue sleep eyes, lashes, painted lower lashes; rooted blond nylon hair; closed mouth. Mark: REGAL TOY/MADE IN CANADA.

Ref.No.: D of C, CI7, p. 233

Mint $65.00 **Ex** $45.00 **G.** $25.00 **F.** $20.00

CANDY
1967 - 14 in.

1967. 14 in. (36 cm). Plastic body, jointed hips, shoulders and neck. Vinyl head; blue sleep eyes, plastic lashes; rooted blond curls; closed mouth. Mark: on head, REGAL TOY/MADE IN CANADA; on back REGAL/CANADA. Original Maple Leaf Tartan jumper and matching beret, red socks, black shoes.

Ref.No.: 2C5

Mint   **$50.00**   **Ex.**   **$40.00**   **G.**   **$20.00**   **F.**   **$15.00**

SAUCY SUE

1967. 13 in. (33 cm). Five-piece plastic body. Vinyl head; blue sleep eyes, lashes, painted lowers; rooted dark blond hair; closed mouth. Originally wore a cotton dress, socks and shoes.

Ref.No.: SW24

Mint   **$25.00**   **Ex.**   **$20.00**   **G.**   **$15.00**   **F.**   **$10.00**

BABY DEAR
1967 - 13 in.

1967. 13 in. (33 cm). Plastic body, jointed hips, shoulders and neck. Vinyl head; blue sleep eyes, lashes; rooted red-gold hair; open-mouth nurser. Original Maple Leaf Tartan skirt and matching beret, white blouse, red socks and black shoes.

Ref.No.: 2C18

Mint   **$45.00**   **Ex.**   **$35.00**   **G.**   **$20.00**   **F.**   **$15.00**

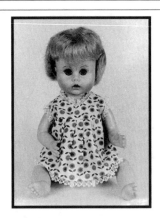

TINY TEARS
Rock-a-bye Eyes

1967. 12 in. (30.5 cm). Vinyl body, jointed hips, shoulders and neck. Vinyl head; blue sleep eyes, lashes; rooted blond curls; open-mouth nurser. Mark: on head, REGAL TOY/CANADA. The doll cries tears and has Rock-a-Bye blue sleep eyes, Unmarked.. Redressed in similar style to the original.

Ref.No.: 2B1

Mint   **$50.00**   **Ex.**   **$40.00**   **G.**   **$30.00**   **F.**   **$20.00**

INDIAN PRINCESS
ca.1968 - 13 in.

ca.1968. 13 in. (33 cm). Brown plastic body, jointed hips, shoulders and neck. Vinyl head; brown plastic sleep eyes, lashes, four upper lashes; rooted black long straight hair; closed mouth. Mark: on head, C REGAL TOY/MADE IN CANADA. Original natural fur clothing.

Ref.No.: D of C, CJ27, p. 233

Mint **$50.00** **Ex.** **$40.00** **G.** **$20.00** **F.** **$10.00**

Note: Common doll but very well-dressed. Probably dressed by natives, not by Regal.

REGAL
ca.1968 - 23 in.

ca.1968. 23 in. (58.5 cm). Cloth body, vinyl arms and legs. Vinyl head; blue sleep eyes, lashes and three painted outer lashes; rooted blond hair; closed smiling mouth. Mark: on head, REGAL TOY LTD./MADE IN CANADA/19C68.

Ref.No.: D of C, CG3, p. 234

Mint **$55.00** **Ex.** **$45.00** **G.** **$35.00** **F.** **$25.00**

KIMMIE CLOWN
With Hat

1968. 10 in. (25.5 cm). Vinyl body, jointed hips, shoulders and neck. Vinyl head with attached red vinyl hat; white painted clown face; painted black eyes; rooted orange hair; watermelon mouth. Mark: on head, REGAL/MADE IN CANADA; on body, REGAL/CANADA. Original red and white polka dot cotton costume with yellow collar and pompoms, shoes missing.

Ref.No.: DH4

Mint **$45.00** **Ex.** **$35.00** **G.** **$25.00** **F.** **$20.00**

KIMMIE CLOWN
Without Hat

1968. 10 in. (25.5 cm). Vinyl body, jointed hips, shoulders and neck. Vinyl head; white painted clown face; painted eyes; rooted orange curly hair; watermelon mouth. Mark: on head, REGAL/MADE IN CANADA; on body, REGAL/CANADA. Original cotton clown suit in red and blue, hat and shoes missing.

Ref.No.: GK14

Mint **$40.00** **Ex.** **$25.00** **G.** **$20.00** **F.** **$15.00**

BABY DEAR
ca.1968 - 18 in.

ca.1968. 18 in. (45.5 cm). Plastic body, jointed hips, shoulders and neck. Vinyl head; brown sleep eyes, lashes; rooted honey blond hair; open-mouth nurser. Mark: on body, REGAL/CANADA. Original pink cotton print dress with attached organdy apron. Socks and shoes missing.

Ref.No.: 2K33

Mint **$45.00** **Ex.** **$35.00** **G.** **$20.00** **F.** **$15.00**

BABY MINE
1968 - 20 in.

1968. 20 in. (51 cm). Cloth body, vinyl three-quarter arms and legs. Vinyl head; blue stencilled eyes and upper lashes; blond rooted hair; open-closed mouth. Mark: on head, REGAL TOY/MADE IN CANADA. Original dress and panties. Hairbow missing.

Ref.No.: D of C, CF20, p. 235

Mint **$45.00** **Ex.** **$35.00** **G.** **$25.00** **F.** **$20.00**

Note: Advertised in Eaton's 1968 catalogue.

POPPI
1968 - 12 in.

1968. 12 in. (30.5 cm). Plastic body, jointed hips, shoulders and neck. Vinyl head; brown stencilled eyes, dark eye shadow; rooted honey blond hair in braids; closed mouth. Mark on head: REGAL/CANADA. Redressed.

Ref.No.: 2I11

Mint **$30.00** **Ex.** **$25.00** **G.** **$20.00** **F.** **$15.00**

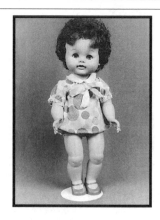

DRINK AND WET BABY DEAR

1969. 18 in. (45.5 cm). Plastic body and legs, vinyl arms, jointed hips, shoulders and neck. Vinyl head; blue sleep eyes, three upper lashes; rooted brown curly hair; open mouth nurser. Mark: on body, REGAL/CANADA. Original cotton dress and panties.

Ref.No.: D of C, AN35, p. 234

Mint **$30.00** **Ex.** **$25.00** **G.** **$20.00** **F.** **$15.00**

GAIL TODDLER

1969. 12 in. (30.5 cm). Plastic body, jointed hips, shoulders and neck. Vinyl head; blue sleep eyes, moulded lashes; rooted blond hair; closed mouth. Mark: on head, REGAL TOY LTD./MADE IN CANADA/129T; on body, REGAL/CANADA. Doll has been redressed in a copy of the original green and white polka dot dress, original shoes and socks.

Ref.No.: DF9

Mint $35.00 **Ex.** $30.00 **G.** $25.00 **F.** $15.00

DRINK AND WET BABY
1969 - 14 in.

1969. 14 in. (35.5 cm). Plastic body, jointed hips, shoulders and neck. Vinyl head; blue inset eyes; brown moulded hair; open-mouth nurser. Mark: on head, REGAL; on body, REGAL/CANADA. Original green cotton print sunsuit, plastic bathtub, soap, bottle and accessories.

Ref.No.: DH2

Mint $30.00 **Ex.** $20.00 **G.** $15.00 **F.** $10.00

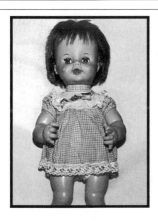

BABY DEAR
ca.1969 - 15 in.

ca.1969. 15 in. (38 cm). Five-piece plastic body. Vinyl head; brown sleep eyes, lashes; rooted red hair. Redressed similar to original, with blue calico dress with lace trim.

Ref.No.: DR5

Mint $35.00 **Ex.** $25.00 **G.** $20.00 **F.** $15.00

RENEE BOUDOIR
1969 - 18 in.

1969. 18 in. (45.5 cm). Five-piece plastic body. Vinyl head; sleep eyes; rooted blond hair; closed mouth.

Ref.No.: ES47

Mint $35.00 **Ex.** $25.00 **G.** $20.00 **F.** $15.00

CAROL
1969 - 15 in

1969. 15 in. (38 cm). Plastic body, jointed hips, shoulders and neck. Vinyl head; blue sleep eyes, lashes; rooted blond nylon hair; open-closed mouth. Mark: on head, REGAL TOY LTD./MADE IN CANADA. Original pale green dress with lace trim. Originally had a pendant on a chain around her neck.

Ref.No.: PGL12

Mint $35.00 **Ex.** $25.00 **G.** $20.00 **F.** $10.00

KIMMIE
1969 - 10 in.

1969. 10 in. (25.5 cm). Plastic body, jointed hips, shoulders and neck. Vinyl head; side-glancing brown eyes; rooted straight black hair; watermelon mouth. Mark: on head, REGAL/MADE IN CANADA. Original fake fur parka with hood, flannelette snow pants.

Ref.No.: 2A22

Mint $40.00 **Ex.** $30.00 **G.** $20.00 **F.** $15.00

KIMMIE
ca.1970 - 10 in.

ca.1970. 10 in. (25.5 cm). Plastic body, jointed hips, shoulders and neck. Vinyl head with freckles; blue stencilled side-glancing eyes, painted upper lashes; rooted short blond curly hair; closed watermelon mouth. Mark: on head, REGAL/MADE IN CANADA. Redressed.

Ref.No.: D of C, CS6, p. 234

Mint $35.00 **Ex.** $30.00 **G.** $20.00 **F.** $15.00

VICKI WALKER
ca.1970 - 18 in.

ca.1970. 18 in. (45.5 cm). Plastic body, jointed hips, shoulders and neck. Vinyl head; blue sleep eyes, lashes, three painted upper lashes on the outside of the eye; rooted long black hair; closed mouth. Mark: on head, REGAL/MADE IN/CANADA; on body, REGAL/CANADA. Originally wore an "A" line dress, pantyhose and shoes.

Ref.No.: D of C, AN31, p. 235

Mint $35.00 **Ex.** $25.00 **G.** $20.00 **F.** $15.00

CATHY
1970 - 18 in.

1970. 18 in. (45.5 cm). Plastic body, jointed hips, shoulders and neck. Vinyl head; blue sleep eyes, lashes, painted; long, rooted auburn hair; closed mouth. Mark: on head, REGAL TOY/MADE IN CANADA; on body, REGAL/CANADA. Originally wore an "A" line dress, pantyhose and shoes.

Mint   **$45.00**   **Ex.**   **$30.00**   **G.**   **$20.00**   **F.**   **$15.00**

WENDY WALKER
ca.1970 - 24 in.

ca.1970. 24 in. (61 cm). Plastic body, jointed hips, shoulders and neck. Vinyl head; brown sleep eyes, lashes; rooted blond nylon hair; closed mouth. Mark: on head, REGAL TOY LTD./MADE IN CANADA/249T. Redressed.

Ref.No.: D of C, BL7, p. 236

Mint   **$35.00**   **Ex.**   **$25.00**   **G.**   **$20.00**   **F.**   **$15.00**

CAROL TODDLER
1970 - 15 in.

1970. 15 in. (38 cm). Plastic body, jointed hips, shoulders and neck. Vinyl head; brown sleep eyes, lashes; rooted auburn hair; closed mouth. Mark: on head, REGAL TOY/MADE IN CANADA; on body, REGAL/CANADA. Original pink knit pant suit and print blouse.

Ref.No.: 2M35

Mint   **$35.00**   **Ex.**   **$25.00**   **G.**   **$20.00**   **F.**   **$15.00**

CAROL TODDLER
ca.1970 - 16 in.

ca.1970. 16 in. (40.5 cm). Five-piece plastic body. Vinyl head; blue sleep eyes; rooted dark brown hair. Mark: on head, 2851/13EVE/REGAL TOY LTD; on body, 159T REGAL CANADA. Originally wore a very short A-line dress and white fishnet hose.

Ref.No.: DR4

Mint   **$35.00**   **Ex.**   **$25.00**   **G.**   **$20.00**   **F.**   **$15.00**

LIZA
1970 - 18 in.

1970. 18 in. (45.5 cm). Brown plastic body; jointed hips, shoulders and neck. Vinyl head; brown sleep eyes, lashes; black rooted hair; closed mouth. Original cream blouse and blue, green and white striped pants; necklace missing. Mark: on head, REGAL TOY - MADE IN CANADA; on body, REGAL - CANADA.

Ref.No.: ES37

Mint $35.00   **Ex.** $30.00   **G.** $20.00   **F.** $15.00

SNUGGLES IN CHRISTENING GOWN

1970. 14 in. (35.5 cm). Cloth body, vinyl arms and legs. Vinyl head; blue sleep eyes, lashes; rooted blond hair; open-closed mouth. Mark: on head, REGAL TOY. Original long gown with lace overskirt, bonnet tied with pink ribbon.

Ref.No.: PRL7

Mint $45.00   **Ex.** $40.00   **G.** $25.00   **F.** $15.00

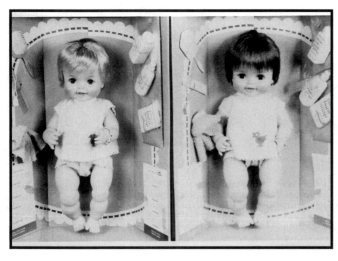

BABY BROTHER
AND BABY SISTER
1970 - 17 in.

1970. 17 in. (43 cm). Plastic bent-limb baby bodies, anatomically correct, jointed hips, shoulders and neck. Vinyl head; blue plastic sleep eyes, lashes, three painted upper lashes; rooted nylon hair; open-closed mouth. Mark: on head, REGAL TOY CO. LTD./MADE IN CANADA. Original short jacket, diaper and accessories. Also came in pyjamas. Boys are more in demand than girls.

Ref.No.: D of C, BN10, p. 235

GIRL:
Mint $45.00   **Ex.** $35.00
G. $25.00   **F.** $20.00

BOY:
Mint $50.00   **Ex.** $40.00
G. $30.00   **F.** $25.00

SOUVENIR DOLL
1970 - 12 in.

1970. 12 in. (30.5 cm). One-piece, fake-fur body. Cloth face. Gold jacket, original ribbon. Label: REGAL TOY LTD. TORONTO, CANADA.

Ref.No.: DR14

Mint   **$10.00**

BABY JILL
1970 - 18 in.

1970. 18 in. (46 cm). Plastic body, jointed hips, shoulders and neck. Vinyl head; sleep eyes, lashes; rooted dark hair; open-mouth nurser. Mark: on head, REGAL TOY/MADE IN CANADA. Redressed. Originally came in five different dresses with matching bonnets and one with dress, coat and matching hat.

Ref.No.: 2G11

Mint   **$40.00**   **Ex.**   **$30.00**   **G.**   **$25.00**   **F.**   **$20.00**

BABY BROTHER AND BABY SISTER
1971 - 12 in.

1971. 12 in. (30.5 cm). Plastic bent-limb baby bodies, anatomically correct, jointed hips, shoulders, and neck. Vinyl heads; blue plastic sleep eyes, lashes, three painted lashes on upper outside of eyes; rooted blond saran hair; open-closed mouth. Mark: on head, REGAL TOY LTD./MADE IN CANADA/129G. Dolls came in a plastic bath tub, dressed in panties and short jacket.

Ref.No.: D of C, BN7, p. 236

GIRL:
Mint $35.00 Ex. $25.00 G. $20.00 F. $15.00
BOY:
Mint $40.00 Ex. $30.00 G. $25.00 F $20.00

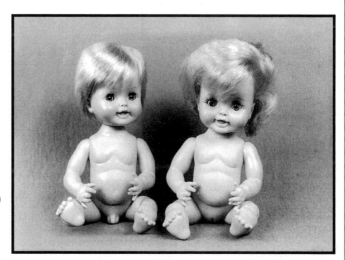

WENDY WALKER
1971 - 24 in.

1971. 24 in. (61 cm). Plastic body, jointed hips, shoulders and neck. Vinyl head; blue sleep eyes, lashes, painted lowers; rooted brown hair; closed mouth. Mark: on head, REGAL TOY LTD./MADE IN CANADA/248T; on body, REGAL/CANADA. Original pink jumper dress with white top, pantyhose, shoes missing.

Reg.No.: 2P25

Mint $35.00 **Ex.** $25.00 **G.** $20.00 **F.** $15.00

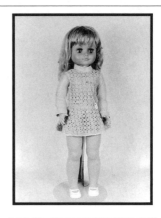

MIMI THE TALKING DOLL

1971. 24 in. (61 cm). Plastic body, jointed hips, shoulders and neck. Talking mechanism requires batteries. Vinyl head; blue sleep eyes, lashes, painted lowers; rooted blond nylon hair; closed mouth. Mark: on head, REGAL TOY LTD./MADE IN CANADA/249T. Blue cotton dress, lace overlay, net sleeves, replaced shoes. Banner "I speak English." Also available speaking French. Came with three nursery rhyme records.

Ref.No.: 2K22

Mint $85.00 **Ex.** $75.00 **G.** $45.00 **F.** $30.00

Note: Mint and Ex. prices are for dolls with working speakers.

CINDY
1971 - 15 in.

1971. 15 in. (38 cm). Five-piece plastic body. Vinyl head; blue eyes looking right; rooted brown hair; came with an extra-long hair piece. Mark: on head, REGAL TOY; on body, REGAL CANADA.

Ref.No.: ES32

Mint $35.00 **Ex.** $30.00 **G.** $20.00 **F.** $15.00

ESKIMO TODDLER

1971. 18 in. (45.5 cm). Plastic body, jointed hips, shoulders and neck. Vinyl head; brown sleep eyes, lashes, painted upper lashes at outside of eyes; rooted black nylon hair; closed mouth. Unmarked.

Ref.No.: D of C, BF26, p. 236

Mint $35.00 **Ex.** $30.00 **G.** $20.00 **F.** $15.00

BABY SOFTINA

1973. 14 in. (35.5 cm). One-piece vinyl body. Vinyl head; blue stencilled eyes and upper lashes; rooted auburn nylon hair; open-closed mouth. Mark: on head, 21/140 SPE/REGAL; on body, 1423 REGAL/12.

Ref.No.: D of C, CG31, p. 237

Mint $20.00   **Ex.** $15.00   **G.** $10.00   **F.** $5.00

BONNIE AND RONNIE RAG DOLLS

1973. 20 in. (51 cm). Cloth body and legs, vinyl hands. Vinyl head with freckles; blue sleep eyes, three painted upper lashes; rooted nylon hair; closed watermelon mouth. Mark: REGAL TOY Co./MADE IN CANADA/30 C (in a circle) O8.

Ref.No.: D of C, BZ9, p. 237

BONNIE
Mint $45.00   **Ex.** $35.00   **G.** $30.00   **F.** $20.00
RONNIE:
Mint $55.00   **Ex.** $45.00   **G.** $35.00   **F.** $25.00

Note: Ronnie is the scarcer doll.

BABY JILL
1973 - 15 in.

1973. 15 in. (38 cm). Plastic body, jointed hips, shoulders and neck. Vinyl head; blue sleep eyes, lashes, three painted upper lashes; rooted blond hair; open-mouth nurser. Mark: on head, REGAL TOY/MADE IN CANADA; on body, REGAL/CANADA. Original green overalls and green checked blouse, matching hat, red shoes. Doll was available in four different outfits.

Ref.No.: DF12

Mint $35.00   **Ex.** $30.00   **G.** $20.00   **F.** $15.00

WENDY WALKER
Mark: REGAL TOY LTD

1973. 30 in. (76 cm). Plastic body, jointed hips, shoulders, and neck. Vinyl head; blue sleep eyes, lashes, painted lower lashes; rooted blond hair; closed mouth. Mark: on head, REGAL TOY LTD./MADE IN CANADA; on body, REGAL/ CANADA. Original dress.

Ref.No.: D of C, CS24A, p. 237

Mint $35.00   **Ex.** $25.00   **G.** $20.00   **F.** $15.00

WENDY WALKER
Mark: REGAL

1973. 30 in. (76 cm). Plastic body, jointed hips, shoulders and neck. Vinyl head; blue sleep eyes, lashes; rooted blond hair; closed mouth. Mark: on back, REGAL. Original leatherette coat with fake fur trim, hat and boots.

Ref.No.: 2I20

Mint $55.00 **Ex.** $45.00 **G.** $20.00 **F.** $15.00

DRINK AND WET BABY
1973 - 14 in.

1973. 14 in. (35.5 cm). Plastic body, jointed hips, shoulders and neck. Vinyl head; stencilled blue eyes, upper lashes; reddish brown moulded hair; open mouth nurser. Mark: on head, REGAL TOY/MADE IN CANADA/141 B P.E. Originally wore a diaper.

Ref.No.: D of C, AM17, p. 238

Mint $15.00 **Ex.** $12.00 **G.** $10.00 **F.** $5.00

BABY ELLEN
1973 - 14 in.

1973. 14 in. (35.5 cm). Plastic body, jointed hips, shoulders and neck. Vinyl head; blue sleep eyes, lashes, painted upper lashes; rooted brown hair; open mouth nurser. Mark: on head, REGAL; on back, REGAL/CANADA.

Mint $25.00 **Ex.** $20.00 **G.** $15.00 **F.** $10.00

RENEE TODDLER

1974. 18 in. (45.5 cm). Plastic body, jointed hips, shoulders and neck. Vinyl head; blue plastic sleep eyes, lashes, painted lower lashes; rooted auburn nylon hair; closed mouth. Mark: on head, REGAL/MADE IN CANADA. Original bridal gown and veil.

Ref.No.: D of C, CS12, p. 238

Mint $25.00 **Ex.** $20.00 **G.** $15.00 **F.** $10.00

GRANNY

ca.1974. 15 in. (38 cm). Plastic body, jointed hips, shoulders, and neck. Vinyl head with glasses painted on her face; stencilled blue eyes and upper lashes; rooted streaked black and white nylon hair; open-closed mouth. Mark: on head, 11/REGAL TOY LTD./MADE IN CANADA/151 P TE. Original gown.

Ref.No.: D of C, BM36, p. 239

Mint   **$35.00**   **Ex.**   **$25.00**   **G.**   **$15.00**   **F.**   **$10.00**

Note: Granny originally had a baby granddaughter and wore a mop cap.

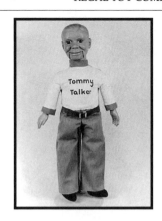

TOMMY TALKER

ca.1974. 26 in. (66 cm). Cloth body and legs, vinyl hands. Hard vinyl head; painted blue eyes; moulded hair; mouth opens when string at back of neck is pulled. Mark: on head, 273V/REGAL TOY CO./CANADA. Original clothing.

Ref.No.: 2A19

Mint   **$65.00**   **Ex.**   **$50.00**   **G.**   **$35.00**   **F.**   **$20.00**

Note: In 1975 "Tommy" wore a suit, shirt and bow tie.

TRIXIE BEAN BAG DOLL

1974. 12 in. (30.5 cm). Body made of green tricot cloth, stuffed with beans, vinyl hands. Vinyl head; black side-glancing eyes; rooted blond fringe of hair under hat; watermelon mouth. Mark: on head, REGAL/MADE IN CANADA.

Ref.No.: 2M22

Mint   **$25.00**   **Ex.**   **$20.00**   **G.**   **$15.00**   **F.**   **$10.00**

VICKI TODDLER
1974 - 18 in.

1974. 18 in. (45.5 cm). Plastic body, jointed hips, shoulders and neck. Vinyl head; brown sleep eyes, lashes; rooted straight blond hair; closed mouth. Mark: on head, REGAL/MADE IN/CANADA; on body, REGAL/CANADA. Original tan vinyl coat with fake fur and red braid trim, tan vinyl boots, hat missing.

Ref.No.: DH16

Mint   **$35.00**   **Ex.**   **$30.00**   **G.**   **$20.00**   **F.**   **$15.00**

POPPI
1975 - 14 in.

1975. 14 in. (35.5 cm). Foam filled cloth body, vinyl hands. Vinyl head; painted eyes; blond rooted hair; closed mouth. Mark: on head, REGAL TOY/CANADA. Original blue gingham dress with white apron and blue hair bow.

Ref.No.: DF7

Mint   **$18.00**   **Ex.**   **$15.00**   **G.**   **$10.00**   **F.**   **$6.00**

BUTTONS
Auburn Hair

ca.1975. 15 in. (38 cm). Plastic body jointed hips, shoulders and neck. Vinyl head; blue stencilled eyes and upper lashes; rooted nylon streaked auburn hair; open-closed mouth. Mark: on head, REGAL TOY LTD./MADE IN CANADA/1817 TPE; on body, REGAL/CANADA.

Ref.No.: D of C, AM28, p. 239

Mint   **$25.00**   **Ex.**   **$20.00**   **G.**   **$15.00**   **F.**   **$10.00**

HUG-A-BYE BABY
1975 - 10 in.

1975. 10 in. (25.5 cm). One-piece vinyl body. Vinyl head; stencilled blue eyes, upper lashes; reddish brown moulded hair; open-closed mouth. Mark: on head, REGAL TOY LTD./MADE IN CANADA/10 B 3 P5.

Ref.No.: D of C, AN10, p. 239

Mint   **$15.00**   **Ex.**   **$12.00**   **G.**   **$10.00**   **F.**   **$5.00**

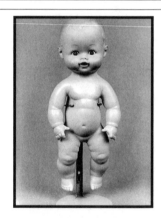

HUG-A-BYE BABY
1975 - 14 in.

1975. 14 in. (35.5 cm). One-piece vinyl body. Vinyl head; stencilled blue eyes, upper lashes; reddish brown moulded hair; open-closed mouth. Mark: on head, REGAL TOY/MADE IN CANADA/141 B P.E.

Ref.No.: D of C, AN15, p. 240

Mint   **$15.00**   **Ex.**   **$12.00**   **G.**   **$10.00**   **F.**   **$5.00**

WENDY WALKER
Rooted Long Blond Nylon Hair

ca.1975. 24 in. (61 cm). Plastic body, jointed hips, shoulders, and neck. Vinyl head; blue sleep eyes, lashes, painted lower lashes; rooted long blond nylon hair; closed mouth. Mark: on head, REGAL TOY LTD./MADE IN CANADA/249T; on body, REGAL/CANADA/PAT. PEND.

Ref.No.: D of C, AO5, p. 240

Mint $30.00   **Ex.** $25.00   **G.** $15.00   **F.** $10.00

INDIAN GIRL
ca.1975 - 18 in.

ca.1975. 18 in. (45.5 cm). Brown plastic body, jointed hips, shoulders and neck. Vinyl head; brown sleep eyes, lashes, three painted upper lashes; rooted black hair; closed mouth. Mark: on head, REGAL TOY/MADE IN CANADA.

Ref.No.: D of C, AO25, p. 240

Mint $30.00   **Ex.** $25.00   **G.** $15.00   **F.** $12.00

HIGHLAND LASS

1975. 16 in. (40.5 cm). Plastic body and legs, vinyl arms, jointed hips, shoulders and neck. Vinyl head; blue stencilled eyes, painted upper lashes; rooted long blond hair; open-closed mouth. Mark: on head, REGAL TOY LTD./MADE IN CANADA/151 TPE.

Ref.No.: D of C, BP3, p. 241

Mint $40.00   **Ex.** $35.00   **G.** $25.00   **F.** $15.00

HUG-A-BYE
1975 - 16 1/2 in.

1975. 16 1/2 in. (42 cm). Body and head are one-piece vinyl. Blue painted side-glancing eyes, three painted upper lashes; light brown moulded hair; watermelon mouth. Mark: on body, 163/REGAL/MADE IN CANADA.

Ref.No.: D of C, CS14, p. 241

Mint $25.00   **Ex.** $20.00   **G.** $15.00   **F.** $10.00

Note: This doll is often mistaken for a Campbell's Soup doll.

WENDY WALKER
Rooted Blond Curls with Bangs

1975. 24 in. (61 cm). Plastic body, jointed hips, shoulders and neck. Vinyl head; plastic sleep eyes, lashes, painted lower lashes; rooted blond curls with bangs; closed mouth. Mark: on head, 249T. Original gown and bonnet.

Ref.No.: D of C, BF13, p. 241

Mint $30.00   **Ex.** $25.00   **G.** $20.00   **F.** $10.00

BUTTONS
Blond Hair

1975. 15 in. (38 cm). Plastic body, jointed hips, shoulders and neck. Vinyl head; blue stencilled eyes, painted upper lashes, upper eyeshadow; rooted long blond hair with bangs; closed mouth. Mark: REGAL. Original clothing.

Ref.No.: D of C, BX14, p. 242

Mint $30.00   **Ex.** $25.00   **G.** $15.00   **F.** $10.00

LUV & KISSES

1976. 16 in. (40.5 cm). One-piece vinyl body. Vinyl head; blue sleep eyes, eyelashes, painted brows; rooted blond curls; open mouth. Makes a kissing sound when the leg is pressed. Mark: REGAL/MADE IN CANADA/166K; on body, 1616/REGAL TOY/MADE IN CANADA. Original pink cotton dress.

Ref.No.: D of C, AN17, p. 242

Mint: $30.00   **Ex.** $25.00   **G.** $15.00   **F.** $10.00

OFFICIAL CANADIAN OLYMPIC HOSTESS

1976. 15 in. (38 cm). Plastic body and legs, vinyl arms, jointed hips, shoulders and neck. Vinyl head; stencilled blue eyes and upper lashes; rooted blond hair with bangs; closed mouth. Mark: on head, REGAL TOY LTD./MADE IN CANADA/151 T PE. Original costume.

Ref.No.: D of C, AZ18, p. 242

15-inch size
Mint $40.00   **Ex.** $30.00   **G.** $20.00   **F.** $15.00
30-inch size
Mint $100.00   **Ex.** $85.00   **G.** $45.00   **F.** $25.00

HUG-A-BYE BABY
1976 - 14 in.

1976. 14 in. (35.5 cm). One-piece vinyl body. Vinyl head; blue stencilled eyes and upper lashes; rooted black curls; open-closed mouth. Mark: on head, REGAL TOY/MADE IN CANADA/141 B P.E.

Ref.No.: D of C, AN20, p. 243

Mint $18.00 **Ex.** $15.00 **G.** $10.00 **F.** $8.00

REGAL
ca.1976 - 18 in.

ca.1976. 18 in. (45.5 cm). Cloth body, vinyl bent-limb arms and legs. Vinyl head; brown sleep eyes, lashes; rooted black hair; closed watermelon mouth. Mark: on head, REGAL/MADE IN CANADA. Leather dress. May have been dressed by natives.

Ref.No.: D of C, CH10, p. 243

Mint $75.00 **Ex.** $60.00 **G.** $45.00 **F.** $25.00

Note: A very unusual doll. Not shown in the catalogue.

DRINK AND WET BABY
1976 - 14 in.

1976. 14 in. (35.5 cm). Plastic body, jointed hips, shoulders and neck. Vinyl head; blue stencilled eyes, painted upper lashes; reddish brown moulded hair; open mouth nurser. Mark: on head, REGAL TOY/MADE IN CANADA/141B P.E. Original costume. Hood missing.

Ref.No.: D of C, CE10, p. 243

Mint $20.00 **Ex.** $15.00 **G.** $10.00 **F.** $5.00

MUSICAL DOLL
ca.1976 - 15 in.

ca.1976. 15 in. (38 cm). Cotton print body, cloth head. Blue painted side-glancing eyes, painted upper lashes; yellow wool hair; painted smiling mouth. Mark: label on side, REGAL TOY LIMITED. Music box inside doll plays Brahms Lullaby.

Ref.No.: D of C, BX20, p. 244

Mint: $25.00 **Ex.** $20.00 **G.** $15.00 **F.** $8.00

Note: Mint price is for doll with working music box.

POPPI
1976 - 17 in.

1976. 17 in. (43 cm). Pink cotton body, vinyl hands, black cotton sewn on shoes. Vinyl head; stencilled blue side-glancing eyes and upper lashes; rooted blond hair; closed pouting mouth. Mark: on head, REGAL TOY/CANADA. Originally wore flowered dress and matching bonnet.

Ref.No.: D of C, CE11, p. 244

Mint $20.00 **Ex.** $15.00 **G.** $10.00 **F.** $5.00

WENDY WALKER
Canadiana Series

1976. 18 in. (45.5 cm). Plastic body, jointed hips, shoulders and neck. Vinyl head; blue stencilled eyes; rooted blond hair; closed mouth. Mark: on head, REGAL/MADE IN CANADA; on body, REGAL/CANADA/PAT. PEND. Original red and white checked gingham dress and matching bonnet.

Ref.No.: 2KA12

Mint $35.00 **Ex.** $25.00 **G.** $20.00 **F.** $10.00

HUG-A-BYE-BABY
1976 - 12 in.

1976. 12 in. (30.5 cm). Vinyl one-piece body and head. Painted side-glancing eyes; moulded blond hair; watermelon mouth. Mark: on back, 124/10/REGAL. Originally wore a print sun-suit and matching hat.

Ref.No.: GK7

Mint $20.00 **Ex.** $15.00 **G.** $12.00 **F.** $8.00

Note: Campbell's Kid look-alike.

RENEE BOUDOIR
1977 - 18 in.

1977. 18 in. (45.5 cm). Plastic body, jointed hips, shoulders and neck. Vinyl head; blue plastic sleep eyes, lashes, painted upper lashes on outside of eye; rooted long blond hair; closed mouth. Mark: on head, REGAL TOY/MADE IN CANADA; on body, REGAL/CANADA/PAT. PEND. Original costume.

Ref.No.: D of C, CG22, p. 244

Mint $35.00 **Ex.** $25.00 **G.** $20.00 **F.** $15.00

SUCK-A-THUMB

1977. 16 in. (40.5 cm). Cloth body and legs, vinyl hands. Vinyl head with freckles; black painted eyes with highlights, painted upper and lower lashes; rooted auburn hair; open-closed mouth shaped to hold her thumb. Mark: on head, 30TS6/REGAL/CANADA.

Ref.No.: D of C, CD2, p. 245

Mint **$25.00** **Ex.** **$20.00** **G.** **$15.00** **F.** **$10.00**

VICKI TODDLER
1977 - 18 in.

1977. 18 in. (46 cm). Plastic body, jointed hips, shoulders and neck. Vinyl head; blue sleep eyes, lashes, painted uppers; rooted straight blond hair; closed mouth. Mark: on head REGAL TOY/MADE IN CANADA; on body, REGAL/CANADA/PAT. PEND. Original one piece costume with white cotton top, pants and headband are blue & green print with green sash, red plastic sandals.

Ref.No.: DH17

Mint **$30.00** **Ex.** **$25.00** **G.** **$20.00** **F.** **$15.00**

VICKI WALKER
ca.1977 - 18 in.

ca.1977. 18 in. (46 cm). Plastic body, jointed hips, shoulders and neck. Vinyl head; light blue sleep eyes, lashes, painted uppers; rooted red hair; closed mouth. Mark: on head, REGAL TOY/MADE IN CANADA; on body, REGAL/CANADA. Original blue denim jumpsuit.

Ref.No.: 2F20

Mint **$30.00** **Ex.** **$25.00** **G.** **$20.00** **F.** **$15.00**

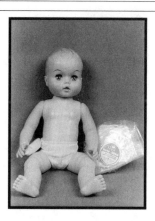

BABY DRINK AND WET

1978. 21 in. and 24 in. (53.5 cm and 61 cm). Plastic body and legs, vinyl arms. Vinyl head; blue plastic sleep eyes, lashes, painted lower lashes; reddish blond moulded hair; open mouth nurser. Mark: on body, REGAL (in script)/CANADA; on hip, REGAL/CANADA.

Ref.No.: D of C, CE15, p. 245

Mint **$25.00** **Ex.** **$20.00** **G.** **$15.00** **F.** **$10.00**

Note: Prices shown are for the 24-inch doll.

CHUBBY WALKER

1978. 20 in. (51 cm). Plastic body, jointed hips, shoulders and neck. Vinyl head; blue sleep eyes, lashes; rooted blond hair over moulded; open-mouth nurser. Mark: on body, REGAL/CANADA. Redressed. Originally wore a patchwork dress with lace trim, socks and a bottle.

Ref.No.: 2F36

Mint $30.00 **Ex.** $25.00 **G.** $20.00 **F.** $15.00

JUDY

ca.1978. 11 1/2 in. (29 cm). Plastic body. Vinyl head; painted blue, side-glancing eyes, brown eye-liner, blue shadow; rooted brown hair; closed mouth. Redressed. In 1978, 18 different outfits were available.

Ref.No.: DR13

Mint $35.00 **Ex.** $25.00 **G.** $20.00 **F.** $10.00

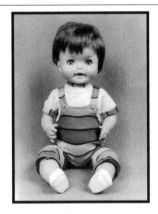

LAFFY CATHY

1979. 17 in. (43 cm). Plastic bent-limb body with on-off switch for battery operated laughing mechanism; jointed hips, shoulders and neck. Vinyl head; blue sleep eyes, lashes, three painted upper lashes on the outside of eyes; rooted straight auburn hair; open-closed mouth. Mark: on head, REGAL TOY CO. LTD./MADE IN CANADA. Original striped overalls and T-shirt.

Ref.No.: D of C, BN24, p. 246

Mint $45.00 **Ex.** $35.00 **G.** $25.00 **F.** $15.00

Note: Mint price includes wand.

MOUSEKETEERS

1979. 8 in. (20 cm). Plastic bodies, jointed hips, shoulders and neck. Vinyl heads; blue painted eyes; blond rooted hair; closed mouths. Mark: on heads, HONG KONG; on box, REGAL/MADE IN CANADA. Original white knit tops with blue denim pants and skirt. Girl has replaced shoes and socks. Mouseketeer hats, one decal missing.

Ref.No.: GK9

Mint $35.00 **Ex.** $30.00 **G.** $20.00 **F.** $10.00

Note: Dolls priced individually.

INDIAN
Canadiana Series

1979. 15 in. (38 cm). Plastic body, jointed hips, shoulders and neck. Vinyl head; brown sleep eyes, lashes; rooted black hair; closed mouth. Mark: on head, REGAL TOY/MADE IN CANADA/1397; on back, REGAL/CANADA. Original leatherette dress with fringe, boots and head band.

Ref.No.: 2F18

Mint $35.00 **Ex.** $25.00 **G.** $15.00 **F.** $10.00

COLOURFUL CANDY

1979. 20 in. (51 cm). Plastic teen body, jointed hips, shoulders and neck. Vinyl head; blue stencilled eyes with black line over eye, painted upper lashes; rooted blond curls; open-closed mouth. Mark: on head, 5/REGAL TOY LTD./MADE IN CANADA/151 TPE. Came with extra clothing, a hairpiece, accessories. Hair could be coloured in different colours by the child.

Ref.No.: D of C, CI31, p. 246

Mint $35.00 **Ex.** $25.00 **G.** $20.00 **F.** $15.00

THE REGAL COLLECTION SERIES
1979 - 20 in.

1979. 20 in. (51 cm). Plastic teen body and legs, vinyl arms, jointed hips, shoulders and neck. Vinyl head; blue sleep eyes, lashes, blue eyeshadow; rooted blond curls; open-closed mouth. Mark: on head, REGAL TOY/CANADA/207 T. All original.

Ref.No.: D of C, CI18, p. 246

Mint $35.00 **Ex.** $25.00 **G.** $20.00 **F.** $15.00

THE REGAL COLLECTION SERIES
1979 -20 in.

1979. 20 in. (51 cm). Plastic teen body, jointed hips, shoulders and neck. Vinyl head; blue sleep eyes, lashes, blue eyeshadow; rooted blond curly hair; open-closed mouth. Mark: REGAL TOY/CANADA/207 F. All original.

Ref.No.: D of C, CI19, p. 247

Mint $35.00 **Ex.** $25.00 **G.** $20.00 **F.** $15.00

THE REGAL COLLECTION SERIES
1979 - 16 in.

1979. 16 in. (40.5 cm). Five-piece plastic body. Vinyl head; blue sleep eyes, lashes; rooted blond hair; closed mouth. Original red velveteen dress with cream lace underskirt. Tiny brooch at neck missing.

Ref.No.: DR12

Mint $30.00 **Ex.** $25.00 **G.** $20.00 **F.** $15.00

WENDY WALKER
1979 - 24 in.

1979. 24 in. (61 cm). Plastic body, jointed hips, shoulders and neck. Vinyl head; blue sleep eyes, lashes, eyeshadow; rooted blond hair; closed mouth. Mark: on head, REGAL TOY CO./MADE IN CANADA/219T. All original.

Ref.No.: D of C, BS36, p. 247

Mint $30.00 **Ex.** $25.00 **G.** $20.00 **F.** $15.00

THE REGAL COLLECTION SERIES
ca.1980 - 20 in.

ca.1980. 20 in. (51 cm). Plastic teen body and legs, vinyl arms, jointed hips, shoulders, and neck. Vinyl head; blue sleep eyes, lashes, blue eyeshadow; rooted blond hair; open-closed mouth. All original.

Ref.No.: D of C, CI17, p. 247

Mint $35.00 **Ex.** $25.00 **G.** $20.00 **F.** $15.00

RUFFLES AND BOWS

1980. 18 in. (45.5 cm). Cloth body, vinyl arms and legs. Vinyl head; blue plastic sleep eyes, lashes; rooted straight blond hair; closed mouth. Mark: on head, REGAL TOY/M '1' C/200 M8. All original.

Ref.No.: D of C, CI16, p. 248

Mint $30.00 **Ex.** $25.00 **G.** $20.00 **F.** $15.00

Note: This doll is from The Regal Collection Series.

DRINK AND WET BABY
ca.1980 - 20 in.

ca.1980. 20 in. (51 cm). Plastic body, jointed hips, shoulders and neck. Vinyl head; brown sleep eyes, lashes; rooted auburn hair; open-closed mouth. Mark: on back, REGAL. Redressed. Originally wore a dress, coat and matching hat, shoes and socks and came with a bottle.

Ref.No.: 2O15

Mint $30.00 **Ex.** $25.00 **G.** $20.00 **F.** $15.00

PRETTY BABY
1980 - 15 in.

1980. 15 in. (38 cm). Cloth body, vinyl arms and legs. Vinyl head; brown sleep eyes, lashes; rooted brown hair; open-closed mouth shaped so thumb can be inserted. Mark: on head, REGAL TOY/CANADA. Original white cotton dress and headscarf with lace trim, panties, shoes and socks.

Ref.No.: 2M14

Mint $40.00 **Ex.** $35.00 **G.** $25.00 **F.** $20.00

TEAR DROPS
1980 - 16 in.

1980. 16 in. (40.5 cm). Plastic body. Vinyl head; blue sleep eyes, lashes; rooted hair; open mouth nurser with pacifier. Redressed.

Ref.No.: DR8

Mint $35.00 **Ex.** $25.00 **G.** $20.00 **F.** $15.00

LACY ELEGANCE
1980 - 20 in.

1980. 20 in. (51 cm). Plastic teen body, jointed hips, shoulders and neck. Vinyl head; brown sleep eyes, lashes, blue eye shadow; rooted short curly brown hair with two long side ringlets; open-closed mouth. Mark: on head, REGAL TOY/CANADA/207T Original white bridal gown trimmed with lace. Hat trimmed with large nylon bow on the back and flowers in the front, high-heeled shoes.

Ref.No.: 2G25

Mint $35.00 **Ex.** $25.00 **G.** $20.00 **F.** $15.00

Note: This doll is from The Regal Collection Series.

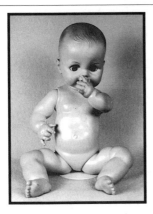

CHUBBY BABY
1980 - 20 in.

1980. 20 in. (51 cm). Plastic body, jointed hips, shoulders and neck. Vinyl head; blue sleep eyes, lashes; moulded light brown hair; open-mouth nurser, shaped to fit thumb. Mark: on head, a crown over REGAL TOY / MADE IN CANADA. Originally wore a sleeveless lace trimmed dress, bonnet and socks and came with a bottle.

Ref.No.: PGC1

Mint $50.00 **Ex.** $45.00 **G.** $35.00 **F.** $25.00

LACY ELEGANCE
1980 - 18 in.

1980. 18 in. (46 cm). Plastic body, jointed hips, shoulders and neck. Vinyl head; blue sleep eyes, lashes; blond rooted long hair; closed mouth. Mark: on head, REGAL TOY / MADE IN CANADA. Original white lace gown with pink ribbon trim and matching bonnet.

Ref.No.: PGL12

Mint $35.00 **Ex.** $25.00 **G.** $20.00 **F.** $15.00

Note: This doll is from The Regal Collections Series.

VELVET PAGEANT

1980. 18 in. (46 cm). Plastic body, jointed hips, shoulders and neck. Vinyl head; blue sleep eyes, lashes; rooted brown long hair; closed mouth. Mark: on head, REGAL / CANADA; on body, REGAL / CANADA. All original.

Ref.No.: 2B5

Mint $35.00 **Ex.** $30.00 **G.** $25.00 **F.** $15.00

Note: This doll is from The Regal Collections Series.

REGAL BABY

1980. 15 in. (38 cm). Plastic body, jointed hips, shoulders and neck. Vinyl head; blue sleep eyes, lashes; rooted auburn curly hair; open-mouth nurser. Mark: on head, REGAL TOY / MADE IN CANADA; on body, REGAL / CANADA.

Ref.No.: 2A23

Mint $30.00 **Ex.** $25.00 **G.** $20.00 **F.** $15.00

ESKIMO
1981 - 19 in.

1981. 19 in. (48 cm). Brown plastic body, jointed hips, shoulders and neck. Brown vinyl head; stencilled brown eyes, painted upper lashes; rooted straight black hair; closed mouth. Mark: on head, 3604/174 PE/REGAL/MADE IN CANADA; on body, REGAL/CANADA/PAT. PEND. Original costume.

Ref.No.: D of C, AO33, p. 248

Mint $30.00   **Ex.** $25.00   **G.** $20.00   **F.** $15.00

KOWEEKA
ca.1981 - 15 in.

ca.1981. 15 in. (38 cm). Plastic body, jointed hips, shoulders and neck. Vinyl head; brown painted eyes; rooted straight black hair; open-closed mouth. Mark: on head, REGAL TOY LTD./MADE IN CANADA/151TPE; on body, REGAL/CANADA. Original tag says "KOWEEKA"/MADE IN CANADA/EXCLUSIVELY FOR HUDSON'S BAY CO. BY REGAL TOY LTD. Original parka.

Ref.No.: 2DF8

Mint $50.00   **Ex.** $45.00   **G.** $30.00   **F.** $20.00

PRETTY BABY
La Collection Regal Series

1981. 18 1/2 in. (47 cm). Cloth body, bent-limb vinyl arms and legs. Vinyl head; blue sleep eyes, lashes; rooted straight blond hair over moulded hair; closed mouth. Mark: on head, G/200 BE/REGAL/CANADA. Original gown and matching bonnet.

Ref.No.: D of C, BU35, p. 249

Mint $30.00   **Ex.** $25.00   **G.** $20.00   **F.** $15.00

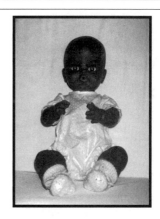

CHUBBY BABY
Black Moulded Hair

1981. 20 in. (50.5 cm). Brown vinyl body, jointed hips, shoulders and neck. Vinyl head; brown sleep eyes, lashes; black moulded hair; open nurser mouth. Mark: on head, REGAL TOY MADE IN CANADA; on body, 209 BD REGAL CANADA.

Ref.No.: ES45

Mint $55.00   **Ex.** $45.00   **G.** $35.00   **F.** $25.00

KIMMIE
ca.1981 - 12 in.

ca.1981. 12 in. (30.5 cm). Brown plastic body, vinyl arms and legs, jointed hips, shoulders and neck. Vinyl head; three dimensional black side-glancing eyes; rooted straight black hair; watermelon mouth. Mark: on body, REGAL (in script)/CANADA. Original fake fur parka.

Ref.No.: D of C, CY10, p. 24

Mint $45.00 **Ex.** $35.00 **G.** $25.00 **F.** $20.00

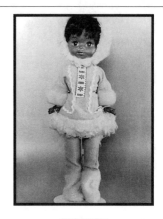

ESKIMO
Canadiana Series

1981. 15 in. (38 cm). Plastic body, jointed hips, shoulders and neck. Vinyl head; brown sleep eyes, lashes; rooted straight black hair; closed mouth. Mark: on head, REGAL TOY LTD./MADE IN CANADA/159T; on body, REGAL/CANADA. Original parka.

Ref.No.: 2DFK13

Mint $30.00 **Ex.** $25.00 **G.** $20.00 **F.** $15.00

WENDY WALKER
1981 - 30 in.

1981. 30 in. (76 cm). Plastic body, jointed hips, shoulders and neck. Vinyl head; blue sleep eyes, lashes; rooted platinum blond hair; closed mouth. Mark: on head, REGAL TOY LTD./MADE IN CANADA; on body, REGAL/CANADA. Original cotton gown.

Ref.No.: 2K18

Mint $30.00 **Ex.** $25.00 **G.** $20.00 **F.** $15.00

MOPPSY

1981. 18 in. (46 cm). Cloth body, vinyl hands. Vinyl head; stencilled blue eyes; rooted yellow yarn hair; closed mouth. Mark: on head, REGAL/CANADA. Original blue print dress and hair band.

Ref.No.: 2N2

Mint $20.00 **Ex.** $15.00 **G.** $12.00 **F.** $8.00

INDIAN PRINCESS
1981 - 15 in.

1981. 15 in. (38 cm). Plastic body, jointed hips, shoulders and neck. Vinyl head; black stencilled eyes; rooted long black hair; open-closed mouth. Unmarked. Original leatherette dress, headband and shoes.
Ref.No.: 2C35

Mint $35.00   **Ex.** $25.00   **G.** $20.00   **F.** $15.00

Note: This doll is from the Canadiana Series.

CHUBBY BABY
Rooted Curly Hair

1981. 20 in. (51 cm). Brown plastic body, jointed hips, shoulders and neck. Brown vinyl head; brown sleep eyes, lashes; rooted black curly hair; open mouth nurser. Mark: on head, 209 BD / REGAL / CANADA. Original pink nylon dress with white lace trim.
Ref.No.: 2H15

Mint $60.00   **Ex.** $50.00   **G.** $40.00   **F.** $30.00

KIMMIE, INDIAN PRINCESS

1981. 12 in. (30.5 cm). Plastic body, jointed hips, shoulders and neck. Vinyl head; three dimensional black eyes; rooted straight black hair; watermelon mouth. Mark: REGAL/CANADA. Original leatherette dress. Headband and shoes missing.
Ref.No.: 2N32

Mint $45.00   **Ex.** $35.00   **G.** $25.00   **F.** $20.00

CHUBBY BABY
1982 - 20 in.

1982. 20 in. (51 cm). Brown plastic body, jointed hips, shoulders and neck. Brown vinyl head; brown sleep eyes, lashes; black rooted curly hair; open mouth nurser. Mark: on head, REGAL/CANADA/200 BDM; on body, 209BD/REGAL.CANADA. Original beige lace dress, hairbow, panties and bottle marked REGAL/CANADA.
Ref.No.: 2DHK

Mint $60.00   **Ex.** $50.00   **G.** $40.00   **F.** $30.00

REGAL
1983 - 15 in.

1983. 15 in. (38 cm). Plastic body, jointed hips shoulders and neck. Vinyl head; painted blue eyes; rooted bright red yarn hair; open-closed mouth. Mark: on head, REGAL TOY LTD./MADE IN CANADA/151TPE; on body, REGAL/CANADA.

Ref.No.: 2I3

Mint $25.00 **Ex.** $20.00 **G.** $15.00 **F.** $10.00

Note: Yarn hair originally tied in twin pony tails.

MUSICAL BABY WIGGLES

1983. 11 in. (28 cm). Cloth body. Vinyl head; blue painted eyes; blond moulded hair; closed mouth. Mark: on head, REGAL CANADA/137 SCPE. Blue cotton cloth body, white print bib, hands and feet, lace trim. Plays Brahms Lullaby and head moves side to side.

Ref.No.: 2M20

Mint $25.00 **Ex.** $20.00 **G.** $15.00 **F.** $10.00

SNOW WHITE
1983 - 15 in.

1983. Disney Classics series. 15 in. (38 cm). Plastic body, jointed hips, shoulders and neck. Vinyl head; blue sleep eyes, lashes; rooted black hair; closed mouth. Original yellow and blue gown with red hood and cape.

Ref.No.: 2B7

Mint $65.00 **Ex.** $55.00 **G.** $40.00 **F.** $20.00

YOUR CUDDLY FRIEND
1983 - 12 in.

1983. 12 in. (30.5 cm). Cloth body. Vinyl head; painted clown eyes; rooted orange yarn hair; closed mouth. Mark: on head, REGAL TOY/CANADA/704 PE; on body, REGAL TOY. Original white cotton sateen body and cap, red felt heart, black cotton feet.

Ref.No.: 2M21

Mint $25.00 **Ex.** $20.00 **G.** $15.00 **F.** $10.00

WENDY WALKER
Rooted Red Yarn Hair

1983. 24 in. (61 cm). Plastic body, jointed hips, shoulders and neck. Vinyl head; blue sleep eyes, lashes; rooted red yarn hair; closed mouth. Mark: on head REGAL TOY LTD./MADE IN CANADA/24GT; on body, REGAL/CANADA/PAT. PEND. Original orange and blue perma-press cotton jump-suit.

Ref.No.: 2KA7

Mint $30.00 **Ex.** $25.00 **G.** $20.00 **F.** $15.00

LUV-KINS AND HER DOLL

1983. 22 in. (56 cm). Five-piece vinyl body. Vinyl head; flange neck; brown sleep eyes, lashes; rooted red curls; open mouth nurser. Mark: on head of small doll, EEGEE CO C#3A; on body, REGAL CANADA. Original white flannelette sleeper with red and green print.

Ref.No.: DR9

Mint $35.00 **Ex.** $25.00 **G.** $20.00 **F.** $15.00

WENDY WALKER
1983 - 24 in.

1983. 24 in. (61 cm). Five-piece plastic body. Vinyl head; brown sleep eyes; light brown hair. Original blue sweat suit with white band and "Regal" in red, red sweat band and shoes.

Ref.No.: ES22

Mint $30.00 **Ex.** $25.00 **G.** $20.00 **F.** $15.00

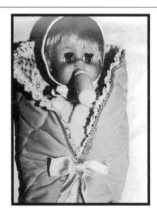

BABY CARE

1983. 10 in. (25.5 cm). Five-piece vinyl body. Vinyl head; blue sleep eyes, lashes; open mouth nurser. Original hooded blue flannel top trimmed with white tape and pompons, white panties, blue quilted wrap lined and trimmed with white lace, white plastic bottle, soap and Johnson Baby Shampoo.

Ref.No.: DR11

Mint $30.00 **Ex.** $25.00 **G.** $20.00 **F.** $15.00

TRIXY RAINBOW

1984. 12 in. (30.5 cm). Cloth body. Vinyl head; blue stencilled eyes; rooted red hair; watermelon mouth. Mark: on head, REGAL/CANADA/704. Original pinafore and hairbow.

Ref.No.: 2I36

Mint $20.00 **Ex.** $15.00 **G.** $10.00 **F.** $5.00

HUG-A-BYE
1984 - 11 in.

1984. 11 in. (28 cm). One-piece vinyl body. Vinyl head; black painted eyes; brown moulded hair; open-mouth nurser. Mark: on head, REGAL TOY LTD./MADE IN CANADA/10B3PE. Original bunting bag and hat.

Ref.No.: 2K16

Mint $15.00 **Ex.** $12.00 **G.** $10.00 **F.** $5.00

YOUR CUDDLY FRIEND
1984 - 12 in.

1984. 12 in. (30.5 cm). Cloth body in red polka-dot, stuffed, removable cotton apron. Vinyl head; blue painted eyes; rooted red yarn hair; closed smiling mouth.

Ref.No.: ES102

Mint $15.00 **Ex.** $12.00 **G.** $10.00 **F.** $5.00

WENDY WALKER
1984 - 32 in.

1984. 32 in. (81 cm). Plastic body, jointed hips, shoulders and neck. Vinyl head; blue sleep eyes, lashes; rooted blond curls; closed mouth. Mark: on head, cCANADA; on body, REGAL/CANADA. Original red print cotton dress and white sandals.

Ref.No.: 2DHK18

Mint $35.00 **Ex.** $30.00 **G.** $25.00 **F.** $20.00

RELIABLE TOY COMPANY LIMITED
1920 -

Reliable is owned by Allied Plastic Products Inc., located at 1655 Dupont Street, Toronto, Ontario. They produce a varied line of plastic toys, including cars, ride-on tractors and trucks, pails and shovels, pull toys and rocking horses. Reliable produced vinyl baby dolls and 24-inch dolls on a very limited scale from 1990 to 1994. The manufacturing of dolls was discontinued in 1995.

The Canadian Toy Manufacturers Association honoured S.F. Samuels, Alex Samuels and Ben Samuels, founders of the Reliable Toy Company, by adding their names to the association's Hall of Fame. Their photographs and achievements were prominently displayed at the 1996 Canadian Toy Show in Toronto.

CHUBBY
1924 - 15 in.

1924. 15 in. (38 cm). Cloth body, composition arms and legs. Composition head; blue tin sleep eyes, lashes; caracul wig; open mouth with two teeth. Unmarked. Original pink cotton rompers.

Ref.No.: PGL14

Mint $235.00 **Ex.** $165.00 **G.** $120.00 **F.** $75.00

Note: Doll exactly as advertised in a Reliable ad of 1924. The parts were undoubtedly imported, assembled and dressed at Reliable.

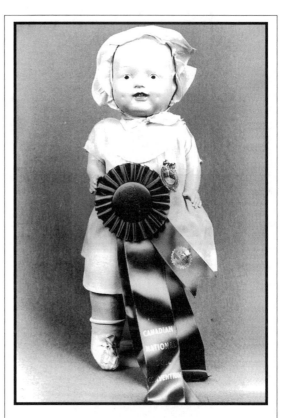

BABY BUBBLES
1929 - 18 in.

1929. 18 in. (45.5 cm). Cloth body and legs, composition arms. Composition head; painted blue eyes, upper lashes and brows; moulded hair painted blond, open-closed mouth showing two painted teeth. Unmarked. All original clothing.

Ref.No.: D of C, AP15, p. 252

Mint $210.00 **Ex.** $160.00 **G.** $95.00 **F.** $50.00

RELIABLE
1929 - 18 in.

ca.1929. 18 in. (45.5 cm). Cloth body and legs, composition arms. Composition shoulderhead; painted blue eyes; mohair wig; open-closed mouth showing painted teeth. Unmarked. Original tag, MADE IN CANADA, A RELIABLE DOLL, A BRITISH EMPIRE PRODUCT, MFD. BY RELIABLE TOY CO. LTD. CANADA. Original cotton print dress and matching bonnet. Missing socks and shoes.

Ref.No.: HX19

Mint **$225.00** **Ex.** **$175.00** **G.** **$110.00** **F.** **$50.00**

BABY TOOTSIE
ca.1929 - 15 in.

ca.1929. 15 in. (38 cm). Cloth body and legs, composition forearms. Composition shoulderhead; painted blue eyes and upper lashes; moulded reddish brown hair; open-closed mouth showing two painted teeth. Unmarked, Original tag, pink dress, bonnet and socks.

Ref.No.: 2B19

Mint **$150.00** **Ex.** **$110.00** **G.** **$65.00** **F.** **$35.00**

HIAWATHA
ca.1929 - 12 in.

ca.1929. 12 in. (30.5 cm). All composition, one-piece head and body, jointed hips and shoulders. Painted brown eyes, black line over eye; black mohair wig in braids; open-closed mouth. Mark: on head, RELIABLE/MADE IN CANADA. Original leather dress, beaded mocassins and headband, necklace.

Ref.No.: D of C, BY13, p. 253

Mint **$160.00** **Ex.** **$100.00** **G.** **$60.00** **F.** **$40.00**

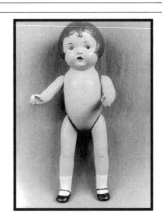

PATSY TYPE

ca.1930. 12 in. (30.5 cm). All composition, one-piece head and body, jointed hips and shoulders. Blue eyes, black line over eye, moulded hair, closed mouth. Mark: on head, RELIABLE/MADE IN/CANADA.

Ref.No.: D of C, BW29, p. 253

Mint **$150.00** **Ex.** **$95.00** **G.** **$60.00** **F.** **$40.00**

Note: The doll illustrated has been repainted.

RELIABLE
ca.1930 - 26 in.

ca.1930. 26 in. (66 cm). Excelsior stuffed cloth body, legs, and upper arms, composition 3/4 arms. Composition shoulderhead; painted blue eyes with black line over eye, painted upper lashes; moulded brown hair; closed mouth. Mark: on shoulderplate, RELIABLE DOLL/MADE IN CANADA. Redressed.

Ref.No.: D of C, CC2, p. 253.

Mint. $150.00 Ex. $105.00 G. $55.00 F. $40.00

RELIABLE
ca.1931 - 19 in.

ca.1931. 19 in. (48 cm). Excelsior stuffed cloth body and legs, composition 3/4 arms, crier. Composition shoulderhead; painted blue eyes; moulded brown hair; closed mouth. Mark: on shoulderplate, A/RELIABLE/DOLL/MADE IN CANADA. Original white cotton dress, panties and bonnet.

Ref.No.: DF16

Mint $130.00 Ex. $75.00 G. $55.00 F. $35.00

RELIABLE
ca.1931 - 17 in.

ca.1931. 17 in. (43 cm). Cloth body, composition arms and straight legs. Composition shoulderhead; blue metal eyes, lashes and painted lower lashes; moulded hair; open mouth showing two teeth. Mark: on shoulderplate, A/RELIABLE/DOLL/MADE IN CANADA. Redressed.

Ref.No.: D of C, CP3, p. 254

Mint. $140.00 Ex. $105.00 G. $75.00 F. $40.00

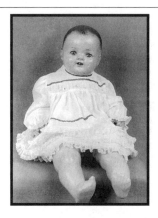

RELIABLE
ca.1932 - 22 in.

ca.1932. 22 in. (56 cm). Cloth body, composition arms and straight legs. Composition head; green tin eyes, lashes, painted lower lashes; moulded brown hair; open mouth, two inset teeth. Mark: on head, A RELIABLE DOLL/MADE IN CANADA. Redressed.

Ref.No.: D of C, CB34A, p. 254

Mint. $225.00 Ex. $195.00 G. $140.00 F. $60.00

RELIABLE
ca.1932 - 25 in.

ca.1932. 25 in. (63.5 cm). Cloth body, composition arms and straight legs. Composition head; blue glassene sleep eyes, lashes, painted lower lashes; brown mohair wig; closed mouth. Mark: on head, RELIABLE/MADE IN CANADA. Redressed.

Ref.No.: D of C, BX2, p. 254

Mint $250.00 **Ex.** $215.00 **G.** $150.00 **F.** $65.00

BABY FONDA

ca.1933. 25 in. (63.5 cm). Cloth body, composition arms and straight legs. Composition head; blue tin sleep eyes, lashes, painted lower lashes; brown moulded hair; open mouth showing two teeth and tongue. Mark: on head, A RELIABLE/DOLL/MADE IN CANADA.

Ref.No.: D of C, AO10, p. 255

Mint. $260.00 **Ex.** $215.00 **G.** $150.00 **F.** $60.00

Note: This doll is not factory dressed and is wearing a Snuggles dress by D.&C.

RELIABLE
ca.1933 - 20 in.

ca.1933. 20 in. (51 cm). Cloth body, composition arms and straight legs. Composition head; blue tin sleep eyes, lashes, painted lower lashes; brown moulded hair; closed mouth. Mark: on head, A RELIABLE/DOLL MADE IN CANADA.

Ref.No.: D of C, CR20, p. 255

Mint $135.00 **Ex.** $110.00 **G.** $65.00 **F.** $45.00

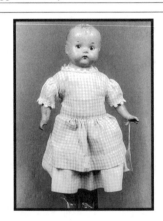

RELIABLE
ca.1933 - 18 in.

ca.1933. 18 in. (45.5 cm). Cloth body, composition arms and straight legs. Composition shoulderhead; blue sleep eyes, lashes; brown moulded hair; closed mouth. Mark: on shoulderplate, RELIABLE/MADE IN CANADA.

Ref.No.: D of C, CH29, p. 255

Mint $130.00 **Ex.** $95.00 **G.** $55.00 **F.** $40.00

RELIABLE
ca.1934 - 16 in.

ca.1934. 16 in. (40.5 cm). Cloth body with crier; composition arms and straight legs. Composition head; blue tin sleep eyes, lashes, painted lower lashes; brown moulded hair, closed mouth. Mark: on head, RELIABLE DOLL/MADE IN CANADA. Redressed in old cotton print dress.

Ref.No.: D of C, CR22, p. 256

Mint $125.00 Ex. $90.00 G. $50.00 F. $35.00

HAIRBOW PEGGY
ca.1934 - 18 in.

ca.1934. 18 in. (45.5 cm). Cloth body and legs, compostion arms. Composition shoulderhead; blue painted eyes; deeply moulded hair with hole for ribbon; closed mouth. Mark: on shoulderplate, A/RELIABLE/DOLL/MADE IN CANADA. Original green and white cotton dress with red rick-rack.

Ref.No.: DH22

Mint $150.00 Ex. $110.00 G. $55.00 F. $35.00

SHIRLEY TEMPLE
1935 - 18 in.

1935. 18 in. (45.5 cm). Composition body, jointed hips, shoulders and neck. Composition head with dimples; green sleep eyes, lashes, painted lower lashes; blond mohair wig; open mouth showing teeth. Mark: on head, SHIRLEY TEMPLE/COP. IDEAL/N.& T. CO.; on dress, A GENUINE/SHIRLEY TEMPLE/DOLL DRESS/RELIABLE TOY CO. LTD., along the side, MADE IN CANADA. Original pale orange flounced dress, white pantalettes, socks and shoes. The Little Colonel costume is worth more.

Ref.No.: D of C, AW23, p. 256

Mint $900.00 Ex. $700.00 G. $400.00 F. $175.00

HAIRBOW PEGGY
ca.1935 - 18 in.

ca.1935. 18 in. (45.5 cm). Excelsior stuffed cloth body and legs, composition forearms. Composition shoulderhead; blue painted eyes, black line over eye; well-defined moulded hair with a hole for ribbon; closed mouth. Mark: on shoulderplate, A/RELIABLE/DOLL/MADE IN CANADA. Original cotton dress.

Ref.No.: D of C, BY9, p. 257

Mint $150.00 Ex. $110.00 G. $60.00 F. $35.00

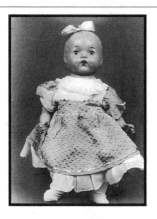

RELIABLE
Composition Body
ca.1935 - 18 in.

ca.1935. 18 in. (45.5 cm). Cloth body, composition bent arms and straight legs. Composition shoulderhead; blue sleep eyes, lashes, painted lower lashes; moulded hair, originally had a wig; closed mouth. Mark: on shoulderplate, A/RELIABLE/DOLL/MADE IN CANADA.

Ref.No.: D of C, CW27, p. 257

Mint $125.00 **Ex.** $ 95.00 **G.** $50.00 **F.** $35.00

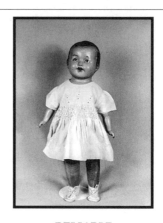

RELIABLE
ca.1935 - 27 in.

ca.1935. 27 in. (68.5 cm). Cloth body and legs, composition arms. Composition shoulderhead; blue glass sleep eyes; painted lower lashes; moulded brown hair; open-closed mouth. Mark: on shoulderplate, A/RELIABLE/DOLL. Original teddy underwear. Redressed.

Ref.No.: PGC12

Mint $150.00 **Ex.** $100.00 **G.** $60.00 **F.** $40.00

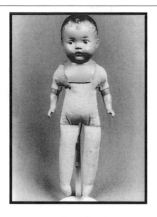

RELIABLE
Stuffed Cloth Body
ca.1935 - 18 in.

ca.1935. 18 in. (45.5 cm). Excelsior stuffed cloth body, upper arms and legs, composition 3/4 arms. Composition shoulderhead; blue painted side-glancing eyes, black line over eye; brown moulded hair; closed mouth. Mark: on shoulderplate, A/RELIABLE/DOLL/MADE IN CANADA.

Ref.No.: D of C, AP20, p. 257

Mint $90.00 **Ex.** $65.00 **G.** $45.00 **F.** $30.00

BABY BUNTING
ca.1935 - 14 in.

ca.1935. 14 in. (35.5 cm). Cloth body and bent legs softly stuffed, composition arms. Composition head; blue sleep eyes; brown moulded hair; open mouth with two teeth. Mark: RELIABLE DOLL/MADE IN CANADA. Original dress and bonnet.

Ref.No.: D of C, CG11, p. 257

Mint $115.00 **Ex.** $75.00 **G.** $50.00 **F.** $35.00

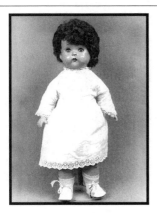

CHUBBY
ca.1935 - 17 in.

ca.1935. 17 in. (43 cm). Cloth body, composition arms and straight legs. Composition head; blue tin sleep eyes, lashes, painted lower lashes; brown caracul wig; closed mouth. Mark: on head, RELIABLE/MADE IN CANADA.

Ref.No.: D of C, BF21, p. 258

Mint **$235.00** **Ex.** **$160.00** **G.** **$120.00** **F.** **$75.00**

SHIRLEY TEMPLE
ca.1935 - 25 in.

ca.1935. 25 in. (63.5 cm).Composition body, jointed hips, shoulders, and neck. Composition head with dimples; green glassene sleep eyes, lashes, painted lower lashes; blond mohair wig; open mouth showing teeth and tongue. Unmarked. Original label on the dress, A GENUINE/SHIRLEY TEMPLE/DOLL DRESS/RELIABLE TOY CO. LTD.; along one side, MADE IN CANADA. Original clothing. Dress from Curly Top.

Ref.No.: D of C, AM11, p. 258

Mint $1,150.00 **Ex.** **$850.00** **G.** **$450.00** **F. $225.00**

SHIRLEY TEMPLE LOOK ALIKE
ca.1936 - 15 in.

ca.1936. 15 in. (38 cm). Composition body, jointed hips, shoulders, and head. Composition head with dimples; green sleep eyes, lashes, painted lower lashes; blond mohair wig; closed mouth. Mark: on head, RELIABLE/MADE IN CANADA. Original clothing.

Ref.No.: D of C, CD20, p. 259.

Mint **$175.00** **Ex.** **$125.00** **G.** **$95.00** **F.** **$50.00**

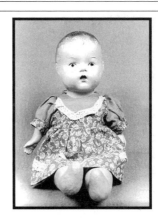

RELIABLE
ca.1936 - 14 in.

ca.1936. 14 in. (35.5 cm). Cloth body and legs, composition forearms. Composition shoulderhead; blue painted eyes, black line over eye, painted upper lashes; moulded brown hair; closed mouth. Mark: on shoulderplate, A RELIABLE DOLL/MADE IN CANADA. Original cotton print dress.

Ref.No.: D of C, BN2, p. 259.

Mint **$85.00** **Ex.** **$50.00** **G.** **$40.00** **F.** **$25.00**

RELIABLE
ca.1936 - 17 in.

ca.1936. 17 in. (43 cm). Cloth body, composition arms and straight legs. Composition head; blue sleep eyes, lashes; brown moulded hair; open mouth showing two teeth. Mark: on head, RELIABLE/MADE IN CANADA. Original pink voile dress and matching bonnet, socks and shoes.

Ref.No.: D of C, BZ6, p. 259

Mint **$150.00** **Ex.** **$115.00** **G.** **$85.00** **F.** **$45.00**

MOUNTIE AND HORSE

1936. 17 in. (43 cm). Excelsior stuffed cloth body and legs; composition arms. Composition head; brown painted eyes; brown moulded hair; closed mouth. Mark: on head, RELIABLE/MADE IN CANADA. Original costume. Cloth covered horse with wire backrest to hold the Mountie. Wooden platform with metal wheels.

Ref.No.: D of C, AO29, p. 260

Mint **$450.00** **Ex.** **$350.00** **G.** **$260.00** **F.** **$160.00**

Note: This doll appeared on a commemorative postage stamp issued June 8, 1990, which adds to its value.

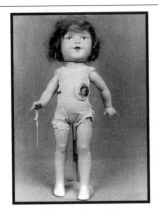

SHIRLEY TEMPLE LOOK ALIKE
ca.1937 - 13 in.

ca.1937. 13 in. (33 cm). Composition body, jointed hips, shoulders, and neck. Composition head with dimples; blue painted eyes with highlights, black painted upper lashes; light brown mohair wig; closed mouth. Mark: on head, RELIABLE/MADE IN CANADA; on body, SHIRLEY TEMPLE.

Ref.No.: D of C, CA32, p. 260.

Mint **$160.00** **Ex.** **$120.00** **G.** **$85.00** **F.** **$45.00**

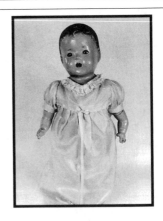

RELIABLE
ca.1937 - 15 in.

ca.1937. 15 in. (38 cm). Cloth body and legs, composition 3/4 arms. Composition shoulderhead; blue tin sleep eyes; moulded brown hair; closed mouth. Mark: on shoulderplate, A RELIABLE DOLL. Redressed.

Ref.No.: 2H19

Mint **$95.00** **Ex.** **$55.00** **G.** **$40.00** **F.** **$25.00**

CURLY LOCKS
ca.1937 - 21 in.

ca.1937. 21 in. (53 cm). Composition body, jointed hips, shoulders and neck. Composition head; blue sleep eyes, lashes, painted lowers; blond mohair wig; open mouth showing teeth. Mark: on head, RELIABLE/MADE IN CANADA. Original skirt and blouse, replaced shoes and socks.

Ref.No.: 2K8

Mint $250.00 **Ex.** $195.00 **G.** $130.00 **F.** $75.00

SHIRLEY TEMPLE
ca.1937 - 13 in.

ca.1937. 13 in. (33 cm). Composition body, jointed hips, shoulders and neck. Composition head; brown sleep eyes, lashes, painted lowers; blond mohair wig; open mouth with teeth and felt tongue. Mark: on head and body, SHIRLEY TEMPLE. Original white cotton dress with green trim is tagged, A GENUINE/SHIRLEY TEMPLE/DOLL DRESS/RELIABLE TOY CO. LTD./MADE IN CANADA. Replaced shoes.

Ref.No.: 2M10

Mint $750.00 **Ex.** $650.00 **G.** $275.00 **F.** $150.00

SHIRLEY TEMPLE
1937 - 18 in.

1937. 18 in. (45.5 cm). All composition body, jointed hips, shoulders and neck. Composition head; blue tin sleep eyes, lashes, painted lower lashes; replaced blond wig (should be mohair); open mouth showing upper teeth. Mark: on head, RELIABLE/MADE IN CANADA. Costume from the film of "Wee Willie Winkie." Velveteen jacket may not be original. Replaced socks and shoes.

Ref.No.: 2W30

Mint $850.00 **Ex.** $750.00 **G.** $375.00 **F.** $175.00

SHIRLEY TEMPLE
1938 - 19 in.

1938. 19 in. (48 cm). Composition body, jointed hips, shoulders, and neck. Composition head; hazel glassene sleep eyes; lashes; blond mohair wig; open mouth showing teeth. Mark: on head, 16 SHIRLEY TEMPLE; original label on dress, A GENUINE SHIRLEY TEMPLE DOLL DRESS. RELIABLE TOY CO. LTD. MADE IN CANADA. Curly Top dress

Ref.No.: D of C, BF22, p. 261

Mint $800.00 **Ex.** $650.00 **G.** $375.00 **F.** $175.00

SALLY ANN
ca.1938 - 20 in.

ca.1938. 20 in. (51 cm). Cloth body, composition arms and straight legs. Composition shoulderhead; blue metal sleep eyes; lashes, painted lower lashes; blond mohair wig; open mouth showing teeth. Mark: on head, RELIABLE/MADE IN CANADA. Probably original dress.

Ref.No. D of C; CQ7 p. 261

Mint $220.00 Ex. $185.00 G. $125.00 F. $70.00

BABY MARILYN
ca.1938 - 14 in.

ca.1938. 14 in. (35.5 cm). All composition, jointed hips, shoulders, and neck. Composition head; brown sleep eyes,, lashes, painted lower lashes; brown moulded hair; closed mouth. Unmarked. Original label GENUINE/BABY MARILYN/DOLLS/RELIABLE TOY CO. LTD./MADE IN CANADA. Original green and white cotton dress, matching bonnet, socks and shoes.

Ref.No.: D of C, BT4A, p. 261

Mint $150.00 Ex. $120.00 G. $90.00 F. $50.00

SNOW WHITE
ca.1938 - 15 in.

ca.1938. 15 in. (38 cm). Cloth body and legs, composition forearms. Composition shoulderhead; blue painted eyes, black line over eye; brown moulded hair with hair bow moulded in; closed mouth. Mark: on shoulderplate, A RELIABLE DOLL/MADE IN CANADA. Redressed.

Ref.No.: D of C, BZ17, p. 262

Mint $150.00 Ex. $115.00 G. $75.00 F. $45.00

TOUSLEHEAD

1939. 17 in. (43 cm). Cloth body, composition arms and straight legs. Composition head; blue tin sleep eyes, lashes, brown caracul wig; open mouth showing two teeth and tongue. Mark: on head, A RELIABLE DOLL/MADE IN CANADA. Original yellow cotton dress, slip and panties, socks and shoes.

Ref.No.: D of C, BJ7, p. 256

Mint $235.00 Ex. $160.00 G. $120.00 F. $75.00

SHIRLEY TEMPLE
ca.1939 - 16 in.

ca.1939. 16 in. (40.5 cm). Composition body, jointed hips, shoulders, and neck. Composition head with dimples; green sleep eyes, lashes, painted lower lashes; blond mohair wig; open mouth showing six teeth. Mark: on head, SHIRLEY TEMPLE; on arms, 14; on body, SHIRLEY TEMPLE 14; on dress, A GENUINE/SHIRLEY TEMPLE/DOLL DRESS/RELIABLE TOY CO. LTD.; on side of label, MADE IN CANADA. Original clothing.

Ref.No. D of C; BZ18 p. 262

Mint $800.00 Ex. $700.00 G. $350.00 F. $175.00

LADDIE
ca.1939 - 12 in.

ca.1939. 12 in. (30.5 cm). All composition, jointed hips and shoulders. Composition head; blue painted eyes, black line over eye; light brown moulded hair; closed mouth. Mark: on back, RELIABLE/MADE IN/CANADA. Original clothing.

Ref.No.: D of C, BH29, p. 262.

Prices per doll:

Mint $130.00 Ex. $90.00 G. $60.00 F. $35.00

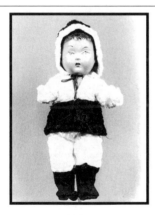

ESKIMO
ca.1939 - 14 in.

ca.1939. 14 in. (35.5 cm). All composition, jointed hips, shoulders, and neck. Composition head; black, almond shaped painted eyes, black line over eyes; black moulded hair; closed mouth. Mark: on head, 1/RELIABLE/MADE IN CANADA. Original clothing.

Ref.No.: D of C, AT12, p. 263

Mint $140.00 Ex. $105.00 G. $75.00 F. $45.00

BABY MARILYN
ca.1939 - 15 in.

ca.1939. 15 in. (38 cm). All composition body, jointed hips, shoulders, and neck. Composition head; blue tin sleep eyes, lashes, painted lower lashes; blond mohair curly wig; open mouth showing two teeth. Mark: on head, RELIABLE/MADE IN CANADA. Original blue and white dotted Swiss dress with matching bonnet, socks and shoes.

Ref.No.: D of C, BZ24, p. 263

Mint $180.00 Ex. $150.00 G. $105.00 F. $55.00

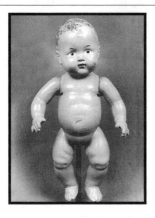

WETUMS
ca.1939 - 17 in.

ca.1939. 17 in. (43 cm). All composition, jointed hips, shoulders, and neck. Composition head; blue painted eyes; brown moulded hair; open mouth nurser. Mark: on head, RELIABLE TOY/MADE IN CANADA.

Ref.No.: D of C, CW17, p. 263

Mint **$95.00** **Ex.** **$70.00** **G.** **$50.00** **F.** **$30.00**

PIGTAILS
ca.1939 - 18 1/2 in.

ca.1939. 18 1/2 in. (47 cm). Composition body, jointed hips, shoulders, and neck. Composition head; blue sleep eyes, lashes, painted lower lashes, grey eyeshadow over eyelids; honey blond mohair wig in original braids with curled bangs; open mouth showing four teeth. Mark: on head, RELIABLE/MADE IN CANADA. Original white taffeta dress with red dots, attached panties. Pinafore and bonnet of white cotton with tiny red flowers and dark blue dots, socks and red shoes, matching hair ribbons.

Ref.No. D of C; CD13 p. 264

Mint **$185.00** **Ex.** **$150.00** **G.** **$95.00** **F.** **$60.00**

BABYKINS
ca.1939 - 12 in.

ca.1939. 12 in. (30.5 cm). All composition, jointed hips and shoulders. Composition head; blue painted eyes, black line over eye, painted upper lashes; brown moulded hair; closed mouth. Mark: on head, RELIABLE/MADE IN CANADA. Original gold label, MADE IN CANADA/BABYKINS/A RELIABLE DOLL/A BRITISH EMPIRE PRODUCT.

Ref.No.: D of C, BW21, p. 264

Mint **$80.00** **Ex.** **$60.00** **G.** **$40.00** **F.** **$25.00**

PANTALETTE LADY

1940. 17 in. (43 cm). Cloth body and legs, composition arms. Composition shoulderhead; blue tin sleep eyes; blond mohair wig; open mouth showing teeth. Mark: on shoulderplate, A/RELIABLE/DOLL/MADE IN CANADA. Original cotton print dress with black trim, matching bonnet and pantalettes.

Ref.No.: 2E5

Mint **$125.00** **Ex.** **$95.00** **G.** **$55.00** **F.** **$35.00**

TODDLES
1940 - 20 in.

1940. 20 in. (51 cm). Composition body, jointed hips, shoulders and neck. Composition head; blue tin sleep eyes, lashes, painted lowers; blond mohair wig; open mouth showing two teeth. Mark: on head, RELIABLE/MADE IN CANADA. Original name tag. Original pink flocked organdy dress with matching bonnet, socks and shoes.
Ref.No.: PGL6

Mint $210.00 **Ex.** $175.00 **G.** $115.00 **F.** $60.00

Note: This doll also came in a 14-inch size and with moulded hair.

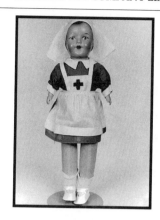

NURSE
ca.1940 - 18 in.

ca.1940. 18 in. (46 cm). Cloth body and legs, composition arms. Composition shoulderhead; painted blue eyes and upper lashes; moulded brown hair; closed mouth. Mark: on shoulderplate, A/RELIABLE/DOLL. Original blue and white nurse uniform, replaced shoes.
Ref.No.: PGL5

Mint $140.00 **Ex.** $110.00 **G.** $75.00 **F.** $40.00

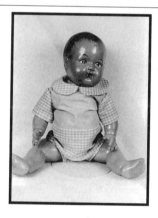

WETUMS
1940 - 17 in.

1940. 17 in. (43 cm). Composition body, jointed hips, shoulders and neck. Composition head; painted blue eyes and upper lashes; moulded brown hair; open mouth nurser. Mark: on head, RELIABLE TOY/MADE IN CANADA. Redressed. Originally came with a layette including dress, bonnet, extra diaper and a glass bottle.
Ref.No.: 2P27

Mint $95.00 **Ex.** $70.00 **G.** $50.00 **F.** $35.00

HIGHLAND LASSIE
ca.1940 - 15 in.

ca.1940. 15 in. (38 cm). All composition, jointed hips, shoulders, and neck. Composition head; blue sleep eyes, lashes, painted lower lashes; brown wig; closed mouth. Mark: on head, RELIABLE/MADE IN CANADA. Original costume. Hat missing.
Ref.No.: D of C, BJ5, p. 264

Mint $140.00 **Ex.** $95.00 **G.** $60.00 **F.** $35.00

RELIABLE
ca.1940 - 14 in.

ca.1940. 14 in. (35.5 cm). Brown composition, jointed hips, shoulders, and neck. Composition head; black painted side-glancing eyes; black braided wool wig over moulded hair; open-closed mouth. Mark: on head, RELIABLE/MADE IN CANADA.

Ref.No.: D of C, BN17, p. 265

Mint $165.00 **Ex.** $110.00 **G.** $80.00 **F.** $50.00

Note: Brown composition dolls are hard to find. The wig on this doll is very unusual.

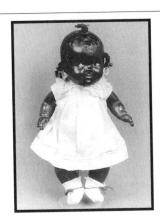

TOPSY
ca.1940 - 17 in.

ca.1940. 17 in. (43 cm). All composition, dark brown, jointed hips, shoulders, and neck. Composition head; black painted side-glancing eyes, painted upper lashes; black moulded hair with three inset wool braids; open-closed mouth with two painted teeth. Mark: on head, RELIABLE/MADE IN CANADA.

Ref.No.: D of C, BH12, p. 266

Mint $225.00 **Ex.** $185.00 **G.** $125.00 **F.** $65.00

BETTY CO-ED

1940. All composition, slim, teen, five-piece body. Sleep eyes, closed mouth; mohair wig. Redressed. MARK: RELIABLE/MADE IN CANADA on head.

Mint $150.00 **Ex.** $100.00 **G.** $75.00 **F.** $50.00

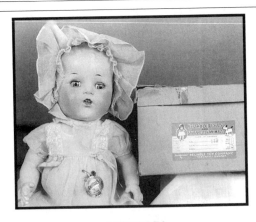

CHUCKLES
1940 - 20 in.

1940. 20 in. (51 cm). All composition jointed hips, shoulders, and neck. Composition head; blue tin sleep eyes, lashes, painted lower lashes; brown moulded hair; open mouth showing two teeth and tongue. Mark: on head, RELIABLE/MADE IN CANADA. Original label, MADE IN CANADA/CHUCKLES/RELIABLE TOY CO. Original clothing.

Ref.No.: D of C, CN31, p. 265

Mint $205.00 **Ex.** $165.00 **G.** $95.00 **F.** $50.00

KENNY-TOK
1940 - 16 in.

1940. 16 in. (40.5 cm). Cloth body and legs, composition hands. Composition head with moveable jaw that opens when the string at the back of the neck is pulled. Painted brown eyes; painted black hair. Unmarked. Original name tag. Original black cotton suit and white shirt. Top hat only came with the 24 in. size doll.

Ref.No.: 2B16

Mint $150.00 **Ex.** $120.00 **G.** $90.00 **F.** $55.00

KENNY-TOK
1940 - 24 in.

1940. 24 in. (61 cm). Sawdust filled cloth body, composition forearms. Composition head with moveable jaw that opens when the string at the back is pulled; painted brown side-glancing eyes; moulded hair painted black; five painted teeth. Mark: on head, MFG. BY/RELIABLE TOY CO/CANADA.

Ref.No.: D of C, BZ2, p. 266

Mint $215.00 **Ex.** $185.00 **G.** $140.00 **F.** $95.00

Note: Regional price differences, lower in the western provinces and the Maritimes. Top hat missing.

SALLY ANN
1940 - 18 in.

1940. 18 in. (45.5 cm). Cloth body, composition arms and straight legs. Composition head; blue tin sleep eyes, lashes; brown mohair wig; open mouth showing teeth. Mark: on head, A RELIABLE DOLL/MADE IN CANADA. Redressed.

Ref.No.: D of C, BH13, p. 266

Mint $175.00 **Ex.** $150.00 **G.** $95.00 **F.** $50.00

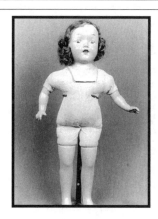

GLORIA
1940 - 18 in.

1940. 18 in. (45.5 cm). Cloth body, composition 3/4 arms and straight legs. Composition shoulderhead; dark blue tin eyes, painted upper lashes; brown mohair wig parted on one side; open mouth showing teeth. Mark: on shoulderplate, A/RELIABLE/DOLL/MADE IN CANADA. Originally wore organdy dress and matching hat.

Ref.No.: D of C, CL36, p. 267

Mint $125.00 **Ex.** $95.00 **G.** $65.00 **F.** $35.00

JOAN
1940 - 20 in.

1940. 20 in. (51 cm). All composition body, jointed hips, shoulders and neck. Composition head; blue glassene sleep eyes, lashes, painted lower lashes; blond mohair curly wig; open mouth showing two teeth and tongue. Mark: on head, RELIABLE/MADE IN CANADA.

Ref.No.: D of C, CM11, p. 267

Mint $220.00 **Ex.** $175.00 **G.** $115.00 **F.** $65.00

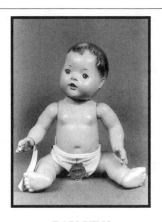

BABYKINS
1940 - 12 in.

1940. 12 in. (3.5 cm). All composition, jointed hips, shoulders and neck. Composition head; blue sleep eyes, lashes, painted lower lashes; brown moulded hair; open mouth showing two teeth and tongue. Unmarked. Original tag, MADE IN CANADA/BABYKINS/A RELIABLE/DOLL/MADE BY RELIABLE TOY CO.

Ref.No.: D of C, CG14, p. 267

Mint $85.00 **Ex.** $60.00 **G.** $50.00 **F.** $30.00

RELIABLE
ca.1940 - 16 in.

ca.1940 16 in. (40.5 cm). All composition, jointed hips, shoulders and neck. Composition head; blue sleep eyes, lashes, painted lower lashes; light brown moulded hair; closed mouth. Mark: on head, RELIABLE/MADE IN CANADA.

Ref.No.: D of C, BY10, p. 268

Mint $105.00 **Ex.** $75.00 **G.** $60.00 **F.** $35.00

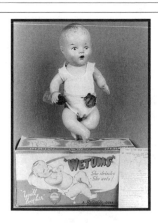

WETUMS
1940 - 11 in.

1940. 11 in. (28 cm). All composition, jointed hips and shoulders. Blue painted eyes, black line over eye; light brown moulded hair; open mouth nurser. Mark: on head, RELIABLE/MADE IN/CANADA. Original tag, MADE IN CANADA/RELIABLE/A RELIABLE DOLL (in script)/A BRITISH EMPIRE PRODUCT/RELIABLE TOY CO. LIMITED.

Ref.No.: D of C, CD18, p. 268

Mint $75.00 **Ex.** $50.00 **G.** $30.00 **F.** $25.00

CUDDLEKINS
1940 - 19 in.

1940. 19 in. (48 cm). All composition, jointed hips, shoulders and neck. Composition head; blue metal sleep eyes, lashes, painted lower lashes; light brown moulded curls, originally had a wig; open mouth showing two teeth. Mark: on head, RELIABLE/MADE IN CANADA.

Ref.No.: D of C, CC13, p. 268

Mint $205.00 **Ex.** $160.00 **G.** $85.00 **F.** $45.00

GIBSON GIRL
1941 - 30 in.

1941. 30 in. (76 cm). Cloth body and legs, composition arms and lower legs with moulded high heel shoes. Composition shoulderhead; blue painted eyes, painted upper lashes, eye shadow and beauty spot on her cheek; blond mohair wig; closed mouth. Unmarked. Original satin gown with print overskirt, trimmed in rick-rack with a matching hat.

Ref.No.: 2J1

Mint $200.00 **Ex.** $150.00 **G.** $110.00 **F.** $70.00

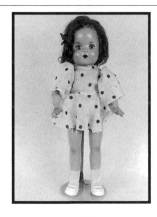

RELIABLE
ca.1941 - 14 in.

ca.1941. 14 in. (35.5 cm). Composition body, jointed hips, shoulders and neck. Composition head; blue sleep eyes, lashes; brown mohair wig; open mouth with four teeth. Mark: on head, RELIABLE/CANADA. Redressed.

Ref.No.: 2H3

Mint $130.00 **Ex.** $95.00 **G.** $60.00 **F.** $40.00

NURSE
1941 - 24 in.

1941. 24 in. (61 cm). Excelsior stuffed cloth body and legs, composition forearms. Composition shoulderhead; blue painted eyes, painted upper lashes; moulded light brown curls; closed mouth. Mark: on shoulderplate, RELIABLE DOLL/MADE IN/CANADA. Original blue cotton dress and navy cape lined with red. Replaced socks and shoes. Missing apron and cap.

Ref.No.: D of C, CT3, p. 269

Mint $160.00 **Ex.** $125.00 **G.** $90.00 **F.** $50.00

OLD FASHIONED GIRL

1941. 15 1/2 in. (39 cm). All composition, jointed hips, shoulders and neck. Composition head; blue tin sleep eyes, lashes, painted lower lashes; blond mohair wig; open mouth showing four teeth. Mark: on head, RELIABLE/MADE IN CANADA.

Ref.No.: D of C, BJ8, p. 269

Mint $155.00 **Ex.** $105.00 **G.** $70.00 **F.** $45.00

TODDLES
ca.1941 - 14 in.

ca.1941. 14 in. (35.5 cm). Composition body, jointed hips, shoulders and neck. Composition head; blue sleep eyes, lashes, painted lowers; light brown mohair wig; open mouth, two teeth. Mark: on head, RELIABLE/MADE IN CANADA. Original name tag. Original pale yellow printed organdy dress, matching bonnet, socks and shoes.

Ref.No.: 2X16

Mint $170.00 **Ex.** $150.00 **G.** $90.00 **F.** $55.00

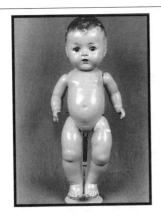

BABYKINS
1941 - 20 in.

1941. 20 in. (51 cm). All composition, jointed hips, shoulders, and neck. Composition head; blue glassene eyes, lashes, painted lower lashes; brown moulded hair; open mouth showing two teeth. Mark: on head, RELIABLE/MADE IN CANADA.

Ref.No.: D of C, AM31, p. 269

Mint $155.00 **Ex.** $115.00 **G.** $65.00 **F.** $45.00

CUDDLEKINS
1941 - 15 in.

1941. 15 in. (38 cm). Cloth body, composition arms and straight legs. Composition shoulderhead, dimples; blue tin sleep eyes, lashes, painted lower lashes; brown moulded hair; open mouth showing two teeth. Mark: on shoulderplate, RELIABLE/DOLL/MADE IN CANADA. Original pink and white dress and matching bonnet, socks and shoes.

Ref.No.: D of C, BZ33, p. 270

Mint $135.00 **Ex.** $100.00 **G.** $60.00 **F.** $35.00

RELIABLE
ca.1941

ca. 1941. All composition, jointed hips, shoulders and neck. Composition head; blue tin sleep eyes, lashes, painted lower lashes; brown mohair wig, moulded hair underneath; open mouth showing two teeth and tongue. Mark: on head, RELIABLE/MADE IN CANADA. Original cotton print dress and matching bonnet.

Ref.No.: D of C, BH35, p. 270

Mint $175.00   Ex. $150.00   G. $75.00   F. $45.00

ARMY DOLL
1942 - 13 in.

1942. 13 in. (33 cm). Excelsior stuffed body and legs, composition forearms. Composition shoulderhead; blue painted eyes, fine black line over eye; light brown moulded hair; closed mouth. Mark: on shoulderplate, RELIABLE DOLL/MADE IN CANADA.

Ref.No.: D of C, CI30, p. 270

Mint $115.00   Ex. $90.00   G. $50.00   F. $30.00

Note: The same doll was also available in an 18-inch size. Both sizes also came dressed in air force blue.

ARMY DOLL
ca.1942 - 18 in.

ca.1942. 18 in. (45.5 cm). Cloth body and legs, composition arms. Composition shoulderhead; blue painted eyes; moulded brown hair; closed mouth. Mark: on head, RELIABLE/MADE IN CANADA. Original army battledress and cap.

Ref.No.: 2B17

Mint $225.00   Ex. $165.00   G. $110.00   F. $50.00

SAILOR

ca.1942. 16 in. (40.5 cm). Cloth body and legs, composition arms. Composition shoulderhead; blue painted eyes; moulded brown hair; closed mouth. Mark: on shoulderplate, RELIABLE DOLL/MADE IN CANADA. Original navy blue sailor suit, black shoes, sailor hat with H.M.S. RELIABLE, in gold print on hat band.

Ref.No.: 2N16

Mint $175.00   Ex. $125.00   G. $65.00   F. $35.00

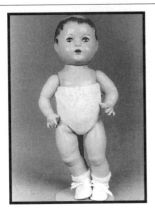

RELIABLE
ca.1942 - 14 in.

ca.1942. 14 in. (35.5 cm). All composition, jointed hips, shoulders and neck. Composition head; blue tin sleep eyes, lashes; brown moulded hair, originally wore a wig; open mouth, showing two teeth. Mark: RELIABLE/MADE IN CANADA.

Ref.No.: D of C, CL2, p. 271

Mint $115.00 **Ex.** $90.00 **G.** $55.00 **F.** $40.00

ROSALYN
ca.1942 - 19 in.

ca.1942. 19 in. (48 cm). Composition body, jointed hips, shoulders and neck. Composition head; blue tin sleep eyes, lashes, painted lower lashes; brown mohair wig with bangs; open mouth showing teeth and tongue. Mark: on head, RELIABLE/MADE IN CANADA. Original cotton print dress, velveteen coat and matching bonnet, socks and shoes.

Ref.No.: D of C, CY5, p. 271

Mint $220.00 **Ex.** $180.00 **G.** $120.00 **F.** $60.00

RELIABLE
ca.1942 - 21 1/2 in.

ca.1942. 21 1/2 in. (54.5 cm). Excelsior stuffed cloth body, legs and upper arms, composition 3/4 arms. Composition shoulderhead; blue painted eyes, black line over eye; brown moulded hair; closed mouth. Mark: on shoulderplate, A RELIABLE DOLL/MADE IN CANADA. Redressed.

Ref.No.: D of C, CC3, p. 271

Mint $115.00 **Ex.** $70.00 **G.** $50.00 **F.** $35.00

STANDING DOLL, NURSE

1942. 8 in. (20.5 cm). All composition, jointed shoulders. Black painted side-glancing eyes, painted upper lashes; blond mohair wig; closed mouth. Mark: on back, RELIABLE/MADE IN CANADA.

Ref.No.: D of C, BW19, p. 272

Mint $50.00 **Ex.** $40.00 **G.** $30.00 **F.** $20.00

NURSE
1942 - 18 in.

1942. 18 in. (45.5 cm). Excelsior stuffed cloth body, composition arms and straight legs. Composition shoulderhead; blue painted eyes, black line over eye, painted upper lashes; blond mohair wig; closed mouth. Mark: on shoulderplate, RELIABLE DOLL/MADE IN CANADA. Original clothing.

Ref.No.: D of C, CI34, p. 272

Mint **$140.00** **Ex.** **$110.00** **G.** **$75.00** **F.** **$40.00**

BABY LOVUMS
1942 - 17 in.

1942. 17 in. (43 cm). Cloth body, composition hands and bent limb legs. Composition head; green sleep eyes, lashes, painted lower lashes; brown mohair curly wig; closed mouth. Mark: on head, A/RELIABLE/DOLL.

Ref.No.: D of C, CD4, p. 283

Mint **$210.00** **Ex.** **$160.00** **G.** **$95.00** **F.** **$55.00**

STANDING DOLL, ARMY

ca.1943. 8 in. (20.5 cm). Composition body and head, jointed shoulders. Painted side-glancing eyes; mohair wig, closed mouth. Mark: on body, RELIABLE/MADE IN/CANADA. Original army uniform, moulded painted shoes and socks.

Ref.No.: D of C, BM24, p. 107

Mint. **$50.00** **Ex.** **$40.00** **G.** **$30.00** **F.** **$20.00**

STANDING DOLL, AIR FORCE

ca.1943. 8 in. (20.5 cm). All composition, jointed shoulders. Black painted side-glancing eyes, painted upper lashes; blond mohair wig; closed mouth. Mark: on back, RELIABLE/MADE IN CANADA. Original air force uniform, moulded painted shoes and socks.

Ref.No.: D of C, BW17, p. 272

Mint **$50.00** **Ex.** **$40.00** **G.** **$30.00** **F.** **$20.00**

SALLY ANN
ca.1943 - 18 in.

ca.1943. 18 in. (45.5 cm). All composition body, jointed hips, shoulders, and neck. Composition head; blue tin sleep eyes, lashes; blond mohair wig; open mouth with teeth and felt tongue. Mark: on head, RELIABLE/MADE IN CANADA. Original red cotton dress with attached panties. Matching red cotton print bonnet.

Ref.No. D of C, XH25, p. 273

Mint $175.00 **Ex.** $155.00 **G.** $110.00 **F.** $55.00

AIR FORCE DOLL

ca.1943. 18 in. (45.5 cm). Cloth body and legs, composition arms. Composition head; painted brown eyes, black line over eye; brown moulded hair; closed mouth. Mark: on head, RELIABLE/MADE IN/CANADA. Original cotton uniform.

Ref.No.: D of C, CA2, p. 273

Mint $235.00 **Ex.** $175.00 **G.** $115.00 **F.** $50.00

Note: Dolls in military uniform and wartime nurse dolls have increased in price, probably because of the 50th anniversary of the end of World War II.

BABY PRECIOUS
1943 - 19 in.

1943. 19 in. (48 cm). Cloth body, composition arms and straight legs. Composition head; blue tin sleep eyes, lashes, painted lower lashes; light brown mohair wig over moulded hair; closed mouth. Mark: on head, A RELIABLE DOLL. Original dress and bonnet.

Ref.No.: D of C, BN35, p. 273

Mint $190.00 **Ex.** $165.00 **G.** $100.00 **F.** $55.00

TOPSY
ca.1943 - 15 in.

ca.1943. 15 in. (38 cm). White cloth body with black cloth legs and brown composition arms. Brown composition shoulderhead; black painted side-glancing eyes; black moulded hair with three inset wool braids; open-closed mouth with two painted teeth. Mark: on head, A/RELIABLE/DOLL/MADE IN CANADA. Redressed.

Ref.No.: HX27

Mint $135.00 **Ex.** $105.00 **G.** $70.00 **F.** $50.00

BABY PRECIOUS
ca.1944 - 17 in.

ca.1944. 17 in. (43 cm). Cloth body with crier, composition arms and legs. Composition head; blue sleep eyes, lashes; light brown mohair wig in original set; closed mouth. Unmarked. Original name tag. Original organdy and lace dress and matching bonnet, socks and shoes.

Ref.No.: 2B11

Mint **$175.00** **Ex.** **$150.00** **G.** **$90.00** **F.** **$50.00**

NURSE DOLL

1944. 24 in. (61 cm). Excelsior stuffed cloth body and legs, composition arms. Composition shoulder head; blue painted eyes, white highlights, fine black line over eye, painted upper lashes; brown moulded hair; closed mouth. Mark: A RELIABLE DOLL / MADE IN CANADA. Original dress and apron, cap missing.

Ref.No.: D of C, CW28, p. 274

Mint **$160.00** **Ex.** **$125.00** **G.** **$90.00** **F.** **$50.00**

STANDING DOLL, INDIAN GIRL

1944. 8 in. (20.5 cm). All composition, jointed shoulders. Black painted side-glancing eyes, painted upper lashes; black synthetic wig in braids; closed mouth. Mark: on body, RELIABLE / MADE IN / CANADA.

Ref.No.: D of C, CN18, p. 274

Mint **$45.00** **Ex.** **$35.00** **G.** **$25.00** **F.** **$20.00**

STANDING DOLL

ca.1945. 8 in. (20.5 cm). All composition, jointed shoulders. Black painted side-glancing eyes, painted upper lashes; blond mohair wig; closed mouth. Mark: on back, RELIABLE / MADE IN / CANADA.

Ref.No.: D of C, BP8, p. 274

Mint **$45.00** **Ex.** **$35.00** **G.** **$25.00** **F.** **$20.00**

MINIATURE DOLL

1945. 11 in. (28 cm). All hard plastic, jointed shoulders and neck. Hard plastic head; blue plastic side-glancing sleep eyes, painted upper lashes; blond mohair wig; closed mouth. Mark: on body, RELIABLE/MADE IN CANADA.

Ref.No.: D of C, CL8, p. 275

Mint   **$20.00**   **Ex.**   **$15.00**   **G.**   **$10.00**   **F.**   **$8.00**

BABY PRECIOUS
ca.1945 - 17 in.

ca.1945. 17 in. (43 cm). Cloth body, composition arms and straight legs. Composition head; blue sleep eyes, lashes, painted lower lashes; light brown mohair wig; closed mouth. Mark: RELIABLE/DOLL/MADE IN CANADA.

Ref.No.: D of C, CJ35, p. 275

Mint   **$175.00**   **Ex.**   **$150.00**   **G.**   **$90.00**   **F.**   **$50.00**

BABY LOVUMS
ca.1945 - 23 in.

ca.1945. 23 in. (58.5 cm). Cloth body, composition hands and legs. Composition head; blue sleep eyes, lashes; reddish gold mohair wig; open-closed mouth. Unmarked. Original mauve taffeta dress and bonnet, socks and shoes.

Ref.No.: 2I31

Mint   **$255.00**   **Ex.**   **$195.00**   **G.**   **$120.00**   **F.**   **$65.00**

BABY MARILYN
1945 - 20 in.

1945. 20 in. (51 cm). All composition body, jointed hips, shoulders, and neck. Composition head; blue sleep eyes, lashes, painted lower lashes; blond wig; closed mouth. Unmarked. Original Reliable tag. Original plaid jumper and tam.

Ref.No.: 2I7

Mint   **$200.00**   **Ex.**   **$165.00**   **G.**   **$115.00**   **F.**   **$50.00**

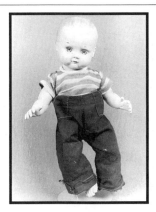

RELIABLE
ca.1946 - 14 in.

ca.1946. 14 in. (35.5 cm). All composition bent limb baby, jointed hips, shoulders, neck and wrists. Composition head; glassene sleep eyes, lashes, painted lower lashes; painted hair; closed mouth. Mark: RELIABLE/MADE IN CANADA.

Ref.No.: D of C, BF27, p. 275

Mint **$120.00** **Ex.** **$90.00** **G.** **$65.00** **F.** **35.00**

CUTIE DOLL
ca.1946 - 6 in.

ca.1946. 6 in. (15 cm). One-piece hard plastic with hole for hair bow. Moulded with a finger in the mouth; pants, socks and shoes. Painted side-glancing eyes. Mark: R over P within a diamond shape/MADE IN CANADA.

Ref.No.: 2PGGK21

Mint **$20.00** **Ex.** **$15.00** **G.** **$10.00** **F.** **$5.00**

FARINA DOLL

ca.1946. 6 in. (15 cm). One-piece hard plastic with hole for hair bow. Moulded with a finger in the mouth, pants, socks and shoes. Painted side-glancing eyes. Mark: R over P within a diamond shape/MADE IN CANADA.

Ref.No.: 2F9

Mint **$25.00** **Ex.** **$20.00** **G.** **$15.00** **F.** **$10.00**

Note: This is the same as the "Cutie Doll," but made of brown plastic.

RELIABLE PLASTICS
ca.1946

ca.1946. Three dolls of various height made of hard plastic.

Ref.No.: GK11

Left - 2 3/4 in.: **Mint - $15.00**
Centre - 4 in.: **Mint - $20.00**
Right - 2 1/2 in.: **Mint - $15.00**

Note: Reliable Plastics was a division of Reliable Toy Co.

COWBOY AND HORSE

ca.1947. 6 in. (15 cm). Both made of hard plastic; features and clothing painted. Mark: on back of cowboy, RELIABLE/MADE IN CANADA.

Ref.No.: 2J6

Mint $60.00 **Ex.** $40.00 **G.** $30.00 **F.** $20.00

STANDING DOLL, SCOTTISH

ca.1947. 8 in. (20.5 cm). All composition, jointed shoulders. Black painted side-glancing eyes; light brown mohair wig; closed mouth. Mark: RELIABLE/MADE IN CANADA. Original tartan skirt and tam, green velvet jacket, red bow.

Ref.No.: 2J28

Mint $50.00 **Ex.** $35.00 **G.** $25.00 **F.** $15.00

BABY LOVUMS
ca.1947 - 24 in.

ca.1947. 24 in. (61 cm). Cloth body with crier, composition hands and bent-limb legs. Composition head; blue sleep eyes, lashes, painted lower lashes, black eye shadow over eye; light brown moulded hair; closed mouth. Mark: on head, RELIABLE.

Ref.No.: D of C, CB7, p. 276

Mint $255.00 **Ex.** $200.00 **G.** $115.00 **F.** $60.00

BABY LOVUMS
ca.1947 - 26 in.

ca.1947. 26 in. (66 cm). Cloth body with crier, composition bent-limb arms and legs. Composition head; blue sleep eyes, lashes, painted lower lashes; brown mohair wig; closed mouth. Mark: on head, RELIABLE. Original organdy dress and bonnet, socks and shoes. Original tag.

Ref.No.: D of C, BZ22, p. 276

Mint $265.00 **Ex.** $225.00 **G.** $150.00 **F.** $70.00

MAGGIE MUGGINS
1947 - 15 in.

1947. 15 in. (38 cm). All composition, jointed hips, shoulders, and neck. Composition head; blue sleep eyes, lashes, painted lower lashes and freckles; red mohair wig in pigtails; open mouth showing teeth. Mark: on head, RELIABLE/MADE IN CANADA.

Ref.No.: D of C, AP10, p. 276

Mint $385.00 Ex. $300.00 G. $170.00 F. $105.00

Note: This doll appeared on a commemorative postage stamp issued June 8, 1990, which adds to its value.

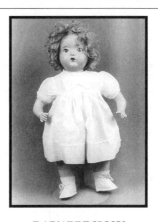

BABY PRECIOUS
ca.1947 - 20 in.

ca.1947. 20 in. (51 cm). Cloth body, composition arms and straight legs. Composition head; blue sleep eyes, lashes, painted lower lashes; blond mohair wig; closed mouth. Mark: on head, A/RELIABLE/DOLL. Original cotton dress.

Ref.No.: D of C, BF28, p. 277

Mint $200.00 Ex. $175.00 G. $110.00 F. $60.00

LADDIE
ca.1947 - 12 in.

ca.1947. 12 in. (30.5 cm). All composition, jointed hips and shoulders. Blue painted eyes, black line over eye; light brown moulded hair; closed mouth. Mark: on head, RELIABLE/MADE IN/CANADA.

Ref.No.: D of C, AO23, p. 277

Mint $130.00 Ex. $90.00 G. $60.00 F. $35.00

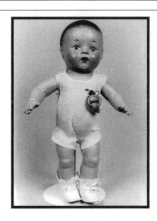

BABY JEAN
1947 - 12 in.

1947. 12 in. (30.5 cm). All composition, jointed hips and shoulders. One-piece head and body. Painted blue eyes; moulded brown curls; closed mouth. Mark: on body, RELIABLE/MADE IN/CANADA; label, BABY JEAN. Original teddy.

Ref.No.: D of C, CX13, p. 277

Mint $85.00 Ex. $60.00 G. $50.00 F. $25.00

BABY MARILYN
1947 - 20 in.

1947. 20 in. (51 cm). All composition, jointed hips, shoulders, and neck. Composition head; blue plastic sleep eyes, lashes, painted lower lashes; blond mohair wig; closed mouth. Mark: on head, RELIABLE/MADE IN CANADA; original gold name label. Original blue cotton dress and matching bonnet, replaced socks and shoes.

Ref.No.: D of C, CT4, p. 278

Mint $200.00 **Ex.** $165.00 **G.** $115.00 **F.** $50.00

RELIABLE
ca.1947 - 15 in.

ca.1947. 15 in. (38 cm). All composition, jointed hips, shoulders and neck. Composition head; brown sleep eyes, lashes, painted lowers; blond mohair wig; closed mouth. Mark: on head, RELIABLE/MADE IN/CANADA. Original mauve cotton dress and hat, replaced shoes. Original tag.

Ref.No.: 2Q32

Mint $115.00 **Ex.** $95.00 **G.** $55.00 **F.** $35.00

GLORIA
ca.1948 - 18 in.

ca.1948. 18 in. (45.5 cm). Cloth body, composition arms and straight legs. Composition shoulderhead; blue sleep eyes, lashes; blond mohair wig; closed mouth. Mark: on shoulderplate, RELIABLE /MADE/IN CANADA.

Ref.No.: D of C, CF28, p. 278

Mint $120.00 **Ex.** $95.00 **G.** $50.00 **F.** $35.00

HIAWATHA
1948 - 12 in.

1948. 12 in. (30.5 cm). All composition, jointed hips and shoulders. Brown painted eyes, black line over eye; black wig in braids; closed mouth. Mark: on back, RELIABLE/MADE IN CANADA.

Ref.No.: D of C, BH6, p. 278

Mint $135.00 **Ex.** $105.00 **G.** $55.00 **F.** $30.00

PIGTAILS
1948 - 15 in.

1948. 15 in. (38 cm). All composition, jointed hips, shoulders, and neck. Composition head; blue sleep eyes, lashes, painted lower lashes; blond mohair wig in pigtails with curled bangs; closed mouth. Mark: on head, RELIABLE/MADE IN CANADA. Original red and white checked cotton dress, socks and shoes. White organdy pinafore missing.

Ref.No.: D of C, CD26, p. 279

Mint **$125.00** **Ex.** **$95.00** **G.** **$55.00** **F.** **$35.00**

HIGHLAND LASSIE
1948 - 15 in.

1948. 15 in. (38 cm). Composition body, jointed hips, shoulders, and neck. Composition head; blue tin sleep eyes, lashes, painted lower lashes; blond mohair wig with bangs; closed mouth. Mark: on head, RELIABLE/MADE IN CANADA. All original costume.

Ref.No.: D of C, CY8, p. 279

Mint **$140.00** **Ex.** **$100.00** **G.** **$55.00** **F.** **$35.00**

BABY MARILYN
1948 - 20 in.

1948. 20 in. (51 cm). All composition toddler, jointed hips, shoulders, and neck. Composition head; blue sleep eyes, lashes, painted lower lashes; blond wig; closed mouth. Unmarked. Original Reliable tag. All original red cotton dress and matching beret, socks and shoes. Dress on backward, should have buttons down the front.

Ref.No.: D of C, BF32, p. 279

Mint **$200.00** **Ex.** **$165.00** **G.** **$115.00** **F.** **$50.00**

BRIDE
ca.1948 - 17 in.

ca.1948. 17 in. (43 cm). All composition, jointed hips, shoulders and neck. Composition head; blue sleep eyes, lashes; blond mohair wig; closed mouth. Mark: on head, RELIABLE/MADE IN/CANADA. Original satin gown with bow at hem. Original tulle veil and bouquet.

Ref.No.: 2I0

Mint **$160.00** **Ex.** **$110.00** **G.** **$80.00** **F.** **$40.00**

BABY JEAN
ca.1948 - 14 in.

ca.1948. 14 in. (35.5 cm). All composition, jointed hips, shoulders and neck. Composition head; blue sleep eyes, lashes, painted lowers; blond mohair wig; closed mouth. Mark: RELIABLE/MADE IN CANADA. Original mauve organdy dress trimmed in lace, matching bonnet.

Ref.No.: 2R5

Mint $120.00 **Ex.** $90.00 **G.** $55.00 **F.** $40.00

BABY TOOTSIE
1948 - 18 in.

1948. 18 in. (45.5 cm). Cloth body and legs, composition arms. Composition shoulderhead; blue painted eyes, moulded brown hair; open-closed mouth showing two teeth. Mark: on shoulderplate, A/RELIABLE DOLL/MADE IN CANADA. Original red print cotton dress. Bonnet missing.

Ref.No.: 2E4

Mint $95.00 **Ex.** $65.00 **G.** $45.00 **F.** $25.00

GLORIA
1948 - 18 in.

1948. 18 in. (45.5 cm). Cloth body, composition arms and straight legs. Composition shoulderhead; blue sleep eyes, lashes, painted lower lashes; blond mohair wig; closed mouth. Mark: on shoulderplate, A/RELIABLE/DOLL/MADE IN CANADA.

Ref.No.: D of C, CO18, p. 280

Mint $120.00 **Ex.** $95.00 **G.** $50.00 **F.** $35.00

BABY PRECIOUS
1948 - 24 in.

1948. 24 in. (61 cm). Cloth body, composition forearms and straight legs. Composition head; blue tin sleep eyes, lashes, painted lower lashes; replaced blond mohair wig over moulded hair; closed mouth. Unmarked. Original tag, BABY PRECIOUS/MADE IN CANADA/A RELIABLE DOLL/MFD. BY RELIABLE TOY CO. CANADA/A BRITISH EMPIRE PRODUCT. Original dress, replaced socks.

Ref.No.: D of C, CD5, p. 280

Mint $235.00 **Ex.** $200.00 **G.** $110.00 **F.** $60.00

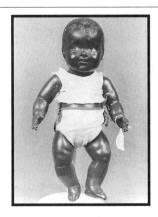

TOPSY
1948 - 17 in.

1948. 17 in. (43 cm). Brown composition body, jointed hips, shoulders and neck. Composition head, dimpled cheeks; black painted side-glancing eyes; open-closed mouth showing two painted teeth. Mark: on head, RELIABLE/MADE IN CANADA.

Ref.No.: D of C, BQ0, p. 280

Mint $175.00 **Ex.** $160.00 **G.** $95.00 **F.** $65.00

TOPSY
1948 - 10 1/4 in.

1948. 10 1/4 in. (26 cm). Brown hard plastic, five-piece body. Hard plastic head; black, side-glancing sleep eyes, painted upper lashes; moulded black hair with three woolly top-knots; open mouth. Mark: on back, RELIABLE/MADE IN CANADA.

Mint $60.00 **Ex.** $45.00 **G.** $35.00 **F.** $30.00

BABYKINS
Open Mouth With Two Teeth

1948. 17 in. (43 cm). All composition, five-piece body. Blue tin sleep eyes; moulded brown hair; open mouth with two teeth showing; dimples. Originally dressed in diaper and undershirt.

Mint $125.00 **Ex.** $95.00 **G.** $60.00 **F.** $50.00

TODDLES
1948 - 17 in.

1948. 17 in. (43 cm). All composition. Sleep eyes; moulded hair. Original print dress with matching bonnet.

Mint $135.00 **Ex.** $100.00 **G.** $60.00 $50.00

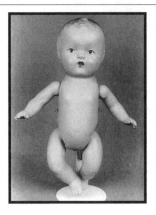

JOAN
1948 - 9 1/2 in.

1948. 9 1/2 in. (24 cm). All composition bent-limb baby, jointed hips and shoulders. Blue painted eyes, black line over eye; brown moulded hair; closed mouth. Mark: on back, RELIABLE/MADE IN CANADA.

Ref.No.: D of C, CL5, p. 281

Mint $60.00 **Ex.** $45.00 **G.** $35.00 **F.** $25.00

SALLY ANN
1948 - 22 in.

1948. 22 in. (56 cm). All composition, jointed hips, shoulders and neck. Composition head with dimpled cheeks; blue metal sleep eyes, lashes, painted lower lashes; red mohair wig; open smiling mouth showing six teeth. Mark: on head, RELIABLE/MADE IN CANADA.

Ref.No.: D of C, CA34, p. 281

Mint $225.00 **Ex.** $175.00 **G.** $95.00 **F.** $55.00

PLASSIKINS

1948. 14 in. (35.5 cm). Hard plastic bent-limb baby, jointed hips, shoulders, neck and wrists. Hard plastic head; blue plastic sleep eyes, and lashes; light brown moulded hair; closed mouth. Mark: RELIABLE/MADE IN CANADA.

Ref.No.: D of C, CL3, p. 281

Mint $140.00 **Ex.** $105.00 **G.** $65.00 **F.** $40.00

Note: One of the first hard plastic dolls in Canada.

BABY LOVUMS
1948 - 17 in.

1948. 17 in. (43 cm). Cloth body with crier, composition hands and bent-limb legs. Composition head; blue sleep eyes, lashes; brown moulded hair; closed mouth. Mark: on head, A/RELIABLE/DOLL.

Ref.No.: D of C, BJ6, p. 282

Mint $200.00 **Ex.** $150.00 **G.** $85.00 **F.** $50.00

BABY LOVUMS
1948 - 25 in.

1948. 25 in. (63.5 cm). Cloth body with crier, composition hands and bent-limb legs. Composition head; blue plastic sleep eyes, lashes, painted lower lashes; blond mohair wig; closed mouth. Mark: on head, RELIABLE/MADE IN CANADA. Replaced clothing similar to the original. Original socks and shoes.

Ref.No.: 2W31

Mint $255.00 **Ex.** $205.00 **G.** $125.00 **F.** $65.00

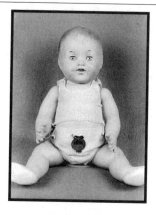

BABYKINS
Open-closed Mouth

1948. 17 in. (43 cm). All composition, jointed hips, shoulders and neck. Composition head with dimpled cheeks; blue tin sleep eyes, lashes, painted lower lashes; reddish brown moulded hair; open-closed mouth, two painted teeth. Mark: on head, RELIABLE/MADE IN CANADA.

Ref.No.: D of C, CJ36, p. 282

Mint $125.00 **Ex.** $95.00 **G.** $60.00 **F.** $40.00

CUDDLES
Blond Moulded Hair

1948. 22 in. (56 cm). Cloth body, composition arms and straight legs. Composition head; blue metal sleep eyes, lashes, painted lower lashes; blond moulded hair; closed mouth. Mark: on head, A/RELIABLE/DOLL/MADE IN CANADA.

Ref.No.: D of C, CO24, p. 282

Mint $225.00 **Ex.** $185.00 **G.** $110.00 **F.** $60.00

WETUMS
1948 - 11 in.

1948. 11 in. (28 cm). Composition, one-piece head and body, jointed hips and shoulders. Painted blue eyes; open mouth nurser. Mark: on head, RELIABLE MADE IN CANADA.

Ref.No.: ES63

Mint $75.00 **Ex.** $50.00 **G.** $30.00 **F.** $25.00

RUTHIE
ca.1949 - 17 in.

ca.1949. 17 in. (43 cm). Cloth body, bent limb, latex arms and legs, crier in the body. Composition head; brown tin sleep eyes, lashes, painted lower lashes; blond mohair wig; closed mouth. Mark: on head, RELIABLE DOLL/MADE IN CANADA. Original costume.

Ref.No.: D of C, AW22, p. 283

Mint **$165.00** **Ex.** **$110.00** **G.** **$65.00** **F.** **$50.00**

CUDDLES
Blond Mohair Hair

1949. 24 in. (61 cm). Cloth body, composition arms and legs. Composition head; blue sleep eyes, lashes, painted lowers; blond mohair wig; closed mouth. Mark: on head, RELIABLE/MADE IN CANADA. Original organdy dress and matching frilled bonnet, socks and shoes.

Ref.No.: HX9

Mint **$240.00** **Ex.** **$200.00** **G.** **$120.00** **F.** **$65.00**

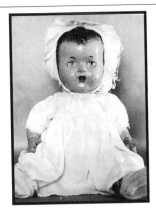

RELIABLE
ca.1949 - 20 in.

ca.1949. 20 in. (51 cm). All composition, jointed hips, shoulders and neck. Composition head; blue tin sleep eyes, lashes, painted lowers; moulded brown hair; closed mouth. Mark: on head, RELIABLE OF CANADA. Original white taffeta dress and matching bonnet.

Ref.No.: DH10

Mint **$175.00** **Ex.** **$125.00** **G.** **$75.00** **F.** **$40.00**

PIGTAILS
1949 - 19 in.

1949. 19 in. (48 cm). Composition body, jointed hips, shoulders and neck. Composition head; blue tin sleep eyes, lashes, painted lowers; blond mohair wig in pigtails and bangs; open mouth showing four teeth and tongue. Mark: on head, RELIABLE/MADE IN CANADA. Original plaid taffeta skirt, attached panties, velveteen jacket, felt hat, shoulder bag purse, socks and shoes.

Ref.No.: D of C, CY6, p. 283

Mint **$195.00** **Ex.** **$150.00** **G.** **$95.00** **F.** **$60.00**

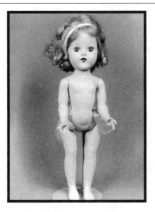

SUSIE STEPPS
ca.1949 - 15 in.

ca.1949. 15 in. (38 cm). All hard plastic walker, jointed hips, shoulders, and neck. Hard plastic head; blue sleep eyes, lashes, painted lower lashes, dark upper eye shadow; synthetic blond wig; open mouth showing four teeth and tongue. Mark: on body, RELIABLE (in script)/MADE IN CANADA. Originally wore plaid dress.

Ref.No.: D of C, CD28, p. 284

Mint **$165.00** **Ex.** **$135.00** **G.** **$90.00** **F.** **$45.00**

BRIDE DOLL
ca.1949 - 15 in.

ca.1949. 15 in. (30.5 cm). Composition body, jointed hips, shoulders and neck. Composition head; blue plastic sleep eyes, lashes, painted lower lashes; blond mohair wig; open mouth. Mark: on head, RELIABLE/MADE IN CANADA.

Ref.No.: D of C, BZ16, p. 284

Mint **$140.00** **Ex.** **$100.00** **G.** **$60.00** **F.** **$35.00**

BABY LOVUMS
1949 - 24 in.

1949. 24 in. (61 cm). Cloth body, composition legs and hands. Composition head; blue sleep eyes, lashes, painted lower lashes, eye shadow over eyes; blond mohair curly wig; closed mouth. Mark: on head, RELIABLE/MADE IN CANADA. Original dress and bonnet. Replaced shoes and socks.

Ref.No.: D of C, BT22, p. 284

Mint **$245.00** **Ex.** **$200.00** **G.** **$125.00** **F.** **$65.00**

BONNIE BRAIDS

1950. 14 in. (35.5 cm). Magic Skin one-piece body and legs, jointed shoulders. Vinyl head; painted blue eyes, painted upper lashes; moulded hair with two inset braids; open-closed mouth. Mark: on head, RELIABLE (in script)/13BVE. Original white cotton gown, lace trim, pale blue rayon jacket, pink hair ribbons.

Ref.No.: D of C, CX15, p. 285

Mint **$125.00** **Ex.** **$ 85.00** **G.** **$55.00** **F.** **$30.00**

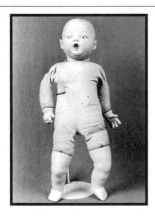

SNOOZIE
Yawning

1950. 17 in. (43 cm). Cloth body and arms, stuffed vinyl hands and legs. Head is an early soft vinyl that feels like sponge rubber; blue painted eyes, painted upper lashes; light brown moulded hair; open-closed yawning mouth. Mark: on head, RELIABLE. Also came in 12 and 14 inch sizes with latex hands and legs.

Ref.No.: D of C, AM5, p. 285

Mint $85.00 **Ex.** $70.00 **G.** $45.00 **F.** $20.00

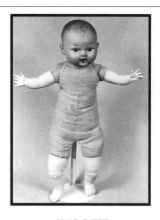

SNOOZIE
Not Yawning

1950. 21 in. (53 cm). Beige linen body, vinyl arms and legs. Stuffed vinyl head: inset blue plastic eyes, painted upper lashes; moulded light brown hair; open-closed mouth. Mark: on head, RELIABLE (script)/6CV8/1. Originally dressed in a nightie and diaper and wrapped in a blanket tied with a ribbon bow.

Ref.No.: PGC7

Mint $105.00 **Ex.** $85.00 **G.** $55.00 **F.** $35.00

TONI
1950 - 14 in.

1950. 14 in. (35.5 cm). Hard plastic body, jointed hips, shoulders and neck. Hard plastic head; blue sleep eyes, lashes, painted lower lashes; dark brown nylon wig (glued on head); closed mouth. Unmarked. Original costume.

Ref.No.: D of C, CD10, p. 285

Mint $195.00 **Ex.** $165.00 **G.** $105.00 **F.** $55.00

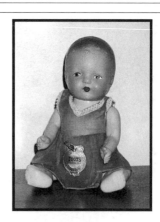

TOOTS

1950. 9 1/2 in. (24 cm). Five-piece composition body. Composition head; painted blue eyes; moulded hair. Unmarked. Original tag. Original pink organdy dress and attached panties.

Ref.No.: ES16

Mint $60.00 **Ex.** $45.00 **G.** $30.00 **F.** $20.00

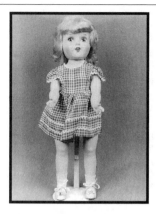

SUSIE STEPPS
1950 - 20 in.

1950. 20 in. (51 cm). Hard plastic body, jointed hips, shoulders and neck. Hard plastic head; brown sleep eyes, lashes, painted lower lashes; light brown saran wig; open mouth showing teeth and tongue. Mark: RELIABLE.

Ref.No. D of C, CF33 p. 286

Mint **$210.00** **Ex.** **$150.00** **G.** **$95.00** **F.** **$50.00**

TICKLE TOES
1950 - 15 in.

1950. 15 in. (38 cm). Cloth body, stuffed latex arms and legs. Composition head; blue plastic eyes, lashes, painted lower lashes; moulded hair, originally wore a semi-wig; closed mouth. Mark: on head, RELIABLE/DOLL/MADE IN CANADA. Original pink organdy dress and matching bonnet. Replaced bootees.

Ref.No.: D of C, CI36, p. 286

Mint **$55.00** **Ex.** **$40.00** **G.** **$25.00** **F.** **$15.00**

STOOPY
Puppet

1950. 9 in. (23 cm). Cloth body with felt hands. Composition head; painted black eyes; open-closed smiling mouth. Unmarked. Wearing dunce hat.

Ref.No.: 2J32

Mint **$30.00** **Ex.** **$25.00** **G.** **$20.00** **F.** **$15.00**

ANNE OF GREEN GABLES
ca.1950 - 8 in.

ca.1950. 8 in. (20 cm). Hard plastic body. Hard plastic head; sleep eyes; red wig; closed mouth. Original costume and box.

Ref.No.: HX12

Mint **$100.00** **Ex.** **$75.00** **G.** **$40.00** **F.** **$20.00**

Note: Possibly issued by Reliable for Lothian's Gift Shop in Stanhope, P.E.I.

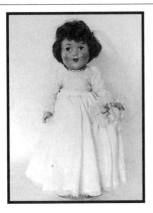

BRIDE
1950 - 15 in.

1950. 15 in. (38 cm). Composition body, jointed hips, shoulders and neck. Composition head: blue sleep eyes, lashes; auburn mohair wig; closed mouth. Mark: on head, RELIABLE/MADE IN/CANADA. Original lace trimmed gown, veil and bouquet.

Ref.No.: 2H36

Mint $140.00 **Ex.** $100.00 **G.** $60.00 **F.** $35.00

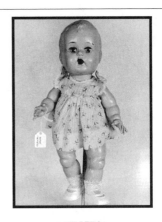

TRUDY
1950 - 12 in.

1950. 12 in. (30.5 cm). All hard plastic body, jointed hips, shoulders and neck. Hard plastic head: blue sleep eyes, lashes; moulded hair; open-closed mouth. Mark: on head, RELIABLE (in script). Original cotton flowered dress and attached panties.

Ref.No.: 2J16

Mint $105.00 **Ex.** $70.00 **G.** $50.00 **F.** $30.00

TOPSY
1950 - 10 in.

1950. 10 in. (25.5 cm). All composition body, jointed hips and shoulders. Black painted side-glancing eyes; black moulded hair; closed mouth. Mark: on back, RELIABLE/MADE IN CANADA.

Ref.No.: D of C, CH8, p. 286

Mint $105.00 **Ex.** $70.00 **G.** $45.00 **F.** $30.00

HAIRBOW PEGGY
1950 - 16 1/2 in.

1950. 16 1/2 in. (42 cm). Cloth body and legs, composition arms. Composition shoulderhead; black painted side-glancing eyes, black line over eye; light brown moulded hair with hole for hair ribbon; closed mouth. Mark: on shoulderplate, RELIABLE DOLL/MADE IN CANADA.

Ref.No.: D of C, BZ29, p. 287

Mint $120.00 **Ex.** $85.00 **G.** $55.00 **F.** $40.00

PEGGY
1950 - 13 in.

1950. 13 in. (33 cm). Cloth body and legs, composition forearms. Composition shoulderhead; painted black side-glancing eyes; moulded brown hair; closed mouth. Mark: on shoulderplate, A/RELIABLE/DOLL/MADE IN CANADA. Original cotton print dress.

Ref.No.: 2N22

Mint $65.00 **Ex.** $50.00 **G.** $35.00 **F.** $25.00

LOVUMS
1950 - 19 in.

1950. 19 in. (48 cm). Cloth body, vinyl arms and legs. Hard plastic head; brown sleep eyes, lashes; brown wig; closed mouth. Mark: on head, RELIABLE (in script). Original blue organdy dress and bonnet, replaced socks and shoes. Transition doll. Made of materials that will not deteriorate.

Ref.No.: PGM7

Mint $170.00 **Ex.** $130.00 **G.** $95.00 **F.** $65.00

PIGTAILS
1951 - 15 in.

1951. 15 in. (38 cm). Composition body, jointed hips, shoulders and neck. Composition head; blue sleep eyes, lashes, painted lower lashes; blond mohair wig in pigtails with bangs; closed mouth. Unmarked. Original hang tag with name. Original cotton dress, socks and shoes.

Ref.No.: D of C, CR24, p. 287

Mint $125.00 **Ex.** $85.00 **G.** $45.00 **F.** $30.00

PIGTAILS
1951 - 18 in.

1951. 18 in. (45.5 cm). Composition body, jointed hips, shoulders and neck. Composition head; blue sleep eyes, lashes, painted lower lashes; honey blond mohair wig in pigtails with curly bangs; open mouth showing four teeth. Mark: on head, RELIABLE/MADE IN CANADA. Originally wore a cotton print dress.

Ref.No.: D of C, BJ13, p. 287

Mint. $185.00 **Ex.** $135.00 **G.** $80.00 **F.** $50.00

PIGTAILS
1951 - 22 in.

1951. 22 in. (56 cm). Composition body, jointed hips, shoulder and neck. Composition head with dimples; blue sleep eyes, lashes, painted lower lashes; light brown mohair pigtails with curly bangs; open mouth showing teeth and tongue. Mark: on head, RELIABLE. Originally wore cotton print dress with white panel in front, white socks and shoes.

Ref.No.: D of C, CO22, p. 288

Mint $220.00 **Ex.** $165.00 **G.** $95.00 **F.** $50.00

BABY SKIN

1951. 12 in. (30.5 cm). Stuffed latex body with coo voice. Composition head with nostril holes; blue plastic sleep eyes, lashes, painted lower lashes; light brown moulded hair; closed mouth. Mark: on head, RELIABLE/MADE IN CANADA.

Ref.No.: D of C, BH11, p. 288

Mint $85.00 **Ex.** $75.00 **G.** $45.00 **F.** $25.00

CUDDLES
Brown Moulded Hair

1951. 20 in. (51 cm). Cloth body, composition arms and legs. Composition head; blue sleep eyes, lashes; moulded brown hair; closed mouth. Mark: on head, RELIABLE/DOLL/MADE IN CANADA. Original white organdy dress and pink slip. Originally wore a matching lace trimmed bonnet, rubber pants and white socks and shoes.

Ref.No.: GK16

Mint $215.00 **Ex.** $175.00 **G.** $95.00 **F.** $55.00

SUSIE STEPPS
Walking Doll

1951. A walking doll. 19 in. (48 cm). Hard plastic body, jointed hips, shoulders and neck. Hard plastic head; blue sleep eyes, lashes, painted lowers; blond saran wig; open mouth showing teeth. Mark: on body, RELIABLE. Original hang tag. Original flowered dress, socks and shoes replaced.

Ref.No.: 2O1

Mint $210.00 **Ex.** $150.00 **G.** $95.00 **F.** $50.00

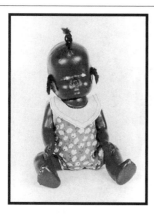

TOPSY
1951 - 10 in.

1951. 10 in. (25.5 cm). Composition body, jointed hips, shoulders and neck. Composition head; painted side-glancing eyes; moulded hair with three inset wool braids; closed mouth. Mark: on head, RELIABLE/MADE IN CANADA. Original sunsuit.

Ref.No.: 2B18

Mint $125.00 **Ex.** $85.00 **G.** $50.00 **F.** $40.00

RELIABLE
ca.1951 - 8 in.

ca.1951. 8 in. (20 cm). Hard plastic body, jointed shoulders and neck. Hard plastic head; sleep eyes; mohair wig; closed mouth. Mark: on back, RELIABLE (in script)/MADE IN CANADA.

Ref.No.: 2G7

Mint $25.00 **Ex.** $20.00 **G.** $15.00 **F.** $10.00

Note: Sold dressed in a variety of costumes.

HIGHLAND LASSIE
1951 - 15 in.

1951. 15 in. (38 cm). Composition body, jointed hips, shoulders and neck. Composition head; blue sleep eyes, lashes, painted lowers; blond mohair wig; open mouth showing teeth. Mark: on head, A/RELIABLE DOLL/MADE IN CANADA. Original flannel plaid skirt and scarf, black velvet jacket and tam. Originally wore black shoes and white socks.

Ref.No.: 2C26

Mint $140.00 **Ex.** $100.00 **G.** $55.00 **F.** $35.00

TODDLES
1951 - 17 in.

1951. 17 in. (43 cm). All composition. Blue plastic sleep eyes, lashes; moulded brown hair; closed mouth. Redressed; Originally wore cotton dress and matching bonnet with rick-rack trim.

Ref.No.: ES18

Mint $75.00 **Ex.** $60.00 **G.** $40.00 **F.** $25.00

SUNSHINE SUSIE
1951 - 13 in.

1951. 13 in. (33 cm). Cloth body. Cloth head with rubberized face, painted features. Original tag on dress: SUNSHINE SUSIE / A RELIABLE DOLL / A BRITISH EMPIRE PRODUCT / MADE IN CANADA / MFD. BY RELIABLE TOY CO. LTD. CANADA.

Ref.No.: 2X3

Mint $25.00 **Ex.** $20.00 **G.** $10.00 **F.** $5.00

DRUM MAJOR

1951. 16 in. (40.5 cm). Cloth and fur fabric body, arms and legs. Composition head; painted black side-glancing eyes; moulded hair; closed mouth. Mark: on head, RELIABLE DOLL / MADE IN CANADA. Original matching removable hat.

Ref.No.: 2J23

Mint $25.00 **Ex.** $20.00 **G.** $15.00 **F.** $10.00

MORTIMER SNERD PUPPET

ca.1951. 10 in. (25.5 cm). Black cotton body. Composition head; painted side-glancing eyes; moulded hair; closed smiling mouth with painted teeth protruding. Mark: on head, RELIABLE / MADE IN CANADA; on gown, EDGAR BERGEN'S MORTIMER SNERD / MADE IN CANADA / BY RELIABLE TOY.

Ref.No.: 2PGGK18

Mint. $30.00 **Ex.** $20.00 **G.** $15.00 **F.** $10.00

DREAM BABY
ca.1952 - 20 in.

ca.1952. 20 in. (51 cm). Cloth body, stuffed vinyl arms and legs. Vinyl head; blue sleep eyes, lashes, painted lower lashes; rooted blond saran hair; open-closed mouth. Mark: on head, RELIABLE / 4CV28.

Ref.No.: D of C, BH17, p. 288

Mint $110.00 **Ex.** $65.00 **G.** $45.00 **F.** $25.00

RELIABLE
ca.1952 - 24 in.

ca.1952. 24 in. (61 cm). Cloth body, stuffed latex arms and legs. Composition shoulderhead; blue sleep eyes, lashes, painted lower lashes; blond saran wig; open mouth showing two teeth and tongue. Mark: on shoulderplate, A/RELIABLE/DOLL/MADE IN CANADA.

Ref.No.: D of C, CF34, p. 289

Mint $85.00 **Ex.** $60.00 **G.** $45.00 **F.** $25.00

RELIABLE
ca.1952 - 14 in.

ca.1952. 14 in. (35.5 cm). Composition body, jointed hips, shoulders and neck. Composition head with freckles; hazel sleep eyes, lashes; auburn saran wig; open mouth showing teeth and tongue. Mark: on head, RELIABLE/MADE IN CANADA.

Ref.No.: D of C, CD23, p. 289

Mint $120.00 **Ex.** $95.00 **G.** $50.00 **F.** $30.00

BOY IN OVERALLS

1952. 24 in. (61 cm). Cloth body, stuffed rubber arms and legs, crier. Composition shoulderhead; Sleep eyes; moulded hair; closed mouth. Mark: on shoulderplate, A RELIABLE DOLL. Original red and yellow costume with matching cap and red rubber boots.

Ref.No.: HX23

Mint $85.00 **Ex.** $60.00 **G.** $35.00 **F.** $20.00

MARY HAD A LITTLE LAMB
1952 - 5 1/2 in.

1952. 5 1/2 in. (14 cm). Hard plastic one-piece body and head with jointed shoulders. Painted side-glancing eyes; mohair wig; closed mouth. Original taffeta and net dress with "Mary had a Little Lamb" around the skirt.

Ref.No.: 2K17

Mint $25.00 **Ex.** $20.00 **G.** $15.00 **F.** $10.00

SUSIE STEPPS
Vinyl Head

1952. 19 in. (48 cm). Hard plastic body, jointed hips, shoulders and neck. Vinyl head; blue sleep eyes, lashes; rooted blond hair; closed mouth. Mark: on head, RELIABLE; on body, RELIABLE (in script)/MADE IN CANADA. Original pink printed taffeta dress, pink shoes.

Ref.No.: 2K28

Mint $180.00 **Ex.** $140.00 **G.** $95.00 **F.** $50.00

SUSIE STEPPS
Hard Plastic Head

1952. 19 in. (48 cm). Hard plastic body, jointed hips, shoulders and neck. Hard plastic head; blue sleep eyes, lashes; saran blond wig; open mouth showing teeth. Mark: RELIABLE. Original green and yellow cotton dress.

Ref.No.: D of C, CT24, p. 289

Mint. $210.00 **Ex.** $150.00 **G.** $95.00 **F.** $50.00

HER HIGHNESS CORONATION DOLL
1953 - 14 in.

1953. 14 in. (35.5 cm). Composition body, jointed hips, shoulders and neck. Composition head; blue sleep eyes, lashes, reddish brown painted lower lashes and brows; auburn wig; open mouth, smiling showing six teeth. Mark: on head, A/RELIABLE DOLL.

Ref.No.: D of C, CA30, p. 290

Mint $250.00 **Ex.** $200.00 **G.** $95.00 **F.** $40.00

HER HIGHNESS CORONATION DOLL
1953 - 15 in.

1953. 15 in. (38 cm). Hard plastic body, jointed hips, shoulders and neck. Hard plastic head; blue sleep eyes, lashes; brown saran wig; closed mouth. Mark: on body, RELIABLE (in script). Original white taffeta and brocade gown with gold rick-rack trim, red velvet cloak lined with taffeta and trimmed with white velvet, red velvet crown, pearl necklace, red ribbon badge with gold lettering, pink shoes, marked Reliable/Made in Canada.

Ref.No.: 2L22

Mint $225.00 **Ex.** $175.00 **G.** $95.00 **F.** $50.00

HER HIGHNESS CORONATION DOLL.
1953 - 11 1/2 in.

1953. 11 1/2 in. (29 cm). Hard plastic body, jointed shoulders and neck. Hard plastic head; blue sleep eyes, moulded lashes; brown mohair wig; closed mouth. Mark: on body RELIABLE (in script)/MADE IN CANADA. Original white taffeta gown with gold trim, red taffeta cape with white taffeta lining and white velvet trim. Replaced crown. Missing ribbon.

Ref.No.: 2M4

Mint $90.00   **Ex.** $70.00   **G.** $40.00   **F.** $25.00

SUSIE STEPPS BRIDE

1953. 20 in. (51 cm). Hard plastic walker, jointed hips, shoulders and neck. Hard plastic head; blue sleep eyes, lashes, painted lowers; blond saran wig; open mouth, felt tongue and teeth. Mark: on body, RELIABLE (in script). Original wedding gown and veil.

Ref.No.: 2K9

Mint $210.00   **Ex.** $150.00   **G.** $95.00   **F.** $50.00

DREAM BABY
1953 - 19 in.

1953. 19 in. (48 cm). Cloth body, vinyl flex arms and legs. Vinyl head; blue sleep eyes, lashes, painted lower lashes; dark brown saran hair; open-closed mouth. Mark: on head, RELIABLE (in script)/MADE IN CANADA/V18.

Ref.No.: D of C, AP13, p. 290

Mint $95.00   **Ex.** $75.00   **G.** $50.00   **F.** $30.00

DRESS ME DOLL

1953. 11 in. (28 cm). Hard plastic body, jointed shoulders and neck. Hard plastic head; sleep eyes; brown wig; closed mouth. Mark: on back, RELIABLE/PAT. PEND. 1953.

Ref.No.: D of C, BQ5, p. 291

Mint $25.00   **Ex.** $20.00   **G.** $15.00   **F.** $10.00

TICKLE TOES
1953 - 23 in.

1953. 23 in. (58.5 cm). One-piece stuffed latex body. Vinyl head; blue sleep eyes, lashes, painted lower lashes; rooted blond hair with bangs; open-closed mouth. Mark: on head, RELIABLE (in script) /MOV19.

Ref.No.: D of C, CJ5, p. 291

Mint $85.00 **Ex.** $60.00 **G.** $45.00 **F.** $30.00

PATTY
1953 - 14 in.

1953. 14 in. (35.5 cm). Hard plastic body, jointed hips, shoulders and neck. Hard plastic head; blue sleep eyes, lashes, painted lower lashes; blond mohair wig; closed mouth. Mark: on back, RELIABLE (in script).

Ref.No.: D. of C, CI12, p. 291

Mint $140.00 **Ex.** $95.00 **G.** $60.00 **F.** $40.00

HIAWATHA
ca.1953 - 8 in.

ca.1953. 8 in. (20 cm). Brown hard plastic body and head, jointed hips, shoulders and neck. Amber sleep eyes; black hair; open mouth. Mark: on body, RELIABLE (in script) MADE IN CANADA. Missing pants, belt and feather in headband.

Ref.No.: DR3

Mint $45.00 **Ex.** $30.00 **G.** $25.00 **F.** $20.00

HONEY
Hard Plastic Head, Moulded Hair

1953. 16 in. (40.5 cm). Cloth body, stuffed latex arms and legs. Hard plastic head; blue painted eyes, black line over eye; brown moulded hair; closed mouth. Mark: on head, RELIABLE (in script). Original dress, bonnet missing.

Ref.No.: D of C, CM2, p. 292.

Mint $75.00 **Ex.** $50.00 **G.** $35.00 **F.** $25.00

HONEY
Composition Head, Saran Hair

1953. 15 in. (38 cm). Cloth body, stuffed latex arms and legs. Composition shoulderhead; blue sleep eyes, lashes; saran hair sewn on bonnet brim; closed mouth. Mark; on head, RELIABLE/MADE IN CANADA. Original blue taffeta and plaid trim dress and matching bonnet, socks and shoes.

Ref.No.: 2C22

Mint $75.00   **Ex.** $50.00   **G.** $35.00   **F.** $25.00

HONEY
Composition Head, Mohair Wig

1953. 20 in. (51 cm). Cloth body, stuffed latex arms and legs. Composition shoulderhead; blue sleep eyes, lashes, painted lowers; brown mohair wig over moulded hair. Mark: on shoulderplate, RELIABLE/DOLL/MADE IN CANADA. Original rose dress with plaid trim and matching bonnet.

Ref.No.: 2E19

Mint $85.00   **Ex.** $60.00   **G.** $40.00   **F.** $30.00

SNOOZIE
1953 - 11 in.

1953. 11 in. (28 cm). One-piece magic skin (stuffed latex) body, with coo voice. Vinyl head; blue plastic inset eyes, painted upper lashes; light brown moulded hair; open-closed yawning mouth. Mark: on head, RELIABLE (in script)/121131. Replaced nightie.

Ref.No.: D of C, CJ23, p. 292

Mint $65.00   **Ex.** $45.00   **G.** $25.00   **F.** $20.00

SUSIE WALKER
1953 - 13 in.

1953. 13 in. (33 cm). Hard plastic body, jointed hips, shoulders, and neck. Hard plastic head; blue sleep eyes, moulded lashes, painted lower lashes; dark brown synthetic wig; closed mouth. Mark: RELIABLE (in script)/MADE IN CANADA.

Ref.No.: D of C, CO32, p. 292

Mint $115.00   **Ex.** $85.00   **G.** $45.00   **F.** $35.00

PATTY BRIDE
1953 - 15 in.

1953. 15 in. (38 cm). Hard plastic body, jointed hips, shoulders and neck. Hard plastic head; hazel sleep eyes, lashes, painted lowers; brown wig; closed mouth. Mark: RELIABLE (in script)/MADE IN CANADA. Original bridal gown and veil.

Ref.No.: 2N30

Mint $145.00 **Ex.** $115.00 **G.** $70.00 **F.** $40.00

RELIABLE
1953 - 24 in.

1953. 24 in. (61 cm). Cloth body, composition arms and legs. Composition head; blue sleep eyes, lashes, painted lowers; blond saran wig in braids; closed mouth. Mark: on head, RELIABLE/MADE IN CANADA. Original blue, flocked cotton dress with matching bonnet, replaced shoes.

Ref.No.: 2A20

Mint $195.00 **Ex.** $150.00 **G.** $95.00 **F.** $60.00

SAUCY WALKER
1953 - Open Mouth

1953. 22 in. (56 cm). Hard plastic body with crier, jointed hips, shoulders and neck. Hard plastic head; plastic flirty eyes, lashes, painted lower lashes; blond saran wig; open mouth showing two teeth and tongue. Mark: RELIABLE/MADE in CANADA. Original jumper dress.

Ref.No.: D of C, CG21, p. 293.

Mint $220.00 **Ex.** $160.00 **G.** $100.00 **F.** $55.00

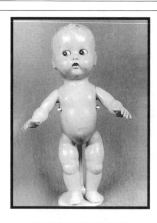

SOUVENIR DOLL
1954 - 10 in.

1954. 10 in. (25.5 cm). Hard plastic body, jointed hips and shoulders. Blue sleep side-glancing eyes; light brown moulded hair; open mouth. Mark: on back, RELIABLE (in script)/MADE IN CANADA. Originally dressed as a Mountie or in a Scottish costume.

Ref.No.: D of C, BP16, p. 293

Mint $45.00 **Ex.** $35.00 **G.** $20.00 **F.** $15.00

RELIABLE
ca.1954 - 19 1/2 in.

ca.1954. 19 1/2 in. (49.5 in). One-piece vinyl-flex body. Vinyl head; blue sleep eyes, lashes, painted lower lashes; rooted blond saran curly hair; closed mouth. Mark: on head, RELIABLE/1581.

Ref.No.: D of C, BH18, p. 293

Mint **$75.00** **Ex.** **$65.00** **G.** **$40.00** **F.$ 25.00**

SUSIE WALKER
1954 - 15 in.

1954. 15 in. (38 cm). Hard plastic body, jointed hips, shoulders, and neck. Hard plastic head; brown sleep eyes, plastic lashes, painted lower lashes; blond wig in braids with bangs; open-closed mouth showing two moulded teeth. Mark: on back, RELIABLE (in script)/MADE IN CANADA. Original cotton dress.

Ref.No.: D of C, BX7, p. 294

Mint **$150.00** **Ex.** **$95.00** **G.** **$65.00** **F.** **$40.00**

JOAN
1955 - 19 in.

1955. 19 in. (48 cm). One-piece stuffed latex body. Vinyl head; blue sleep eyes, lashes, painted lowers; brown deeply moulded hair; open-closed mouth. Mark: on head, RELIABLE. Original blue flocked dress and bonnet, replaced shoes and socks.

Ref.No.: 2K35

Mint **$60.00** **Ex.** **$40.00** **G.** **$30.00** **F.** **$15.00**

WALKING DOLL
1955 - 15 in.

1955. 15 in. (38 cm). Hard plastic walker, jointed hips, shoulders and neck. Vinyl head; blue sleep eyes, lashes, painted lowers; deeply moulded brown hair in ringlets, moulded red hairbow; closed mouth. Mark: on head, RELIABLE (in script); on body, RELIABLE (in script). Replaced costume. Original red shoes and white socks. Originally wore printed cotton pique jacket with crushed ice dress trimmed with bows.

Ref.No.: 2M8

Mint **$75.00** **Ex.** **$55.00** **G.** **$40.00** **F.** **$30.00**

WALKING DOLL
Plastisol Head

1955. 15 in. (38 cm). Hard plastic body. Plastisol head; grey sleep eyes; rooted hair; closed mouth. Mark: on head, 157 WD / RELIABLE 13; on body, RELIABLE MADE IN CANADA. Original red dress with print inset and rick-rack trim.

Mint $75.00   **Ex.** $55.00   **G.** $40.00   **F.** $30.00

POSIE
1955 - 23 in.

1955. 23 in. (58.5 cm). Hard plastic body, jointed knees, hips, and shoulders. Vinyl head; blue sleep eyes, lashes, painted lowers; rooted long blond curly hair; closed mouth. Mark: on head, 17/RELIABLE. Original blue nylon dress with lace trim. Shown in catalogue with knee-length dress with rick-rack trim.

Ref.No.: PGC10

Mint $175.00   **Ex.** $130.00   **G.** $65.00   **F.** $45.00

SAUCY WALKER
1955 - 22 in.

1955. 22 in. (56 cm). Plastic body, jointed hips, shoulders and neck. Vinyl head; hazel sleep eyes, lashes, painted lower lashes; rooted blond curly hair; closed mouth. Mark: on head, 1391/RELIABLE (in script). Original dress.

Ref.No.: D of C, CE16, p. 294

Mint $160.00   **Ex.** $120.00   **G.** $65.00   **F.** $40.00

MARGARET ANN
1955 - 20 in.

1955. 20 in. (51 cm). One-piece vinyl-flex body. Vinyl head; blue sleep eyes, lashes, painted lower lashes; rooted blond saran hair; closed mouth. Mark: on head, 1481/RELIABLE (in script). Original costume.

Ref.No.: D of C, CE14, p. 294

Mint $75.00   **Ex.** $60.00   **G.** $40.00   **F.** $25.00

NANCY LEE

1955. 25 in. (63.5 cm). One-piece stuffed vinyl body. Vinyl head; sleep eyes; rooted brown hair. Unmarked. Original pink and cream dress and bonnet; replaced socks and shoes.

Ref.No.: ES46

Mint $75.00 **Ex.** $60.00 **G.** $40.00 **F.** $25.00

GLAMOUR GIRL
1956 - 15 in.

1956. 15 in. (38 cm). One-piece vinyl skin body. Vinyl head; blue inset eyes, painted upper lashes; rooted blond hair; closed mouth. Mark: on back, R-15X; on shoes, RELIABLE/950-O/MADE IN CANADA.

Ref.No.: D of C, BC17, p. 295

Mint $45.00 **Ex.** $35.00 **G.** $25.00 **F.** $20.00

MAGGIE MUGGINS
1956 - 16 in.

1956. 16 in. (40.5 cm). One-piece magic skin (stuffed latex) body. Vinyl head with freckles; blue sleep eyes, lashes, painted lower lashes; rooted red saran hair in pigtails with curly bangs; closed mouth. Mark: on head, RELIABLE. Original green print dress and white pinafore, white socks and green shoes.

Ref.No.: D of C, CF9, p. 296

Mint $140.00 **Ex.** $110.00 **G.** $65.00 **F.** $35.00

Note: Few of these dolls have survived, as the rubber skin deteriorated so rapidly.

DAVY CROCKETT

1956. 12 in. (30.5 cm). One-piece magic skin (stuffed latex) body with coo voice. Vinyl head; plastic inset eyes; moulded hair; closed mouth. Original tag, MADE IN TORONTO, CANADA/BY RELIABLE TOY CO. LIMITED./WALT DISNEY'S OFFICIAL DAVY CROCKETT.

Ref.No.: D of C, BH36, p. 296

Mint $60.00 **Ex.** $40.00 **G.** $20.00 **F.** $15.00

Note: The same doll sold in 1957 as Pierre Radisson.

RELIABLE
1956 - 9 1/2 in.

1956. 9 1/2 in. (24 cm). One-piece stuffed vinyl body. Vinyl head; inset blue plastic eyes; rooted blond curls; open-closed mouth. Mark: on head, RELIABLE. Original cotton print dress.

Ref.No.: 2R11

Mint   **$25.00**   **Ex.**   **$20.00**   **G.**   **$15.00**   **F.**   **$10.00**

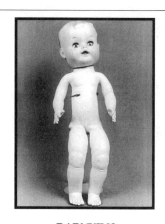

BABYKINS
1956 - 20 in.

1956. 20 in. (51 cm). One-piece vinyl-flex body. Vinyl head; blue sleep eyes, lashes, painted lower lashes; brown moulded hair; open-closed mouth. Mark: on head, RELIABLE 1590. Originally sold wearing only a diaper.

Ref.No.: D of C, AN28, p. 296

Mint   **$30.00**   **Ex.**   **$25.00**   **G.**   **$20.00**   **F.**   **$15.00**

BETSY WETSY
1956 - 13 in.

1956. 13 in. (33 cm). Vinyl body, jointed at hips, shoulders and neck. Hard plastic head; blue sleep eyes, lashes, painted lower lashes; grey eyeshadow; brown moulded hair; open mouth nurser. Mark: RELIABLE (in script) MADE IN CANADA.

Ref.No.: ES17

Mint   **$60.00**   **Ex.**   **$45.00**   **G.**   **$30.00**   **F.**   **$25.00**

MARGARET ANN
1956 - 17 in.

1956. 17 in. (43 cm). One-piece vinyl-flex body. Vinyl stuffed head; blue sleep eyes, lashes, painted lowers; platinum blond rooted hair in a pony-tail with bangs; closed mouth. Mark: on head, 14. Original pink and white nylon dress with dark blue ribbons and straw hat, socks and shoes missing.

Ref.No.: 2K10

Mint   **$60.00**   **Ex.**   **$45.00**   **G.**   **$25.00**   **F.**   **$15.00**

RELIABLE
ca.1956 - 18 in.

ca.1956. 18 in. (46 cm). One-piece stuffed vinyl-flex body. Vinyl head; blue sleep eyes, lashes; brown mohair wig; open-closed mouth with two painted teeth. Mark: on head, RELIABLE/CANADA. Original red dress trimmed with white lace, red slip attached to panties, socks and shoes.

Ref.No.: 2H18

Mint $75.00 **Ex.** $55.00 **G.** $40.00 **F.** $30.00

BRIDE
1956 - 15 in.

1956. 15 in. (38 cm). One-piece stuffed vinyl body. Vinyl head; blue sleep eyes, lashes; rooted blond hair; closed mouth. Mark: on head, RELIABLE. Original white gown trimmed with net and lace, pink panties, white socks and shoes, black net covering hair, net veil.

Ref.No.: 2N14

Mint $50.00 **Ex.** $40.00 **G.** $25.00 **F.** $20.00

RUTHIE
1956 - 14 in.

1956. 14 in. (35.5 cm). One-piece stuffed vinyl body. Vinyl head; blue sleep eyes, lashes; rooted blond curls; closed mouth. Mark: on head, RELIABLE. Original red and white cotton dress with blue rick-rack, blue hair ribbon, original name tag.

Ref.No.: PGM12

Mint $40.00 **Ex.** $30.00 **G.** $25.00 **F.** $15.00

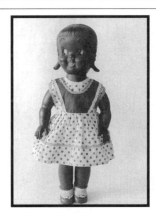

TOPSY
1956 - 12 in.

1956. 12 in. (30.5 cm). One-piece vinyl body. Vinyl head; side-glancing black eyes; hair moulded in braids; open-closed mouth. Mark: on head, 2/1132/RELIABLE. Original red and white cotton dress, red moulded shoes and white socks. Hairbows missing.

Ref.No.: PGL23

Mint $45.00 **Ex.** $35.00 **G.** $20.00 **F.** $15.00

RELIABLE
Washable Doll

1957. 9 1/2 in. (24 cm). One-piece vinyl body. Vinyl head; blue, painted side-glancing eyes, painted upper lashes; light brown moulded hair; open mouth nurser. Mark: on head, RELIABLE/MADE IN CANADA/1029. Originally wore bathrobe.

Ref.No.: 2O31

Mint $20.00 **Ex.** $15.00 **G.** $10.00 **F.** $5.00

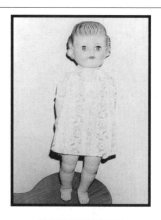

BABY BUBBLES
1957 - 21 in.

1957. 21 in. (53.5 cm). One-piece vinyl-flex body with coo voice. Vinyl head; blue sleep eyes, lashes; deeply moulded blond curls with bangs; closed mouth. Unmarked. Originally wore printed taffeta dress.

Ref. No.: D of C, CT18, p. 297

Mint $95.00 **Ex.** $75.00 **G.** $50.00 **F.** $35.00.

SUSIE THE WALKING DOLL
Blond Wig

1957. 9 in. (23 cm). Hard plastic body, jointed hips, shoulders and neck. Hard plastic head; blue plastic sleep eyes, moulded lashes; blond wig; closed mouth. Mark: on back, RELIABLE (in script)/MADE IN CANADA.

Ref.No.: D of C, BP5, p. 297

Mint $115.00 **Ex.** $85.00 **G.** $45.00 **F.** $35.00

BALLERINA DOLL
1957 - 20 in.

1957. 20 in. (51 cm). Plastic body and legs, vinyl arms, jointed knees, hips, shoulders and neck. Vinyl head; blue sleep eyes, lashes, painted lower lashes; rooted brown saran hair; closed mouth. Mark: on head, RELIABLE.

Ref.No.: D of C, CF26, p. 297

Mint $130.00 **Ex.** $95.00 **G.** $60.00 **F.** $30.00

POSIE
1957 - 23 in.

1957. 23 in. (58.5 cm). Hard plastic body, jointed knees, hips, shoulders and neck. Vinyl head; blue sleep eyes, lashes, painted lower lashes; rooted blond saran hair; closed mouth. Mark: on head and body, RELIABLE.

Ref.No.: D of C, CF10, p. 298

Mint $175.00 **Ex.** $130.00 **G.** $65.00 **F.** $45.00

TOPSY
1957 - 14 in.

1957. 14 in. (35.5 cm). One-piece vinyl-flex body. Vinyl head; golden brown sleep eyes, lashes, painted lower lashes; rooted black saran curly hair; closed mouth. Original tag: TOPSY/RELIABLE/MADE IN CANADA.

Ref.No.: D of C, BQ2, p. 298

Mint $60.00 **Ex.** $45.00 **G.** $30.00 **F.** $20.00

BETSY WETSY
1957 - 14 in.

1957. 14 in. (35.5 cm). Vinyl body, jointed hips, shoulders and neck. Vinyl head; brown sleep eyes, lashes, painted lower lashes; rooted brown curly saran hair; open mouth nurser. Mark: on back, RELIABLE (in script)/12.

Ref.No.: D of C, AM16, p. 298

Mint $50.00 **Ex.** $40.00 **G.** $25.00 **F.** $15.00

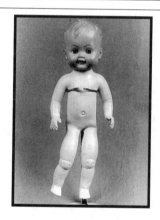

SLEEPYHEAD

1957. 14 in. (35.5 cm). One-piece vinyl-flex body. Vinyl head; inset plastic eyes, painted upper lashes; moulded hair; open-closed mouth. Mark: on head, RELIABLE (in script); on body, R-15X. Originally wore pyjamas.

Ref.No.: D of C, BU12, p. 299

Mint $20.00 **Ex.** $15.00 **G.** $12.00 **F.** $8.00

SUSIE THE WALKING DOLL
Brown Wig In Braids

1957. 9 in. (23 cm). Hard plastic body, jointed hips, shoulders and neck. Hard plastic head; blue sleep eyes, moulded lashes; brown wig in braids; closed mouth. Mark: on back, RELIABLE.

Ref.No.: D of C, CO3, p. 299

Mint $115.00 **Ex.** $85.00 **G.** $40.00 **F.** $35.00

MARY ANN
1957 - 23 in.

1957. 23 in. (58.5 cm). One-piece vinyl-flex body. Vinyl head; blue sleep eyes, lashes, painted lower lashes; rooted brown curls; closed mouth. Unmarked.

Ref.No.: D of C, CR14, p. 300

Mint $75.00 **Ex.** $60.00 **G.** $45.00 **F.** $25.00

BABY TEAR DROPS

1957. 11 in. (28 cm). Vinyl body, jointed hips, shoulders and neck. Hard plastic head; blue sleep eyes, moulded lashes; brown moulded hair; open mouth nurser. Mark: on head, RELIABLE (in script)/7.

Ref.No.: D of C, CO30, p. 300

Mint $50.00 **Ex.** $40.00 **G.** $30.00 **F.** $20.00

MISS CANADA PEDAL PUSHER

1957. 10 in. (25.5 cm). Plastic body, jointed hips, shoulders and neck. Vinyl head; blue sleep eyes, lashes; rooted brown hair; closed mouth. Mark: on head, P. Original red velvet pedal pushers, white nylon blouse, sandals, earrings. Originally included sunglasses and head scarf.

Ref.No.: 2K11

Mint $95.00 **Ex.** $60.00 **G.** $35.00 **F.** $25.00

Note: A wide variety of costumes were sold separately.

SUSIE STEPPS PARTY DRESS

1957. 20 in. (51 cm). Hard plastic walker, jointed hips, shoulders and neck; crier. Vinyl head; blue sleep eyes, lashes; rooted red hair; closed mouth. Mark: on head, RELIABLE ; on body, RELIABLE (in script). Original long, pink, flared taffeta gown with flocked marquisette overskirt, trimmed with ribbon.

Ref.No.: 2K2

Mint $185.00 Ex. $140.00 G. $95.00 F. $50.00

GLAMOUR GIRL
1957 - 15 in.

1957. 15 in. (38 cm). One-piece stuffed vinyl-flex body. Vinyl head; blue sleep eyes; rooted green hair; closed mouth. Mark: on head, RELIABLE. Original ski suit. Doll also came with pink or blue hair. Very unusual.

Ref.No.: HX24

Mint $75.00 Ex. $60.00 G. $45.00 F. $30.00

QUEEN OF DIAMONDS
REVLON DOLL

1957. 18 in. (45.5 cm). Plastic body, jointed hips, shoulders and neck. Vinyl head; blue sleep eyes, lashes, painted lowers; rooted light brown hair; closed mouth. Mark: on head, 14RA; on body, 918. Original taffeta skirt with a gold thread, red velvet blouse, fur collar, nylons, high-heeled shoes, earrings and diamond ring. Original white ribbon with red print, Revlon Doll by Reliable, Made in Canada.

Ref.No.: PGL21

Mint $135.00 Ex. $100.00 G. $70.00 F. $40.00

Note: May also be called a working doll.

KISSING PINK
REVLON DOLL

1957. 18 in. (45.5 cm). Vinyl body, jointed hips, shoulders and neck. Vinyl head; blue sleep eyes, lashes, painted lower lashes; rooted blond hair; closed mouth. Mark: on head, 326. Original dress. Original white ribbon with red print, Revlon Doll by Reliable, Made in Canada.

Mint $135.00 Ex. $100.00 G. $70.00 F. $40.00

Note: May also be called a working doll.

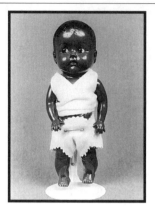

RELIABLE
ca.1958 - 7 1/2 in.

ca.1958. 7 1/2 in. (19 cm). Brown plastic baby, jointed hips and shoulders. Black side-glancing sleep eyes; moulded hair; closed mouth. Mark: on body, RELIABLE (in script)/MADE IN CANADA/PAT. PEND.

Ref.No.: D of C, BM32, p. 300

Mint $45.00 **Ex.** $35.00 **G.** $20.00 **F.** $15.00

MISS CANADA
1958 - 10 1/2 in.

1958. 10 1/2 in. (26.5 cm). Hard plastic body and legs, vinyl arms, jointed hips, waist, shoulders and neck. Vinyl head with earrings; blue sleep eyes, moulded lashes; rooted brown hair; closed mouth. Mark: on head, P.

Ref.No.: D of C, BQ18, p. 301

Mint $95.00 **Ex.** $70.00 **G.** $40.00 **F.** $30.00

MISS CANADA
PARTY FORMAL DRESS

1958. 20 in. (51 cm). Heavy quality vinyl body, jointed hips, shoulder, waist and neck. Vinyl head; brown sleep eyes, lashes, painted lower lashes; brown rooted hair; closed mouth. Mark: on head, 6. Original white gown with flocked black design, delicate underclothes, earrings, net headdress.

Ref.No.: DF21

Mint $125.00 **Ex.** $100.00 **G.** $65.00 **F.** $30.00

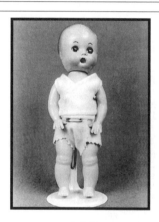

TRUDY
1958 - 8 in.

1958. 8 in. (20.5 cm). Plastic body, jointed hips, shoulders, and neck. Plastic head; sleep eyes, moulded lashes; moulded hair; open mouth nurser. Mark: on body, RELIABLE (in script)/MADE IN CANADA/Pat. 1958.

Ref.No.: D of C, BM31, p. 301

Mint $40.00 **Ex.** $30.00 **G.** $25.00 **F.** $15.00

PEGGY
1958 - 8 1/2 in.

1958. 8 1/2 in. (21.5 cm). Five-piece hard plastic body. Blue eyes; blond hair; closed mouth. Original bridal dress, bouquet, veil and pearl necklace. Missing shoes and socks.

Mint $115.00 **Ex.** $85.00 **G.** $40.00 **F.** $35.00

JUDY BRIDESMAID
1958 - 17 in.

1958. 17 in. (43 cm). One-piece vinyl body. Vinyl head with earrings; blue sleep eyes, moulded lashes, painted lower lashes; rooted blond saran curls; closed mouth. Mark: on head, RELIABLE.

Ref.No.: D of C, BU13, p. 301

Mint $55.00 **Ex.** $40.00 **G.** $25.00 **F.** $20.00

JUDY BRIDE
Blond Hair - 19 in.

1958. 19 in. (48 cm). One-piece stuffed vinyl-flex body. Vinyl head; blue sleep eyes, lashes, painted lowers; rooted blond curls; open-closed mouth. Mark: on head, RELIABLE. Original white taffeta gown with lace overskirt, veil.

Ref.No.: 2P15

Mint $55.00 **Ex.** $45.00 **G.** $25.00 **F.** $20.00

JUDY BRIDE
Black Hair - 24 in.

1958. 24 in. (61 cm). One-piece stuffed vinyl-flex body. Vinyl head; brown sleep eyes, lashes, painted lowers; black rooted hair; closed mouth. Mark: on body, VH. Original tag. Original tiered gown with lace overskirt, veil and flowers.

Ref.No.: 2O26

Mint $65.00 **Ex.** $55.00 **G.** $35.00 **F.** $20.00

TOPSY
1958 - 12 in.

1958. 12 in. (30.5 cm). One-piece vinyl body. Vinyl head with dimples; black painted side-glancing eyes, painted upper lashes; hair moulded in braids tied with ribbons; open-closed mouth. Mark: on head, RELIABLE.

Ref.No.: D of C, BQ8, p. 302

Mint $45.00   **Ex.** $35.00   **G.** $20.00   **F.** $15.00

ROSALYN
1958 - 18 in.

1958. 18 in. (45.5 cm). Plastic body, jointed hips, shoulders and neck. Vinyl head with dimples; brown sleep eyes, lashes, painted lower lashes; rooted brown saran hair in curls; open-closed smiling mouth showing teeth. Mark: on head, RELIABLE. All original.

Ref.No.: D of C, BQ19, p. 302

Mint $125.00   **Ex.** $85.00   **G.** $45.00   **F.** $30.00

BARBARA ANN
1958 - 20 in.

1958. 20 in. (51 cm). Plastic teen body, jointed hips, waist, shoulders and neck. Vinyl head; blue plastic sleep eyes, lashes, painted lower lashes; rooted black curls; closed mouth. Unmarked.

Ref.No.: D of C, CT5, p. 302

Mint $125.00   **Ex.** $95.00   **G.** $50.00   **F.** $30.00

Note: This doll appeared on a commemorative postage stamp issued June 8, 1990, which adds to its value.

BARBARA ANN
(Semi-formal)

1958. 20 in. (51 cm). Plastic teen body, jointed hips, waist, shoulders and neck. Vinyl head; blue sleep eyes, lashes, painted lowers; rooted black hair; closed mouth. Original strapless short formal dress, high-heeled shoes, choker, earrings.

Ref.No.: 2X11

Mint $115.00   **Ex.** $95.00   **G.** $50.00   **F.** $30.00

SNOWSUIT DOLL

1958. 8 in. (20 cm). One-piece moulded vinyl body and head. Painted side-glancing eyes; deeply moulded blond hair covered in hood; open-closed mouth. Mark: on body, R (inside a triangle). Moulded snowsuit and teddy bear.

Ref.No.: 2I27

Mint   **$20.00**   **Ex.**   **$15.00**   **G.**   **$12.00**   **F.**   **$10.00**

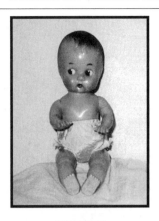

WETUMS
1958 - 8 in.

1958. 8 in. (20 cm.). Five-piece, hard plastic body. Side-glancing sleep eyes; moulded hair. Originally had a bottle.

Ref.No.: ES27

Mint   **$45.00**   **Ex.**   **$35.00**   **G.**   **$25.00**   **F.**   **$15.00**

ZORRO HAND PUPPET

1958. 9 1/2 in. (24 cm). Cloth body, felt hands. Vinyl head; painted side-glancing eyes; moulded painted black hair; open-closed mouth showing teeth. Mark: tag on body, ZORRO / COPYRIGHT WALT DISNEY PROD / "CANADA'S FINEST" / RELIABLE / TRADE-MARK / RELIABLE TOY CO. LIMITED, TORONTO. Originally came with cape and sword.

Ref.No.: 2PGGK20

Mint   **$20.00**   **Ex.**   **$15.00**   **G.**   **$10.00**   **F.**   **$5.00**

BEDTIME DOLL

1958. 10 in. (25.5 cm.). One-piece moulded vinyl body, jointed neck. Vinyl head; painted side-glancing eyes; deeply moulded hair; closed smiling mouth. Mark: on body, RELIABLE. Moulded sleepers and teddy bear.

Ref.No.: 2I28

Mint   **$20.00**   **Ex.**   **$15.00**   **G.**   **$12.00**   **F.**   **$10.00**

PATSY
ca.1959 - 9 in.

ca.1959. 9 in. (23 cm). Hard plastic body, jointed hips, shoulders and neck. Hard plastic head; blue sleep eyes, moulded lashes; brown moulded hair; closed mouth. Mark: on back, RELIABLE (in script).

Ref.No.: D of C, BM29, p. 303

Mint $75.00   **Ex.** $45.00   **G.** $30.00   **F.** $20.00

PEGGY
1959 - 9 in.

1959. 9 in. (23 cm). Hard plastic walker, jointed hips, shoulders and neck. Hard plastic head; blue sleep eyes, moulded plastic lashes; honey blond saran wig in braids; closed mouth. Mark: on back, RELIABLE/MADE IN CANADA.

Ref.No.: D of C, CL7, p. 303.

Mint $110.00   **Ex.** $85.00   **G.** $40.00   **F.** $35.00

ROSALYN
1959 - 18 in.

1959. 18 in. (46 cm). Plastic body, vinyl head; jointed hips, shoulder and neck; blue sleep lashes, painted lowers; rooted blond hair, pigtails and bangs; open-closed mouth showing upper teeth. All original.

Ref.No.: 2W38

Mint $125.00   **Ex.** $75.00   **G.** $45.00   **F.** $25.00

TOPSY WETUMS

1959. 18 in. (46 cm). Plastic body, jointed hips, shoulders and neck. Vinyl head; brown sleep eyes, lashes; rooted black curls; open mouth nurser. Mark: on head, RELIABLE (in script). Original red and white dress, replaced socks and shoes. Missing red hair ribbon.

Ref.No.: DC3

Mint $90.00   **Ex.** $60.00   **G.** $40.00   **F.** $30.00

SWEETIE, GIRL
WASHTUB BABY, BOY

1959. 6 in. (15 cm). Hard plastic bodies and heads, jointed shoulders. Painted side-glancing eyes; "Sweetie" has a dark brown wig, boy has moulded hair; closed mouths. Mark: on body, RELIABLE, (in script)/MADE IN CANADA. Boy redressed. Originally, both dolls were sold undressed and the boy came with a plastic bathtub, bar of soap and brush.
Ref.No.: 2R31

Mint $20.00 **Ex.** $15.00 **G.** $10.00 **F.** $5.00

Note: Prices are per doll.

GLAMOUR GIRL
1959 - 15 in.

1959. 15 in. (38 cm). One-piece stuffed vinyl-flex body. Vinyl head; blue sleep eyes, lashes; blond rooted hair; closed mouth. Mark: on head, RELIABLE. Original hang tag. Original green and white striped taffeta with organdy bodice, red trim and red hair ribbon.
Ref.No.: 2KA10

Mint $40.00 **Ex.** $30.00 **G.** $25.00 **F.** $15.00

JUDY BRIDE
Rooted Brown Hair

1959. 17 in. (43 cm). One-piece Rigidsol body. Vinyl head; brown sleep eyes, lashes, painted lower lashes; rooted brown hair; closed mouth. Mark: on head, RELIABLE; on body, H-17. Original clothing.
Ref.No.: D of C, CW21A, p. 306

Mint $55.00 **Ex.** $40.00 **G.** $25.00 **F.** $20.00

MARY ANN
ca.1959 - 26 in.

ca.1959. 26 in. (66 cm). One-piece stuffed vinyl-flex body. Vinyl head; blue sleep eyes, lashes; rooted auburn curls; open-closed mouth. Mark: on head, RELIABLE. Original pink organdy dress and bonnet, socks and shoes.
Ref.No.: PGM18

Mint $95.00 **Ex.** $75.00 **G.** $45.00 **F.** $30.00

Note: These large one-piece dolls were heavy and cumbersome to play with and difficult to position.

MISS CANADA
1960 - 18 in.

1960. 18 in. (45.5 cm). Plastic teen body, jointed hips, shoulders and neck. Vinyl head; blue sleep eyes, lashes, painted lower lashes; rooted auburn curls; closed mouth. Mark: on body, RELIABLE (in script)/CANADA. Replaced strapless dress a copy of the original.

Ref.No.: D of C, CS8, p. 303

Mint $75.00 **Ex.** $50.00 **G.** $35.00 **F.** $20.00

Note: Doll was sold in three different costumes, including one with a coat and hat. It was also available in a 20 and 25-inch size.

TICKLETOES
1960 - 18 in.

1960. 18 in. (45.5 cm). One-piece vinyl-flex body. Vinyl head; blue sleep eyes, lashes, painted lower lashes; rooted blond saran hair; closed mouth. Unmarked. Original pink floral taffeta dress, matching bonnet.

Ref.No.: D of C, BH10, p. 304

Mint $55.00 **Ex.** $45.00 **G.** $30.00 **F.** $20.00

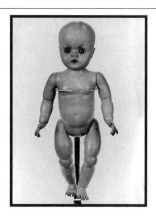

BABY HONEY
1960 - 25 in.

1960. 25 in. (63.5 cm). Plastic body, jointed hips, shoulders, and neck. Vinyl head; blue sleep eyes, lashes, painted lower lashes; light brown moulded hair; open mouth nurser. Mark: on back, RELIABLE (in script). Originally wore print dress and matching bonnet.

Ref.No.: D of C, AE8, p. 295

Mint $80.00 **Ex.** $55.00 **G.** $45.00 **F.** $35.00

PATTY SUE PLAYMATE

1960. 35 in. (89 cm). Plastic body, jointed hips, shoulders and neck. Vinyl head; blue sleep eyes, lashes, painted lower lashes; rooted blond saran hair; closed mouth. Unmarked. Original nylon party dress, socks and shoes.

Ref.No.: D of C, BH9, p. 304

Mint $135.00 **Ex.** $100.00 **G.** $65.00 **F.** $50.00

BARBARA ANN
1960 - 16 in.

1960. 16 in. (40.5 cm). Plastic body and legs, vinyl arms. Vinyl head; blue sleep eyes, lashes, painted lower lashes; rooted blond curly hair; open mouth nurser. Mark: RELIABLE (in script)/CANADA. Redressed.

Ref.No.: D of C, CJ26, p. 304

Mint $55.00 **Ex.** $40.00 **G.** $30.00 **F.** $20.00

GRENADIER GUARD
1960 - 16 in.

1960. 16 in. (40.5 cm). Plastic body, jointed hips, shoulders and neck. Vinyl head; blue sleep eyes, lashes, painted lower lashes; brown moulded hair; closed mouth. Mark: on back, RELIABLE (in script)/CANADA. Original clothing.

Ref.No.: D of C, BN36, p. 305

Mint $65.00 **Ex.** $50.00 **G.** $30.00 **F.** $20.00

TOPSY
ca.1960 - 20 in.

ca.1960. 20 in. (51 cm). Brown plastic body, jointed hips, shoulders and neck. Vinyl head; brown sleep eyes, lashes; rooted black curls; open mouth nurser. Mark: on body, RELIABLE (in script). Replaced costume. Originally came with a bottle and was dressed in a shirt and diaper.

Ref.No.: 2F22

Mint $80.00 **Ex.** $60.00 **G.** $40.00 **F.** $30.00

Note: Topsy came in three sizes.

LITTLE SISTER
1960 - 30 in.

1960. 30 in. (76 cm). Plastic body, jointed hips, shoulders and neck. Vinyl head; blue sleep eyes, lashes, painted lower lashes; rooted brown saran curls; closed mouth. Mark: on back, RELIABLE. Original clothing.

Ref.No.: D of C, BQ16, p. 305

Mint $110.00 **Ex.** $90.00 **G.** $50.00 **F.** $35.00

RELIABLE
ca.1960 - 13 in.

ca.1960. 13 in. (33 cm). Plastic body, jointed hips, shoulders and neck. Vinyl head; brown sleep eyes, lashes; deeply moulded brown curls; open mouth nurser. Mark: on body, RELIABLE (in script). Redressed.

Ref.No.: PGB20

Mint $55.00 **Ex.** $45.00 **G.** 35.00 **F.** $25.00

Note: This doll was not shown in the Reliable catalogues with this body.

PATTY
1960 - 14 in.

1960. 14 in. (35.5 cm). Hard plastic walker, jointed hips, shoulders and neck. Vinyl head; blue sleep eyes, lashes; blond rooted hair in a pony tail; closed mouth. Mark: on head, RELIABLE; on body, RELIABLE (in script). Original blue organza dress, white ribbon trim.

Ref.No.: 2M7

Mint $80.00 **Ex.** $60.00 **G.** $40.00 **F.** $30.00

SOUVENIR DOLL
1960 - 16 in.

1960. 16 in. (40.5 cm). Plastic body and legs, vinyl arms, jointed hips, shoulders and neck. Vinyl head; brown sleep eyes, lashes, painted lower lashes; rooted long black hair; closed mouth. Unmarked. Original costume.

Ref.No.: D of C, BQ4, p. 305

Mint $50.00 **Ex.** $40.00 **G.** $30.00 **F.** $15.00

BRIDE
1960 - 18 in.

1960. 18 in. (45.5 cm). Plastic teen body, jointed hips, waist, shoulders and neck. Vinyl head; blue sleep eyes, lashes; rooted blond curls; closed mouth. Mark: on head, 14RA; on body, B18. Original taffeta and net gown, veil, panties, high-heeled shoes, earrings and bouquet.

Ref.No.: DH19

Mint $65.00 **Ex.** $40.00 **G.** $25.00 **F.** $20.00

RELIABLE BOY

1961. 12 in. (30.5 cm). One-piece vinyl body. Vinyl head; black painted side-glancing eyes, painted upper lashes; brown moulded hair; open-closed mouth showing tongue. Mark: on head, 1/1104/RELIABLE/MADE IN CANADA. Original clothing.

Ref.No.: D of C, CG30, p. 306

Mint **$50.00** **Ex.** **$40.00** **G.** **$30.00** **F.** **$15.00**

Note: The boy is harder to find than the girl.

RELIABLE GIRL

1961. 12 in. (30.5 cm). One-piece vinyl body. Vinyl head, dimples; black painted side-glancing eyes, painted upper lashes; yellow moulded hair in braids; open-closed mouth. Mark: on head, RELIABLE (in script). Original cotton dress.

Ref.No.: D of C, CM5, p. 307

Mint **$35.00** **Ex.** **$25.00** **G.** **$15.00** **F.** **$10.00**

Note: This is a common doll.

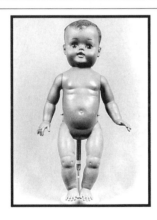

WETUMS
1961 - 20 in.

1961. 20 in. (51 cm). Brown plastic body and legs, vinyl arms, jointed hips, shoulders and neck. Vinyl head; brown sleep eyes, lashes, painted lower lashes; black moulded hair; open mouth nurser. Mark: on body, RELIABLE (in script)/MADE IN CANADA. Originally wore an undershirt and diaper and came with a bottle.

Ref.No.: D of C, AT13, p. 306

Mint **$60.00** **Ex.** **$45.00** **G.** **$30.00** **F.** **$20.00**

COLOURED NURSE WALKING DOLL

1961. 30 in. (76 cm). Brown plastic body, jointed hips, shoulders and neck. Vinyl head; brown sleep eyes, lashes, painted lower lashes; rooted black curls; closed mouth. Mark: on head, RELIABLE TOY/MADE IN CANADA. Originally came with a white nurse's costume with cap but no cape. She wore an imitation pendant watch, carried an 8-inch doll in a blanket and wore white socks and shoes.

Ref.No.: D of C, CP17, p. 307

Mint **$135.00** **Ex.** **$110.00 G.** **$60.00** **F.** **$40.00**

LOVUMS
1961 - 14 in.

1961. 14 in. (35.5 cm). Plastic body, jointed hips, shoulders and neck. Vinyl head; blue sleep eyes, lashes, painted lowers; rooted dark brown curly hair; closed watermelon mouth. Mark: on head, RELIABLE/MADE IN CANADA; on body, RELIABLE/CANADA. Original nylon dress, red bow and flower trim. Missing frilled bonnet.

Ref.No.: 2B24

Mint   **$45.00**   **Ex.**   **$35.00**   **G.**   **$30.00**   **F.**   **$20.00**

Note: This doll is also available in larger sizes.

SAUCY WALKER
1961 - 15 in.

1961. 15 in. (38 cm). Five-piece plastic body. Vinyl head; blue sleep eyes; rooted blond hair; closed mouth. Original blue and white dress, white socks and blue shoes.

Mint   **$80.00**   **Ex.**   **$60.00**   **G.**   **$45.00**   **F.**   **$35.00**

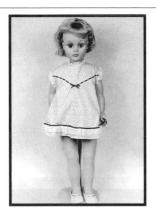

SUSIE WALKER
1961 - 30 in.

1961. 30 in. (76 cm). Plastic body, jointed hips, shoulders and neck with new slender proportions. Vinyl head; blue sleep eyes, lashes, painted lowers; rooted blond hair; closed mouth. Mark: on head, RELIABLE/MADE IN CANADA/1961; on body, RELIABLE/CANADA. Redressed. Originally dressed in two different cotton print dresses with puff sleeves, socks and black suedine shoes. Also available in a new suntan shade of skin colour.

Ref.No.: 2F37

Mint   **$75.00**   **Ex.**   **$55.00**   **G.**   **$40.00**   **F.**   **$30.00**

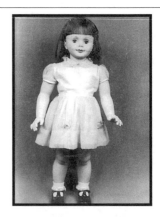

SAUCY WALKER
1961 - 35 in.

1961. 35 in. (89 cm). Plastic body, jointed hips, shoulders and neck. Vinyl head; blue sleep eyes, lashes, painted lower lashes; rooted auburn saran straight hair with bangs; closed mouth. Mark: on body, RELIABLE (in script). Replaced dress, similar to the original.

Ref.No.: D of C, CW12, p. 307

Mint   **$135.00**   **Ex.**   **$100.00**   **G.**   **$65.00**   **F.**   **$50.00**

MITZI FASHION MODEL DOLL

1961. 12 in. (30.5 cm). Plastic teen body, jointed hips, shoulders and neck. Vinyl head; painted eyes with black line around the eye; rooted dark brown pony tail with bangs; closed mouth. Mark: on body, RELIABLE (in script). Original bathing suit, earrings, hair bow and stand.

Ref.No.: DD8, DD9

Mint **$75.00** **Ex.** **$50.00** **G.** **$25.00** **F.** **$15.00**

Note: Mitzi resembles the early Barbies, which may explain her increase in price.

CINDY LOU

ca.1961. 14 in. (35.5 cm). Plastic body and legs, vinyl arms, jointed hips, shoulders and neck. Vinyl head; blue sleep eyes, lashes, painted lower lashes; rooted brown saran hair in ponytail and bangs; closed mouth. Mark: on head, RELIABLE. Original dress.

Ref.No.: D of C, BQ13, p. 309

Mint **$45.00** **Ex.** **$35.00** **G.** **$25.00** **F.** **$15.00**

LITTLE SISTER
ca.1961 - 30 in.

ca.1961. 30 in. (76 cm). Good quality heavy plastic body, jointed hips, shoulders and neck, with crier. Vinyl head; blue sleep eyes, lashes; light brown rooted hair; closed mouth. Mark: on head, RELIABLE TOY; on body, RELIABLE (in script). Original red and white gingham dress.

Ref.No.: DH20

Mint **$100.00** **Ex.** **$85.00** **G.** **$50.00** **F.** **$30.00**

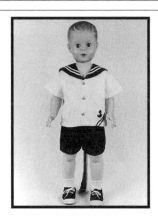

PETER PLAY PAL WALKING DOLL

1961. 30 in. (76 cm). Plastic body, jointed hips, shoulders and neck. Vinyl head; blue sleep eyes, lashes; moulded brown hair. Mark: on head, RELIABLE. Redressed. Originally wore tailored cuffed short pants, short sleeved white shirt and plaid vest, socks and suedine shoes.

Ref.No.: 2A18

Mint **$125.00** **Ex.** **$100.00** **G.** **$65.00** **F.** **$50.00**

Note: Boy dolls of this size are scarce.

WEST INDIES POLICEMAN

1961. 8 in. (20 cm). One-piece hard plastic body with stand. Painted features and uniform. Mark: on stand, RELIABLE (in script); on front of stand, BAHAMAS.

Ref.No.: 2X3

Mint $25.00 **Ex.** $20.00 **G.** $15.00 **F.** $10.00

Note: This doll is also available as a London bobby, a guardsman and an R.C.M.P. officer.

LITTLE MISTER BAD BOY
ca.1961 - 18 in.

ca.1961. 18 in. (45.5 cm). Plastic body, jointed hips, shoulders and neck. Vinyl head, blue sleep eyes, lashes, painted lower lashes; moulded brown hair; closed mouth. Mark: on body, RELIABLE (in script). Original striped cotton suit and hat.

Ref.No.: D of C, CY7, p. 309

Mint $75.00 **Ex.** $50.00 **G.** $30.00 **F.** $20.00

DRUM MAJORETTE

1961. 30 in. (76 cm). Five-piece vinyl body. Original ivory uniform and hat with red and gold trim.

Ref.No.: ES15

Mint $185.00 **Ex.** $160.00 **G.** $90.00 **F.** $55.00

LOUISA

1961. 30 in. (76 cm). Plastic body, jointed waist, hips, shoulders, swivel-jointed upper legs, wrists and ankles. Vinyl head; blue sleep eyes, lashes, painted lower lashes; rooted red saran hair; closed mouth. Unmarked. Original glazed cotton dress and cotton print overdress, saddle shoes and socks.

Ref.No.: D of C, CS21A, p. 308

Mint $185.00 **Ex.** $160.00 **G.** $90.00 **F.** $55.00

Note: In 1962 this doll wore a two-tone, glazed dress with a crinoline, and in 1963, a taffeta dress and princess-style coat with matching hat.

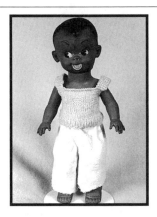

COLOURED RELIABLE BOY

1962. 12 in. (30.5 cm). One-piece brown vinyl body, jointed neck. Vinyl head; black painted side-glancing eyes, painted uppers; moulded black hair; open-closed smiling mouth. Mark: on head, RELIABLE (in script). Redressed. Originally wore cotton polka dot shorts, white shirt and bow-tie.

Ref.No.: PGB24

Mint $55.00   **Ex.** $45.00   **G.** $30.00   **F.** $20.00

MISS CAPRI

1962. 22 in. (56 cm). Heavy plastic body, jointed hips, shoulders and neck; a waist that twists, bends and turns. Vinyl head; freckles; blue sleep eyes, lashes, upside down "V" eyebrows; rooted straight blond hair; closed mouth with watermelon smile. Mark: on head, RELIABLE TOY/ MADE IN CANADA; on body, RELIABLE (in script).

Ref.No.: 2Y25

Mint $110.00   **Ex.** $80.00   **G.** $55.00   **F.** $35.00

Note: This costume not shown in the catalogue, but may be original. The catalogue shows a slack suit with striped pants, straw hat with striped ties, sandals and sunglasses.

RELIABLE
1962 - 24 in.

1962. 24 in. (61 cm). Plastic body, jointed hips, shoulders and neck. Vinyl head; blue sleep eyes, lashes, painted lowers; dark brown rooted hair; open-closed mouth. Mark: on head, RELIABLE/MADE IN CANADA. Original dress, white cotton blouse with dark pink suedine jumper.

Ref.No.: 2K23

Mint $55.00   **Ex.** $45.00   **G.** $35.00   **F.** $25.00

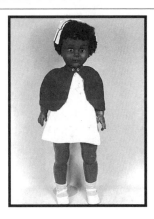

COLOURED NURSE WALKER

1962. 31 in. (78.5 cm). Brown plastic body, jointed hips, shoulders and neck. Vinyl head; brown sleep eyes, lashes, painted lowers; rooted black curls; closed mouth. Mark: on body, RELIABLE (in script)/MADE IN CANADA. Original nurse's costume, white dress and cap, blue cotton cape lined with red, original shoes and socks. Imitiation pendant watch missing. Originally carried an 8-inch baby doll in a blanket.

Ref.No.: PGM19

Mint $135.00   **Ex.** $110.00   **G.** $60.00   **F.** $35.00

PATSY
1962 - 11 in.

1962. 11 in. (28 cm). Plastic body, jointed hips, shoulders and neck. Vinyl head; blue sleep eyes, lashes, painted lowers; rooted red hair; closed mouth. Mark: RELIABLE/MADE IN CANADA.

Ref.No.: 2J17

Mint $50.00 **Ex.** $40.00 **G.** $30.00 **F.** $20.00

Note: Patsy was also available with pastel-coloured hair.

COLOURED TODDLER
1962 - 14 in.

1962. 14 in. (35.5 cm). Brown plastic body, jointed hips, shoulders and neck. Vinyl head; brown sleep eyes, lashes, painted lowers; rooted black hair in pony tails; open-closed mouth. Mark: on head, RELIABLE. Original pink nylon dress, socks and shoes. Hair ribbon missing.

Ref.No.: 2K13

Mint $60.00 **Ex.** $45.00 **G.** $30.00 **F.** $25.00

COLOURED TODDLER
1962 - 16 in.

1962. 16 in. (40.5 cm). Brown plastic body and legs; vinyl arms; jointed hips, shoulders and neck. Vinyl head; brown sleep eyes, lashes, painted lowers; rooted black hair in pigtails; open nurser mouth. Mark: on head, RELIABLE; on body, RELIABLE - MADE IN CANADA. Original white nylon dress with pink dots and ribbon and pink ribbons in hair.

Ref.No.: ES38

Mint $65.00 **Ex.** $50.00 **G.** $35.00 **F.** $25.00

TODDLES
1962 - 20 in.

1962. 20 in. (50.5 cm). Five-piece plastic body. Vinyl head; blue sleep eyes, lashes, painted lowers; rooted strawberry blond hair; open mouth with tongue. Mark: on body, RELIABLE (in script) MADE IN CANADA. Redressed. Originally wore cotton print dress with matching bonnet.

Ref.No.: SW20

Mint $35.00 **Ex.** $30.00 **G.** $25.00 **F.** $20.00

BARBARA ANNE, DRUM MAJORETTE
Rooted Red Curls

1962. 16 in. (40.5 cm). Plastic body, jointed hips, shoulders and neck. Vinyl head; blue sleep eyes, lashes, painted lowers; rooted red curls; closed mouth. Mark: on head, RELIABLE, on body, RELIABLE (in script). All original costume, cream taffeta dress with dark orange front panel and cuffs, black belt, matching cream hat, gold trim, leatherette boots with red trim and tassles.

Ref.No.: 2N21

Mint $60.00 **Ex.** $45.00 **G.** $25.00 **F.** $15.00

NELL GET WELL

1962. Three faced doll. 16 in. (40.5 cm). Plastic body, jointed hips, shoulders and neck. Vinyl head with three faces and a knob on top to turn the head; painted features. Mark: RELIABLE (in script)/CANADA. Redressed. Originally wore flannelette sleeping bag with a hood.

Ref.No.: 2KA22-23-24

Mint $85.00 **Ex.** $60.00 **G.** $45.00 **F** $35.00

RELIABLE
ca.1962 - 17 in.

ca.1962. 17 in. (43 cm). Plastic body, jointed hips, shoulders and neck. Vinyl head; blue sleep eyes, lashes, painted lower lashes; rooted blond saran hair; open-closed mouth. Mark: on head, RELIABLE; on body, Reliable (in script). Original clothing.

Ref.No.: D of C, CW24, p. 310

Mint $45.00 **Ex.** $35.00 **G.** $20.00 **F.** $15.00

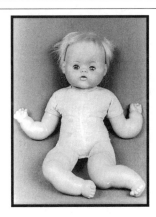

WRIGGLES

ca.1962. 19 in. (48 cm). Cloth body, vinyl bent-limb arms and legs, has a pull cord in the back of the body. Vinyl head; blue sleep eyes, lashes; rooted straight blond baby hair; open-closed mouth. Mark: on head, RELIABLE. Wind up mechanism causes head and body to wriggle in a realistic way when string is pulled. Originally wore printed knit top and short pants.

Ref.No.: D of C, CW2, p. 309

Mint $60.00 **Ex.** $30.00 **G.** $25.00 **F.** $15.00

Note: Mint price is for doll in working order.

PATTY TODDLER

ca.1962. 16 in. (40.5 cm). Plastic body, jointed hips, shoulders and neck. Vinyl head; blue sleep eyes, lashes, painted lower lashes; rooted dark brown hair in twin pony tails and bangs; open-closed mouth. Mark: on head, RELIABLE; on body, RELIABLE (in script)/CANADA. Original clothing.

Ref.No.: D of C, CW26, p. 310

Mint $45.00 **Ex.** $35.00 **G.** $25.00 **F.** $15.00

BOY TODDLER

ca.1962. 16 in. (40.5 cm). Plastic body, jointed hips, shoulders and neck. Vinyl head; blue sleep eyes, lashes, painted lower lashes; black moulded hair; closed mouth. Mark: on body, RELIABLE (in script)/CANADA.

Ref.No.: D of C, CG16, p. 310

Mint $50.00 **Ex.** $40.00 **G.** $30.00 **F.** $20.00

Note: The same outfit was worn by Peter Play Pal in 1962.

DOCTOR TODDLER

1963. 15 1/2 in. (39.5 cm). Plastic body, jointed hips, shoulders and neck. Vinyl head; blue sleep eyes, lashes, painted lower lashes; black moulded hair; closed mouth. Mark: on body, RELIABLE (in script)/CANADA. Original clothing.

Ref.No.: D of C, CW20A, p. 311

Mint $60.00 **Ex.** $40.00 **G.** $30.00 **F.** $20.00

CAROLYN WALKER
1963 - 30 in.

1963. 30 in. (76 cm). Plastic body, jointed hips, shoulders and neck. Vinyl head; blue sleep eyes, lashes; auburn rooted hair; open-closed mouth with four moulded teeth. Mark: on body, RELIABLE (in script)/CANADA. Redressed in a close copy of the original cotton print dress.

Ref.No.: 2KA1

Mint $80.00 **Ex.** $65.00 **G.** $40.00 **F.** $30.00

BARBARA ANNE, DRUM MAJORETTE
Rooted Blond Hair

1963. 15 1/2 in. (39 cm). Plastic body and legs, vinyl arms, jointed hips, shoulders and neck. Vinyl head; blue sleep eyes, lashes; rooted blond hair; closed mouth. Mark: on head, RELIABLE; on body, RELIABLE (in script)/CANADA. Original clothing.

Ref.No.: D of C, XH22, p. 312.

Mint $60.00 **Ex.** $45.00 **G.** $25.00 **F.** $15.00

SAUCY WALKER
1963 - 14 in.

1963. 14 in. (35.5 cm). Hard plastic body, jointed hips, shoulders and neck. Vinyl head; blue sleep eyes, lashes; rooted blond curls; closed mouth. Mark: on head, RELIABLE; on body, RELIABLE/MADE IN CANADA. Original pink voile dotted dress, socks and shoes.

Ref.No.: 2C10

Mint $70.00 **Ex.** $50.00 **G.** $35.00 **F.** $30.00

Note: This costume was not shown in the catalogue.

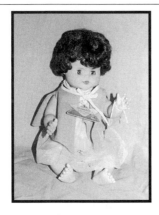

BABY PRECIOUS
1963 - 16 in.

1963. 16 in. (40.5 cm). Plastic body, jointed hips, shoulders and neck. Vinyl head; sleep eyes, lashes; rooted brown curls; open mouth nurser. Mark: on head, RELIABLE; on body, RELIABLE (in script). Original tag. Original organdy dress and cape.

Ref.No.: HX22

Mint $45.00 **Ex.** $35.00 **G.** $25.00 **F.** $15.00

MARY, MARY QUITE CONTRARY

1963. 18 in. (45.5 cm). Plastic body and legs, vinyl arms. Vinyl head; green sleep eyes, lashes, painted lower lashes; rooted blond saran hair; closed mouth. Mark: on head, RELIABLE/MADE IN/CANADA. Original clothing.

Ref.No.: D of C, BH30, p. 311.

Mint $60.00 **Ex.** $40.00 **G.** $25.00 **F.** $20.00

Note: Tommy Tucker, Little Miss Muffet and Little Bo-peep dolls were also available.

THUMBELINA

1963. 20 in. (51 cm). Cloth body, vinyl arms and legs. Vinyl head; painted blue eyes; rooted blond curls; open-closed mouth. Mark: on head, IDEAL TOY CORP./OTT-10. A key-wind doll. Mama voice. Original pink knit suit. Knitted bootees added.

Ref.No.: 2W27

Mint   **$55.00**   **Ex.**   **$45.00**   **G.**   **$30.00 F. $25.00**

Note: Mint and Ex. prices are for dolls in working order.

KISSY

1963. 22 in. (56 cm). Plastic body, jointed hips, shoulders neck and wrists. Vinyl head; blue sleep eyes, lashes, painted lowers; rooted auburn hair; open mouth nurser. Mark: head and body have Ideal markings but original box says; Mfg. in Canada by Reliable Toy Co. Ltd., under license from Ideal Toy Corp. U.S.A. Original red and white sunsuit and red shoes. Kissy puckers up and gives a realistic sound effects kiss, when you press her arms together.

Ref.No.: DF15

Mint   **$90.00**   **Ex.**   **$65.00**   **G.**   **$45.00 F. $35.00**

RAG DOLL

1963. 24 in. (61 cm). Fabric body and hat, firmly stuffed. Plastic mask face; side-glancing eyes; closed mouth. Pink and black costume.

Ref.No.: PS8

Mint   **$20.00**   **Ex.**   **$15.00**   **G.**   **$10.00 F. $5.00**

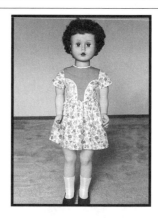

SUSIE WALKER
1963 - 36 in.

1963. 36 in. (91.5 cm). Five-piece plastic body. Vinyl head; blue sleep eyes, lashes, painted lowers; rooted curly auburn hair; closed mouth. Mark: on head, RELIABLE (in script) CANADA. Original print dress, white socks and black shoes.

Ref.No.: SW21

Mint   **$120.00**   **Ex.**   **$85.00**   **G.**   **$55.00 F. $40.00**

NEGRO TODDLER

1963. (official catalogue name) 14 in. (35.5 cm). Vinyl body, jointed hips, shoulders and neck. Vinyl head with moulded bonnet; brown plastic inset eyes; moulded black hair; open-closed mouth. Mark: on head, Reliable (in script)/CANADA. Original red felt coat. Missing scarf. Replaced socks and shoes.

Ref.No.: 2B4

Mint **$50.00** **Ex.** **$40.00** **G.** **$30.00** **F.** **$20.00**

RELIABLE GIRL, BONNET HEAD

1963. 14 in. (35.5 cm). Plastic body, jointed hips, shoulders and neck. Vinyl head with bonnet moulded on the head; blue plastic fixed eyes, painted upper lashes; yellow moulded hair; open-closed mouth. Mark: on back, RELIABLE/CANADA.

Ref.No.: D of C, BC21, p. 312

Mint **$45.00** **Ex.** **$35.00** **G.** **$25.00** **F.** **$15.00**

BARBARA ANNE NURSE

1963. 16 in. (40.5 cm). Plastic body, jointed hips, shoulders and neck. Vinyl head; blue sleep eyes, lashes, painted lower lashes; rooted brown curls; closed mouth. Mark: on head, RELIABLE. Original clothing.

Ref.No.: D of C, BH20, p. 313

Mint **$60.00** **Ex.** **$40.00** **G.** **$20.00** **F.** **$15.00**

PATTY SUE WALKER

1963. 36 in. (91 cm). Five-piece vinyl body. Redressed; originally wore sheer party dress with lace trim.

Ref.No.: ES6

Mint **$135.00** **Ex.** **$100.00** **G.** **$60.00** **F.** **$45.00**

ESKIMO
1963 - 11 in.

1963. 11 in. (28 cm). Brown hard plastic body, jointed hips, shoulders and neck. Hard plastic head; brown sleep eyes, moulded lashes; black moulded hair with added black fringe glued on; open mouth nurser. Mark: on head, Reliable. Original 3/4 length parka and hood, matching pants trimmed in rick-rack.

Ref.No.: 2N34

Mint $50.00 **Ex.** $40.00 **G.** $35.00 **F.** $30.00

CUTIE-PIE TODDLER

1963. 14 in. (35.5 cm). Plastic body, jointed hips, shoulders and neck. Vinyl head; googly side-glancing blue eyes; moulded hair plus rooted orange single curl; closed watermelon mouth. Mark: on body, RELIABLE (in script)/CANADA. Redressed. Originally dressed in slacks and a lace trimmed top with matching peaked cap.

Ref.No.: PGB22

Mint $30.00 **Ex.** $25.00 **G.** $15.00 **F.** $10.00

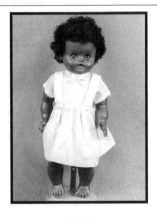

TOPSY
1963 - 16 in.

1963. 16 in. (40.5 cm). Brown plastic body, jointed hips, shoulders and neck. Vinyl head; golden brown sleep eyes, lashes, painted lower lashes; rooted black curls; open mouth nurser. Mark: on head, RELIABLE (in script); on body, RELIABLE (in script)/CANADA. Redressed. Originally wore cotton print dress.

Ref.No.: D of C, BP26, p. 313

Mint $50.00 **Ex.** $40.00 **G.** $30.00 **F.** $20.00

BABY CUDDLES
1963 - 20 in.

1963. 20 in. (51 cm). Vinyl bent-limb body. Vinyl head; blue sleep eyes, lashes; rooted blond hair over moulded hair; open-closed mouth. Mark: on head, RELIABLE.

Ref.No.: D of C, CN22, p. 313

Mint $70.00 **Ex.** $55.00 **G.** $40.00 **F.** $25.00

MUSICAL MOUNTIE

1963. 7 in. (18 cm). One-piece hard plastic body. Painted features and clothing. Standing on a block which plays, "O Canada."

Ref.No.: 2R10

Mint $30.00 **Ex.** $25.00 **G.** $15.00 **F.** $10.00

Note: Mint and Ex. prices are for dolls in working order.

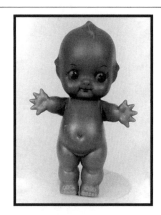

CUTIE DOLL
1963 - 9 1/2 in.

1963. 9 1/2 in. (24 cm). Brown vinyl one-piece body, jointed neck. Brown vinyl head; Black side-glancing googly eyes; moulded hair; watermelon mouth. Mark: on body, RELIABLE. Sold undressed.

Ref.No.: 2N33

Mint $25.00 **Ex.** $20.00 **G.** $15.00 **F.** $10.00

Note: Also available in white vinyl.

TAMMY

1964. 12 in. (30.5 cm). Plastic body, jointed hips, shoulders and neck. Vinyl head; blue painted side-glancing eyes, painted upper lashes; rooted honey blond curls; closed mouth. Mark: on head, C. IDEAL TOY CORP.; on back, RELIABLE/CANADA.

Ref.No.: D of C, BN34, p. 314

Mint $50.00 **Ex.** $40.00 **G.** $20.00 **F.** $15.00

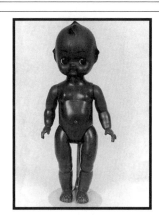

JEMIMA TODDLER

1964. 15 in. (38 cm). Brown plastic body, jointed hips, shoulders and neck. Vinyl head; painted side-glancing black eyes; moulded hair; closed watermelon mouth. Mark: on head, RELIABLE/MADE IN CANADA. Originally wore a sleeveless cotton print dress, white socks and shoes.

Ref.No.: 2O29

Mint $35.00 **Ex.** $30.00 **G.** $25.00 **F.** $20.00

CUTIE DRUM MAJORETTE

1964. 14 in. (35.5 cm). Five-piece vinyl body. Blue eyes; red hair; smiling mouth. Red, white and blue costume; hat and baton missing.

Ref.No.: ES7

Mint $30.00 **Ex.** $25.00 **G.** $15.00 **F.** $10.00

GIGI
1964 - 17 in.

1964. 17 in. (43 cm). Five-piece plastic body. Vinyl head; suntan complexion; sleep eyes; rooted hair. Original cream cotton blouse and turquoise velveteen jumper.

Mint $55.00 **Ex.** $40.00 **G.** $30.00 **F.** $20.00

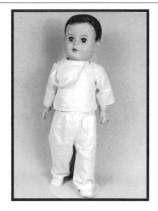

DOCTOR DOLL
ca.1964 - 25 in.

ca.1964. 25 in. (63.5 cm). Plastic body, jointed hips, shoulders and neck. Vinyl head; blue sleep eyes, lashes, painted lowers; moulded black hair; closed mouth. Mark: on head, RELIABLE/MADE IN CANADA; on body, RELIABLE/MADE IN CANADA. Original white cotton uniform and mask. Originally wore a cap and came with medical equipment.

Ref.No.: 2O7

Mint $80.00 **Ex.** $65.00 **G.** $45.00 **F.** $30.00

CAROLYN WALKER
1964 - 32 in.

1964. 32 in. (81 cm). Plastic body, jointed hips, shoulders and neck. Vinyl head, freckles; blue sleep eyes, lashes; rooted blond hair; open mouth showing teeth. Mark: on body, RELIABLE (in script)/CANADA. Original clothing with replaced blouse. Black velvet vest, trimmed with beads and sequins, organdy skirt trimmed with rows of various coloured ribbon.

Ref.No.: 2I9

Mint $110.00 **Ex.** $75.00 **G.** $45.00 **F.** $35.00

WETUMS
1964 - 13 in.

1964. 13 in. (33 cm). Plastic body, jointed hips, shoulders and neck. Vinyl head; inset blue plastic eyes; rooted brown curls; open-mouth nurser. Mark: on head, RELIABLE (in script); on body, RELIABLE (in script). Dress not shown in Reliable catalogue. Originally sold with a polka dot shirt, diaper and bottle.

Ref.No.: PGB21

Mint $30.00   **Ex.** $25.00   **G.** $20.00   **F.** $15.00

GIGI
1964 - 14 in.

1964. 14 in. (35.5 cm). Plastic body, jointed hips, shoulders and neck. Vinyl head; blue sleep eyes, lashes; rooted auburn curls; closed mouth. Mark: on head, RELIABLE/19c64/MADE IN CANADA. Original pink lace trimmed dress. Missing white socks and shoes, two hairbows and a knitted coat.

Ref.No.: 2I15

Mint $50.00   **Ex.** $40.00   **G.** $30.00   **F.** $20.00

BARBARA ANNE
1965 - 16 in.

1965. 16 in. (40.5 cm). Plastic body, jointed hips, shoulders and neck. Vinyl head; blue sleep eyes, lashes, painted lowers; rooted honey blond hair; closed smiling mouth. Mark: on head, RELIABLE (in script); on body, RELIABLE (in script)/CANADA. Original cotton print dress.

Ref.No.: 2R20

Mint $45.00   **Ex.** $35.00   **G.** $25.00   **F.** $15.00

RUTHIE
1965 - 18 in.

1965. 18 in. (45.5 cm). Plastic body, jointed hips, shoulders and neck. Vinyl head; blue sleep eyes, lashes, painted lower lashes; rooted honey blond hair; closed mouth. Mark: on head, RELIABLE (in script); on body, RELIABLE (in script). Original blue nylon dress. Replaced socks and shoes.

Ref.No.: D of C, AO21, p. 314

Mint $45.00   **Ex.** $35.00   **G.** $25.00   **F.** $15.00

BABY JOY

1965. 12 in. (30.5 cm). Plastic body, jointed hips, shoulders and neck. Vinyl head; painted blue side-glancing eyes; rooted auburn hair; closed mouth. Mark: on body, RELIABLE (in script)/CANADA. Original polka dot dress, socks and shoes.

Ref.No.: 2I5

Mint **$25.00** **Ex.** **$20.00** **G.** **$15.00** **F.** **$10.00**

MARY POPPINS
1965 - 12 1/2 in.

1965. 12 1/2 in. (32 cm). Hard plastic body and legs, vinyl arms, jointed hips, shoulders and neck. Vinyl head; painted side-glancing eyes; rooted black hair; closed mouth. Mark: on body, RELIABLE. Original dress, coat and hat plus extra polka dotted dress. Originally included umbrella and large hand bag.

Ref.No.: HX25

Mint **$75.00** **Ex.** **$50.00** **G.** **$25.00** **F.** **$20.00**

Note: Mary Poppins was also available dressed in a checked dress and white apron and included a plastic teaset.

MARY POPPINS
1965 - 12 1/2 in.

1965. 12 1/2 in. (32 cm). Plastic body, jointed hips, shoulders and neck. Vinyl head; painted side-glancing blue eyes; rooted black hair; closed mouth. Mark: on body, RELIABLE (in script)/CANADA. Original red polka dot dress, matching hat umbrella and bag.

Ref.No.: 2C6

Mint **$65.00** **Ex.** **$45.00** **G.** **$25.00** **F.** **$20.00**

SWEETIE PIE

1965. 18 in. (45.5 cm). Plastic body, jointed hips, shoulders and neck. Vinyl head, freckles; green sleep eyes, lashes; rooted long dark brown hair with bangs; closed mouth. Mark: on head, RELIABLE; on body, RELIABLE (in script)/CANADA. Original red corduroy jumper with attached white cotton blouse.

Ref.No.: DF19

Mint **$45.00** **Ex.** **$40.00** **G.** **$30.00** **F.** **$20.00**

DOLLY IN BATHTUB

1965. 8 in. (20 cm). Hard plastic body, jointed hips, shoulders and neck. Hard plastic head; sleep eyes; moulded hair; open mouth nurser. Mark: on body, RELIABLE (in script)/MADE IN CANADA/PAT. PEND. Bath set included plastic bath, soap and brush. Original box.

Ref.No.: 2J36

Mint   **$30.00   Ex.**   **$25.00   G.**   **$20.00   F. $15.00**

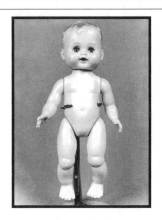

RELIABLE
ca.1966 - 12 in.

ca.1966. 12 in. (30.5 cm). Plastic body, jointed hips, shoulders and neck. Vinyl head; blue sleep eyes, lashes, painted lower lashes; brown moulded hair; open mouth nurser. Mark: on body, RELIABLE (in script)/CANADA. Originally wore cotton print sunsuit.

Ref.No.: D of C, AN7, p. 314

Mint   **$25.00   Ex.**   **$20.00   G.**   **$15.00   F. $10.00**

BABY SWEETHEART

1966. 13 in. (33 cm). Plastic body, jointed hips, shoulders and neck. Vinyl head; blue sleep eyes, lashes; rooted straight blond hair; closed watermelon mouth. Mark: on head, RELIABLE (in script); on back, RELIABLE /CANADA. Original dress with eyelet skirt and velveteen bodice and bows. Missing socks and shoes.

Ref.No.: 2H25

Mint   **$30.00   Ex.**   **$25.00   G.**   **$20.00   F. $15.00**

SUSIE STEPPS
1966 - 21 in.

1966. 21 in. (53.5 cm). Hard plastic body and legs, vinyl arms, jointed hips, shoulders and neck. Body has a battery box with an on/off switch. Vinyl head; blue sleep eyes, lashes; rooted blond straight hair; closed mouth. Mark: RELIABLE/MADE IN CANADA. Original coat and hat, replaced shoes.

Ref.No.: D of C, BC14, p. 315

Mint $105.00   Ex.   **$85.00   G.**   **$50.00   F. $35.00**

Note: Rarely found in working condition.

PEEWEES

1966. 4 in. (10 cm). One-piece vinyl body. Vinyl head; painted side-glancing blue eyes; rooted blond hair. Mark: on body, RELIABLE HONG KONG; left foot, U.D.CO. 1965 c; right foot, PEEWEES T.U. Dolls came in 12 different costumes. This is probably not the original outfit.

Ref.No.: DR27

Mint $15.00   Ex. $12.00   G. $10.00   F. $8.00

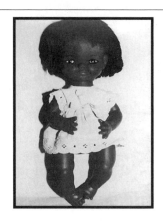

BABY TICKLETOES
Black Hair

1966. 9 in. (23 cm). Five-piece brown vinyl baby body with bent limbs. Brown vinyl head; painted black eyes; rooted black hair in shag cut; closed smiling mouth. Original white cotton dress with eyelet trim. Originally came with bootees, hair bow and matching pillow.

Ref.No.: DR26

Mint $35.00   Ex. $25.00   G. $20.00   F. $15.00

BABY TICKLETOES
Orange Hair

1966. 9 in. (23 cm). Vinyl five-piece body. Sleep eyes; rooted orange hair; smiling mouth. Redressed.

Ref.No.: ES62

Mint $35.00   Ex. $25.00   G. $20.00   F. $15.00

Note: This doll came dressed in a variety of dresses and sleepers.

GINNY LOU

1966. 17 in. (43 cm). Plastic body, jointed hips, shoulders and neck. Vinyl head; blue sleep eyes, lashes; rooted blond hair; closed watermelon mouth. Probably original blue print dress. Missing socks and shoes.

Ref.No.: 2J0

Mint $30.00   Ex. $25.00   G. $20.00   F. $15.00

HONEY TODDLER

1967. 14 in. (35.5 cm). Plastic body jointed hips, shoulders and neck. Vinyl head; blue plastic sleep eyes, lashes; rooted auburn hair trimmed with black grosgrain ribbon; closed mouth. Mark: on back, RELIABLE (in script)/MADE IN CANADA.

Ref.No.: D of C, CD21, p. 315

Mint $35.00 **Ex.** $30.00 **G.** $20.00 **F.** $15.00

TOPSY BABY

1967. 16 in. (40.5 cm). Plastic body, jointed hips, shoulders and neck. Vinyl head; brown plastic sleep eyes, lashes; rooted black straight hair; closed smiling mouth. Mark: on head, RELIABLE/MADE IN CANADA. Original clothing.

Ref.No.: D of C, BN22, p. 315

Mint $75.00 **Ex.** $55.00 **G.** $30.00 **F.** $25.00

STAR BRIGHT
1967 - 16 in.

1967. 16 in. (40.5 cm). Plastic body, jointed hips, shoulders and neck. Vinyl head; blue-black painted eyes with star high-lights; brown rooted hair; closed mouth. Mark: on head, RELIABLE TOY LTD./MADE IN CANADA; on body, RELIABLE/CANADA. Redressed. Originally available in sleepers with matching night caps; or in cotton dresses with puffed sleeves; or a two-piece sun-suit with eyelet trim.

Ref.No.: GK21

Mint $35.00 **Ex.** $30.00 **G.** $25.00 **F.** $20.00

STAR BRIGHT
1967 - 17 in.

1967. 17 in. (43 cm). Five-piece vinyl body. Vinyl head; painted blue eyes with small white stars; brown rooted hair; closed mouth. Original pink print dress. Came in several different dresses.

Mint $45.00 **Ex.** $30.00 **G.** $25.00 **F.** $20.00

ESKIMO
1967 - 10 in.

1967. 10 in. (25.5 cm). Brown plastic body, jointed hips, shoulders and neck. Brown vinyl head with ethnic features; slanted painted black eyes; rooted straight black hair; open-closed mouth, showing teeth. Mark: on back, RELIABLE/CANADA. Original white fur parka and hood. Brown leather snowpants.

Ref.No.: 2B15

Mint $75.00 **Ex.** $55.00 **G.** $45.00 **F.** $35.00

Note: This doll may have been dressed by native Canadians. Reliable shows the same doll in a nylon fleece pile parka.

TOPSY
ca.1967 - 11 in.

ca.1967. 11 in. (28 cm). Brown plastic body, jointed hips, shoulders and neck. Brown vinyl head; painted eyes, glancing up, slanted brows; rooted straight black hair; closed watermelon mouth. Mark: on head, RELIABLE (in script); on back, RELIABLE (in script). Original peasant dress.

Ref.No.: 2B21

Mint $45.00 **Ex.** $35.00 **G.** $30.00 **F.** $25.00

Note: This doll is not shown in the Reliable catalogues.

GINGER
Closed Mouth

1967. 15 in. (38 cm). Plastic body, jointed hips, shoulders and neck. Vinyl head; green sleep eyes, lashes; rooted orange hair; closed watermelon mouth. Mark: on head and body, RELIABLE TOY/MADE IN CANADA. Redressed. Originally wore short dress with matching shorts, socks and shoes.

Ref.No.: GK17

Mint $30.00 **Ex.** $25.00 **G.** $20.00 **F.** $15.00

GINGER
Open Mouth

1967. 15 in. (38 cm). Plastic body, jointed hips, shoulders and neck. Vinyl head, orange freckles; slanted green sleep eyes, lashes; rooted orange hair; open-closed mouth. Mark: on head and body, RELIABLE (in script). Original gold and green sundress with matching panties, green shoes.

Ref.No.: 2N24

Mint $30.00 **Ex.** $25.00 **G.** $20.00 **F.** $15.00

TICKLETOES BABY
1967 - 9 in.

1967. 9 in. (23 cm). Vinyl bent-limb body, jointed hips, shoulders and neck. Vinyl head; side-glancing painted eyes; rooted straight blond hair; closed watermelon mouth. Original Scottish costume.

Ref.No.: 2C2

Mint $35.00 **Ex.** $30.00 **G.** $20.00 **F.** $15.00

INDIAN BOY

1967. 11 in. (28 cm). Brown hard plastic body, jointed hips, shoulders and neck. Brown hard plastic head; brown sleep eyes, moulded lashes; black wig in braids; open-mouth nurser. Mark: on back, RELIABLE (in script). Original felt clothing.

Ref.No.: GK20

Mint $50.00 **Ex.** $40.00 **G.** $35.00 **F.** $25.00

INDIAN GIRL
1967 - 11 in.

1967. 11 in. (28 cm). Brown hard plastic body, jointed hips, shoulders and neck. Brown hard plastic head; brown sleep eyes, moulded lashes; black wig in braids; open-mouth nurser. Mark: on back, RELIABLE (in script). Original felt clothing.

Ref.No.: 2J21

Mint $50.00 **Ex.** $40.00 **G.** $35.00 **F.** $25.00

CHUBBY
1967 - 14 in.

1967. 14 in. (35.5 cm). Plastic body, jointed hips, shoulders and neck. Vinyl head; brown sleep eyes, lashes, painted lowers; rooted blond hair; open-closed mouth. Mark: on head, RELIABLE TOY CO. LTD./19C67/MADE IN CANADA/2654 10 EYE 11. Original white cotton dress with checked pink trim, matching bonnet, panties and socks.

Ref.No.: 2F34

Mint $30.00 **Ex.** $25.00 **G.** $20.00 **F.** $15.00

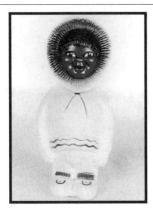

ESKIMO
1967 - 6 in.

1967. 6 in. (15 cm). One-piece moulded vinyl head and body. Face painted brown; hair painted black. Smiling open-closed mouth. Mark: on bottom, RELIABLE (in script).

Ref.No.: 2R23

Mint   **$20.00**   **Ex.**   **$15.00**   **G.**   **$10.00**   **F.**   **$5.00**

SWEETIE PIE RELIABLE

1967. 17 in. (43 cm). Plastic body, jointed hips, shoulders and neck. Vinyl head; blue sleep eyes, lashes, painted lower lashes; rooted blond hair; closed mouth. Mark: on head, RELIABLE/MADE IN CANADA; on body, RELIABLE (in script)/CANADA. Redressed.

Mint   **$30.00**   **Ex.**   **$25.00**   **G.**   **$20.00**   **F.**   **$15.00**

JACQUELINE

1968. 16 in. (40.5 cm). Plastic body, jointed hips, shoulders and neck. Vinyl head; blue sleep eyes, lashes; rooted long blond straight hair; closed mouth. Mark: on head, RELIABLE TOY CO./MADE IN CANADA; on body, RELIABLE/CANADA. Redressed. Originally wore an "A-line" dress or a slacks set and the hair hung loose.

Ref.No.: 2F33

Mint   **$45.00**   **Ex.**   **$40.00**   **G.**   **$30.00**   **F.**   **$25.00**

SWEETIE PIE BABY

1968. 16 in. (40.5 cm). Plastic body, jointed hips, shoulders and neck. Vinyl head; brown sleep eyes, lashes, painted lowers; rooted honey blond hair; open-mouth nurser. Mark: on head, RELIABLE/MADE IN CANADA (in script); on body, RELIABLE (in script)/CANADA. Redressed. Originally came in a variety of pretty lace trimmed dresses or in a batiste dress with a nylon fleece coat and matching hat.

Ref.No.: 2G15

Mint   **$30.00**   **Ex.**   **$25.00**   **G.**   **$20.00**   **F.**   **$15.00**

PERKY ESKIMO

1968. 10 in. (25.5 cm). Brown plastic body, jointed hips, shoulders and neck. Brown vinyl head; painted black eyes; rooted straight black hair; closed watermelon mouth. Mark: on head, RELIABLE (in script); on body, RELIABLE (in script)/CANADA. Original red pants with rick-rack trim, white parka with painted design and white fur trim. Hood missing.

Ref.No.: 2F13

Mint $40.00   **Ex.** $30.00   **G.** $25.00   **F.** $20.00

BLACK STAR BRIGHT

1968. 16 in. (40.5 cm). Brown plastic body, jointed hips, shoulders and neck. Brown vinyl head; painted black, side-glancing eyes with star high-lights, heavily painted lashes; rooted black curls; closed mouth. Mark: on head, RELIABLE TOY LTD./MADE IN CANADA. Original red "A-line" cotton dress, red and white striped trim, white socks and black shoes.

Ref.No.: 2E14

Mint $60.00   **Ex.** $45.00   **G.** $35.00   **F.** $25.00

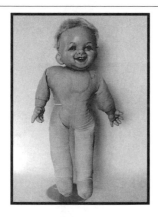

CHUCKLES
1968 - 17 in.

1968. 17 in. (43 cm). Cloth body and legs, vinyl hands. Vinyl head; painted blue eyes and lashes; rooted platinum blond hair; open-closed mouth, laughing and showing two top teeth. Mark: on head, C1967/RELIABLE/MADE IN CANADA. Originally had a straight shag hairdo and came dressed in a coat, leggings and a matching hat. Also available in a polka-dot clown suit.

Ref.No.: 2H35

Mint $55.00   **Ex.** $45.00   **G.** $35.00   **F.** $25.00

LITTLE BROTHER
1968 - 21 in.

1968. 21 in. (53 cm). Plastic baby body, jointed hips, shoulders and neck. Vinyl head; blue sleep eyes, lashes; rooted straight blond hair; open-closed mouth, showing two teeth. Mark: on head, RELIABLE/MADE IN CANADA. Originally wore a short top and panties.

Ref.No.: 2C8

Mint $65.00   **Ex.** $50.00   **G.** $35.00   **F.** $30.00

BABY MARILYN
1968 - 13 in.

1968. 13 in. (33 cm). Five-piece plastic body. Vinyl head; blue sleep eyes, lashes, painted lowers; rooted auburn hair; open mouth nurser. Mark: on head, RELIABLE TOY CO. LTD. MADE IN CANADA. Redressed.

Ref.No.: SW17

Mint $25.00   **Ex.** $20.00   **G.** $15.00   **F.** $10.00

SUNSUIT DOLL
1968 - 16 in.

1968. 16 in. (40.5 cm). Plastic body and legs, jointed hips, shoulders and neck. Vinyl head and arms; blue painted eyes; rooted blond hair. Mark: on back, RELIABLE / CANADA. Redressed; originally wore a sunsuit.

Mint $25.00   **Ex.** $20.00   **G.** $15.00   **F.** $10.00

SUNSHINE SUSIE
1968 - 20 in.

1968. 20 in. (51 cm). Red and white striped cloth body. Cloth head; printed black side-glancing eyes; yellow yarn hair; printed watermelon mouth. Mark: label, RELIABLE TOY CO. LTD. Removable apron.

Ref.No.: HX21

Mint $20.00   **Ex.** $15.00   **G.** $10.00   **F.** $5.00

Note: Sunshine Susie is a name that Reliable has used for cloth dolls since the thirties.

RELIABLE BABY

1969. 14 in. (35.5 cm). Plastic body, jointed hips, shoulders and neck. Vinyl head; blue stencilled, side-glancing eyes; rooted honey blond curls; open-mouth nurser. Mark: on head, O26914/RELIABLE TOY CO. LTD./19c69/MADE IN CANADA; on body, RELIABLE (in script)/CANADA. Originally wore a sleeveless "A-line" dress, socks and shoes.

Ref.No.: AN11A

Mint $25.00   **Ex.** $20.00   **G.** $15.00   **F.** $10.00

SUNSUIT DOLL
1969 - 16 in.

1969. 16 in. (40.5 cm). Plastic body, jointed hips, shoulders and neck. Vinyl head; blue stencilled eyes; rooted blond hair; open mouth nurser. Mark: on head, RELIABLE TOY CO. LTD./19c68/MADE IN CANADA; on body, RELIABLE (in script)/CANADA. Originally wore a printed cotton sunsuit.

Ref.No.: D of C, AN18, p. 316.

Mint $25.00   **Ex.** $20.00   **G.** $15.00   **F.** $10.00

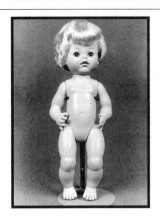

BABY LOVUMS
1969 - 16 in.

1969. 16 in. (40.5 cm). Plastic body, jointed hips, shoulders and neck. Vinyl head, with earrings; blue sleep eyes, lashes, painted lower lashes; rooted blond hair; open mouth nurser. Mark: on head, RELIABLE TOY CO. LTD./19c68/MADE IN CANADA. Sold in a variety of lace-trimmed dresses.

Ref.No.: D of C, AN24, p. 316.

Mint $30.00   **Ex.** $25.00   **G.** $20.00   **F.** $10.00

BABY PRECIOUS
1969 - 18 in.

1969. 18 in (45.5 cm). Cloth body, vinyl bent-limb arms and legs. Vinyl head; sleep eyes, lashes; rooted blond nylon curls; open-closed mouth. Mark: on head, RELIABLE. Original brushed lace dress, bonnet and bootees.

Ref.No.: D of C, BJ24, p. 317

Mint $50.00   **Ex.** $40.00   **G.** $30.00   **F.** $20.00

MARY ANNE WALKER
1969 - 30 in.

1969. 30 in. (76 cm). Plastic body, jointed hips, shoulders and neck. Vinyl head; blue sleep eyes, lashes, painted lower lashes; rooted blond hair; closed mouth. Mark: on head, RELIABLE (in script)/MADE IN CANADA.

Ref.No.: D of C, BW1, p. 317

Mint $50.00   **Ex.** $40.00   **G.** $30.00   **F.** $25.00

RUTHIE A-GO-GO

1969. 17 1/2 in. (44.5 cm). Vinyl and plastic body, fully jointed. Blue sleep eyes, heavy eye makeup; white hair. Mark: on head, RELIABLE MADE IN CANADA; on back, RELIABLE. Redressed; originally wore an A-line mini or a low-waisted mini-dress with fishnet pantyhose and boots.

Ref.No.: ES52

Mint **$45.00** **Ex.** **$35.00** **G.** **$20.00** **F.** **$15.00**

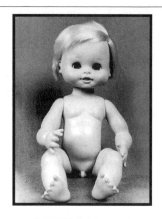

LITTLE BROTHER
1969 - 16 in.

1969. 16 in. (40.5 cm). Vinyl body, jointed hips, shoulders and neck. Vinyl head; blue sleep eyes; lashes; rooted blond saran hair; open-closed mouth. Mark: on head, 2054/15EYE/10/RELIABLE TOY CO. LTD./C1967/MADE IN CANADA. Originally wore a short jacket and panties.

Ref.No.: D of C, BN8, p. 317

Mint **$50.00** **Ex.** **$40.00** **G.** **$30.00** **F.** **$25.00**

Note: Also available in a toter seat.

GISELLE

1969. 18 in. (45.5 cm). Five-piece vinyl body. Vinyl head; blue sleep eyes; lashes, painted lowers; rooted black nylon curls around her face, long hair at back swept to the right side in a ringlet tied with a bow; closed mouth. Original pink dress with lace trim. White lace leotards missing.

Ref.No.: DR25

Mint **$30.00** **Ex.** **$25.00** **G.** **$20.00** **F.** **$15.00**

BABY CUDDLES
1969 - 9 in.

1969. 9 in (23 cm). Plastic body, jointed hips, shoulders and neck. Vinyl head; blue sleep eyes; lashes; three painted upper lashes; rooted blond saran curls; open mouth nurser. Mark: on head, RELIABLE TOY CO./19C69. Originally wore printed sleepers.

Ref.No.: D of C, BX25, p. 318

Mint **$25.00** **Ex.** **$20.00** **G.** **$15.00** **F.** **$10.00**

NICOLE

1969. 16 in. (40.5 cm). Plastic body and legs, vinyl arms, jointed hips, shoulders and neck. Vinyl head; blue sleep eyes; lashes; rooted brown straight hair; closed smiling mouth. Mark: on head, RELIABLE (in script); on body, RELIABLE (in script)/CANADA. Originally available in a variety of "A-line" dresses or a leatherette raincoat and matching hat.

Ref.No.: D of C, CS13, p. 318

Mint $45.00 **Ex.** $35.00 **G.** 20.00 **F.** 15.00

ROSALYN
1969 - 18 in.

1969. 18 in. (45.5 cm). Plastic body, jointed hips and shoulders. Vinyl head; blue sleep eyes, lashes, painted lower lashes; rooted blond curls with bangs; closed mouth. Mark: on head, 22/RELIABLE (in script); on body, RELIABLE (in script). Came in a variety of dresses, coat and hats.

Ref.No.: D of C, CR11, p. 318

Mint $45.00 **Ex.** $35.00 **G.** $20.00 **F.** $15.00

THREE-FACED DOLL

1969. 17 in. (43 cm). Plastic body, jointed hips, shoulders and neck. Vinyl head with three faces and a knob on top to turn the head. One face sleeps, one laughs and one cries. Original sleeper with a hood.

Ref.No.: 2I24-25-26

Mint $85.00 **Ex.** $60.00 **G.** $40.00 **F.** $35.00

RELIABLE
ca.1969 - 11 in.

ca.1969. 11 in. (28 cm). Plastic body, jointed hips, shoulders and neck. Vinyl head; one eye shut and one side-glancing; rooted straight blond hair; open-closed mouth with tip of tongue protruding and one tooth showing. Mark: on head, 2899/RELIABLE TOY CO LTD./MADE IN CANADA; on body, RELIABLE/CANADA; original tag reads, "HELLO, I AM A RELIABLE DOLL." Original red short overalls, hat, with red and white striped scarf.

Ref.No.: DF14

Mint $50.00 **Ex.** $40.00 **G.** $30.00 **F.** $25.00

RELIABLE
ca.1970 - 12 in.

ca.1970. 12 in. (30.5 cm). Plastic body, jointed hips, shoulders and neck. Vinyl head; blue stencilled side-glancing eyes, black line over eye, four painted upper lashes; rooted blond hair; open-closed mouth. Mark: on head, RELIABLE. Original "A-line" dress.

Ref.No.: D of C, CJ12, p. 319

Mint   **$30.00**   **Ex.**   **$25.00**   **G.**   **$20.00**   **F.**   **$15.00**

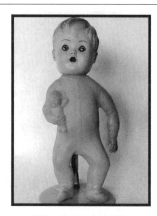

SQUEEZE ME DOLL

1970. 10 in. (25.5 cm). One-piece moulded vinyl body. Vinyl head; inset plastic eyes; moulded blond hair; open-closed mouth. Sleeper and teddy bear moulded on.

Ref.No.: 2I29

Mint   **$20.00**   **Ex.**   **$15.00**   **G.**   **$10.00**   **F.**   **$5.00**

TERRY TALKER

ca.1970. 24 in. (61 cm). Cloth body, arms and legs. Vinyl mask face over cloth head; inset plastic eyes; blond yarn hair; closed mouth. Original tag, RELIABLE/MADE IN CANADA. Cotton print skirt removable. Inset voice box with handle in the back; when activated doll sings "Rockabye Baby on the Tree Top."

Ref.No.: 2X1

Mint   **$40.00**   **Ex.**   **$35.00**   **G.**   **$15.00**   **F.$10.00**

BABY LOVUMS
1971 - 16 in.

1971. 16 in. (40.5 cm). Plastic body, jointed hips, shoulders and neck. Vinyl head; blue sleep eyes, lashes, painted lowers; rooted blond curls; open mouth nurser. Mark: on head, RELIABLE (in script). Original flannelette nightie and mob-cap. Missing bottle.

Ref.No.: PGL8

Mint   **$30.00**   **Ex.**   **$25.00**   **G.**   **$20.00**   **F.**   **$10.00**

Note: Mint and Ex. prices are for dolls in working order.

LORRIE WALKER
1971 - 30 in.

1971. 30 in. (76 cm). Plastic body, jointed hips, shoulders and neck. Vinyl head; blue sleep eyes, lashes, painted lowers; rooted long blond hair; closed mouth. Mark: on head, RELIABLE MADE IN CANADA; on back, RELIABLE CANADA. Redressed.

Ref.No.: ES44

Mint $35.00 **Ex.** $30.00 **G.** $25.00 **F.** $20.00

INDIAN GIRL
1973 - 16 in.

1973. 16 in. (40.5 cm). Brown plastic body, jointed hips, shoulders and neck. Vinyl head; painted brown eyes, painted upper lashes; rooted black hair; closed mouth. Mark: on head, 2-RELIABLE TOY CO. LTD. MADE IN CANADA; on back, RELIABLE - CANADA. Original felt dress; missing mocassins, head band and pendant.

Ref.No.: ES39

Mint $35.00 **Ex.** $30.00 **G.** $25.00 **F.** $20.00

BUNTING BAG CAT DOLL

1974. 13 1/2 in. (34.5 cm). Five-piece vinyl body. Originally wore orlon pile bunting bag (missing) and hood.

Mint $35.00 **Ex.** $30.00 **G.** $20.00 **F.** $15.00

CAROL WALKER
ca.1974 - 24 in.

ca. 1974. 24 in. (61 cm). Plastic body, jointed hips, shoulders and neck. Vinyl head; blue sleep eyes, lashes, painted lower lashes; rooted blond curls; closed mouth. Mark: on body, RELIABLE (in script)/CANADA.

Ref.No.: D of C, AN32, p. 319

Mint $35.00 **Ex.** $25.00 **G.** $20.00 **F.** $10.00

Note: Bunting bags came in lion, cat or dog styles.

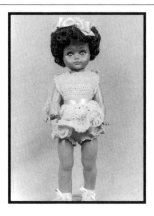

BLACK GLORIA

1974. 16 in. (40.5 cm). Brown plastic body, jointed hips, shoulders and neck. Vinyl head; brown stencilled eyes, black line over eye, painted upper lashes; rooted black curls; closed mouth. Mark: on head, RELIABLE TOY CO. LTD./MADE IN CANADA. Originally wore a bright multi-coloured long gown with a flounce around the bottom.

Ref.No.: D of C, CI13, p. 319

Mint $35.00 **Ex.** $30.00 **G.** $25.00 **F.** $20.00

JACKIE
1974 - 18 in.

1974. 18 in. (45.5 cm). Plastic body, jointed hips, shoulders and neck. Vinyl head; blue sleep eyes; rooted long blond hair; closed mouth. Mark: on head, RELIABLE TOY CO. LTD/cMADE IN CANADA; on back, RELIABLE. Original white cotton dress, brushed nylon coat, blue felt hat and boots.

Ref.No.: 2B9

Mint $40.00 **Ex.** $30.00 **G.** $25.00 **F.** $20.00

MAGIC SKIN BABY

1974. 14 in. (35.5 cm). One-piece, stuffed-vinyl body. Vinyl head; blue sleep eyes, lashes, painted lowers; rooted blond hair; smiling closed mouth. Mark: on head, RELIABLE (script). Redressed. Originally wore a dress in two styles and knit bootees, with a piece of hair tied in a topknot with a ribbon.

Ref.No.: SW18

Mint $25.00 **Ex.** $20.00 **G.** $15.00 **F.** $10.00

Note: Not the old rubber magic skin but a very soft vinyl.

MITZI
Short Blond Hair - Blue Eyes

1974. 18 in. (45.5 cm). Plastic teen body, jointed hips, shoulders and neck. Vinyl head; blue plastic sleep eyes, lashes, painted lowers; rooted blond hair; open-closed mouth. Mark: on head, RELIABLE; on back, RELIABLE/CANADA. Original cotton floral print jacket, pink cuffs and collar, attached yellow dickie, pink bell bottoms with print cuffs.

Ref.No.: 2G14

Mint $30.00 **Ex.** $25.00 **G.** $20.00 **F.** $15.00

MITZI
Long blond hair - Blue Eyes

1974. 18 in. (45.5 cm). Plastic teen body, jointed hips, shoulders and neck. Vinyl head; blue plastic sleep eyes, lashes, painted lowers; rooted blond long hair; open-closed mouth. Mark: on head, RELIABLE (in script); on back, RELIABLE (in script)/CANADA. Original pink cotton top sewn to long cotton print beige skirt, yellow suedine waist inset with green bow, high-heeled shoes.

Ref.No.: 2G16

Mint **$30.00** **Ex.** **$25.00** **G.** **$20.00** **F.** **$15.00**

MITZI
Long blond hair - Violet Eyes

ca.1974. 18 in. (45.5 cm). Five-piece vinyl teen body. Vinyl head; violet sleep eyes, lashes; rooted blond hair; open-closed mouth. Mark: on head, 3121 13 EYE RELIABLE MADE IN CANADA. Redressed similar to original.

Ref.No.: DR23

Mint **$30.00** **Ex.** **$25.00** **G.** **$20.00** **F.** **$15.00**

SOFT BODY BABY

1974. 18 in. (45.5 cm). Cloth body, vinyl arms and legs. Vinyl head; blue sleep eyes, lashes; rooted straight blond hair; closed mouth. Mark: on head, RELIABLE/MADE IN CANADA; label on body, RELIABLE TOY/TORONTO, CANADA. Original white brushed lace sleepsuit and hood.

Ref.No.: 2G6

Mint **$30.00** **Ex.** **$25.00** **G.** **$20.00** **F.** **$15.00**

LORRIE WALKER
ca.1975 - 32 in.

ca.1975. 32 in. (81.5 cm). Plastic body, jointed hips, shoulders and neck. Vinyl head; blue sleep eyes, lashes, painted lower lashes; rooted black hair with bangs; closed mouth. Mark: on head, RELIABLE (in script)/MADE IN CANADA; on body, RELIABLE (in script)/CANADA. Original costume.

Ref.No.: D of C, AO11, p. 320

Mint **$35.00** **Ex.** **$30.00** **G.** **$25.00** **F.** **$20.00**

BABY LOVUMS
ca.1975 - 13 in.

ca. 1975. 13 in. (33 cm). Plastic body, jointed hips, shoulders and neck. Vinyl head; blue sleep eyes, lashes, painted lower lashes; rooted straight blond hair; open mouth nurser. Mark: RELIABLE TOY CO. LTD./10c00/MADE IN CANADA.

Ref.No.: D of C, CG32, p. 321

Mint $25.00   **Ex.** $20.00   **G.** $15.00   **F.** $10.00

RELIABLE
ca.1975 - 16 in.

ca.1975. 16 in. (40.5 cm). Plastic body, jointed hips, shoulders and neck. Vinyl head; black stencilled side-glancing eyes, painted upper lashes; black moulded tufts of hair; closed mouth. Mark: RELIABLE. Redressed.

Ref.No.: D of C, CA7, p. 321

Mint $35.00   **Ex.** $30.00   **G.** $25.00   **F.** $20.00

RELIABLE
ca.1975 - 16 1/2 in.

ca.1975. 16 1/2 in (42 cm). Plastic body, jointed hips, shoulders and neck. Vinyl head; blue sleep eyes, lashes; rooted blond curls; open mouth nurser. Mark: on head, RELIABLE/MADE IN CANADA; on body, RELIABLE (in script)/CANADA. Original print top and plain leggings.

Ref.No.: D of C, AN22, p. 321

Mint $25.00   **Ex.** $20.00   **G.** $15.00   **F.** $10.00

CAROL
ca.1975 - 24 in.

ca.1975. 24 in. (61 cm). Plastic body, jointed hips, shoulders and neck. Vinyl head; blue sleep eyes, lashes, painted lowers; rooted red-gold hair; closed mouth. Mark: on head, RELIABLE TOY CO. LTD./MADE IN CANADA. Original sweater and slacks.

Ref.No.: 2P36

Mint $30.00   **Ex.** $25.00   **G.** $20.00   **F.** $15.00

RELIABLE
ca.1976 - 19 in.

ca.1976. 19 in. (48 cm). Plastic body, jointed hips, shoulders and neck. Vinyl head; green sleep eyes, lashes, painted lower lashes; rooted brown curls; closed mouth. Mark: on head, RELIABLE. Original print dress.

Ref.No.: D of C, CJ28, p. 322

Mint $30.00 **Ex.** $25.00 **G.** $20.00 **F.** $15.00

CINDERELLA
ca.1976 - 30 in.

ca.1976. 30 in. (76 cm). Plastic body, jointed hips, shoulders and neck. Vinyl head; blue sleep eyes, lashes, painted lower lashes; rooted black curly hair with long hair on each side; closed mouth. Mark: on head, RELIABLE 9 (in script)/MADE IN CANADA; on body, RELIABLE (in script)/CANADA; on shoe, CINDERELLA/NO. 5. Original flocked pink long gown.

Ref.No.: D of C, CH2, p. 322

Mint $40.00 **Ex.** $35.00 **G.** $25.00 **F.** $20.00

RELIABLE
1977 - 13 in.

ca.1977. 13 in. (33 cm). Jointed hips, shoulders and neck. Soft vinyl head; light brown moulded hair; stencilled eyes; open mouth nurser. Mark: RELIABLE (in script) CANADA. Redressed.

Ref.No.: D of C, CG27, p. 323

Mint $20.00 **Ex.** $15.00 **G.** $10.00 **F.** $5.00

MITZI
ca.1977 - 18 in.

ca.1977. 18 in. (45.5 cm). Five-piece vinyl teen body. Vinyl head; painted blue eyes; rooted long blond hair. Mark: on head, RELIABLE TOY CO LTD 1977; on body, RELIABLE MADE IN CANADA CANADA. Original pink jumpsuit with white, green and violet print and violet straps.

Ref.No.: DR22

Mint $30.00 **Ex.** $25.00 **G.** $20.00 **F.** $15.00

RELIABLE
ca.1978 - 18 in.

ca.1978. 18 in. (45.5 cm). Plastic body, jointed hips, shoulders and neck. Vinyl head; blue sleep eyes, lashes, painted lower lashes; rooted blond hair; closed mouth. Mark: on head, 27/RELIABLE (in script); on body, RELIABLE (in script). Original gown with lace trim.

Ref.No.: D of C, AN33, p. 323

Mint **$30.00** **Ex.** **$25.00** **G.** **$20.00** **F.** **$15.00**

INUIT DOLL

1978. 12 in. (30.5 cm). Plastic body, jointed hips, shoulders and neck. Vinyl head; black stencilled eyes, eyes outlined in black; rooted straight black hair; open-closed mouth. Mark: on head, RELIABLE TOY CO. LTD./19c68/MADE IN CANADA. Fur parka, hood and boots.

Ref.No.: D of C, BU30, p. 322

Mint **$45.00** **Ex.** **$35.00** **G.** **$25.00** **F.** **$20.00**

BABY BRENDA

1978. 19 in. (48 cm). Cloth body, vinyl arms and legs. Vinyl head; blue sleep eyes, lashes; moulded brown hair; closed mouth. Mark: on head, RELIABLE/MADE IN CANADA. Original white snowsuit.

Ref.No.: 2K15

Mint **$30.00** **Ex.** **$25.00** **G.** **$20.00** **F.** **$15.00**

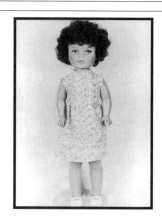

RELIABLE
ca.1979 - 24 in.

ca.1979. 24 in. (61 cm). Sun tan coloured plastic body, jointed hips, shoulders and neck. Sun tan vinyl head; blue stencilled eyes; rooted dark curly hair; open-closed mouth. Mark: on head, RELIABLE TOY CO. LTD./c1978; on body, RELIABLE/CANADA. Redressed.

Ref.No.: 2G1

Mint **$35.00** **Ex.** **$30.00** **G.** **$25.00** **F.** **$20.00**

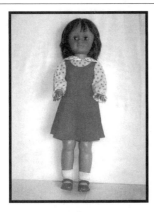

RELIABLE
ca.1979 - 24 in.

ca.1979. 24 in. (61 cm). Plastic body, jointed hips, shoulders and legs. Vinyl head; blue sleep eyes, lashes, painted lower lashes; closed mouth; rosy cheeks; suntanned complexion; rooted, straight dark brown hair. Mark: on head, RELIABLE TOY CO. LTD. MADE IN CANADA; on back, RELIABLE - CANADA. Redressed.

Ref.No.: ES43

Mint $35.00   **Ex.** $30.00   **G.** $25.00   **F.** $20.00

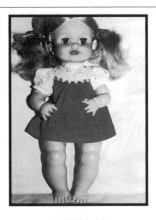

LOVUMS
1980 - 16 in.

1980. 16 in. (40.5 cm). Five-piece vinyl baby body. Vinyl head; green sleep eyes, lashes; rooted blond hair with two pony tails; open mouth nurser. Mark: on head, RELIABLE MADE IN CANADA; on body, RELIABLE MADE IN CANADA. Original red and white dress.

Ref.No.: DR29

Mint $25.00   **Ex.** $20.00   **G.** $15.00   **F.** $10.00

RELIABLE
ca.1980 - 18 in.

ca.1980. 18 in. (45.5 cm). Plastic body, jointed hips, shoulders and neck. Vinyl head; blue sleep eyes, lashes, painted lower lashes; rooted blond curls; closed mouth. Mark: on body, RELIABLE (in script). Original clothing.

Ref.No.: D of C, CW29, p. 320

Mint $30.00   **Ex.** $25.00   **G.** $20.00   **F.** $15.00

RELIABLE
ca.1980 - 16 in.

ca.1980. 16 in. (40.5 cm). Plastic body, jointed hips, shoulders and neck. Vinyl head; blue plastic sleep eyes, lashes, painted lower lashes; rooted blond hair; open mouth nurser. Mark: on head, RELIABLE (in script); on body, RELIABLE/CANADA. Redressed.

Ref.No.: D of C, CG26, p. 323

Mint $30.00   **Ex.** $25.00   **G.** $20.00   **F.** $15.00

RELIABLE
1980 - 16 in.

1980. 16 in. (40.5 cm). Five-piece vinyl body. Vinyl head; painted blue eyes; rooted blond hair in braids; closed mouth. Mark: on head, RELIABLE TOY CO LTD/MADE IN CANADA; on body, RELIABLE/CANADA. Original cotton print skirt, white blouse, black vest and white apron. Black shoes are missing.

Ref.No.: DR21

Mint $35.00 **Ex.** $30.00 **G.** $25.00 **F.** $20.00

Note: This doll is from the Fairy Tale Collection.

RELIABLE
1980 - 32 in.

1980. 32 in. (81 cm). Plastic body, jointed hips, shoulders and neck. Vinyl head; stencilled blue eyes; rooted blond hair; closed mouth. Mark: on body, RELIABLE (in script)/CANADA. Original slacks suit.

Ref.No.: 2N35

Mint $35.00 **Ex.** $30.00 **G.** $25.00 **F.** $20.00

GLORIA
1980 - 16 in.

1980. 16 in. (40.5 cm). Plastic body, jointed hips, shoulders and neck. Vinyl head; blue stencilled eyespainted upper lashes; rooted long blond hair; closed mouth. Mark: on head, 8/RELIABLE TOY CO. LTD./MADE IN CANADA; on back, RELIABLE (in script)/CANADA. Original dress.

Mint $30.00 **Ex.** $25.00 **G.** $20.00 **F.** $15.00

GLORIA BOUDOIR

ca.1981. 17 in. (43 cm). Plastic body, jointed hips, shoulders and neck. Vinyl head; blue stencilled eyes; rooted long blond hair; closed mouth. Original long blue gown with circular lace-trimmed skirt.

Ref.No.: 2H22

Mint $35.00 **Ex.** $30.00 **G.** $20.00 **F.** $15.00

RELIABLE
ca.1981 - 32 in.

ca.1981. 32 in. (81 cm). Plastic body, jointed hips, shoulders and neck. Vinyl head; blue plastic sleep eyes; rooted blond hair; closed mouth. Mark: on head, RELIABLE/MADE IN CANADA/19c61; on body, RELIABLE (in script)/CANADA. Original flowered long gown, lace collar, vest and sandals.

Ref.No.: PGC15

Mint $30.00 **Ex.** $25.00 **G.** $20.00 **F.** $15.00

Note: This mould was used for many years.

CAROL
ca.1982 - 25 in.

ca.1982. 25 in. (63.5 cm). Plastic body, jointed hips, shoulders and neck. Vinyl head; brown sleep eyes, lashes, painted lowers; rooted long black hair; closed mouth. Mark: on head, RELIABLE TOY CO. LTD./MADE IN CANADA. Original long gown with a red cotton print skirt and yellow bodice.

Ref.No.: PGM22

Mint $30.00 **Ex.** $25.00 **G.** $20.00 **F.** $15.00

ROSALYN
1982 - 18 in.

1982. 18 in. (45.5 cm). Five-piece vinyl body. Vinyl head; blue sleep eyes, lashes, painted lowers; rooted brown curls; closed mouth. Original long flowered dress with lace collar and ribbon at waist.

Ref.No.: DR24

Mint $25.00 **Ex.** $20.00 **G.** $15.00 **F.** $10.00

MITZI
1982 - 18 in.

1982. 18 in. (45.5 cm). Vinyl and plastic body, fully jointed. Blue-black painted eyes; rooted auburn hair. Original blue pants and cap, white fleece vest, red top and white sandals. Mark: on head, RELIABLE TOY CO.; on back, RELIABLE / CANADA.

Ref.No.: ES12

Mint $30.00 **Ex.** $25.00 **G.** $20.00 **F.** $15.00

RELIABLE
1982 - 14 1/2 in.

1982. 14 1/2 in. (36 cm). Vinyl one-piece body. Vinyl head; stencilled blue and black eyes, painted lashes; moulded hair; open-closed mouth. Mark: on head, RELIABLE TOY CO./1981. Originally wore diaper or sleepers.

Mint   **$18.00**   **Ex.**   **$15.00**   **G.**   **$10.00**   **F.**   **$5.00**

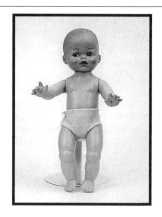

RELIABLE
1982 - 13 in.

1982. 13 in. (33 cm). Plastic body; jointed hips, shoulders and neck. Vinyl head; stencilled blue eyes, painted lashes; moulded hair; open-closed mouth. Mark: on back, RELIABLE (in script)/CANADA. Originally wore diaper or was dressed in a jacket and diaper and included a plastic cradle.

Mint   **$15.00**   **Ex.**   **$10.00**   **G.**   **$8.00**   **F.**   **$5.00**

GLORIA
ca.1983 - 16 in.

ca.1983. 16 in. (40.5 cm). Plastic body, jointed hips, shoulders and neck. Vinyl head; blue stencilled eyes, black upper lashes and upper eye-liner; rooted blond hair tied at each side; closed mouth. Mark: RELIABLE. Original blue cotton dress with white pinafore.

Ref.No.: D of C, BX12, p. 324

Mint   **$30.00**   **Ex.**   **$25.00**   **G.**   **$20.00**   **F.**   **$15.00**

CHUBBY
1984 - 21 in.

1984. 21 in. (53.5 cm). Plastic body, vinyl arms and legs, jointed hips, shoulders and neck. Vinyl head; blue plastic sleep eyes, lashes, painted lower lashes; rooted blond curls; open-closed mouth showing two moulded teeth. Mark: on head, RELIABLE/MADE IN CANADA. Original fleece sleepers.

Ref.No.: D of C, BU2, p. 324

Mint   **$30.00**   **Ex.**   **$25.00**   **G.**   **$20.00**   **F.**   **$15.00**

BALLERINA DOLL
1984 - 16 in.

1984. 16 in. (40.5 cm). Plastic body, jointed hips, shoulders and neck. Vinyl head; blue stencilled eyes with black upper lashes; rooted blond hair; closed mouth. Mark: on head, RELIABLE TOY CO. LTD./MADE IN CANADA; on back, RELIABLE (in script)/CANADA. Original ballet costume and slippers.

Ref.No.: D of C, AO18, p. 324

Mint $30.00 **Ex.** $25.00 **G.** $20.00 **F.** $15.00

JACKIE
1984 - 17 in.

1984. 17 in. (43 cm). Plastic teen body, jointed hips, shoulders and neck. Vinyl head; brown stencilled eyes with black upper lashes; rooted black curls; closed mouth. Mark: on head, 8/RELIABLE TOY CO. LTD./MADE IN CANADA; on back, RELIABLE (in script)/CANADA. Original lace gown and matching hat.

Ref.No.: D of C, AO20, p. 324

Mint $35.00 **Ex.** $30.00 **G.** $25.00 **F.** $15.00

MITZI
1984 - 18 in.

1984. 18 in. (45.5 cm). Brown five-piece, vinyl body. Vinyl head; painted brown eyes; rooted black hair; closed mouth. Mark: RELIABLE MADE IN CANADA. Original white dress with mauve polka dots, mauve ribbon trim, white lacy tights, white leg warmers and high-heels.

Ref.No.: DR20

Mint $35.00 **Ex.** $30.00 **G.** $25.00 **F.** $20.00

BLACK BABY BRENDA
1984 - 18 in.

1984. 18 in. (45.5 cm). Cloth body, 3/4 brown vinyl arms and legs. Brown vinyl head; brown sleep eyes; lashes; moulded brown hair; closed mouth. Mark: on head, RELIABLE/MADE IN CANADA; on label on body, RELIABLE TOY CO. LTD. Original pink flannel leggings and pink fur fabric jacket and hood.

Ref.No.: GK21

Mint $45.00 **Ex.** $40.00 **G.** $35.00 **F.** $25.00

BLACK BABY BRENDA
1984 - 17 in.

1984. 17 in. (43 cm). Brown cloth body, vinyl baby arms and legs, cryer and scented. Brown vinyl head; brown sleep eyes, lashes; moulded black hair; closed mouth. Mark: on head, RELIABLE MADE IN CANADA. Original yellow flannelette sleeper with attached hood.

Ref.No.: DR28

Mint $45.00 **Ex.** $35.00 **G.** $30.00 **F.** $25.00

CHUBBY
1984 - 21 in.

1984. 21 in. (53 cm). Plastic baby body, jointed hips, shoulders and neck. Vinyl head; blue sleep eyes, lashes; rooted blond curls; open-closed mouth showing two moulded teeth. Mark: on head, RELIABLE (in script)/MADE IN CANADA. Redressed in a copy of the original dress and panties.

Ref.No.: 2KA2

Mint $30.00 **Ex.** $25.00 **G.** $20.00 **F.** $15.00

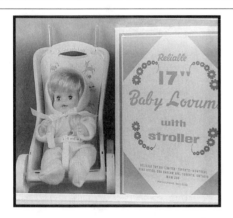

BABY LOVUMS WITH STROLLER

1985. 15 in. (38 cm). Plastic body, vinyl arms and legs, jointed hips, shoulders and neck. Vinyl head; blue plastic sleep eyes, lashes, painted lower lashes; rooted blond hair; open mouth nurser. Mark: on head, RELIABLE (in script); on body, RELIABLE (in script). Original clothing.

Ref.No.: D of C, BW23, p. 325

Mint $35.00 **Ex.** $30.00 **G.** $20.00 **F.** $15.00

Note: Mint and Ex. prices include stroller.

BRENDA

1985. 17 in. (43 cm). Cloth body with crier, vinyl arms and legs. Vinyl head; blue plastic sleep eyes, lashes; light brown moulded hair; closed mouth. Mark: on head, RELIABLE/MADE IN CANADA. Original pink and white bloomers, jacket and matching bonnet.

Ref.No.: D of C, BW24, p. 325

Mint $30.00 **Ex.** $25.00 **G.** $20.00 **F.** $15.00

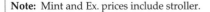

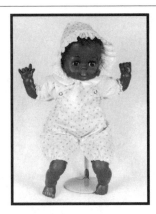

BLACK BABY BRENDA
1985 - 17 in.

1985. 17 in. (43 cm). Brown cloth body, brown vinyl 3/4 vinyl arms and legs. Brown vinyl head; brown sleep eyes, lashes; moulded black hair; closed mouth. Mark: on head, RELIABLE/MADE IN CANADA; label on body, RELIABLE TOY CO. LTD. Original blue floral romper, white blouse, pink lace trim and matching bonnet.

Ref.No.: 2F17

Mint $45.00 **Ex.** $35.00 **G.** $30.00 **F.** $25.00

SOUVENIR INUIT DOLL

ca.1985. 16 in. (40.5 cm). Five-piece brown plastic body. Vinyl head; brown painted eyes; rooted black hair. Mark: on head, RELIABLE TOY CO LTD MADE IN CANADA; on body, RELIABLE CANADA. Original brown felt parka, hood and pants trimmed with white fur.

Ref.No.: ES23

Mint $30.00 **Ex.** $25.00 **G.** $20.00 **F.** $15.00

MARYANNE

1985. 16 in. (40.5 cm). Plastic baby body, jointed hips, shoulders and neck. Vinyl head; blue sleep eyes, lashes, painted lowers; rooted straight dark brown hair; closed mouth. Mark: on head, RELIABLE/MADE IN CANADA; on body, RELIABLE (in script)/CANADA. Original blue and white paisley jumpsuit and mob-cap, shoes and socks.

Ref.No.: 2L24

Mint $30.00 **Ex.** $25.00 **G.** $20.00 **F.** $15.00

BUBBLES

ca.1986. 21 in. (53 cm). Plastic body, jointed hips, shoulders and neck. Vinyl head; blue sleep eyes, lashes; rooted blond hair; open-closed mouth. Mark: on back, RELIABLE (in script). Original one-piece white blouse and orange and white striped overalls, blue trim and white shoes.

Ref.No.: 2N27

Mint $35.00 **Ex.** $30.00 **G.** $20.00 **F.** $15.00

RELIABLE - 1990

1990. 30 in. (76 cm). Plastic body, jointed hips, shoulders and neck. Vinyl head; sleep eyes, lashes; rooted curly hair, in blond and dark brown; closed mouth. Doll came in four different costumes.

Ref.No.: 2Y4, 5, 6, 7.

Mint. $30.00 **Ex.** $25.00 **G.** $20.00 **F.** $15.00

Note: In 1990 Reliable also sold small baby dolls with cloth bodies and vinyl heads, arms and legs, dressed in five different costumes.

REMPEL MFG. (CAN.) LTD.
1952 - 1968

STANDARD TOYS LTD
ca.1917

Rempel was a Canadian branch of an American company. It produced small rubber character dolls that were more novelties than dolls. These were caricatures rather than realistic portrayals. Some of the characters, including the Indian doll, were copyrighted in the United States under the name Fred G. Reinhart.

INDIAN
ca.1958 - 6 1/2 in.

ca.1958. 6 1/2 in. (16 cm). One-piece brown rubber body.
Mark: MADE IN CANADA/REMPEL.
Ref.No.: 2M23

Mint $20.00   **Ex.** $15.00   **G.** $10.00   **F.** $5.00

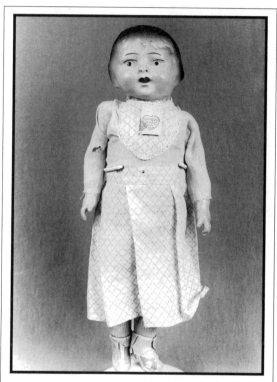

STANDARD
ca.1917 - 14 1/2 in.

ca.1917. 14 1/2 in. (36 cm). Excelsior stuffed cloth body, metal disc hip and shoulder joints. Composition head; blue painted eyes; moulded reddish-brown hair; closed mouth. Mark: on head, H.B.CO.; label on dress, STANDARD QUALITY/DOLLS/MADE/IN/CANADA.
Ref.No.: D of C, CN14, p. 326

Mint $200.00   **Ex. $175.00**   **G. $85.00**   **F. $60.00**

STAR DOLL MANUFACTURING COMPANY
Toronto, Ontario
1952 - 1970

The company was established by two American dollmakers. In 1960, Harry Zigelstein, a Canadian, became president. Star dolls were made of rubber skin or plastic and vinyl, as the composition era had ended by the time Star began production.

Do not confuse the dolls of Wis-Ton Mfg., Star Doll Division (1983 -) with this earlier company. Both companies marked their moulds STAR DOLL.

STAR DOLL
ca.1952 - 24 in.

ca.1952. 24 in. (61 cm). One-piece stuffed rubber skin body. Vinyl head; blue sleep eyes, lashes, painted lowers; rooted brown hair; open-closed mouth. Unmarked. Original box, STAR DOLL CO., TORONTO, ONT. Original yellow nylon lace-trimmed dress, socks and shoes.

Ref.No.: 208

Mint $50.00 **Ex.** $40.00 **G.** $30.00 **F.** $20.00

Note: The rubber skin body devalues the doll due to its short lifespan.

STAR DOLL
ca.1954 - 22 in.

ca.1954. 22 in. (56 cm). One-piece stuffed vinyl body. Vinyl head; blue sleep eyes, upper lashes, painted lowers; closed mouth. Marked: head, STAR 20.

Ref.No.: SW23

Mint $50.00 **Ex.** $40.00 **G.** $30.00 **F.** $20.00

STAR DOLL
ca.1955 - 17 in.

ca.1955. 17 in. (43 cm). One-piece stuffed vinyl body. Stuffed vinyl head; blue sleep eyes, lashes, painted lowers; rooted brown hair; open-closed mouth. Mark: on head, 14/STAR. Redressed.

Ref.No.: 2I16

Mint $45.00 **Ex.** $35.00 **G.** $20.00 **F.** $15.00

STAR DOLL
ca.1956 - 15 in.

ca.1956. 15 in. (38 cm). Cloth body, vinyl bent-limb arms and legs. Vinyl head; green sleep eyes, moulded lashes; rooted straight blond hair; open-closed mouth. Mark: on head, STAR DOLL. Redressed.

Ref.No.: 2I13

Mint $45.00 **Ex.** $35.00 **G.** $25.00 **F.** 15.00

STAR DOLL
ca.1957 - 13 in.

ca.1957. 13 in. (34 cm). Cloth body, vinyl bent-limb arms and legs. Vinyl head; blue sleep eyes, lashes; rooted blond hair; closed mouth. Mark: on body tag, STAR DOLL MFG. CO. LTD./TORONTO, CANADA. Original white chiffon and lace christening gown with ribbon trim.

Ref.No.: GK19

Mint $40.00 **Ex.** $20.00 **G.** $20.00 **F.** $15.00

STAR DOLL
ca.1957 - 17 in.

ca.1957. 17 in. (43 cm). One-piece stuffed vinyl body. Vinyl head; green sleep eyes, lashes, painted lower lashes; rooted honey blond hair; closed mouth. Mark: on head, 14R ; on body, A. Original box marked, STAR DOLL CO. 7182

Ref.No.: D of C, XH21, p. 327

Mint $60.00 **Ex.** $45.00 **G.** $35.00 **F.** $25.00

BRIDE
1957 - 24 in.

1957. 24 in. (51 cm). Stuffed rubber skin body. Vinyl head; blue sleep eyes, lashes, painted lowers; blond rooted saran hair; closed mouth. Mark: on neck, STAR. Original lace bridal dress with muslin underskirt, long veil, oilcloth shoes, rayon ribbed socks.

Ref.No.: 2N10

Mint **$50.00** **Ex.** **$40.00** **G.** **$25.00** **F.** **$20.00**

BALLERINA
ca.1958 - 20 in.

ca.1958. 20 in. (50.5 cm). Hard plastic body, jointed neck, shoulders, waist, hips, knees and ankles. Vinyl head; blue sleep eyes, lashes; blond rooted hair; closed mouth. Mark: on head, 14 R.

Ref.No.: DR33

Mint **$130.00** **Ex.** **$95.00** **G.** **$50.00** **F.** **$30.00**

DRINK AND WET
1959 - 19 1/2 in.

1959. 19 1/2 in. (49 cm). Plastic body, jointed hips, shoulders and neck. Vinyl head; blue sleep eyes, lashes; moulded brown hair; open mouth nurser. Unmarked. Doll came undressed. Original wrapping bag.

Ref.No.: 2J24

Mint **$40.00** **Ex.** **$35.00** **G.** **$25.00** **F.** **$15.00**

STAR DOLL
ca.1959 - 13 in.

ca.1959. 13 in. (33 cm). Five-piece vinyl body. Vinyl head; blue plastic inset eyes, painted upper lashes; open-closed mouth. Probably originally dressed in a diaper.

Ref.No.: DR7

Mint **$25.00** **Ex.** **$20.00** **G.** **$15.00** **F.** **$10.00**

BRIDE DOLL
ca.1959 - 18 in.

ca.1959. 18 in. (45.5 cm). Five-piece plastic body. Vinyl head; sleep eyes, lashes; blond hair; closed mouth. White gown and net veil.

Ref.No.: PS4

Mint $60.00   **Ex.** $45.00   **G.** $35.00   **F.** $25.00

STAR DOLL
ca.1960 - 16 in.

ca.1960. 16 in. (40.5 cm). Plastic body, jointed hips, shoulders and neck. Vinyl head; blue sleep eyes, lashes, painted lower lashes; rooted blond hair, open mouth nurser. Mark: on head, STAR.

Ref.No.: D of C. BQ7, p. 327

Mint $50.00   **Ex.** $40.00   **G.** $30.00   **F.** $20.00

STAR DOLL
1961 - 20 1/2 in.

1961. 20 1/2 in. (52 cm). Cloth body, vinyl bent-limb arms and legs. Vinyl head; blue sleep eyes, lashes; rooted honey blond hair; open-closed mouth. Mark: on head, PLATED MOULDS INC./C1961; tag sewn into body, MADE BY/STAR DOLL MFG. CO.

Ref.No.: D of C, BF7, p. 328

Mint $50.00   **Ex.** $40.00   **G.** $30.00   **F.** $20.00

STAR DOLL
ca.1962 - 24 in.

ca.1962. 24 in. (61 cm). Plastic body, jointed hips, shoulders and neck. Vinyl head; blue sleep eyes, lashes; rooted blond curls; open-closed mouth. Mark: on head, STAR DOLL/CANADA. Original dress and panties. Bodice is white cotton on red taffeta with a royal blue check. Replaced shoes.

Ref.No.: 2KA6

Mint $45.00   **Ex.** $35.00   **G.** $25.00   **F.** $15.00

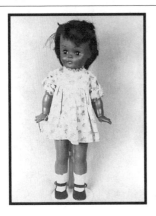

STAR DOLL
ca.1963 - 18 in.

ca.1963. 18 in. (46 cm). Brown plastic body, jointed hips, shoulders and neck. Brown vinyl head; brown sleep eyes, lashes, painted lowers; rooted long black hair with bangs; closed mouth. Mark: on head, STAR DOLL. Original flowered dress.

Ref.No.: PGC5

Mint **$55.00** **Ex.** **$45.00** **G.** **$35.00** **F.** **$25.00**

STAR DOLL
ca.1963 - 18 in.

ca.1963. 18 in. (45.5 cm). Plastic body, jointed hips, shoulders and neck. Vinyl head; blue sleep eyes, lashes, painted lower lashes; rooted light brown curls; closed mouth. Mark: on head, STAR DOLL.

Ref.No.: D of C, CO16, p. 328

Mint **$45.00** **Ex.** **$30.00** **G.** **$20.00** **F.** **$15.00**

STAR DOLL
ca.1964 - 18 in

ca.1964. 18 in. (46 cm). Plastic body, jointed hips, shoulders and neck. Vinyl head; blue sleep eyes, lashes, rooted honey blond hair; closed mouth. Mark: on head, STAR DOLL. Original red cotton dress with lace trim, red shoes and white socks, original label.

Ref.No.: 2D3

Mint **$45.00** **Ex.** **$30.00** **G.** **$20.00** **F.** **$!5.00**

STAR DOLL
1965 - 23 in.

1965. 23 in. (58.5 cm). Plastic body, jointed hips, shoulders and neck. Vinyl head; blue sleep eyes, lashes, painted lower lashes; rooted blond hair with bangs; closed mouth. Mark: on head, STAR DOLL / c1965 CANADA.

Ref.No.: D of C, AN26, p. 329

Mint **$50.00** **Ex.** **$35.00** **G.** **$25.00** **F.** **$20.00**

STAR DOLL
1965 - 24 in.

ca.1965. 24 in. (61 cm). Plastic body, jointed hips, shoulders and neck. Vinyl head; blue sleep eyes, lashes, painted lowers; rooted long blond hair; closed mouth. Mark: on head, STAR DOLL/C1965/CANADA. Original pink cotton dress with matching hat.

Ref.No.: PGC8

Mint $50.00 **Ex.** $35.00 **G.** $25.00 **F.** $20.00

STAR DOLL
ca.1965 - 16 in.

ca.1965. 16 in. (41 cm). Plastic body, jointed hips, shoulders and neck. Vinyl head; blue sleep eyes, lashes, painted lowers; rooted blond hair; open mouth nurser. Mark: on head, STAR DOLL. Original red, white and blue dress.

Ref.No.: 2M36

Mint $35.00 **EX.** $25.00 **G.** 15.00 **F.** $10.00

LAURA LEE
1966 - 15 in.

1966. 15 in. (38 cm). Five-piece plastic body. Vinyl head; blue sleep eyes, lashes, painted lowers; rooted blond hair; closed mouth. Original red and white checked dress with white lace trim and a red bow at the waist.

Ref.No.: DR15

Mint $35.00 **EX.** $25.00 **G.** 15.00 **F.** $10.00

STAR DOLL
1967 - 18 in.

1967. 18 in. (45.4 cm). Cloth body, vinyl bent-limb arms and legs. Vinyl head; blue sleep eyes, lashes; rooted auburn hair; closed mouth. Mark: STAR DOLL/MADE IN CANADA.

Ref.No.: D of C, CG28, p. 330

Mint $45.00 **Ex.** $40.00 **G.** $30.00 **F.** $25.00

STAR DOLL
ca.1967 - 24 in.

ca.1967. 24 in. (61 cm). Plastic body, jointed hips, shoulders and neck. Vinyl head, blue sleep eyes, lashes, painted lowers; rooted blond hair; closed mouth. Mark: on head, STAR DOLL/c1965/CANADA. Original pink nylon dress with lace trim.

Ref.No.: 2P28

Mint $50.00   **Ex.** $35.00   **G.** $25.00   **F.** $20.00

STAR DOLL
ca.1967 - 24 in.

ca.1967. 24 in. (61 cm). Plastic body, jointed hips, shoulders and neck. Vinyl head; blue sleep eyes, lashes, painted lowers; rooted honey blond hair; open-closed mouth. Mark: on head, STAR DOLL/CANADA. Original pink and white dress, white socks and shoes.

Ref.No.: 2R14

Mint $50.00   **Ex.** $35.00   **G.** $25.00   **F.** $20.00

STAR DOLL
1967 - 12 in.

1967. 12 in. (30.5 cm). Plastic body and legs. Vinyl head and arms. Jointed hips, shoulders and neck; grey-blue sleep eyes, lashes; rooted blond hair; open-closed mouth. Mark: on head, STAR DOLL. Original dresS.

Mint $30.00   **Ex.** $25.00   **G.** $15.00   **F.** $10.00

STAR DOLL
ca.1968 - 24 in.

ca.1968. 24 in. (61 cm). Plastic body, jointed hips, shoulders and neck. Vinyl head; blue sleep eyes, lashes; rooted dark brown hair in ponytail and bangs; open-closed mouth. Mark: on head, STAR DOLL/CANADA. Original blue flocked nylon party dress with net flounce and lace trim, socks and shoes.

Ref.No.: PGM16

Mint $50.00   **Ex.** $35.00   **G.** $25.00   **F.** $20.00

STAR DOLL
1968 - 14 in.

1968. 14 in. (35.5 cm). Plastic body, jointed hips, shoulders and neck. Vinyl head; blue sleep eyes, lashes, painted lower lashes; rooted platinum curls; closed mouth. Mark: on head, STAR DOLL; on body, 13 G.

Ref.No.: D of C, AN8, p. 330

Mint $35.00 **Ex.** $25.00 **G.** $15.00 **F.** $10.00

STAR DOLL
1969 - 15 in.

1969. 15 in. (38 cm). Five-piece plastic body. Vinyl head; blue sleep eyes, lashes, pale blue eye-shadow; rooted long blond hair; closed mouth. Mark: on head, STAR. Probably the original blue cotton dress with red and white polka dots and red insert.

Ref.No.: DR17

Mint $30.00 **Ex.** $25.00 **G.** $15.00 **F.** $10.00

STAR DOLL
ca.1969 - 18 in.

ca.1969. 18 in. (45.5 cm). Cloth body, vinyl bent-limb arms and legs. Vinyl head; blue plastic sleep eyes, lashes, painted lower lashes; rooted straight blond hair; closed mouth. Mark: on head, STAR DOLL/MADE IN CANADA.

Ref.No.: D of C, CW15, p. 331

Mint $50.00 **Ex.** $40.00 **G.** $30.00 **F.** $25.00

STAR DOLL
ca.1969 - 18 in.

ca.1969. 18 in. (46 cm). Plastic body, jointed hips, shoulders and neck. Vinyl head; brown sleep eyes, lashes; rooted long blond hair; closed mouth. Mark: on head, STAR DOLL. Original lace pant-suit trimmed with red braid.

Ref.No.: KP9

Mint $35.00 **Ex.** $25.00 **G.** $20.00 **F.** $15.00

STAR DOLL
ca.1969 - 14 in.

ca.1969. 14 in. (36 cm). Plastic body, jointed hips, shoulders and neck. Vinyl head; blue sleep eyes, lashes; rooted blond curls; open mouth nurser. MARK: on head, STAR DOLL. Redressed.

Ref.No.: 2M37

Mint $30.00 **Ex.** $25.00 **G.** $15.00 **F.** $10.00

STAR DOLL
ca.1969 - 11 in.

ca.1969. 11 in. (28 cm). Five-piece vinyl body. Vinyl head; blue sleep eyes, moulded lashes; rooted blond hair; open-closed mouth. MARK: on head, STAR DOLL MADE IN CANADA. Original pink cotton dress.

Ref.No.: DR16

Mint $25.00 **Ex.** $20.00 **G.** $15.00 **F.** $10.00

STAR DOLL
ca.1969 - 12 in.

ca.1969. 12 in. (30.5 cm). Cloth one-piece body. Soft vinyl head; gre-blue sleep eyes, plastic lashes; rooted blond hair; closed mouth. MARK: on head, STAR DOLL. Original.

Mint $25.00 **Ex.** $20.00 **G.** $15.00 **F.** $10.00

STAR DOLL
ca.1970 - 15 in.

ca.1970. 15 in. (38 cm). Plastic body, jointed hips, shoulders and neck. Vinyl head; blue sleep eyes, lashes, painted lowers; rooted blond hair; closed mouth. Mark: on head, STAR DOLL. Original blue party dress, lace and net overskirt, socks and shoes.

Ref.No.: PGL11

Mint $35.00 **Ex.** $25.00 **G.** $20.00 **F.** $15.00

TILCO INTERNATIONAL INC.
1940 - ca.1967

Tilco is the parent company of Tilly Toy of St. Jean, Quebec. Both companies made rubber and soft vinyl dolls.

TWO-FACE BABY

ca.1955. 8 in. (20 cm). One-piece vinyl moulded body wrapped in a blanket. Vinyl head with moulded hair and a knob to turn the head. Mark: on back, TILLY-TOY/MADE IN CANADA.

Ref.No.: 2R33

Mint $25.00 **Ex.** $20.00 **G.** $15.00 **F.** $10.00

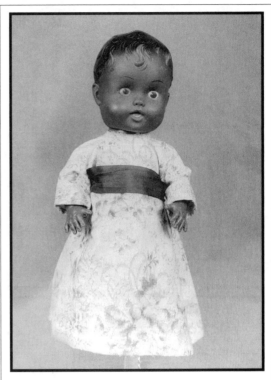

TILCO
ca.1958 - 10 in.

ca.1958. 10 in. (25.5 cm). One-piece brown vinyl body. Black painted eyes, black moulded hair, open-closed mouth.

Ref.No.: D of C, CQ11, p. 332

Mint $35.00 **Ex.** $30.00 **G.** $20.00 **F.** $15.00

TILCO
ca.1965 - 6 1/2 in.

ca.1965. 6 1/2 in. (17 cm). One-piece soft vinyl. Black painted side-glancing eyes, moulded blond hair, open-closed mouth. Mark: on back, TILLY TOY / MADE IN CANADA. Moulded nurses uniform moulded baby in her arms.

Ref.No.: D of C, BX18, p. 332

Mint $25.00   **Ex.** $20.00   **G.** $12.00   **F.** $8.00

TILLY TOY
ca.1966 - 10 1/2 in.

ca.1966. 10 1/2 in. (27 cm). Moulded vinyl body, jointed hips shoulders and neck. Vinyl head; side glancing black eyes; closed mouth. Mark: on body, TILLY TOY / MADE IN CANADA.

Ref.No.: 2R32

Mint $25.00   **Ex.** $20.00   **G.** $12.00   **F.** $8.00

TOPPER TOYS
Deluxe Reading Canada
Toronto, Ontario
ca.1960 - 1972

In the early sixties, Deluxe Reading, a Toronto branch of the Topper Corporation of the U.S.A., specialized in mechanical dolls.

BABY MAGIC

1966. 18 in. (45 cm). Plastic body, jointed hips, shoulders and neck. Vinyl head; blue sleep eyes, with tear ducts, lashes; rooted blond hair; open mouth. Mark: on head, K182/DELUXE READING CORP. Original box, "She sleeps, wakes, cries real tears, stops crying, picks up her bottle, lifts her arms and wets too." Original red and white dress, bootees.

Ref.No.: 2C13

Mint $75.00   **Ex.** $50.00   **G.** $40.00   **F.** $30.00

Note: Mint and Ex. prices are for dolls in working order.

VALENTINE DOLL COMPANY
Toronto, Ontario
1949 - 1959

Most Valentine dolls were unmarked, but some had a small "V" or "VW" on the body.

VALENTINE
ca.1955 - 21 in.

ca.1955. 21 in. (53 cm). One-piece vinyl body, jointed neck. Vinyl head; blue sleep eyes, lashes, three painted upper lashes; rooted blond hair, closed mouth. Mark: on body, V. Original blue taffeta gown with net over-skirt.

Ref.No.: PGC11

Mint   **$60.00**   **Ex.**   **$50.00**   **G.**   **$40.00**   **F.**   **$25.00**

VALENTINE
1958 - 19 in.

1958. 19 in. (48.5 cm). Heavy vinyl body, jointed ankles, knees, hips, waist, shoulders and neck. Vinyl head; thick hair. Mark: on head, 17 VW. Original tutu, stockings and ballet slippers by Capezio; feather missing from headpiece. Came by itself or with a trunk containing a formal gown, slip, pyjamas, housecoat and accesories.

Mint   **$160.00**
(with trunk and wardrobe)
Mint   **$135.00**   **Ex.**   **$90.00**   **G.**   **$60.00**   **F.**   **$40.00**
(ballet costume only)

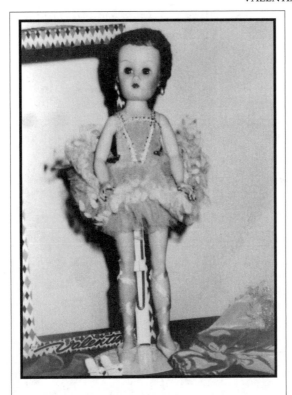

BALLERINA
ca.1959 - 15 in.

ca.1959. 15 in. (37 cm). Plastic body, jointed hips, shoulders and neck. Vinyl head; sleep eyes, moulded lashes; rooted brown curls; closed mouth. Unmarked. Company name on the box. Original blue ballerina costume. Came with a pink taffeta gown, nylons and shoes.

Ref.No.: PGG1

Mint **$125.00** **Ex.** **$80.00** **G.** **$40.00** **F.** **$30.00**

Note: The Ballerina also came in an 11-inch size with wardrobe and accessories. Mint price $115.00.

VICEROY MANUFACTURING COMPANY LIMITED
Toronto, Ontario
1935 -

Viceroy Manufacturing made small dolls of rubber or soft vinyl. It is noted for producing the Gerber Baby in Canada.

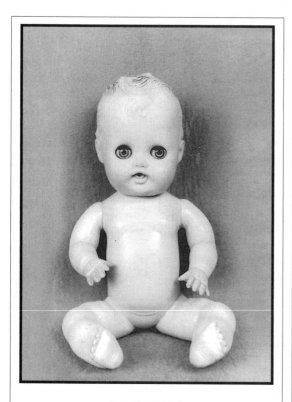

BETTY BOWS

ca.1950. 11 1/2 in. (29.5 cm). All rubber bent-limb baby body, jointed hips, shoulders and neck. Vinyl head; sleep eyes, lashes; moulded hair with a curl on top; open-mouth nurser, Mark: A VICEROY/SUNRUCO DOLL/MADE IN CANADA/PATENT PENDING.

Ref.No.: D of C, BX24, p.334

Mint $45.00   **Ex.** $35.00   **G.** $30.00   **F.** $20.00

Note: The 1954 Betty Bows was dressed in a sunsuit and came with a bottle.

RONNY

ca.1952. 7 in. (17 cm). One-piece rubber body and head. Blue painted side-glancing eyes; moulded hair; open-closed mouth. Mark: RONNY/C.RUTH E.NEWTON/VICEROY/MADE IN CANADA/3. Moulded clothing.

Ref.No.: D of C, CH6, p.334

Mint $25.00   **Ex.** $20.00   **G.** $15.00   **F.** $10.00

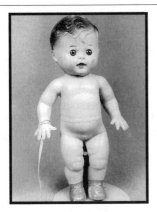

TOD-L-TIM

1953. 10 in. (25.5 cm). One-piece vinyl body and head. Inset blue eyes; black moulded hair; closed mouth. Mark: on foot, TOD-L-TIM/SUN RUBBER CO./MADE IN CANADA/BY VICEROY.

Ref.No.: D of C, CH3, p. 335

Mint **$45.00** **Ex.** **$35.00** **G.** **$25.00** **F.** **$15.00**

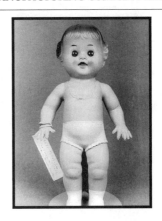

TOD-L-DEE

1953. 10 in. (25.5 cm). One-piece vinyl body and head. Inset brown eyes; brown moulded hair; closed mouth. Mark: on foot, TOD-L-DEE/SUN RUBBER CO./MADE IN CANADA BY VICEROY. Designed by Ruth E. Newton.

Ref.No.: D of C, CH4, p. 335

Mint **$45.00** **Ex.** **$35.00** **G.** **$25.00** **F.** **$15.00**

HONEY BABE BROWNIE

1954. 12 in. (30.5 cm). Brown all rubber bent-limb baby body, jointed hips, shoulders and neck. Brown rubber head; black painted side-glancing eyes, painted upper lashes; black moulded hair; open mouth nurser. Mark: on body, A VICEROY/SUNRUCO DOLL/MADE IN CANADA/PATENT PENDING.

Ref.No.: D of C, CL29, p. 335

Mint **$50.00** **Ex.** **$40.00** **G.** **$30.00** **F.** **$25.00**

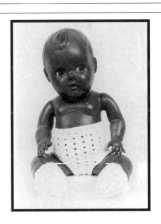

VICEROY
ca.1954 - 11 in.

ca.1954. 11 in. (28 cm). Brown all rubber bent-limb baby body, jointed hips, shoulders and neck. Brown rubber head; brown painted side-glancing eyes; black moulded hair; open-mouth nurser. Mark: on body, A VICEROY/SUNRUCO DOLL/MADE IN CANADA/PATENT PENDING.

Ref.No.: D of C, AZ3, p. 336

Mint **$50.00** **Ex.** **$40.00** **G.** **$30.00** **F.** **$25.00**

HONEY BABE BLONDIE

1954. 11 in. (28 cm). All rubber bent-limb baby body, jointed hips, shoulders and neck. Rubber head; blue painted eyes, painted upper lashes; brown moulded hair; open-closed mouth. Mark: on body, A VICEROY/SUNRUCO DOLL/MADE IN CANADA/PATENT PENDING. Original white lace-trimmed dress and panties.

Ref.No.: D of C, CL4, p. 336

Mint   **$45.00**   **Ex.**   **$35.00**   **G.**   **$30.00**   **F.**   **$20.00**

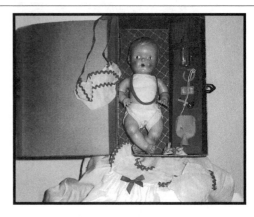

SUNBABE TREASURE CHEST
Sunbabe Blondie in a Travel Set

1954. 12 in. (30.5 cm). Rubber. Drinks, wets and cries. Original white dress, pants, bonnet and bib, all with red trim. Original travelling case with metal fasteners.

Ref.No.: ES21

Mint   **$80.00**   **Ex.**   **$65.00**   **G.**   **$30.00**   **F.**   **$20.00**

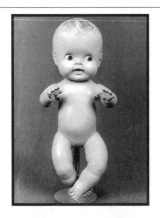

SUNBABE BLONDIE

1955. 12 in. All rubber bent-limb baby body, jointed hips, shoulders and neck. Rubber head; blue painted eyes, painted upper lashes; brown moulded hair; open-closed mouth. Mark: on body, A VICEROY/SUNRUCO DOLL/MADE IN CANADA/PATENT PENDING.

Ref.No.: D of C, AB28, p. 337

Mint   **$45.00**   **Ex.**   **$35.00**   **G.**   **$30.00**   **F.**   **$20.00**

VICEROY
ca.1955 - 7 1/2 in.

ca.1955. 7 1/2 in. (18 cm). One-piece vinyl body and head. Black side-glancing eyes; black moulded hair; open-closed mouth. Mark: on feet, VICEROY/MADE IN CANADA. Moulded snowsuit, hood and boots.

Ref.No.: D of C, BX19, p. 336

Mint   **$25.00**   **Ex.**   **$20.00**   **G.**   **$15.00**   **F.**   **$10.00**

VICEROY
ca.1956 - 11 1/2 in.

ca.1956. 11 1/2 in. (29.5 cm). All rubber bent-limb baby, jointed hips, shoulders and neck. Rubber head; inset blue eyes, painted upper lashes; brown moulded hair; open-mouth nurser. Mark: on body, A VICEROY/SUNRUCO DOLL/MADE IN CANADA

Ref.No.: D of C, BX22, p. 337

Mint $45.00 **Ex.** $35.00 **G.** $30.00 **F.** $20.00

SUN DEE
Golden Brown Sleep Eyes

ca.1956. 15 in. (38 cm). Brown all rubber body, jointed hips, shoulders and neck. Brown rubber head, golden brown sleep eyes, lashes, painted lowers; moulded black hair in curls; open mouth nurser. Mark: on head, SUN DEEc/VICEROY/MADE IN CANADA. Redressed.

Ref.No.: 2B14

Mint $50.00 **Ex.** $40.00 **G.** $35.00 **F.** $25.00

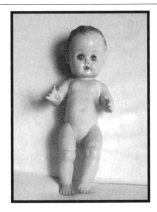

SUN DEE
Blue Sleep Eyes

ca.1956. 15 in. (38 cm). All rubber body, jointed hips, shoulders and neck. Rubber head; blue sleep eyes, lashes, painted lowers; moulded brown hair; open mouth nurser. Mark: on head, SUN DEE - VICEROY - MADE IN CANADA.

Ref.No.: ES41

Mint $45.00 **Ex.** $35.00 **G.** $25.00 **F.** $20.00

VICEROY
ca.1956 - 12 in.

ca.1956. 12 in. (30.5 cm). All rubber bent-limb baby body, jointed hips, shoulders and neck. Rubber head; sleep eyes, lashes, painted lower lashes; brown moulded hair; open-mouth nurser. Mark: on head, W/VICEROY/MADE IN CANADA

Ref.No.: D of C, BX21, p. 337

Mint $45.00 **Ex.** $35.00 **G.** $30.00 **F.** $20.00

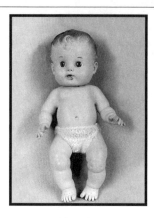

SO-WEE

ca.1957. 10 in. (26 cm). One-piece vinyl body, arms and legs. Vinyl head; inset blue eyes; deeply moulded light brown hair, open-mouth nurser. Mark: on head, SO-WEE/cR.E.N.; on body, VICEROY/MADE IN CANADA. When fed, doll wets diaper.

Ref.No.: DB7

Mint $30.00 **Ex.** $25.00 **G.** $20.00 **F.** $15.00

KEWPIE LOOK A LIKE

ca.1957. 19 in. (26 cm). One-piece vinyl body. Moveable vinyl head; side-glancing painted eyes, lashes, moulded hair in three tufts; open-closed mouth. Mark: on head, VICEROY/MADE IN CANADA; on foot, VICEROY/MADE IN CANADA.

Ref.No.: 2G2

Mint $25.00 **Ex.** $20.00 **G.** $15.00 **F.** $10.00

VICTORIA DOLL & TOY MFG. CO. LTD.
Victoriaville, Quebec
1920

VICTORIA

1920. 14 1/2 in. (37 cm). Cloth body and legs, composition forearms. Composition shoulderhead painted blue eyes; brown mohair wig; open-closed mouth. Mark: on shoulderplate, a V within a wide diamond. Original pink cotton dress and bonnet, trimmed in cotton print, white socks.

Ref.No.: BH31

Mint $200.00   Ex. $175.00   G. $95.00   F. $60.00

WIS-TON TOY MFG. CO. LTD.
STAR DOLL DIVISION
1983 - 1991

Wis-Ton also used the name Star Doll on its dolls and boxes. It was the last remaining manufacturer of vinyl dolls in Canada and made a variety of dolls, from cloth bodied baby dolls to walking dolls.

The president of Wis-Ton, Sam Manganaro, died in 1991, ending a long history of commercial doll production in Canada.

MANDY
1986 - 32 in.

1986. 32 in. (81.5 cm). Plastic body, jointed hips, shoulders and neck. Vinyl head; brown sleep eyes, lashes, painted lower lashes; rooted long streaked brown hair with bangs; closed mouth, Mark: on head, C CANADA/33W. Original red velveteen gown with lace trim.

Ref.No.: D of C, CY13, p. 338

Mint $35.00 **Ex.** $30.00 **G.** $25.00 **F.** $20.00

Hi there!
Let's walk
together.
Bonjour!
Marchons
ensemble

Wendy Walker

A WALKING DOLL
UNE POUPÉE QUI MARCHE

26" / 66 cm

WENDY WALKER
1986 - 26 in.

1986. 26 in. (66 cm). Plastic body, jointed hips, shoulders and neck. Vinyl head; brown sleep eyes, lashes, painted lower lashes, eyeshadow; rooted strawberry blond curls; closed mouth. Mark: on head, C CANADA/26W.

Ref.No.: D of C, CY12, p. 338

Mint $35.00 **Ex.** $30.00 **G.** $25.00 **F.** $20.00

BABY CUDDLE-SOFT
1986 - 17 in.

1986. 17 in. (43 cm). Cloth body with vinyl bent-limb arms and legs. Vinyl head; blue sleep eyes, lashes; rooted blond curls; open-closed mouth. Mark: on head, STAR DOLL/MADE IN CANADA. Label on body, MADE BY WIS-TON MFG.

Ref.No.: D of C, CY11, p. 338

Mint $30.00 **Ex.** $25.00 **G.** $20.00 **F.** $15.00

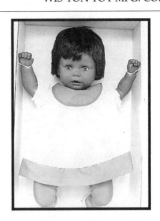

BABY CUDDLE-SOFT
1987 - 25 in.

1987. 25 in. (63 cm). Cloth body, brown vinyl head; brown sleep eyes, lashes; rooted straight black hair; open-closed mouth. Mark: on head, CANADA. Original red-dotted white cotton dress, trimmed in red, cotton bloomers, socks.

Ref.No.: PGM20

Mint $45.00 **Ex.** $35.00 **G.** $30.00 **F.** $25.00

PLAYFUL CHILD

1988. 14 in. (35.5 cm). Cloth body, vinyl arms and legs. Vinyl head; brown sleep eyes, lashes; rooted brown curls; watermelon mouth. Mark: body tag, Wis-Ton Mfg. Co. Ltd./Toronto, Ontario, Canada; on head, Star Doll. Original pink cotton dress with white sailor collar.

Ref.No.: 2KA3

Mint $25.00 **Ex.** $20.00 **G.** $15.00 **F.** $10.00

BABY CUDDLE-SOFT
1988 - 25 in.

1988. 25 in. (63 cm). Cloth body, vinyl arms and legs. Vinyl head; brown sleep eyes, lashes; moulded brown hair; open-closed mouth. Mark: on head, WIS-TON/CANADA; tag on body, MADE BY WIS-TON/MFG. CO. LTD. ONT. Original pink blanket sleeper with white attached bib.

Ref.No.: DF22

Mint $40.00 **Ex.** $30.00 **G.** $20.00 **F.** $15.00

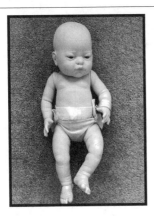

BABY NEW ARRIVAL

1989. 17 in. (43 cm). Realistic wrinkled newborn vinyl body, jointed hips, shoulders and neck. Anatomically correct, boys and girls. Vinyl head; moulded hair; stationary eyes; open-closed mouth. Diaper, naval band and bracelet.

Ref.No.: PGD6

Mint $30.00 **Ex.** $25.00 **G.** $20.00 **F.** $15.00

SATIN N' LACE
Short Satin Dress

1989. 22 in. (56 cm). Cloth body, vinyl arms and legs. Vinyl head; sleep eyes, lashes; moulded painted hair. Cries "Mama." Knee-length satin and lace dress.

Ref.No.: PGE6

Mint $40.00 **Ex.** $25.00 **G.** $20.00 **F.** $15.00

SATIN N' LACE
Long Satin Dress

1989. 22 in. (56 cm). Cloth body, vinyl arms and legs. Vinyl head; sleep eyes, lashes; moulded painted hair. Cries "Mama." Long satin and lace gown and matching bonnet.

Ref.No.: PGE7

Mint $45.00 **Ex.** $25.00 **G.** $20.00 **F.** $15.00

DOCTOR DOLL
1989 - 18 in.

1989. 18 in. (45.5 cm). Five-piece plastic body. Vinyl head; blue sleep eyes; moulded red hair. Redressed; originally wore white cotton doctor's uniform with a toy stethoscope.

Ref.No.: ES35

Mint $35.00 **Ex.** $30.00 **G.** $25.00 **F.** $20.00

WENDY WALKER, DOCTOR

1989. 18 in. (476 cm). Plastic body, jointed hips, shoulders and neck. Vinyl head; sleep eyes; rooted straight hair; closed mouth. Dressed in doctors pant-suit with two accessories.

Ref.No.: PGE5

Mint **$30.00** **Ex.** **$25.00** **G.** **$20.00** **F.** **$15.00**

WENDY WALKER, NURSE

1989. 18 in. (46 cm). Plastic body, jointed hips, shoulders and neck. Vinyl head; sleep eyes; rooted curly hair; closed mouth. White cotton pant-suit and matching cap. Includes toy stethoscope.

Ref.No.: PGE2

Mint **$30.00** **Ex.** **$25.00** **G.** **$20.00** **F.** **$15.00**

WENDY WALKER, NURSES AID

1989. 18 in. (46 cm). Plastic body, jointed hips, shoulders and neck. Vinyl head; sleep eyes; rooted wavy hair; closed mouth. White blouse and striped apron. Includes toy stethoscope.

Ref.No.: PGE3

Mint **$30.00** **Ex.** **$25.00** **G.** **$20.00** **F.** **$15.00**

BABY GIGGLES, BOY

1989. 19 in. (51 cm). Cloth body with mechanism to make the doll giggle when pressed. Vinyl bent-limb arms and legs. Vinyl head with dimples; blue sleep eyes, lashes; rooted blond hair; open-closed mouth showing two top teeth. Mark: on head, MIGHTY STAR/CANADA. Original blue romper suit with white sleeves and lace collar. Girl came in a dress in several pastel colours and bloomers. Both dolls had BABY GIGGLES printed on the front. Dolls were also available in brown vinyl with black hair.

Ref.No.: E11 17

Mint **$45.00** **Ex.** **$40.00** **G.** **$30.00** **F.** **$25.00**

THIRSTY WALKER, GIRL

1990. 24 in. (61 cm). Plastic body, jointed hips, shoulders and neck. Vinyl head; sleep eyes, lashes; moulded hair, open mouth nurser. Nightgown, mob-cap, plush dog and nursing bottle.

Ref.No.: PGE17

Mint $35.00 **Ex.** $30.00 **G.** $25.00 **F.** $15.00

THIRSTY WALKER, BOY

1990. 24 in. (61 cm). Plastic body, jointed hips, shoulders and neck. Vinyl head; sleep eyes, lashes; moulded hair; open-mouth nurser. Cotton print shirt and overalls, plush dog and nursing bottle.

Ref.No.: PGE19

Mint $35.00 **Ex.** $30.00 **G.** $25.00 **F.** $20.00

CHUBBY TUBBY
Moulded Hair

1990. 21 in. (53 cm). Plastic baby body, jointed hips, shoulders and neck. Vinyl head; sleep eyes, lashes; moulded hair; open-mouth nurser. Dress, panties and socks with nursing bottle.

Ref.No.: PGE8

Mint $35.00 **Ex.** $30.00 **G.** $25.00 **F.** $20.00

CHUBBY TUBBY
Rooted Straight Hair

1990. 21 in. (53 cm). Plastic baby body, jointed hips, shoulders and neck. Vinyl head; sleep eyes, lashes; rooted straight hair; open-mouth nurser. Dress, panties, socks and nursing bottle.

PGE9

Mint $40.00 **Ex.** $35.00 **G.** $25.00 **F.** $20.00

PIERROT CLOWN
1990 - 26 in.

1990. 26 in. (66 cm). Cloth body, arms and legs. Vinyl head; blue sleep eyes, lashes, black tear drop; closed mouth. Unmarked. Original black and white satin costume, black lace trim, black knit cap with pompon.

Ref.No.: Z8

Mint $40.00   **Ex.** $35.00   **G.** $25.00   **F.** $20.00

ANNE OF GREEN GABLES
1990 - 19 in.

1990. 19 in. (48 cm). Plastic body, jointed hips, shoulders and neck. Vinyl head with freckles; golden brown sleep eyes, lashes; rooted red hair in braids with bangs; closed mouth. Mark: on head, 14R. Original cotton bloomers, petticoat, cotton print dress and striped pinafore, black stockings and boots, straw hat and a bag.

Ref.No.: 2W32

Mint $125.00   **Ex.** $100.00   **G.** $70.00   **F.** $30.00

Note: This doll was on the market for only a few months and then withdrawn due to copyright reasons.

PIERROT CLOWN
1991 - 18 in.

1991. 18 in. (46 cm). Cloth body, arms and legs. Vinyl head, painted white with black teardrop on the cheek and black eyebrows; blue sleep eyes, lashes; black knit cap with side pompon; closed mouth. Original metallic gold fabric clown costume, trimmed in black lace with white and black neck ruffle.

Ref.No.: 2W7

Mint $35.00   **Ex.** $25.00   **G.** $20.00   **F.** $15.00

MISS TEEN MAKE-UP

1991. 20 in. (51 cm). Plastic teen body, jointed hips, shoulders and neck. Vinyl head; blue sleep eyes, lashes; rooted long blond hair; closed mouth. Original shorts and top plus an extra dress. When Miss Teen is washed with warm water, her make-up disappears and when ice-cold water is applied her make-up reappears.

Ref.No.: 2W13

Mint $35.00   **Ex.** $30.00   **G.** $25.00   **F.** $20.00

ALICE IN WONDERLAND
1991 - 19 in.

1991. 19 in. (48 cm). Plastic body, jointed hips, shoulders and neck. Vinyl head; blue sleep eyes, lashes; rooted blond hair; closed mouth. Original blue cotton dress, white ruffled pinafore.

Ref.No.: 2W10

Mint $40.00 **Ex.** $35.00 **G.** $25.00 **F.** $20.00

GOLDILOCKS

1991. 19 in. (48 cm). Plastic body, jointed hips, shoulders and neck. Vinyl head; blue sleep eyes, lashes; rooted honey blond long hair; closed mouth. Original gold dress and bonnet with brown pinafore.

Ref.No.: 2W12

Mint $40.00 **Ex.** $35.00 **G.** $25.00 **F.** $20.00

SNOW WHITE
1991 - 19 in.

1991. 19 in. (48 cm). Plastic body, jointed hips, shoulders and neck. Vinyl head; blue sleep eyes, lashes; rooted black hair; closed mouth. Original taffeta gown, yellow skirt, blue bodice, red ruffle at the waist.

Ref.No.: 2W11

Mint $40.00 **Ex.** $35.00 **G.** $25.00 **F.** $20.00

LITTLE RED RIDING HOOD

1991. 19 in. (48 cm). Plastic body, jointed hips, shoulders and neck. Vinyl head; blue sleep eyes, lashes; rooted reddish brown hair; closed mouth. Original red and white checked dress, white apron and red hooded cape.

Ref.No.: 2W9

Mint $40 00 **Ex.** $35.00 **G.** $25.00 **F.** $20.00

SANTA

1991. 12 in. (30.5 cm). One-piece cloth body, arms, legs and head. Vinyl face, side-glancing eyes, moulded white hair and beard, open-closed mouth.

Ref.No.: 2W2

Mint **$25.00** **Ex.** **$20.00** **G.** **$15.00** **F.** **$10.00**

YORK TOY SPECIALTY LTD.
Toronto, Ontario
1938 - 1953

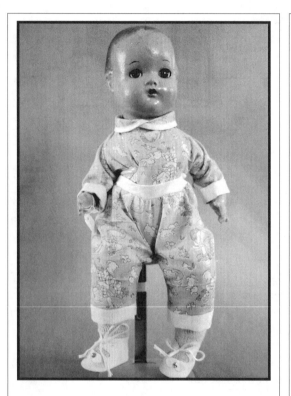

YORK
ca.1939 - 16 in.

ca.1939. 16 in. (41 cm). Cloth body, 3/4 composition arms and legs. Composition head; blue sleep eyes, lashes; brown moulded hair; closed mouth. Mark: on head, YORK TOY/SPECIALTY LTD. Redressed.

Ref.No.:2KA19

Mint $175.00 Ex. $135.00 G. $95.00 F. $60.00

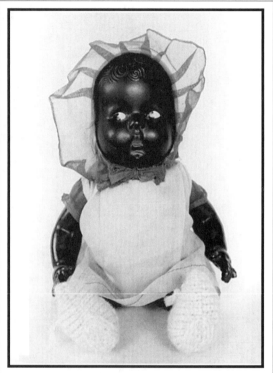

YORK
ca.1940 - 10 in.

ca.1940. 10 in. (26 cm). Dark brown composition one-piece head and body, jointed hips and shoulders. Painted side-glancing eyes; black moulded curls; open-closed mouth. Mark: label on dress, MADE IN CANADA/YORK TOY SPECIALTY LTD./TORONTO. Original white cotton dress and bonnet with red trim. Replaced bootees.

Ref.No.: PGM23

Mint $95.00 Ex. $75.00 G. $45.00 F. $30.00

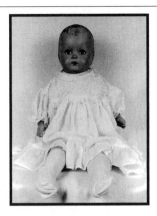

YORK
ca.1942 - 22 in.

ca.1942. 22 in. (56 cm). Cloth body and legs, composition forearms. Composition head; blue sleep eyes, lashes; moulded reddish brown hair; closed mouth. Mark: on head, YORK TOY. Redressed.

Ref.No.: 2P32

Mint $160.00 **Ex.** $110.00 **G.** $70.00 **F.** $50.00

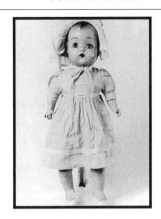

YORK
ca.1947 - 22 in.

ca.1947. 22 in. (56 cm). Cloth body with crier, composition arms and legs. Composition head; blue sleep eyes, lashes, painted lowers; moulded reddish brown hair; closed mouth. Mark: on head, YORK TOY/SPECIALTY CO. Original pink batiste dress with lace trim, matching bonnet. Socks and shoes missing.

Ref.No.: 2W28

Mint $175.00 **Ex.** $135.00 **G.** $80.00 **F.** $60.00

BABY MINE
1949 - 16 in.

1949. 19 in. (48 cm). Cloth body, composition arms and legs. Composition head; blue sleep eyes, lashes, painted lower lashes and painted grey eyebrows; moulded brown hair; closed mouth. Unmarked. Original label: MADE IN CANADA/A BABY MINE DOLL/YORK TOY SPECIALTY/LIMITED, TORONTO. Original white organza dress and bonnet with cotton lace trim. Socks and shoes missing.

Ref.No.: 2K29

Mint $175.00 **Ex.** $140.00 **G.** $85.00 **F.** $60.00

INDEX

DOLLS OF CANADA: A REFERENCE GUIDE
By Evelyn Robson Strahlendorf

   This book is for doll collectors, museums, libraries, antique dealers, doll stores, and flea market operators. It contains the dates, names, and characteristics to identify about one thousand Canadian dolls from prehistoric times to the present, with the emphasis on dolls of this century manufactured commercially and dolls made by Canadian Artists. It may be considered a history of Canadian dolls. Also included are about fifty dolls sold by the T. Eaton Co. Limited labeled as Eaton's Beauties. Many of the Eaton Beauty dolls were made by European companies like J. D. Kestner, Armand Marseille, and Cuno and Otto Dressel. However, they are included because they an integral part of Canadian doll history. Attention is devoted to the doll industry in Canada and how the manufacturing process evolved from bisque and composition dolls through the various plastics to the dolls of today. Reproduction dolls are not presented, although two are shown as working dolls. With few exceptions, every doll described in this book has been personally examined by the author.

   This book is also intended for a special class of doll enthusiast whom we call the closet collector. There are tens of thousands of these doll lovers in North America who have dolls and may also collect dolls, but do not admit this pleasure to others.

DOLLS OF CANADA: A REFERENCE GUIDE
CROSS REFERENCING NUMBERS

For the collectors who have Dolls of Canada: A Reference Guide, this table may be used as a cross reference for the two books.

DofC Ref.No.	DofC Pg. No.	Charlton Pg.No.	DofC Ref.No.	DofC Pg. No.	Charlton Pg.No.	DofC Ref.No.	DofC Pg. No.	Charlton Pg.No.	DofC Ref.No.	DofC Pg. No.	Charlton Pg.No.
AA18	223	195	AP31	75	26	BH19	101	54	BP26	313	320
AB1A	13	5	AP32	225	199	BH20	313	319	BQ0	280	273
AB2	90	40	AR18	14	8	BH23	79	29	BQ1	92	43
AB28	337	368	AR19	10	2	BH24	80	29	BQ2	298	297
AE8	295	306	AR20	11	2	BH25	70	23	BQ4	305	308
AE10	143	91	AR22	9	1	BH26	75	26	BQ5	291	287
AE14	11	2	AT12	263	253	BH27	76	26	BQ6	157	104
AM5	285	278	AT13	306	309	BH29	262	253	BQ7	327	355
AM11	258	249	AW21	91	42	BH30	311	317	BQ8	302	302
AM16	298	297	AW22	283	276	BH32	171	122	BQ11	83	32
AM17	238	224	AW23	256	247	BH35	270	261	BQ13	309	311
AM19	132	76	AW28	189	135	BH36	296	293	BQ15	147	92
AM21	151	99	AZ3	336	367	BJ3	134	79	BQ16	305	307
AM23	145	93	AZ4	188	134	BJ4	133	77	BQ18	301	300
AM24	90	42	AZ5	218	168	BJ5	264	255	BQ19	302	302
AM26	211	164	AZ18	242	228	BJ6	282	274	BQ20	20	150
AM28	239	226	AZ25	9	1	BJ7	256	252	BQ21	158	104
AM31	269	260	AZ27	24	14	BJ8	269	260	BQ24A	75	26
AM34	203	152	AZ32	11	2	BJ10	135	79	BS2A	69	22
AN5	164	113	AZ33	12	3	BJ13	287	281	BS10	82	31
AN7	314	325	AZ34	24	15	BJ23	197	144	BS12	146	93
AN8	330	359	AZ35	25	15	BJ24	317	333	BS32	158	105
AN10	239	226	AZ36	22	12	BL7	236	219	BS36	247	234
AN15	240	226	AZ36A	25	15	BM1	232	209	BT1A	86	38
AN17	242	228	BC3	26	16	BM24	107	263	BT4A	261	252
AN18	316	333	BC4	26	16	BM28	27	17	BT8A	73	24
AN20	243	229	BC7	13	6	BM29	303	304	BT17	70	23
AN22	321	340	BC13	81	30	BM30	21	11	BT22	284	277
AN24	316	333	BC14	315	325	BM31	301	300	BT24	177	128
AN26	329	356	BC15	142	88	BM32	300	300	BU2	324	346
AN28	296	294	BC17	295	293	BM33	99	50	BU3	141	66
AN31	235	218	BC18	136	80	BM35	184	132	BU5	159	106
AN32	319	337	BC19	137	81	BM36	239	225	BU12	299	297
AN33	323	342	BC21	312	319	BN2	259	249	BU13	301	301
AN35	234	216	BC55	22	13	BN4	100	49	BU17	161	111
AO5	240	227	BF4	205	154	BN7	236	221	BU30	322	342
AO7	222	192	BF5	169	119	BN8	317	334	BU31	163	112
AO8	221	191	BF7	328	355	BN9	103	51	BU35	249	237
AO10	255	246	BF13	241	228	BN10	235	220	BW1	317	333
AO11	320	339	BF21	258	249	BN14	207	156	BW8	89	41
AO18	324	347	BF22	261	251	BN15	131	75	BW11	89	39
AO20	324	347	BF25	224	197	BN16	203	152	BW17	272	263
AO21	314	323	BF26	236	222	BN17	265	256	BW19	272	262
AO22	220	178	BF27	275	267	BN19	104	56	BW20	125	71
AO23	277	269	BF28	277	269	BN22	315	327	BW21	264	254
AO25	240	227	BF30	142	89	BN24	246	232	BW23	325	348
AO29	260	250	BF31	136	80	BN25	192	139	BW24	325	348
AO33	248	237	BF32	279	271	BN26	200	149	BW27	185	132
AP3	222	193	BF33	196	143	BN30	202	149	BW28	184	132
AP4	220	179	BF36	131	75	BN32	155	102	BW29	253	244
AP5	85	34	BH5	14	7	BN33	209	159	BW34	166	117
AP8	91	42	BH6	278	270	BN34	314	321	BX2	254	246
AP9	168	119	BH7	12	3	BN35	273	264	BX5	144	92
AP10	276	269	BH9	304	306	BN36	305	307	BX6	155	102
AP11	217	168	BH10	304	306	BO1	103	48	BX7	294	291
AP13	290	287	BH11	288	282	BP3	241	227	BX8	198	144
AP15	252	243	BH12	266	256	BP5	297	296	BX10	164	113
AP19	172	123	BH13	266	257	BP8	274	265	BX11	100	55
AP20	257	248	BH14	197	143	BP11	23	13	BX12	324	346
AP21	214	165	BH16	183	131	BP14	25	13	BX13	162	111
AP27	229	203	BH17	288	284	BP16	293	290	BX14	242	228
AP29A	93	43	BH18	293	291	BP19	73	25	BX15	219	173

DofC Ref.No.	DofC Pg. No.	Charlton Pg.No.	DofC Ref.No.	DofC Pg. No.	Charlton Pg.No.	DofC Ref.No.	DofC Pg. No.	Charlton Pg.No.	DofC Ref.No.	DofC Pg. No.	Charlton Pg.No.
BX16	148	95	CC11	138	81	CG23	140	85	CL26	162	110
BX18	332	362	CC13	268	259	CG25	221	190	CL27	172	122
BX19	336	368	CC14	133	77	CG26	323	343	CL29	335	367
BX20	244	229	CD2	245	231	CG27	323	341	CL31	216	166
BX21	337	369	CD3	156	103	CG28	330	357	CL36	267	257
BX22	337	369	CD4	283	263	CG29	229	203	CM2	292	288
BX24	334	366	CD5	280	272	CG30	306	309	CM5	307	309
BX25	318	334	CD7	169	120	CG31	237	223	CM6	29	17
BX31	24	14	CD8	148	97	CG32	321	340	CM7	31	18
BX32	12	3	CD9	160	110	CG35	84	33	CM8	176	128
BX34	167	117	CD10	285	278	CH2	322	341	CM9	177	128
BY6	26	16	CD13	264	254	CH3	335	367	CM11	267	258
BY9	257	247	CD15	224	197	CH4	335	367	CN3A	122	63
BY10	268	258	CD16	93	44	CH5	102	51	CN7	122	63
BY12	178	129	CD17	228	202	CH6	334	366	CN11	212	164
BY13	253	244	CD18	268	258	CH7	232	211	CN14	326	351
BY14	76	27	CD19	154	101	CH8	286	280	CN18	274	265
BY16	144	90	CD20	259	249	CH9	194	140	CN19	167	118
BZ2	266	257	CD21	315	327	CH10	243	229	CN22	313	320
BZ6	259	250	CD23	289	285	CH11	232	210	CN23	132	77
BZ7	176	127	CD24	101	48	CH12	209	159	CN24	219	171
BZ8	213	164	CD25	159	107	CH18	70	22	CN27	172	124
BZ9	237	223	CD26	279	271	CH22	68	22	CN28	174	125
BZ12	22	11	CD28	284	277	CH24	79	29	CN31	265	256
BZ13	15	8	CD33	175	126	CH26	71	23	CN34	218	169
BZ14	21	10	CE2	15	8	CH29	255	246	CO1A	231	206
BZ15	83	32	CE7	230	205	CH31	72	24	CO3	299	298
BZ16	284	277	CE8	131	76	CH32	77	27	CO16	328	356
BZ17	262	252	CE10	243	229	CI4	137	81	CO17	210	161
BZ18	262	253	CE11	244	230	CI6	205	154	CO18	280	272
BZ19	201	149	CE14	294	292	CI7	233	213	CO20	195	141
BZ20	311	202	CE15	245	231	CI8	168	118	CO22	288	282
BZ21	157	104	CE16	294	292	CI9	151	98	CO24	282	275
BZ22	276	268	CE21	87	38	CI10	141	86	CO27A	29	17
BZ23	198	145	CE29	139	83	CI11	229	203	CO30	300	298
BZ24	263	253	CE31	136	80	CI12	291	288	CO32	292	289
BZ28	147	94	CE34	76	27	CI13	319	338	CP2	81	30
BZ29	287	280	CF2	67	21	CI15	135	80	CP3	254	245
BZ30	233	212	CF4	174	126	CI16	248	234	CP4	82	32
BZ32	204	153	CF5	169	120	CI17	247	234	CP5	160	109
BZ33	270	260	CF8	99	53	CI18	246	233	CP17	307	309
CA2	273	264	CF9	296	293	CI19	247	233	CP20	199	146
CA7	321	340	CF10	298	297	CI30	270	261	CP22,CP28	126,127	72
CA8	170	122	CF12	140	84	CI31	246	233	CP29	14	7
CA16	101	55	CF16	94	44	CI34	272	263	CQ7	261	252
CA18	78	28	CF20	235	216	CI36	286	279	CQ11	332	361
CA23	92	42	CF21	161	109	CJ4	153	100	CQ12	175	127
CA27	216	167	CF25	161	110	CJ5	291	288	CR10	144	91
CA29	82	31	CF26	297	296	CJ10	163	112	CR11	318	335
CA30	290	286	CF27	208	157	CJ11	163	111	CR12	225	198
CA31	173	125	CF28	278	270	CJ12	319	336	CR14	300	298
CA32	260	250	CF29	145	93	CJ13	230	206	CR16	214	165
CA33	217	167	CF30	143	90	CJ17	78	28	CR18	81	30
CA34	281	274	CF31	141	87	CJ19	73	25	CR20	255	246
CA35	186	133	CF32	158	104	CJ20	80	30	CR21	148	99
CA36	156	103	CF33	286	279	CJ23	292	289	CR22	256	247
CA39	28	17	CF34	289	285	CJ26	304	307	CR24	287	281
CB7	276	268	CG3	234	215	CJ27	233	215	CS6	234	218
CB14	145	92	CG5	223	194	CJ28	322	341	CS7	230	204
CB15	13	5	CG6	221	191	CJ35	275	266	CS8	303	306
CB17	159	108	CG7	222	192	CJ36	282	275	CS9	154	101
CB21	139	83	CG8	228	203	CL2	271	262	CS12	238	224
CB24	167	118	CG11	257	248	CL3	281	274	CS13	318	335
CB32	140	85	CG12	186	133	CL4	336	368	CS14	241	227
CB34A	254	245	CG14	267	258	CL5	281	274	CS14A	95	45
CC2	253	245	CG16	310	316	CL6	171	121	CS15A	123	64
CC3	271	262	CG17	196	143	CL7	303	304	CS21A	308	312
CC5	175	126	CG19	149	97	CL8	275	266	CS22A	150	97
CC6	177	128	CG21	293	290	CL22	74	25	CS24A	237	223
CC8	173	125	CG22	244	230	CL25	176	127	CS25A	228	200

DofC Ref.No.	DofC Pg. No.	Charlton Pg.No.	DofC Ref.No.	DofC Pg. No.	Charlton Pg.No.	DofC Ref.No.	DofC Pg. No.	Charlton Pg.No.	DofC Ref.No.	DofC Pg. No.	Charlton Pg.No.
CT1	31	18	CW22	153	99	CZ2	215	167	PL30	192	139
CT3	269	259	CW22A	154	102	CZ10	203	151	PL31	186	134
CT4	278	270	CW23A	231	207	DA1	134	79	PL32	187	134
CT5	302	302	CW24	310	315	DH6	162	111	PL34	191	138
CT6	217	168	CW25	132	76	PL2	197	144	PL35	191	138
CT16	133	78	CW26	310	316	PL4	199	147	PL36	190	137
CT18	297	296	CW27	257	248	PL6	198	147	PL37	191	137
CT20	216	167	CW28	274	265	PL8	202	152	PU0	191	137
CT21	194	141	CW29	320	343	PL10	206	155	PU1	190	136
CT23	157	103	CW31	146	94	PL11	204	153	PU2	189	137
CT24	289	286	CX10	121	62	PL12	207	156	PU4-3	189	136
CV10	84	33	CX13	277	269	PL13	206	153	PU5	187	134
CV12	83	33	CX14	149	96	PL14	201	151	PU6	188	135
CW2	309	315	CX15	285	277	PL15	200	148	PU7	187	135
CW5	74	25	CX16	160	108	PL16	200	148	PU8	188	135
CW6	69	22	CX18	139	82	PL17	201	150	PU10	185	133
CW8	190	138	CX19	143	90	PL18	210	161	PU11	185	133
CW9	124	68	CY1	85	34	PL20	210	160	PU12	184	132
CW10	155	102	CY5	271	262	PL21	208	158	PU13	183	131
CW12	307	310	CY6	283	276	PL23	208	157	XH16	72	23
CW14	199	148	CY7	309	312	PL24	193	139	XH21	327	353
CW15	331	359	CY8	279	271	PL25	193	140	XH22	312	317
CW17	263	254	CY10	24	238	PL26	196	142	XH23	123	64
CW20	231	208	CY11	338	373	PL27	193	140	XH24	123	64
CW20A	311	316	CY12	338	372	PL28	192	139	XH25	273	264
CW21A	306	305	CY13	338	372	PL29	194	140	XH26	209	160
									XH27	223	193

BIBLIOGRAPHY

Anderton, J. G. Twentieth Century Dolls: from bisque to vinyl.
Des Moines, Iowa: Wallace Homestead. 1981.

Anderton, J. G. More Twentieth Century Dolls: from bisque to vinyl.
North Kansas City: Athena. 1974

Charlton Press The Charlton Standard Catalogue of Royal Doulton Figurines.
Toronto: Charlton. 1981

Coleman, D. S. The Collector's Encyclopedia of Dolls. New York: Crown. 1968

Foulke, Jan 9th. Blue Book Dolls & Values. Cumberland Md.: Hobby House. 1989

Foulke, Jan 8th. Blue Book Dolls & Values. Cumberland Md.: Hobby House. 1987

Foulke, Jan 7th. Blue Book Dolls & Values. Cumberland Md.: Hobby House. 1986

Lavitt, Wendy Dolls. (The Knopf Collectors' Guide to American Antiques).
New York: A. A. Knopf. 1983

Smith, Patricia Doll Values: Antique to Modern. Paducah, Ky.: Collector. 1979

Strickler, Eva Inuit dolls: reminders of a heritage. Toronto:
Canadian Stage and Arts Publications. 1968